Contents

Chapter 1:
Basics

Chapter 2:
Formulas and Functions

Chapter 3:
Formats

Chapter 4:
Page Layout and Printing

Chapter 5:
Managing Sheets and Files

Chapter 6:
Excel Views

Chapter 7:
Database Functions

Chapter 8:
Charts

Chapter 9:
Data Exchange

Chapter 10:
Insert Objects

Chapter 11:
Automatic Functions

Chapter 12:
Protection Features

Chapter 13:
Help and Troubleshooting

Glossary

1. Basics

After you have started your PC and Windows has been loaded, you will see the desktop. At the lower border of the desktop, you will see the taskbar with the *Start* button. You will also see several other Windows' icons on the desktop.

Multitasking

After you start an application like *Excel*, this application is shown in a window and represented by a button on the taskbar. Because *Excel* is a Windows application, you can also start additional programs such as *Word* and exchange data between them. You do not have have to exit *Excel* in order to do this, just switch between the applications by clicking the respective buttons on the taskbar.

Starting and Exiting Excel

This is the simplest way to activate *Excel*. But there are several other faster or more convenient methods of starting *Excel*. There are also several ways to quit a Windows application.

Starting Excel

There are several ways to start and exit *Excel*. Try them all out, then decide which way is easiest for you.

Here's how to begin *Excel*:

- Via the *Start* button and the *Start* menu
- Via a shortcut on the desktop
- Together with a workbook
- Automatically after starting Windows

Starting Excel with the *Start* button

You will probably prefer this procedure if you are not yet familiar with *Windows 98*. Open the menus step by step and choose the correct entries.

First click the *Start* button.

The *Start* menu will appear. Point the mouse cursor to the *Programs* item in the menu. You do not have to click the item, all you have to do to open the overlapping menu is to move the cursor over the menu item. In this menu, the programs installed on your PC are displayed. Click on *Microsoft Excel* and *Excel* will start.

Creating a Shortcut

The procedure described above is the simplest but certainly not the fastest way to start *Excel*. If you have already worked with *Excel* in Windows 3.11 or if you are familiar with Windows 95, you may find this procedure too tedious. In this case you should create a shortcut on the desktop to start *Excel* faster.

To create this shortcut, open Windows *Explorer*. To do this, move the mouse pointer over the taskbar, then click with the right mouse button on the *Start* button. Choose the *Explore* item. In the *Explorer* window, the contents of the *Start* menu will be automatically displayed. Open the file *C:\WINDOWS\START MENU\ PROGRAMS* by clicking the little plus sign, located to the left of the file icon in the left part of the window. So that you can see the desktop, arrange and move the *Excel* window and, if necessary, any other application windows.

While pressing the *Ctrl* key, drag and drop the shortcut icon from the *Explorer* window onto the desktop. The moment you release the left mouse button, Windows creates a copy of the shortcut on the desktop.

Microsoft
Excel

The shortcut icon on the desktop

Here, too, you can close the *Explorer* window by clicking the *Close* button ▣. Now you can start *Excel* by double-clicking the shortcut icon on the desktop.

Starting Excel Together with a Workbook

If you know exactly which of your recently used files you want to work on first, you can open them automatically in *Excel*. In this manner, you can start the *Excel* program and open your file in one go.

Activate the *Start* button on the taskbar, then select the *Documents* item. In the overlapping menu which now appears, click on the name of the file you want to work with.

If you want to work for some time on the same project in *Excel*, you can also automatically open the file together with *Excel*. For that you have to save the file you want to work with in the following folder:

```
C:\Program\Microsoft Office\Office\Xlstart
```

Starting Excel Automatically

By default *Excel* can be started by clicking the *Start* button on the Windows taskbar and choosing *Programs/ Microsoft Excel*. If you use *Excel* a lot you may not want to follow this procedure after every reboot of your PC. In this case, you can start *Excel* automatically after loading Windows.

A procedure, which is not fully automatic but still speeds up the start of *Excel*, is already described above. You can start *Excel* immediately after Windows starts or later with a double-click.

StartUp

Windows controls the automatic starting of programs, not the programs themselves. Windows places all programs and documents to be loaded, automatically, in a particular folder called *StartUp*.

In order to start *Excel* automatically, move the *Excel* program file or a shortcut to the program into the *StartUp* folder.

Click the *Start* button on the taskbar and select *Programs/ Windows Explorer*. Since a shortcut to the *Excel* program file, which allows you to start *Excel* in the normal way, already exists in the *Start* menu folder, the fastest and simplest thing to do is just to copy this shortcut into the *StartUp* folder. To do this, click on the plus sign in the left pane of the *Explorer* window, just to the left of the *Programs* folder, to expand it and display its contents.

```
Windows\Start Menu\Programs
```

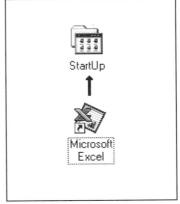

Fig. 1.2:   Folders and shortcut icons

In the *PROGRAMS* folder you will find the icon for the shortcut to the *Excel* program. This shortcut makes it possible for you to start *Excel* via the *Program* menu. One of the folders displayed will be called *StartUp*.

Copy and paste

Holding down the *Ctrl* key, drag-and-drop the *Excel* shortcut icon into the *StartUp* folder. Alternatively you can right-click the *Excel* shortcut and choose *Copy*, then right-click the *StartUp* folder and choose *Paste*.

Now close the *Explorer* window with a click on the *Close* button ⊠ in the window title bar. In the future, *Excel* will start automatically and immediately after Windows is loaded.

Quitting Excel

Exiting

There are also several ways of quitting *Excel*.

These methods use:

- The *File* menu

- The title bar
- The *System* menu
- The *Close* button on the title bar
- The *Excel* button on the taskbar

Quitting Excel Using the *File* Menu

To quit *Excel*, open the *File* menu and choose the *Exit* command. You will find this command at the bottom of the menu. If you have created a new workbook or if you have modified an existing one and you have not yet saved these changes, then you will be prompted to save them.

Quitting Excel Using the Context Menu

A significantly faster method, to quit *Excel*, uses the context menu. Click with the right mouse button either on the title bar or on the *Excel* button on the taskbar. Choose the *Close* option from the context menu. Here too, you are prompted to save your workbooks if necessary.

Quitting Excel Using the *System* Menu

If you have previously worked with *Excel* under Windows 3.11, you may not want to do without the option of quitting the program using the *System* menu. You can still close *Excel* either by clicking the *System* menu and then choosing *Close* or by just double-clicking the *System* menu icon. If required, you will be asked to save your workbooks.

Quitting Excel Using the *Close* Button

Close button

An even faster method of quitting *Excel* is by using the *Close* button ☒, which you find in all Windows applications on the right-hand side of the title bar. You will find it there in *Excel* too. A single click, on this, is all that is required to quit *Excel*. Here also you are prompted to save your work if necessary.

Quitting Excel and Saving All Open Workbooks

Normally, when you quit *Excel*, the program will ask you to save each workbook's changes separately. But a new function in *Excel 97* allows you to save all open workbooks with just one command. After the command *Close* or *Exit* a dialog box appears:

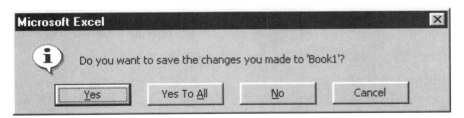

Fig. 1.3:   Yes To All

Select the *Yes To All* button, in order to save all changes in all your open workbooks. Only when you have started a new workbook does the *Save As* dialog box appear, so that you can enter a name for the workbook. All workbooks that have already been saved will be saved again with the same name and in the same folder without further confirmation.

With the *Yes* button, you can save the workbooks individually, and, with the *No* button you can decide not to save changes to a particular workbook.

Working with Excel

After *Excel* starts, an empty sheet is displayed in the workbook window. This window appears within the *Excel* application window. Both the application window and the workbook have all the elements typical to Windows:

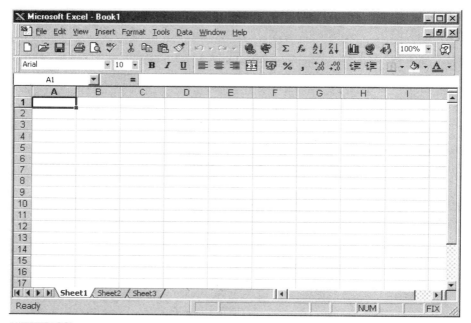

Fig. 1.4: The worksheet area in Excel

- *Title bar*
  Here the name of the application or the workbook is displayed. In addition to that, on the right-hand side of the title bar there are buttons to minimize, maximize, and close the window.

- *Maximize* ▢

  Click this button to maximize the size of the application window or the workbook. If a window is maximized, the desktop is no longer visible. If the
  workbook is maximized, it does not have it's own title
  bar any longer. The name of the workbook is then
  displayed in the title bar of the application window.
  In this case, you will find the *System* menu icon and
  the window control buttons on the menu bar.

- *Minimize* ▬

  Click this button if you want to bring a window to its
  smallest size without closing it. The *Excel* application
  window will then be displayed as a button on the
  taskbar. A workbook will be displayed as a button
  within the application window.

- *Restore* ▣

  A click on this button restores the window to its
  previous size and position.This button replaces the
  Maximize button in the maximized state.

- *Close* ✕

  Click this button to close a window. For the application window this means *Excel* will be closed.
  Clicking this button on the workbook title bar or,
  when a workbook is maximized, on the button of
  the menu bar, will close the present workbook.

- *System* menu icon

  The *System* menu icon always displays the icon of the
  respective window, so it is either the *Excel* program
  icon or the icon for the *Excel* workbook .

- *System* menu icon of *Excel*: ▨

- *System* menu icon of a Workbook: ▨

System menu icon

The icon for the *System* menu of *Excel* is always displayed in the title bar, while you will find the icon for a workbook either in the workbook title bar, or, if the workbook is maximized, at the beginning of the menu bar.

Around the worksheet area, you find a number of useful tools: the toolbars, the formula bar with the *Formula Palette*, the scroll bars and the status bar. These will help you to control the work, move within the workbook and choose commands.

The Menu Bar

Directly beneath the title bar you will find the menu bar. Here the main commands are displayed and each of them opens a menu with further sub-commands. In every command, one letter is underlined. You can execute the command either by clicking on it or using the key combination of ⌊Alt⌋. in conjunction with the letter underlined in the command.

The Toolbars

The toolbars consist of buttons. These buttons can be used to access the commands more quickly than by opening the menus and the respective dialog boxes. By default two toolbars are displayed in *Excel*: the *Standard* toolbar and the *Formatting* toolbar.

Standard toolbar

The *Standard* toolbar consists of buttons that can be used to organize your folders and files, and, to cut, paste and move data within the worksheets. In addition, you find buttons to sort cell contents, execute summations and insert special objects.

Formatting toolbar

The *Formatting* toolbar consists of lists and buttons to format the contents of cells. Part of these are meant for your choice of fonts and their appearance, as well as a selection of the most important number formats.

ScreenTip

If you point the mouse cursor on one of those buttons or menu commands, it will appear raised. In the case of a button you will also see a ScreenTip (or ToolTip), describing the function of the button. Buttons with similar functions are grouped together. The groups are separated from each other by a vertical separation line. You can slide a docked toolbar from left to right and back again by clicking on a separation line or the handle and dragging the toolbar to another screen position.

The Scroll Bars

The scroll bars are found on the border at the right and at the bottom of a workbook window. The vertical scroll bar helps you to move up and down in your table, while the horizontal scroll bar will move the table from left to right. The left side of this bar also contains the worksheet tabs and the tab scrolling buttons.

The Worksheet Tabs

For each table in the workbook, there is a sheet and a sheet tab, located in the worksheet tab bar at the bottom of the workbook window. Three tables are created by default after opening a new workbook in *Excel 97*. They are named Sheet 1, Sheet 2 and Sheet 3.

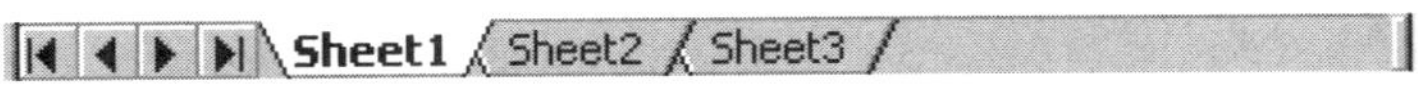

Fig. 1.5:   The sheet tabs

Of course you can add other tables or sheets as well, such as, the presentation of a chart, any time you like. At the left end of the tab bar, you will find the tab scrolling buttons to navigate among the various sheets.

The Status Bar

The status bar displays the active edit mode. You may see, for example, *Ready* if *Excel* is waiting for you to enter a command or some data. Or you may read *Edit* if you selected a cell to edit. Additionally, the right corner of the status bar displays the status of certain special functions; for example, EXT indicates that you have activated the extended selection option with the F8 key.

The Formula Bar and the Formula Palette

The formula bar is displayed directly below the second toolbar. It shows the content of the active cell. You can also edit the content in the cell itself, but with larger cell contents it is easier to do the editing in the formula bar. If you have selected a cell, the formula bar will show buttons to enter or cancel your entry or any changes.

Fig. 1.6:   The formula bar

You can directly activate the Formula Palette with a click on an additional button in the formula bar to start the entry of a formula.

Enter ✔
Click this button to finalize an entry and transfer it to the cell.

Cancel ✖
Select this button if you do not want to transfer the entry or modify the cell in any way.

Edit Formula =
This button opens the Formula Palette and enters an equal sign into a cell, to start a new formula.

The Name Box

The *Name* box is located on the left hand side, at the beginning of the formula bar. Normally the *Name* box displays the address of the selected cell. As soon as you select a range of cells, the address of the upper left cell is displayed in the *Name* box.

| 1R x 2C ▼ |

While you are selecting, and before you release the mouse or press the ◇ key, the size of the selected cell area is shown in the form *R x C*.

You can also use the *Name* box to enter a new name or to go to an existing name. There is a drop-down button on the right hand side of the *Name* box. Click on this arrow and a list of all existing names in the sheet will appear.

The Worksheet

An *Excel* worksheet has a maximum of 65,536 rows and 256 columns. The rows are labelled with numbers and the columns with letters. You can find these labels on the grey buttons to the left of the rows as well as on top of the columns.

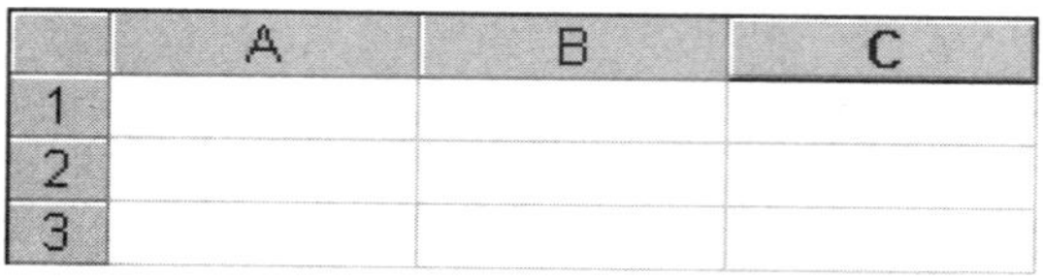

	A	B	C
1			
2			
3			

Fig. 1.7:   Column headings and row headings

The intersection of a row and a column creates a cell. Every cell can be reached by its address, which consists of the column letter and the row number. This address is displayed in the *Name* box as soon as a cell is selected. For example, A1 is the cell address of the first cell and F15 is the address of the cell which occurs at the intersection of column F and row 15.

The Cell Frame

The active or selected cell has a black frame. This is called the cell frame or cell cursor. If you click with the mouse on a cell or if you use the cursor keys, you will move the cell frame and thus move your selection. All entries and commands apply to the selected cell only.

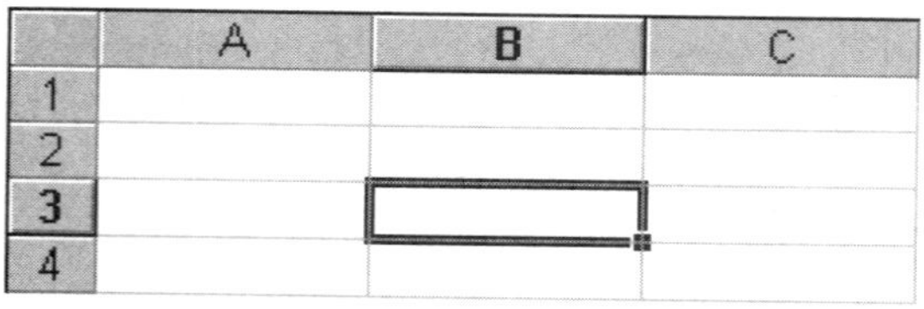

	A	B	C
1			
2			
3			
4			

Fig. 1.8:   The selected cell is B3

The Fill Handle

In the lower right-hand corner of the cell frame is a very small black square, the fill handle. When the mouse pointer is on the fill handle, the pointer changes from an arrow to a crosshair.

The fill handle

You can drag the fill handle to copy the contents of the selected cell to adjacent cells. You can also use this procedure to create series.

Entering Text, Numbers and Special Signs

To enter text, numbers or any other content into an empty cell you have to select the cell by clicking on it with the mouse or by moving the cell frame with the →, ←, ↑ or ↓ keys. Only then can you begin entering data.

Corrections

The *Backspace* key ← can be used during the entry of data to correct information which has already been entered. You cannot use the → and ← keys to move within the contents of the cell, because they insert references into the cell.

During the data entry the cell content is displayed in the cell itself as well as in the formula bar. Click on the place in the formula bar where you want to make the corrections without affecting the remaining cell content.

Finalizing the entry

After you have entered the desired data, you can choose one of the following options to complete the entry procedure:

- Click the *Enter* button ✔.

- Press the ↵ key.

- Select the next cell that you want to edit or in which you want to enter new data.

27

Automatic
alignment

After completing the editing of a cell using the first or second method, the cell frame will automatically move down to the next cell in the same column. By using the third procedure, the selected cell will obviously be the highlighted one. If the data entered is numerical, the cell content will be right-aligned, but if the contents are in the form of text, then it will be left-aligned.

Entering Values

If you want *Excel* to recognize your data as numeric values, you should enter only the following elements.

- Numbers
- Arithmetic operators and signs
- Parentheses
- Decimal delimiters

Further elements like currency symbols, digit grouping symbols, and percentage signs must be specified in the number format dialog and need not be typed in directly.

Entering Text

All entries that *Excel* does not recognize as numeric values or formulas are classified as text, and, are therefore left-aligned. In the case of a formula, you have to put the text in quotation marks in order for *Excel* to differentiate between text and names.

If you want to enter numbers such as telephone numbers as text, select the cell in which you want to enter the data. Then choose *Format/Cells* and double-click the *Text* item in the *Category* list box on the *Number* tab.

Entering Formulas

A formula always begins with an equal sign. This is the only case in which *Excel* recognizes the cell content as a formula. After completing the entry, the cell will not display the formula anymore, it will show the result instead. A value will be right-aligned, a text will be left-aligned.

Correcting Entry Mistakes

If *Excel* repeats the # sign or displays this sign followed by a sequence of numbers, then your entry leads to a mistake that is blocking the further entry of correct data. This error message appears whether you made a logical mistake while entering the formula, or if the cell content is too long for the column width. You can alter the column width in order to display the cell contents properly. Read more about troubleshooting in Chapter 14.

Entering Values with Leading Zeros

You may have already noticed that *Excel* is 'eating up' all the zeros at the beginning of a value. Usually, those values are numbers like article numbers, client numbers, postal or area codes, but not numeric values that are meant for calculation.

However, *Excel* can only distinguish between text and numbers. Everything that consists merely of numbers is classified as a numeric value. By default, *Excel* suppresses the extra zeros at the beginning of a value as well as the decimal zeros after the point at the very end of a value.

To display leading zeros, let *Excel* handle the numbers as text by formatting the cell for text. You have to do this before entering the numbers, otherwise afterwards the zeros will be lost. You can convert the cell to text but you will not get back your zeros.

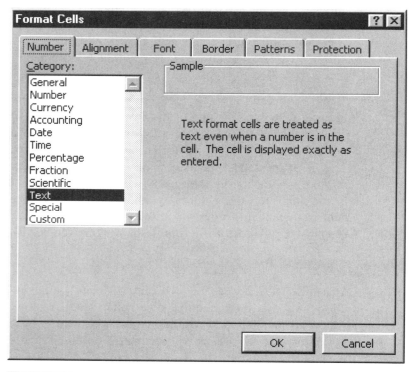

To create such a text-formatted cell, select the cell and then choose *Format/Cells*. On the *Number* tab page there is a list box called *Category*. Choose the *Text* item in this list.

In this category there is only one type of format and this cannot be modified. After choosing the format, close the dialog box with the *OK* button. Now you can enter numbers with leading zeros.

Fixing Decimal Places

Unless you spend your time at the stock market, you will probably be working with integers or with values having two decimal places. But if you have a lot of decimal places to enter, it is annoying to always have to write the decimal point. Therefore *Excel* gives you the option to specify how an entry will be interpreted.

Automatic decimal separator

By default *Excel* displays values with the entered precision and suppresses non-significant zeros. But if you tell *Excel* how many decimal places a value should have, and if you specify this before entering the data, then you do not have to enter the decimal separator anymore. *Excel* automatically sets the decimal point for you.

To avoid mistakes you will now have to consider the specified number of decimal places, even if the value you wish to enter has no decimal places. In this case you have to add the respective number of zeros.

To make the entry of the decimal point unnecessary for future entries, click on *Tools/Options* and choose the *Edit* tab.

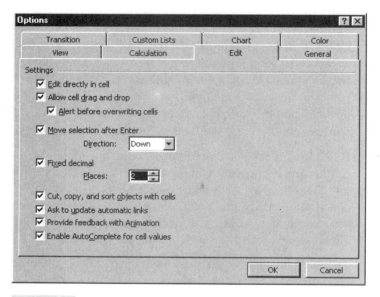

Fig. 1.11: Fixing decimal places

Check the box *Fixed decimal*. You can then adjust the number of decimal places in the *Places* spin box to the right of the check box. This will then be the number of decimal places and *Excel* will automatically separate these from the rest of the data entered with a decimal point.

For example, if you have specified two decimal places *Excel* will convert the data entry as follows:

34	1200	12095	100000
0.34	12	120.95	1000

Close the dialog box with the *OK* button. Now you can start entering the data. This choice of fixed decimal places will remain activated until you uncheck the check box in the *Options* dialog box.

Inserting Special Signs

With an ordinary PC keyboard you can already enter quite a few special characters in your *Excel* tables by using the ⌂ key.

° ^ $ % & ~

But sometimes you may have to enter characters that cannot be found on your keyboard, when not even the combination of the ⌂ or Alt keys can supply the right signs.

Windows special characters

Since *Excel* is a Windows application, you can use the Windows special characters in such a case. Here you will find several character sets which include symbols and characters from different languages, foreign currency symbols, and mathematical and physics symbols, among others.

You will for example find the sign for the British pound '£' or the sign for ø.

Character map

To insert special characters, click the *Start* button on the taskbar and choose *Programs/Accessories/Sytem Tools/ Character Map*. The characters which are displayed in this dialog box depend on the font selected.

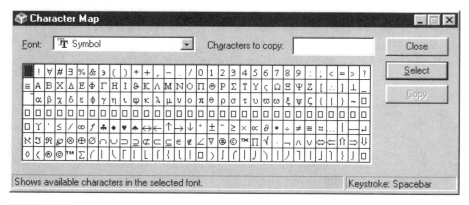

Fig. 1.13:   The Windows Character Map

Open the *Font* drop-down list and select a font. Clicking on a specific character enlarges it. As soon as you click on a character, a keystroke is displayed at the lower right corner of the dialog box. Using this key combination, you can immediately insert the character into the *Excel* cell.

Selecting characters

Click the *Select* button, and choose the highlighted character for transfer. Like this, the selected character is transferred into the *Characters to copy* box. This procedure allows you to select more than one character at a time.

Copying characters

After you have chosen all the special characters that you want to use in your cell, press the *Copy* button to copy all the characters selected into the Windows clipboard. If you need more characters in other locations of the table, switch to *Excel* using the *Excel* button on the taskbar, without closing the *Character Map* dialog box. Later on you can switch back and forth between *Excel* and *Character Map*.

Closing the Character Map

Once you have inserted all the special signs you require, click the *OK* button to close the *Character Map*. In *Excel*, select the cell into which you want to paste the special characters and place the insertion point where you want to insert them. Click the *Paste* button to insert the special characters from the clipboard into the cell.

Selecting the font   Select the special characters, open the *Font* drop-down box and choose the same font which you chose for the special characters in the *Character Map*.

Key combinations   To insert special characters you can also use the key combinations displayed in the *Character Map*. You have to type the numbers in the number pad of your keyboard Here are some examples:

ø	Alt+0216	Arial
£	Alt+0163	Arial
∞	Alt+0165	Symbol

Character Map   If the *Character Map* is not installed on your system, go to the Windows *Control Panel* and install this component by clicking on the *Add/Remove Programs* icon and moving to the *Windows Setup* tab.

Inserting the Date and Time

You can use *Excel* to insert and automatically update the date in a table. To quickly insert the date, you can use a key combination

Ctrl+;   Press the Ctrl+: key combination to insert the date. The manner in which the date is displayed can be controlled using the *Format/Cells* menu item. Choose one of the formats in the *Date* category.

Excel offers you the option of inserting the date into the table in such a way that it will be updated whenever you next edit the worksheet. Insert the following into the cell in which the current date should be displayed:

=TODAY()

Date formats

If you want to manually enter the date use one of the standard formats for dates. Use points, slashes or hyphens as separators.

Thus, the following examples are acceptable:

- 12.01.99
- 12-01-99
- 12/01/99

Time formats

When you enter the time, you have to use the colon to separate the hours, minutes and seconds. You can add AM or PM after the time, but leave a space in front of it so that *Excel* can distinguish it from the time value.

- 12:45:51 AM

You can also insert the time quickly by using the [Ctrl]+[◇]+[:] key combination.

Tip!

Use the function NOW() instead of TODAY(), if you want to display the date as well as the time. With the time format you can restrict the display to the time only.

Creating Series

Excel provides you with the *AutoFill* feature. This function helps you to automatically create series after you have entered a first value.

What are series? Series, in this context, consist of numeric values, dates, times or sequences of symbols that show constant intervals. Series in which the next value is automatically calculated by addition or subtraction are called *Linear Series*. Series in which the following value is obtained by multiplication or division are called *Growth Series*.

A time series can include increments of days, weeks, or months. It can also include different repeating sequences that you specify.

Here are some examples:

▪ Linear series: 1, 5, 9, 13, 17; delivery 1, delivery 2

▪ Growth series: 3, 6, 12, 24, etc.

▪ Date series: Monday, Tuesday, Wednesday

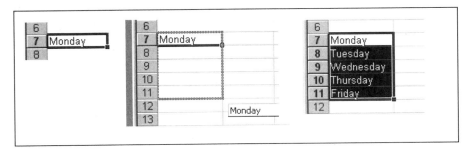

Fig. 1.14: Creating series with the fill handle

For any series that *Excel* can recognize automatically, it is sufficient to enter just the first value. For other series you have to enter the first two values.

Enter the first value or the first two values of the series and select the cells by clicking or by pressing ⟨◇⟩ and clicking. Drag the fill handle in the lower right-hand corner to the right or down until you reach the desired number of cells.

ScreenTip

Excel will always provide you with a *ScreenTip* which lets you know to which value you have dragged the cursor.

Instead of creating a series by dragging the fill handle, you can also use the *Edit/Fill/Series* command. If necessary, you can specify in the *Series in* option group, in which direction *Excel* should create the series. Use either the *Columns* or *Rows* radio button.

Step value

Select the type of series in the *Type* option group and, in case of *Date* series, which *Date* unit should be used. Enter a number into the *Step value* box to indicate the amount by which you want a series to increase or decrease.

If you have not specified the value where you want the series to end by selecting the cells, insert the desired length into the *Stop value* box.

If you want to calculate the trend, check the *Trend* box. In this case *Excel* does not consider the *Step value* and just continues to the specified *Stop value*. After confirming the Series dialog box with *OK*, *Excel* will fill the selected cells up to the chosen *Stop value*.

Creating Series with Your Own Values

Excel provides you with a very practical feature called *AutoFill* to automatically complete series of numbers and character sequences that contain certain increments.

Access this function either by dragging the fill handle or through the command *Edit/Fill/Series*. With series that *Excel* recognizes automatically, it is enough just to enter and select either the first or the first two cells. *Excel* will continue the series using the increment between the first two cell values.

To work with series that you frequently require but that *Excel* does not automatically complete, it is worthwhile to know more about the extended *AutoFill* function.

Choose *Tools/Options* and click the *Custom Lists* tab. In the *Custom lists* list box, the item *NEW LIST* is highlighted by default.

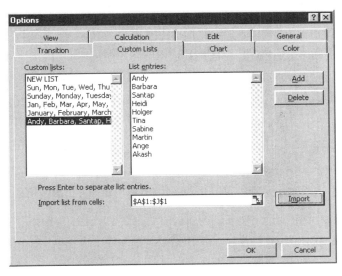

Fig. 1.15:   Creating custom lists

Click on the *List entries* box and enter the terms for your user defined list, one after the other, separated by commas or by pressing *Enter*, and then select the *Add* button. Your entries are added to the custom list. Close the dialog box with the *OK* button.

If you have already entered the items you want to use as a series in a worksheet range, select the list on the worksheet. On the *Tools* menu, click *Options* to call up the *Options* dialog box. In the dialog click the *Custom Lists* tab. In the *Import list from cells* box you will see the selected worksheet range. To use the selected list, click the *Import* button. Excel will add your new list to the items of the custom lists.

From now on, it is enough to enter the first entry of your list and continue the series using the fill handle. Select the cell after you have entered the first list vallue and drag the series with the fill handle to the desired stop value. You do not necessarily have to begin with the first item of the list.

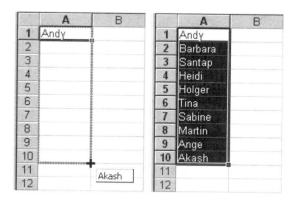

Fig. 1.16:   A user defined list

Moving Within a Worksheet and Among Worksheets.

When you enter data into the various cells of your work-sheet, you have to move around within the document of course to reach the cell into which you want to enter the data.

And when you want to start with the creation of the next table, or if you want to create a link between different sheets using a formula, you should be able to freely move around and between the worksheets of a workbook, and even between different workbooks.

Moving Within a Worksheet

To enter data into a cell you move to the cell and select it. Then you can easily spot the cell, because it has a dark frame around it. You can select a cell by clicking on it with the left mouse button. You can also use the keyboard arrows, as well as the *Go To* command, to move to a new target cell.

If you can already see the cell you want to go to, all you have to do is click on it. If the cell is not visible on the screen, you first have to move the window content in order to display the cell. Only then can you click it.

To move the window content with the mouse, click with the left mouse button on the scroll bar. The scroll bars are situated at the right edge and at the lower edge of the window. Slide the scroll bar box by clicking on it and holding down the left mouse button. Using the scroll bar arrows in the horizontal and vertical scroll bars, you can shift the window content row by row or column by column.

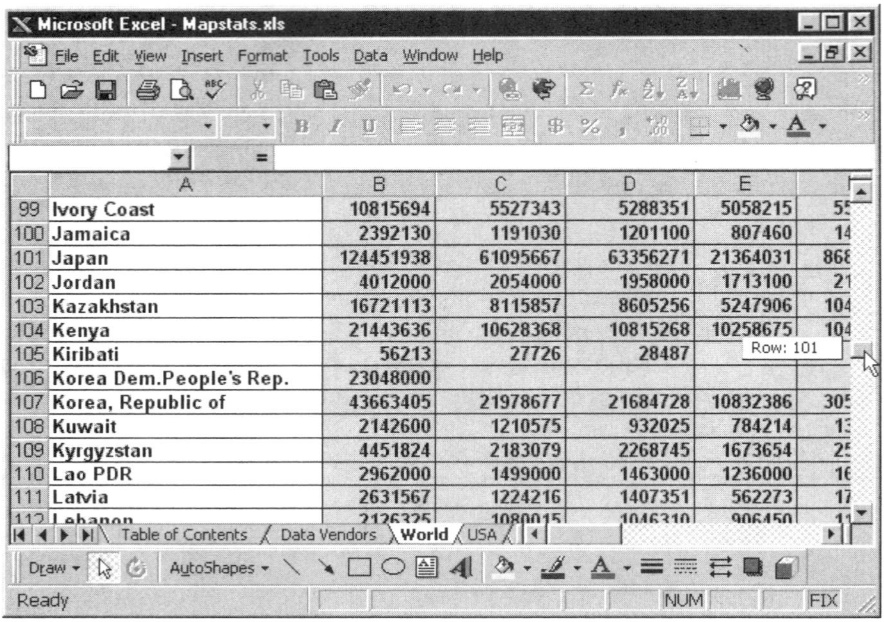

Fig. 1.17: The pointer on the scroll bar box

While scrolling with the scroll bar box, a ScreenTip informs you about your present position. As soon as you release the left mouse button, the table is displayed in such a way that the column or row shown in the ScrollTip appears as the first column or row.

Clicking anywhere on the scroll bar before or after the scroll bar box will scroll through the window content one page at a time. This is the same movement that occurs when you press PgUp and PgDn.

Use the scroll arrows at the end of every scroll bar as follows:

- ◀ Click this button to slide the window content one column to the right and thus display the content of the column beside it on the left.

- ▶ Use this button to slide the window content one column to the left and thus display the content of the column beside it on the right.

- ▲ Click this button to slide the window content one row down and thus display the content of the row above it.

- ▼ This button slides the window content one row up and thus displays the content of the row below it.

Moving with the keyboard

The keyboard can also be used to navigate between columns and rows. Using the mouse, you must first move over the cell and then select it. However, using the keyboard, you can directly select the cell, because you can actually move the cell frame in the desired direction. The window content will shift automatically when you come to the last visible row or column on the screen.

- Press the → or ← key, to move one column to the right or to the left.

- Use the ↑ or ↓ key, to move one row at a time up or down.

- Press the PgDn and PgUp keys to move up or down one screen at a time.

- Press the Ctrl+Home or Ctrl+End key-combination, to jump to the first or last row or column of your table.

- If your table has locked cells, use the Tab⇆ key to move to the next unlocked cell.

The sheet tabs are displayed to the left of the horizontal scroll bar. You can resize the horizontal scroll bar by dragging the tab split bar between the tabs and the scroll bar.

Go To

Another way of going to a certain cell in the table is to use the *Go To* command. You can call up this dialog box by choosing *Edit/GoTo* or by pressing the ⌈Ctrl⌉+⌈g⌉ key combination.

This dialog box can be used in many ways. Enter the address of the cell you want to jump to and click *OK*.

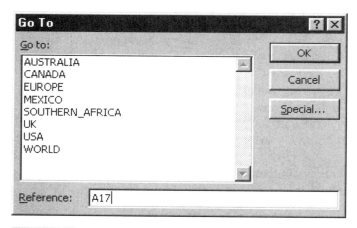

Fig. 1.18:   References in the *Go To* dialog box

Excel displays the respective cell and highlights it. The cell is thus framed. You can as well enter the reference to a cell area, then the respective area will be selected and displayed simultaneously.

The references you entered in the dialog box are stored in the list. The next time you open the dialog box a double-click on the desired entry will be enough to move to this reference.

Fig. 1.19:   Moving with the *Name* box

An entry in the *Name* box on the left side of the formula bar will also enable you to jump to any cell in the worksheet. Write the cell reference into the *Name* box and press the *Enter* key ⏎.

Tip! If your worksheet contains named cells, you can also enter the names of the cell into the *Named* box in order to reach the cell with that name. You can also type the name of the cell into the *GoTo* dialog box.

Moving Among Various Worksheets of a Workbook

If you have completed your task in one worksheet or you want to create a reference to another cell in a different worksheet, then you first have to switch to that worksheet.

You can switch between worksheets using the mouse and the worksheet tabs or using the keyboard. The sheet tabs are at the lower border of the workbook window. There is one tab for every element in the workbook.

You can move to another worksheet by clicking on its sheet tab. The active worksheet tab always appears highlighted. If the tab of the worksheet, that you want to switch to is not visible, first use the tab scrolling buttons at the left end of the bar to scroll through the tabs. These buttons will only scroll through the tabs but do not actually switch to the Worksheet.

- ◄ Click this button to display the first worksheet tab.

- ►► This button will display the last worksheet tab.

- ► Click here to display the next worksheet tab.

- ◄ Use this button to see the previous worksheet tab.

With the keyboard   If you want to use the keyboard to move to the next worksheet, use the Ctrl+PgDn key combination. The Ctrl+PgUp key combination will take you to the previous worksheet.

Toggling Between Worksheets of Different Workbooks

If you have more than one workbook open at a time, you can either display the workbooks next to each other on the screen, or toggle between the workbooks with a simple click. There is also a key combination and a command to execute this task.

Window menu   Open the *Window* menu. At the very end of the menu, a list of all the open workbooks appears. Either click on the name of the workbook you want to see, or enter the respective number.

Ctrl + F6

Instead of the above procedure you can also use the Ctrl+F6 key combination to move through all the workbooks one by one.

After activating the workbook, click on the worksheet tab to reach your destination worksheet and then select the cell you want to edit.

Selecting Cells in a Worksheet

A lot of tasks, like formatting, copying or moving cell contents, proceed once the first step of selecting the cells has been taken. You have to do that, so that *Excel* can apply your commands to the correct cells.

The selecting procedure inverts the color of a cell area, except for the first cell, the one with which you began. This cell remains uninverted but is still included in the selection.

Mouse, keyboard or command ?

You can use the mouse or the keyboard for selecting the cells. Additionally there is a command to select cell areas or cells with certain contents.

Selecting Cells with the Left Mouse Button

Using the mouse click is definitely the simplest way to select cells. You do not have to remember key combinations or commands, you can always use the same basic procedure. And you can speed up the selecting even more if you know the elements of the table that allow you to select whole columns or rows with a single click.

Drag

A procedure that you can use independent of the area to be selected, is the dragging of the mouse over the cells to be highlighted. Click the first cell and drag the mouse, with the left mouse button pressed, to the last cell to be selected.

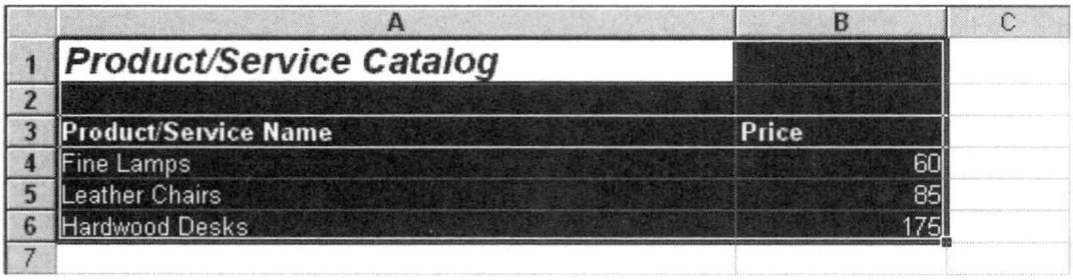

	A	B	C
1	**Product/Service Catalog**		
2			
3	Product/Service Name	Price	
4	Fine Lamps	60	
5	Leather Chairs	85	
6	Hardwood Desks	175	
7			

Fig. 1.21:　　Selected cells, started at the cell A1

Selected cells are displayed in inverted color. The first cell remains the active cell and is therefore not inverted, but it is nevertheless part of the selection.

To select a complete column, click on the column heading with the left mouse button. To highlight several columns, click on the first column heading and drag the mouse over all the column headings to be highlighted.

Fig. 1.22:　　The row heading highlights the row

In order to select an entire row, all you have to do is to click on the row heading. To select several row headings, click on the first row heading and then drag the mouse over all the rows that you want to select.

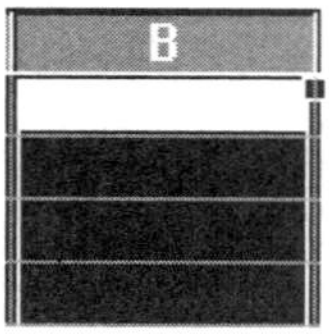

Fig. 1.23:　　The column heading highlights the column

If you want to select the entire table, e.g., in order to choose a different font, click the button which is located to the left of the first column header and on top of the first row header.

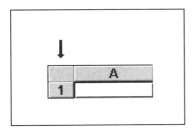

Fig. 1.24: The *Select All* button

To select several non-adjacent cells with the left mouse button, click the first cell or highlight the first area. Then, while holding down the Ctrl key, select further cells or drag over further cell areas.

A	B	C
1 **Product/Service Catalog**		
2		
3 Product/Service Name	Price	
4 Fine Lamps	60	
5 Leather Chairs	85	
6 Hardwood Desks	175	
7		
8		
9		
10		
11		
12		
13		
14		

Fig. 1.25: Multiple selection

You can cancel the current selection by simply clicking anywhere outside the highlighted area.

Selecting Cells with the Keyboard

If you want to perform changes like formatting your cells after entering them, the mouse is a convenient tool.

However, during data entry, moving your hand back and forth between the mouse and keyboard slows down your work significantly and it is advisable to use the keyboard for selecting. Therefore *Excel* also provides keys and key combinations which can be used on the keyboard to highlight all the elements that can otherwise be selected with the mouse.

[⇧]+ arrow keys

To highlight an area of adjacent cells with the keyboard, hold down the [⇧] key and move over the cells using the [←], [→], [↑] or [↓] arrow keys

Fast selecting

With the following key combination you can select cells exceptionally fast:

▣ [Ctrl]+[spacebar]   highlights the whole column.

▣ [⇧]+[spacebar]   highlights the whole row.

▣ [Ctrl]+[a]   highlights the whole table.

If you do not like holding down the [⇧] key all the time while selecting cells using the keyboard, you can also switch on the *Extension* mode using [F8]. This will be indicated in the status bar at the bottom of the application window. Look for the little *EXT*. This mode can be switched off with the [Esc] key or by pressing the [F8] key again.

Fig. 1.26:   The status bar indicating Extended Selection

With the ⌈Ctrl⌉+⌈⇧⌉+⌈Home⌉ and. ⌈Ctrl⌉+⌈⇧⌉+⌈End⌉ key combinations you can extend a highlighted area to the first or
last cell of the table.

Selecting Large Cell Areas

If you want to select the complete worksheet, click on the
button at the top-left side of the first worksheet. This
button highlights all cells in the worksheet, no matter
how many cells the worksheet contains.

Another way to select large cell areas is to temporarily
use the ⌈F8⌉ key. Click the top left cell of the area you
want to highlight and press ⌈F8⌉. The *EXT* will show up in
the status bar to indicate that this feature is now active.

Deactivating the
Extension

Click on the last cell to the far right of the cells that
should be included in your selected range. The entire area
will be displayed inverted. You can then deactivate the
Extension mode by pressing ⌈F8⌉ again.

And here is yet another method of selecting a large range
of cells: Click on the first cell in the left of the desired
area and switch on the *Extension* mode with ⌈F8⌉.

Go To

Then choose *Edit/Go To* and enter the address of the last
cell into the *Reference* box. Close the dialog box with
OK.

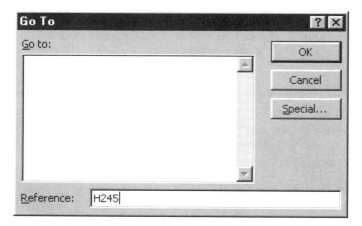

Fig. 1.27:   The *Go To* dialog box

The *Go To* command is normally used for single jumps in
a worksheet but can be of help in selecting a large range
of cells while using the *Extension* select mode.

Selecting Non-adjacent Cells

Often you have to copy a formula into more than one cell
and the target cells are scattered all over your worksheet.

Also, for the creation of references to several non-adjacent single cells, multiple selection is a necessary feature.
With this highlighting procedure you can select all non-
adjacent cells and cell areas.

Ctrl

If you want to highlight non-adjacent cells, select the first
cell and then, while holding down the Ctrl key, click all
the other required cells one by one, or drag the mouse
over the cell areas you need.

Non-adjacent cell areas can also be highlighted with the
keyboard by activating the *Multiple* selection. Click the
first cell or select the first cell area of your multiple
selection.

Press the key combination ⟨⇧⟩+⟨F8⟩. With *ADD* in the status bar the *Multiple* selection will be indicated.

ADD

Fig. 1.28:   The *Multiple Selection* indicator in the status bar

Select the next cell or the next cell area and press the ⟨⇧⟩+⟨F8⟩ key combination again. Repeat the selection and the key combination alternately until all the required cells have been highlighted.

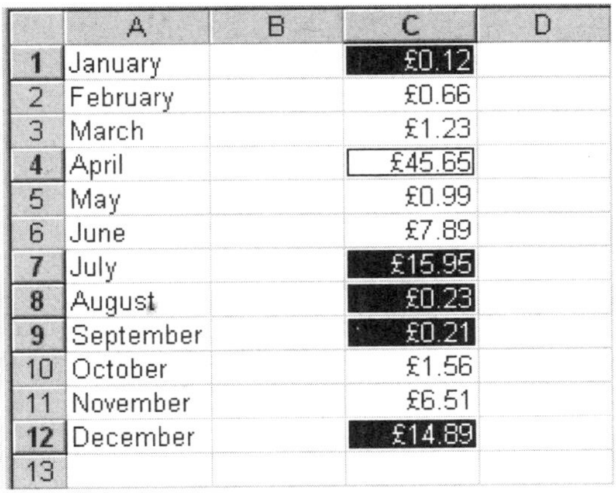

	A	B	C	D
1	January		£0.12	
2	February		£0.66	
3	March		£1.23	
4	April		£45.65	
5	May		£0.99	
6	June		£7.89	
7	July		£15.95	
8	August		£0.23	
9	September		£0.21	
10	October		£1.56	
11	November		£6.51	
12	December		£14.89	
13				

Fig. 1.29:   A multiple selection

Selecting All Cells with a Particular Cell Content

If you want to select or edit all the cells that contain a particular entry, you do not have to search for them one by one in your worksheet.

Edit /Go To

The *Edit/Go To* command is designed to help you navigate within the worksheet, but it can also be used for selecting purposes. If you switch on the *ADD* option before you select the *Go To* command, then all the cells from the activated cell to the cell you are jumping to will be highlighted.

All cells with a particular content can be automatically selected with the *Go To* command. Choose *Edit/Go To* and click the *Special* button in the dialog box.

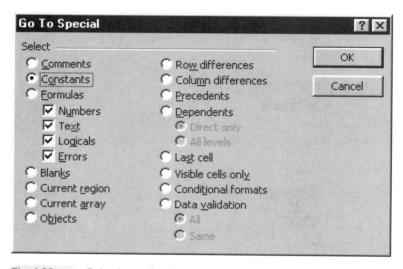

Fig. 1.30:   Selecting cells with special contents

Selecting contents   In the *Go To Special* dialog box you can choose the kind of cell you want to select. For example, you can click the *Constants* radio button, to select all cells with constant values.

Subsequently, using the check boxes, you can select with more precision what kind of constants the cells should contain, say, only text. Uncheck all check boxes indicating types that you are not interested in.

If you want to inspect certain cell references or correct a mistake, you can in addition select all preceding and dependent cells by selecting the *Precedents* and *Dependents* options. This will select all the cells which are logically connected, either backward or forward, with the activated cell.

Click the *OK* button. *Excel* will now highlight all cells in the worksheet that contain the special information. With the ⌜Tab⇆⌟ key, you can jump from selection to selection. Within a highlighted cell area the ⌜Tab⇆⌟ key will jump one by one to all selected cells in the area before it proceeds to the next separate cell or cell area.

Repeating, Undo and Redo commands

In *Excel* you can repeat procedures that you need to perform more than once. Suppose you want to insert several rows or columns. You can do this just once and then repeat the procedure until the job is done, using the key combination for the *Repeat* command.

Particularly helpful for the beginner is the program's capacity to undo, that is, to reverse an action. You should memorize the *Undo* command in order to always be able to withdraw a command or a number of actions if the result does not satisfy you.

Undo Commands

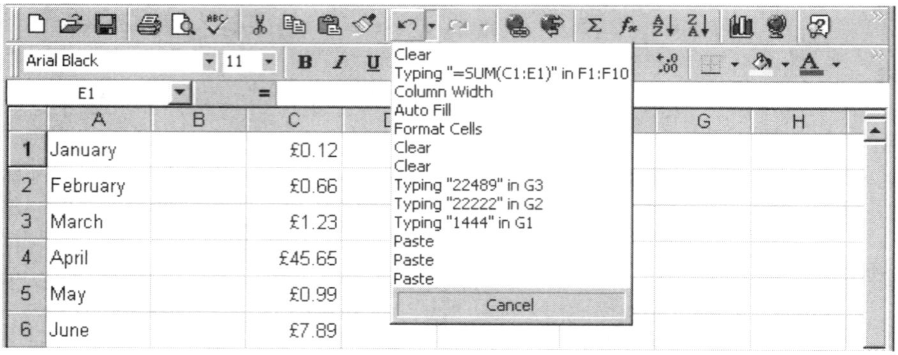

Fig. 1.31: The list of the last operations

To undo an action, perform one of the following procedures:

- Choose *Edit/Undo*: command 'xyz'.

- Press the ⌨Ctrl⌨+⌨z⌨ key combination.

- Click the *Undo* button ↺.

Excel can undo more than one operation. The last 16 operations you performed are stored in a list. Click the drop-
down button next to the *Undo* ↺▾ button and then click
on the command up to which you want to undo your
work.

Redo Actions

In the present version of *Excel* the previous *Repeat* button
has a new definition. It can only be used to redo commands that have been previously undone.

If you used *Undo* for one or more operations, then you
can open the *Redo* drop-down list ↻▾ on the right-hand

side of the *Redo* button. There you will find a list of up to 16 operations which can be redone.

And this is the new *Redo* button. But you can still repeat actions in *Excel 97*. In order to repeat the last executed command, perform one of the following steps:

▣ choose *Edit/Redo*: command 'xyz'.

▣ press the ⌈Ctrl⌋+⌊y⌋ key combination.

There are, however, some cases in which commands cannot be undone, repeated or redone. However, if the action cannot be undone or repeated or redone, at least you get the comforting message: *Can't Undo* etc. It will be displayed in the *Edit* menu next to the respective command.

Inserting Cells, Rows and Columns

While editing a table you often have to shuffle around or update already entered cells, in order to improve the results. In *Excel* you can insert additional cells, rows or columns any time you like.

In order to insert an additional row into your table, click on the heading of the row above which you want to insert a new row. Choose *Insert/Rows*.

If you want to insert an empty column, click on the column heading of the column to the left of which you want to insert the empty column. Choose *Insert/Columns*.

Inserting several
rows or columns

If you want to insert several rows or columns in one go, first select the desired number of row headings or column headings. Then choose the *Insert* command to perform the action.

Inserting Cells

You have to take more care while inserting cells than you would if you were inserting whole rows or whole columns. Cells, if not properly inserted in a table, can upset the existing structure of the table.

If you want to change the position of a cell or a cell area, select the area and choose *Insert/Cells*. You should then decide whether you are going to shift the cells to the right or down.

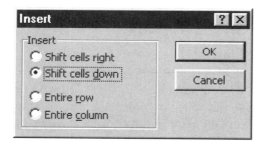

Fig. 1.32:   Inserting cells

Select the correct option from those available in the dialog box and click the *OK* button. The following figure shows the table as it looks before and after inserting the cells.

	A	B	C	D
1	January	Andy	£0.12	
2	February	Barbara	£0.66	
3	March	Martin	£1.23	
4	April	Barbara	£45.65	
5	May	Andy	£0.99	
6	June	Andy	£7.89	
7	July	Barbara	£15.95	
8	August	Martin	£0.23	
9	September	Barbara	£0.21	
10	October	Andy	£1.56	
11	November	Martin	£6.51	
12	December	Martin	£14.89	
13				
14				
15				

Fig. 1.33: The original table

	A	B	C	D
1	January		£0.12	
2	February	Andy	£0.66	
3	March	Barbara	£1.23	
4	April	Martin	£45.65	
5	May	Barbara	£0.99	
6	June	Andy	£7.89	
7	July	Andy	£15.95	
8	August	Barbara	£0.23	
9	September	Martin	£0.21	
10	October	Barbara	£1.56	
11	November	Andy	£6.51	
12	December	Martin	£14.89	
13		Martin		
14				
15				

Fig. 1.34: The cells shifted down by one cell

	A	B	C	D
1	January		Andy	£0.12
2	February	Barbara	£0.66	
3	March	Martin	£1.23	
4	April	Barbara	£45.65	
5	May	Andy	£0.99	
6	June	Andy	£7.89	
7	July	Barbara	£15.95	
8	August	Martin	£0.23	
9	September	Barbara	£0.21	
10	October	Andy	£1.56	
11	November	Martin	£6.51	
12	December	Martin	£14.89	
13				
14				
15				

Fig. 1.35:   The cells shifted to the right by one cell

Deleting and Clearing Cells

When we talk about deleting cells and table contents, we have to differentiate between deleting the data *within* a cell and deleting the cell itself. The deletion of data within the cell is called *clearing* and it leaves the cell empty. It does not change the structure of the table. The order and position of all the table's elements remains unchanged. The cleared cells are displayed as blanks.

However, deleting the cell alters the order of the cells themselves. Therefore a dialog box pops up which prompts you to decide whether the deleted cell should be replaced by cells from the row or by cells from the column.

Deleting Cells, Columns or Rows

The deletion of cells, as well as the deletion of rows or columns is all done using the same command. Always remember that deleting will alter the entire structure of the table.

Select the cells, rows or columns you want to delete, and choose *Edit/Delete.*When you delete cells, a dialog box is called up in which you can specify in which direction the cells are to be shifted in order to immediately close the gap that will be created after the respective cells have been removed.

If you choose the *Shift cells left* option button in the *Delete* dialog box, the cell to the right of the empty place will shift into this position and drag all the adjacent cells with it.

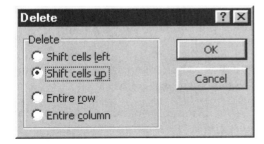

Fig. 1.36:   Deleting single cells

On the other hand, choosing the *Shift cells up* radio button will move all the cells below the empty place up by one cell.

Deleting Cell Contents

There is a difference between deleting and clearing a cell. If you delete cells in a worksheet, the order of all the cells will be rearranged, because either they will move up or to the left in order to fill the gap that was caused by deleting the cell

Clearing the cell contents

On the other hand, clearing the content of the cell does not change the structure of the worksheet. The cell will simply be empty afterwards, or altered if only a part of it was cleared. Cells not only store text and numbers for display, but they can also contain:

- Formats

- Contents

- Comments

Clearing data

You can either clear the contents of a cell completely, or you can delete only a part of the information stored in the cell. In order to clear only the formulas or constants that have been entered into the cell, select the cell and press the Del key. In this manner, all the formatting information in the cell is retained.

Partly clearing the cell

If only a part of the cell is to be removed, double-click on the cell and clear the unwanted part with Del.

Clearing certain contents

To remove certain parts of the information contained in a cell, highlight the cell and select the *Edit/Clear* command and choose one of the following items from the overlapping submenu:

- *All*, to remove all information from the cell.

- *Formats*, to remove only the formatting of the cell.

- *Contents Del*, to remove only the entered constants and formulas.

- *Comments*, to clear linked notes or comments.

Editing Formulas, Values and Other Cell Contents

After having finished entering the data into a cell, *Excel* immediately displays the entered data in the cell. Text is automatically left-aligned, while numeric values are automatically right-aligned. Date and time information is also right-aligned.

If you want to change data once it has been entered in a cell, you should not just go into the cell by double-clicking on it and then start typing. This procedure is perfect for entering new data into empty cells or if you want to completely replace the data in a cell.

Edit mode

However, if the content has to be modified, you should first activate the cell for editing. To do so, change to edit mode. Select the cell to be edited and then proceed in one of the following ways:

▪ Press F2 .

▪ Double-click the cell.

▪ Click directly on the place to be changed in the formula bar.

You can recognize the edit mode by the change in the frame around the cell as well as by the blinking cursor in the cell. The formula bar will show the cell's contents and the edit buttons. The status bar will display the message *Edit* instead of the message *Ready*.

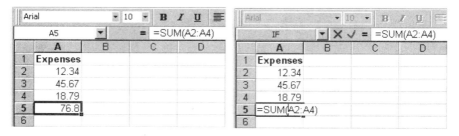

Fig. 1.37: The cell in normal mode and in edit mode

Now make all the corrections, changes and supplements you want. You can type either in the formula bar or in the cell itself. Lengthy cell contents are easier to edit in the formula bar.

- Click with the mouse on the place where additional data is to be entered and start typing.

- Move character by character within the cell or within the formula bar using the →, ←, ↑, and ↓ keys.

- With Home or End you can jump directly to the beginning or to the end of the cell content.

- Use the Del and ← keys to clear the cell.

Overwrite mode

The Ins key switches on the *OVR* mode, which stands for *Overwrite* mode and is indicated in the status bar. In this mode you can overwrite your data starting from the insertion point. This means that the data you enter will not be pushed to the right while you are typing as is normally the case. Press the Ins key again to return to the normal *Insert* mode.

You can select parts of the cell content in order to move, copy or delete them. To do so, click and drag the mouse over the respective characters. With the *Cut* button ✄ you can cut out the data and *Paste* it into another position in the same cell or in another cell. If you click the *Copy* button 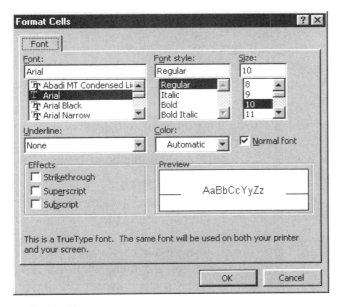 instead of the *Cut* button, you can duplicate the contents you have selected later on by clicking the *Paste* button.

If you want to format part of the cell content, select this part and click the buttons on the *Formatting* toolbar or choose *Format/Cells*.

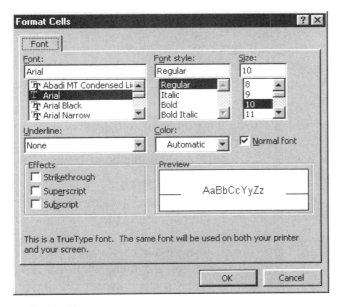

Fig. 1.38:   The *Format Cells* dialog box

The *Format Cells* dialog box shows only one tab page now, the one which is used for fonts. This is because within a cell only formatting related to fonts can be done. Any other formatting always involves the cell as a whole.

Enter the editing

Complete your editing of the formula or the cell content with the *Enter* key or by clicking the *Enter* button on the formula bar.

Entering Data into Several Tables by Grouping Worksheets

It often happens that certain calculations have to be repeated at regular intervals. These include, for example monthly salaries, the year-end closing of the accounts or the weekly or monthly monitoring of the your expenses.

What is grouping?

When creating worksheets which have the same structure and the same formulas in the same places, you should group them together before you enter data that is going to be identical in all the tables. Then you only have to enter the data once, and it will automatically be entered into all the worksheets by *Excel*. In *Excel*, the sharing of the same information between several cells is called *grouping*.

Grouped worksheets are handled in the same way as an individual worksheet. Any command or data you enter in one of the sheets is applied to all of the other sheets in the group.

Grouping

You can group adjacent worksheets, meaning worksheets whose tabs in the sheet tab bar are next to each other, or you can group worksheets that are further apart. To group worksheets that directly neighbour each other, click on the tab of the first worksheet and then, while pressing down the ⌂ key, click the last worksheet tab. If you want to group worksheets that are not located next to each other, click on the tab of the first worksheet and then, while holding down the Ctrl key, all the other tabs of your choice.

The group is indicated in the title bar as well as in the sheet tabs. The title bar of a workbook contains the *[Group]* extension, and the tabs of all grouped worksheets appear highlighted. You can now enter all data and formulas that are common to all the selected worksheets.

You can also perform all the formatting that you need for all the worksheets as well.

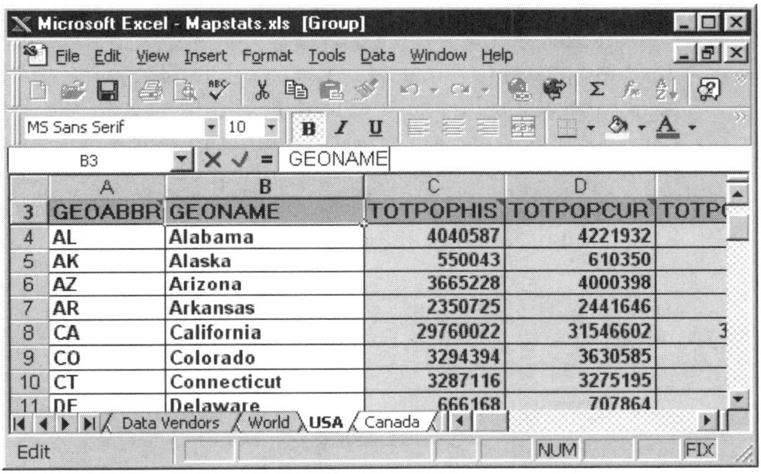

Fig. 1.39:   A group

To cancel a group, click on the tab of a worksheet that does not belong to the group. You can also right-click the tab of a grouped worksheet to open the shortcut menu, and then choose the *Ungroup Sheets* command.

Copying Data Within a Worksheet

Data which is needed in various places in an *Excel* table can be duplicated in several different ways. Save time and energy, do not unnecessarily bang the keyboard!

The simplest way to duplicate cells is to copy the data into adjacent cells. To do this, use the fill handle. It does not matter whether the data contains numeric values, text or formulas. All cell contents are copied using the fill handle.

Besides the fill handle, you can also use the *Copy* and *Fill* commands and buttons. The fill handle itself is the little box you will find in the lower right-hand corner of the active cell.

Copying with the fill handle

To copy data into adjacent cells using the fill handle, first select the cell with the source data and then drag the fill handle either to the left or to the right, or up or down over the cells, depending on where you want to have the copied data. As long as you have not released the mouse button, you can adjust the size of the highlighted area.

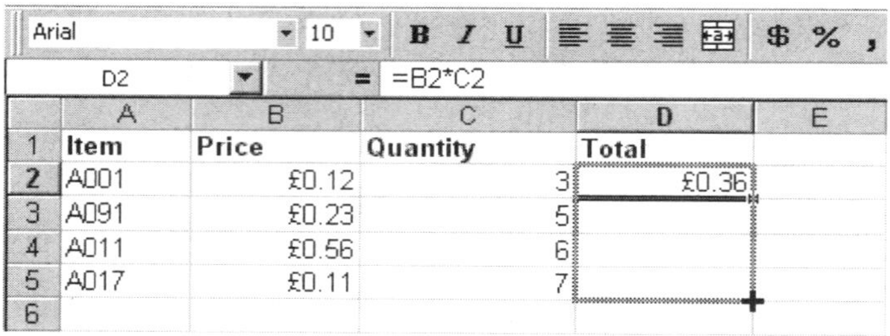

	A	B	C	D	E
1	Item	Price	Quantity	Total	
2	A001	£0.12	3	£0.36	
3	A091	£0.23	5		
4	A011	£0.56	6		
5	A017	£0.11	7		
6					

Arial — 10 — B *I* U $ % ,

D2 = =B2*C2

Fig. 1.40: Copying a formula with the fill handle

You can also use a command to copy existing information into adjacent cells. Select both the cell to be copied and the adjacent cell or cell area into which the data has to be copied.

Fill by command

Choose *Edit/Fill* and select the command to fix the direction in which to move the cells. Choose, for example, *Down* to fill all selected cells below the first cell with the data contained within the cell to be copied.

To fill non-adjacent cells, use the *Copy* command. Here also, the first step is to select the source cell. Then execute one of the following steps:

- Click the *Copy* button 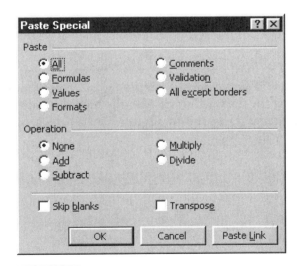.
- Choose *Edit/Copy*.
- Press the `Ctrl`+`C` key combination.

Next, click on the first cell or select the first cell area into which you want to copy the data. Click the *Paste* button , or choose *Edit/Paste*. Repeat these last steps until you have pasted the data into all the cells, and complete the job by pressing the `↵` key.

Copying only formats or contents

Whenever you copy the contents of a cell, you are copying not only the value or the text which is visible in the cell. You are also copying the formatting information, such as the number format, and the comments, if any, which are invisibly linked to the cell. Use the *Paste Special* command instead of the *Paste* command if you want to copy only the data or only the formatting information.

Fig. 1.41: Copying of special contents

In the *Paste Special* dialog box, you can choose which part of the cell content you want to copy by selecting the respective radio button. After clicking the *OK* button, only the elements of the cell content you selected will be copied into the target positions.

Copying and Moving by Drag-and-Drop

As an alternative to using the clipboard, you can work with the mouse and the *Drag-and-Drop* procedure to copy and move selected cells. You can move or copy data:

- within a worksheet,

- from one worksheet to another,

- from one workbook to another,

- from a workbook to a document of another application.

Moving Cell Contents

In order to move cell contents using drag-and-drop, you have to select the data and point with the mouse pointer on the cell frame. Drag the frame to a new position in order to move the data.

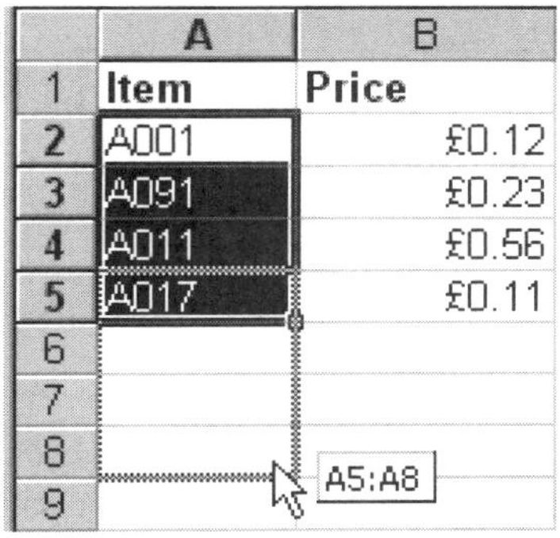

	A	B
1	**Item**	**Price**
2	A001	£0.12
3	A091	£0.23
4	A011	£0.56
5	A017	£0.11
6		
7		
8		A5:A8
9		

Fig. 1.42:   The mouse during drag-and-drop

Copying Cell Contents

While holding down the [Ctrl] key, drag the cell frame to a new position in order to copy the contents of the selected cell into the new cell.

To insert cells, i.e., to copy them into the space between cells that already contain information, just hold down the [⇧] key while dragging.

Copying From One Table to Another

If you want to copy cells from one worksheet to another, open a second window by choosing *Window/New window*. This enables you to see both the source and the destination worksheet on the desktop at the same time. Select the required cell and drag it from the source sheet to the destination sheet while holding down the [Ctrl] key.

To drag data from one workbook to another, open both workbooks and arrange them with the *Window/Arrange* command. Select the data and, while holding down the [Ctrl] key, drag the cell from the source workbook to the destination workbook.

71

Copying to Other Applications

In order to drag data from one application to another, start the destination application and open the destination document there. Select the cell which contains the information, and drag-and-drop it into the destination window.

Creating a Scrap Table

You can also make a little detour: Arrange your *Excel* application window in such a way that you can see a part of the *Windows 98* desktop. Now just drag the selection over to any point on the desktop. A scrap table has been created and you will see the respective icon on the desktop.

Later on you can insert this table into a destination document any time you want. This procedure is necessary if for some reason you do not want to open the other program immediately

Worksheet
Scrap 'Jordan
Kazakhst...'

Fig. 1.43:   A scrap icon

Finding Table Contents

In a large worksheet it is sometimes difficult to locate the cell which contains a particular piece of information. Luckily there is a find command which can search through the whole table to find it.

Excel compares the contents of each cell of the worksheet with the search text you have entered.

Each time *Excel* finds a match, it will halt its search and display the cell. When you find the right cell, you can interrupt the search; otherwise carry on with the search until you find what you are looking for.

To search through a worksheet using this method, choose *Edit/Find* or press the Ctrl+F key combination. In the dialog box, type the text you want to find into the *Find what* box. Specify in the *Search* drop-down list whether *Excel* should search first through rows or columns.

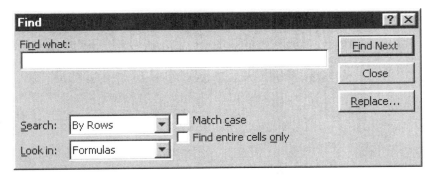

Fig. 1.44:   Find in tables

In the *Look in* drop-down list you can specify which elements you are looking for. Choose *Values* if you want to find the entered keyword as a constant value or formula result.

Formulas

Choose *Formula*, if you want to find the keyword only as a constant value or as a part of a formula, but not as a formula result. If you want to search only comments, choose *Comments* from the list.

Match case

Select the *Match case* check box if you want the search text and result text to match exactly, including lower and uppercase letters, in other words, if you want the search to be case sensitive. Mark the *Find entire cells only* check box if you want *Excel* to search only for cells that contain nothing apart from the keyword you typed in.

Start the search by clicking the *Find Next* button. Keep clicking this button until you find the cell or all the cells you are searching for. You can click the *Replace* button in order to automatically replace the contents of the cell you have found with different information. Complete or interrupt the search by clicking the *Close* button.

A particularly fast method of searching for data that occurs more than once is by activating the *Find Next* feature with the ⌂ + F4 key combination after you have performed the first search and then closed the dialog box.

Replacing Table Contents

In very large workbooks, it is often a very tedious task to tidy up everything and keep the table up to date. To make sure that you do not overlook any data, *Excel* offers not only the *Find* dialog which we already discussed, but also ways to extend this feature and to replace particular entries with new information.

The *Replace* function

The *Replace* function can be used in two ways. Either it can automatically replace all the findings with the new information, or you can control the replacement process by confirming each replacement individually.

To work with this function, choose *Edit/Find*. Type the keyword into the *Find what* text box. The keyword is the expression you are searching for.

Replace

The new expression with which you wish to replace the keyword should be typed into the *Replace with* text box. This is where you put the new data you want to appear in your table.

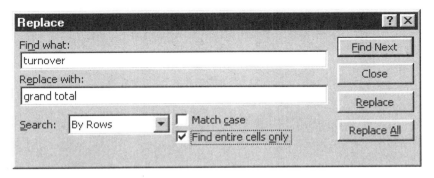

Fig. 1.45:   The replace function

In our example the text 'turnover' is replaced by the text 'grand total' Check the check box *Match case* if you want the search to be case sensitive.

Find entire

cells only

If you want to search only for cells that contain only your keyword, mark the *Find entire cells only* check box.

If you want *Excel* to search row by row choose *By Rows* in the *Search* drop-down list. To search column by column, choose *By Columns*.

Start the search by clicking on the *Find Next* button. When the first match is displayed on the screen, clicking on the *Replace All* button will replace this and all other matches throughout the entire worksheet.

In order to manually control the replacement of each match, click the *Find Next* button. When the first result appears, click on the *Replace* button if you want to replace it, and then click on the *Find Next* button again. Close the dialog box by clicking on the *Close* button.

2. Formulas and Functions

Excel offers you a large number of readymade functions with which you can quickly calculate, verify or change the data on your worksheet.

Among them are, for example, functions that sum up several numeric values or find the average value of a range of numbers, or calculate the smallest and largest values in a range of numbers.

You can also assemble your own formulas and use the readymade functions within your formulas.

Creating Formulas

The entry of a formula always begins with an equal sign. Exceptions are formulas that begin with the entry of a function. A click on the *Paste Function* button on the *Standard* toolbar automatically inserts the equal sign when you enter a function via the *Paste Function* dialog box. Likewise, clicking the *Edit Formula* button `=` in order to display the *Formula Palette* will automatically insert the equal sign.

To assemble a formula you can use the following elements:

- Numeric values

- Cell addresses

- Functions

- Operators

- Cell names or names of cell areas

- Character sequences as function arguments in quotation marks

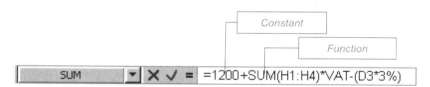

Fig. 2.1:   The formula in the Formula Palette

To create a simple formula with operators and without functions, first type or insert the equal sign.

=

Creating references

Click the cursor on the first cell that should be included in the formula. Then enter the required operator. Now click the cursor over the next cell to be included in the formula.

Close formulas

Type the next operator, click the next cell and repeat these steps until you have included all the necessary cells. Complete the creation of the formula with ⏎, or click the *Enter* button ✓.

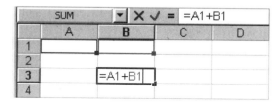

Fig. 2.2:   A simple formula

The buttons you find on the *Formula* bar are there to help you create and edit formulas.

▣ *Edit Formula* =
Click the *Edit Formula* button = to display the *Formula Palette* and to insert an equal sign to start the formula.

■ *Enter* ✅
Use this button to finalize the entry of a formula. You can also press the ⏎ key or click into the next cell that has to be edited.

■ *Cancel* ❌
With this button you can cancel the entry of a formula. The new data or the changes will then be lost.

Function box

The *Function* box at the left end of the formula bar appears when you start a formula with the equal sign. It replaces the *Name* box. Generally, the *Function* box displays the most recently used worksheet function.

Fig. 2.3:   The formula bar with the *Function* box on the left

Only rarely does one deal with such simple formulas as shown in Figure 2.2. Even for the calculation of the sum of a row or column, you will need to use a function in order to speed up the creation of the formula.

Again, start the entry with an equal sign and create the formula to the point where you want to apply a function. Then click the drop-down button on the right side of the *Function* box and choose *More Functions* to open the *Paste Function* dialog box.

In the *Function category* list box choose the category to which the formula you want to use belongs. In the *Function name* list box select the name of the function. Confirm your choice with the *OK* button.

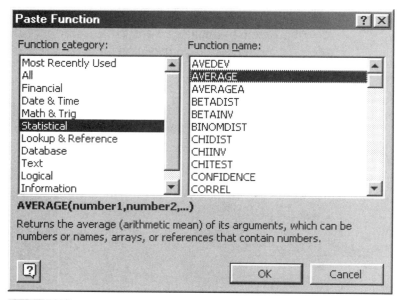

The *Paste Function* dialog box

After the confirmation with *OK*, the *Formula Palette* will be displayed. Here you will find the text boxes for the arguments of the function you had selected. Click into the text boxes and either type the cell references or select the respective cells in the worksheet.

Using the Formula Palette

The *Formula Palette* opens automatically when you click the equal sign button on the *Formula* bar or when you confirm the *Paste Function* dialog box with *OK*.

The *Formula Palette* displays the current result of the function and the current result of the entire formula, lets you know how you can get further Help, and helps you enter worksheet functions.

If the *Formula Palette* is visible you will also see the *Function* box, which lists the recently used functions and offers access to all other functions.

Editing with the Formula Palette

When you select a cell which contains a function and click the *Edit Formula* button on the *Formula* bar, the *Formula Palette* opens and the entry boxes for the function arguments are displayed so that you can quickly edit the formula.

When you insert a new function the *Formula Palette* opens automatically after selecting a function name, and the entry boxes for the function arguments are displayed so that you can enter the formula.

Minimize the palette

On the right-hand side of the text boxes you find the *Collapse Dialog* button 📝. Click the button to minimize the *Formula Palette* in such a way that you can see the entire worksheet and select the cell references or range references.

When the *Formula Palette* is minimized, the button changes to the *Restore Dialog* button 🔲. Use this button to restore the *Formula Palette* to its original size.

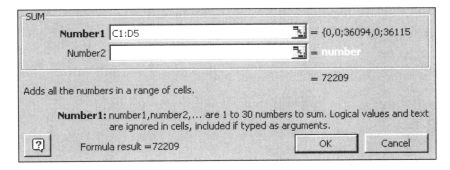

Fig. 2.5:   The Formula Palette ready to use

You can call up the *Office Assistant* by clicking the button with the question mark. Click the *Help with this feature* option and select the Help from topics displayed.

Displaying Formulas

When you enter a formula, it is displayed in the cell itself as well as in the *Formula* bar and the *Formula Palette*. The moment you finish creating the formula, the cell will display the result and not the formula anymore.

In the cells, *Excel* displays either the constants entered there, or text or results; or if results are impossible to attain, an error value.

Formula in the
Formula bar

If you want to see the formula in a cell, you have to select the cell first. Double-clicking the cell will enable you to edit the formula directly in the cell.

You can arrange the display in such a way that formulas are always on view, for example to check references or in order to use the formula shown as template for another formula.

Showing and
hiding formulas

In order to show/hide formulas choose from the *Tools* menu the *Options* item and there activate the *View* tab page. Check the *Formulas* check box in the *Window options* section and close the dialog with the *OK* button.

As an alternative to this procedure you can also press the ⌈Ctrl⌉+⌈`⌉ key combination to switch off or on the display of formulas.

F8 ▼ =				
	A	B	C	D	E
1		1.Shop	2.Shop	3.Shop	
2	1.quarter	1345	2365	2345	=SUM(B2:D2)
3	2.quarter	1254	3456	2344	=SUM(B3:D3)
4	3.quarter	3244	6345	3453	=SUM(E2:E3)
5		=SUM(B2:B4)	=SUM(C2:C4)	=SUM(D2:D4)	

Fig. 2.6:   Permanent display of the formulas

The formulas usually require significantly more space on the worksheet than their results; therefore you should select the columns that contain formulas and size them with *Format/Column/AutoFit Selection*.

Zoom

You can also open the *Zoom* drop-down list or choose the *View/Zoom* command in order to change the display size of the worksheet and show more columns.

If you want to revert to the results display, clear the *Formula* check box in the *Options* dialog box or press the key combination Ctrl+ again.

Hiding the Formula Display Permanently

In every cell that contains a formula, *Excel* stores the formula as well as the result. Normally the result is displayed in the cell itself. But you can also display the formula in the cell as well.

Displaying the formula result

If you switched from displaying formula results to displaying formulas and now you want to suppress the formula display in the worksheet, press the Ctrl+ key combination or clear the *Formulas* check box in the *Tools/Options* dialog box.

Hiding formulas
in the cell and the
Formula bar

By default, *Excel* displays the formulas stored in a cell in the *Formula* bar the moment you select the cell. But even this can be suppressed so that the formulas are not displayed even when a cell is selected. Then both the cell and the *Formula* bar will show only the result of the calculation.

Protecting hidden
formulas

In order to avoid unintentionally clearing a cell that contains formulas, you should generally link the hiding of formulas with a cell protection.

Unlocking cells

To hide formulas in the worksheet and to protect them at the same time from any unwanted changes, you have to tell *Excel* which cells are still enabled for further editing after activating the cell protection.

Select the cells that you want to be able to edit after activating the cell protection. To highlight non-adjacent cells and cell areas, hold down the Ctrl key while clicking all the necessary cells, or while dragging over the cell areas.

If you want to hide formulas without activating the cell protection, skip the following step. Select *Format/Cells* and clear the *Locked* check box on the *Protection* tab page. Click the *OK* button to close.

Select the cells which should not display their formulas. Again choose *Format/Cells* and select the *Hidden* check box. Close with the *OK* button.

Activate the Protection

Locking cells or hiding formulas has no effect unless the worksheet is protected. To protect the worksheet, open the *Tools* menu and choose *Protection/Protect Sheet*. A password is optional.

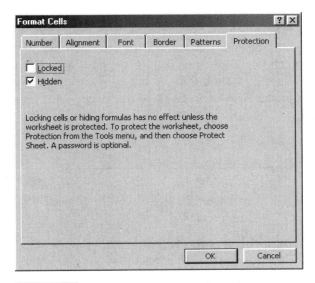

Fig. 2.7:   Locking cells and hide formulas

Enter a password which can have up to 255 characters and may contain numbers, letters or symbols. Then click the *OK* button. You have to confirm your password by entering it again before it will be enabled.

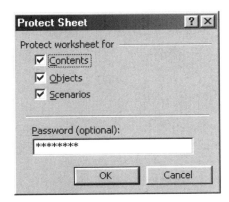

Fig. 2.8:   Activate the worksheet protection

Unhiding Formulas

To deactivate the formula suppression and unprotect the worksheet, choose *Tools/Protection/Unprotect Sheet*. Enter your password and click the *OK* button. Now you have access to in the *Format Cells* dialog box again and you can clear the *Hidden* check box.

Printing Formulas

By default, *Excel* always prints the results of formulas when you print out a worksheet with the *Print* button 🖨 or the *File/Print* command.

However, for archival purposes, while editing worksheets created by someone else and in which you are searching for a mistake, it is helpful to print the formulas themselves, instead of the formula results.

This is indeed possible in *Excel*, but not without first making certain adjustments. You have to consider that formulas need more space in the worksheet than their respective results. Therefore, a little adjustment of the page setup is necessary before you can print a sheet that displays formulas.

	A	B	C	D	E
1	Item	Qty	Unit Rate	Total	
2	A110	3	£3.00	£9.00	
3	C198	6	£0.23	£1.38	
4	B123	6	£1.56	£9.36	
5	A112	3	£0.06	£0.18	
6				£10.92	
7					

Fig. 2.9: A sheet with results

	A	B	C	D
1	**Item**	**Qty**	**Unit Rate**	**Total**
2	A110	3	=IF(ISTEXT(A2),VLOOKUP(A2,Sheet3!$A$2:$B$5,2),"")	=C2*B2
3	C198	6	=IF(ISTEXT(A3),VLOOKUP(A3,Sheet3!$A$2:$B$5,2),"")	=C3*B3
4	B123	6	=IF(ISTEXT(A4),VLOOKUP(A4,Sheet3!$A$2:$B$5,2),"")	=C4*B4
5	A112	3	=IF(ISTEXT(A5),VLOOKUP(A5,Sheet3!$A$2:$B$5,2),"")	=C5*B5
6				=SUM(D3:D5)
7				

Fig. 2.10: The sheet with the formulas

The sheet with the formula results can easily be printed out on paper. Immediately after switching to the formula display, the sheet requires more space for each column. Therefore, the page break appears already before column D (Figure 2.10).

In order to print the formulas they have to be displayed on-screen as well. Choose *Tools/Options* and then activate the *View* tab page if it is not already shown.

Optimizing width

Check the *Formulas* check box and click the *OK* button. To display formulas properly, *Excel* increases the width of columns automatically, but this does not automatically optimize the column width. To *AutoFit* the column width for the formula size, click the *Selct All* button above the row headings to select the whole sheet. Then choose *Format/Column/AutoFit Selection*.

If you use nested functions and the formulas become too long to be displayed on one page with the present settings, you have to decrease the font size step by step and check the result with the *Page Break Preview* in-between.

If the formulas do need that much space, you can also change from *Portrait* to *Landscape* mode. Just go to the *File* menu and choose *Page Setup*. In the *Orientation* option group on the *Page* tab page select the *Landscape* radio button.

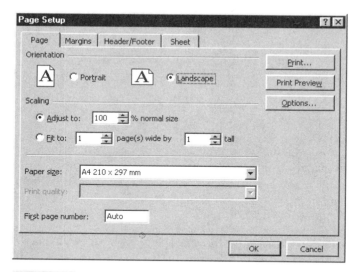

Fig. 2.11: Selecting Landscape

The sheet size can also be controlled by reducing the scaling in the *Scaling* option group. You can then print the sheet. If you want, you can switch off the formula display by choosing *Tools/Options* and activating the *View* tab page. Here you have to clear the *Formulas* check box.

The [Ctrl]+[`] key combination toggles between the formula display and the formula results display.

Replacing Formulas By Their Result

If changes in data should not in any way affect a formula anymore, you can replace the formula by its result.

To do so, you have to copy the formula to the clipboard and then replace it by the result, but in the process, the formula itself will be lost.

Therefore, be careful and make sure that the formula is not still needed somewhere before you execute the following steps.

In order to replace a formula by its result, select the formula and choose *Edit/Copy* or click the *Copy* button 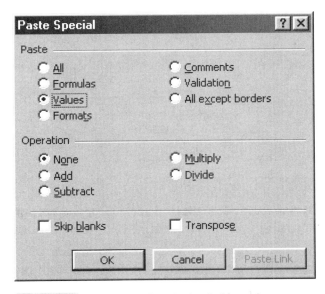.

Next choose *Edit/Paste Special.* The *Paste Special* dialog box will appear. Select the *Values* radio button and close the dialog box with the *OK* button.

Excel replaces the formula of the activated cell by its result. Press ⌈Esc⌉, to end the procedure.

Fig. 2.12:   Inserting values instead of formulas

Undo replace formula

Immediately after the replacement of the formula by its result, the procedure can be undone. To do so, either choose *Edit/Undo* or click the *Undo* button.

Array Formulas

A formula can create a single result or it can create
several results. A formula that creates only one result is
called a single-value formula. A formula that returns more
than one result is called an array formula.

You can apply array formulas instead of single-value formulas to save time, because you only need to create one
formula instead of several. The following single-value
formulas calculate the tax in D2:D5 and in E2:E5 the
total amount. The formulas have been entered in D2 and
E2 and copied to D3:D5 and E3:E5 respectively.

	A	B	C	D	E
	E5		= =(C5+D5)*B5		
1	ID	Qty	Unit Rate	Tax	Total
2	A110	3	=IF(ISTEXT(A2),VLOOKUP(A2,Sheet3!$A$2:$B$5,2),"")	=C2*7%	=(C2+D2)*B2
3	C198	6	=IF(ISTEXT(A3),VLOOKUP(A3,Sheet3!$A$2:$B$5,2),"")	=C3*7%	=(C3+D3)*B3
4	B123	7	=IF(ISTEXT(A4),VLOOKUP(A4,Sheet3!$A$2:$B$5,2),"")	=C4*7%	=(C4+D4)*B4
5	A112	3	=IF(ISTEXT(A5),VLOOKUP(A5,Sheet3!$A$2:$B$5,2),"")	=C5*7%	=(C5+D5)*B5
6					=SUM(E3:E5)
7					

Fig. 2.13: Single-value formulas

The following array formulas calculate all four results in
one go:

	A	B	C	D	E
	E5		= {=(C2:C5+D2:D5)*B2:B5}		
1	ID	Qty	Unit Rate	Tax	Total
2	A110	3	=IF(ISTEXT(A2),VLOOKUP(A2,Sheet3!$A$2:$B$5,2),"")	=C2:C5*7%	=(C2:C5+D2:D5)*B2:B5
3	C198	6	=IF(ISTEXT(A3),VLOOKUP(A3,Sheet3!$A$2:$B$5,2),"")	=C2:C5*7%	=(C2:C5+D2:D5)*B2:B5
4	B123	7	=IF(ISTEXT(A4),VLOOKUP(A4,Sheet3!$A$2:$B$5,2),"")	=C2:C5*7%	=(C2:C5+D2:D5)*B2:B5
5	A112	3	=IF(ISTEXT(A5),VLOOKUP(A5,Sheet3!$A$2:$B$5,2),"")	=C2:C5*7%	=(C2:C5+D2:D5)*B2:B5
6					=SUM(E3:E5)
7					

Fig. 2.14: Array formulas

Creating an array formula

In order to create an array formula, select instead of a cell the cell area in which the results should appear. After completing the formula do not close it with the *Enter* key ⏎, close it with the key combination Ctrl+⇧+⏎ instead. The formula is displayed in the *Formula* bar enclosed in curly braces.

Every cell of the array formula displays the complete formula in the formula bar. You cannot edit cells separately that belong to an array formula.

Editing Array Formulas

In order to edit an array formula you have to always select the whole cell area. To do so, click on any cell in the array range and then press the Ctrl+⇧+/ key combination.

Deleting an Array Formula

The procedure for deleting an array formula also differs from the one used to delete a normal formula. In order to remove an array formula from a cell you first have to select the whole cell area of the array formula. Only then can you delete the formula with Del or by choosing *Edit/Clear/Contents*.

Creating and Using References

The insertion of the address of a cell or cell range into a formula is known as *Referencing*. A reference identifies a cell or a range of cells on a worksheet and tells *Excel* where to look for the values or data you want to use for your calculation. With references, you can use data contained in different cells of a worksheet in one formula.

Excel then uses the flexible content of the cell, instead of constant values.

How to create a reference?

You can insert references into a formula in different ways:

■ By clicking on a cell or cell area.

■ By moving the cell frame with the cursor keys ⟶, ⟵, ⟶ or ⟶ to a single cell or over a cell range with the ⟶ key pressed down.

■ By entering the address of a cell, consisting of column letter and row number.

■ By typing the addresses of the first and the last cell of a cell range separated by a colon.

The reference to a cell is inserted into a formula so that the formula uses the value given in the respective cell. In *Excel*, there are several kinds of references:

■ Relative references

■ Absolute references

■ Mixed references

By default, the first reference type is used as soon as you click on a cell or select it in any way. The relative reference changes with every change of position, regardless of whether this change is caused by an insertion or a deletion in the surrounding cells. Even if you move the cell with the reference, it automatically adjusts to the new location.

The absolute reference is created when you press the (F4) function key after selecting a cell. The absolute reference always remains unchanged, even if you copy or move it.

Reference Operators

The signs used to combine or separate several cell addresses are called reference operators. *Excel* supports the following reference operators:

- : (*Colon*)

  The colon defines the range of a cell range and is called *range operator*. It appears between the first and last cells of this cell range. All the cells between the two references are separated by the colon, the two cells are also a part of the reference.

  ```
  Example: =SUM(A8:D10)
  ```

- , (*Comma*)

  The comma combines multiple cell references into one reference and is called *union operator*. These can be single cells or cell ranges that become arguments in a function.

  ```
  Example: =SUM(A8:A20,D8:D20)
  ```

- (*Single space*)

  The single space is called *intersection operator*, the reference is created for the intersection of the cell range to the left and the cell range to the right of the space.

  ```
  Example: =SUM(A1:D20,B5:C10)
  ```

Relative References

If you insert a cell reference into a formula by clicking or by selecting, or by entering the respective addresses manually, this reference is automatically inserted by *Excel* as a relative reference. It is called relative because the address does not refer to a certain cell but tells *Excel* how to find another cell by starting from the cell that contains

2. Formulas and Functions

the formula, like giving someone directions that explain where to go, for example, 'go up three cells and two cells to the left.'

If, as shown in Figure 2.15, in cell B9, a formula calculates the sum of B5:B8, and you copy this formula into the cell C9 that is located one column to the right, then *Excel* will automatically change the cell reference so that B becomes C.

=SUM(B5:B8)   =SUM(C5:C8)

	A	B	C	D
1	Income and Expenses 1998			
2				
3			Q1	
4	Income	Jan	Feb	Mar
5	concerts	£250.00	£280.00	£100.00
6	recordings	£135.00	£0.00	£210.00
7	teaching	£260.00	£260.00	£260.00
8	sales	£120.00	£0.00	£0.00
9		=SUM(B5:B8)		
10				

	A	B	C	D
1	Income and Expenses 1998			
2				
3			Q1	
4	Income	Jan	Feb	Mar
5	concerts	£250.00	£280.00	£100.00
6	recordings	£135.00	£0.00	£210.00
7	teaching	£260.00	£260.00	£260.00
8	sales	£120.00	£0.00	£0.00
9		£765.00	=SUM(C5:C8)	
10				

Fig. 2.15:   The relative reference and its copy

It is partly because of this automatic adjustment of relative cell references that a spreadsheet program like *Excel* is so convenient. However, in some cases this adjustment is not desirable because the references in the copied formula should still refer to the same cells in the original formula.

Absolute References

In the following worksheet *Excel* has to calculate the discount in the cells D6:D8. The original formula is created in the cell D6 and is copied to D7:D8:

	A	B	C	D	E
1				Discount	
2		Qty	<10	5%	
3		Qty	>10	10%	
4					
5	ID	Qty	Unit Rate	Discount	Total
6	A110	3	£3.00	£0.15	£8.55
7	B123	7	£4.00	£0.40	£25.20
8	C198	3	£5.00	£0.00	£15.00
9					£40.20
10					

	A	B	C	D	E
1				Discount	
2		Qty	<10	5%	
3		Qty	>10	10%	
4					
5	ID	Qty	Unit Rate	Discount	Total
6	A110	3	£3.00	£0.15	£8.55
7	B123	7	£4.00	£0.40	£25.20
8	C198	3	£5.00	=C8*D4	£15.00
9					£40.20
10					

Fig. 2.16: The copied reference calculates the wrong result

The blue lines show how the relative reference to D2 has changed in the copied formulas in cells D7 and D8, and how the wrong results in the cells are created. The solution here is to use an absolute reference that is not altered by the copy procedure.

Creating an absolute reference

To create an absolute reference, press the [F4] key after entering or selecting the cell addresses for the reference. *Excel* then converts the relative reference to an absolute reference. You can recognize the absolute reference by the '$' signs that appear before the column letter as well as before the row number.

- Relative reference: D1

- Absolute reference: $D$1

Absolute to
relative

Instead of converting the relative reference to an absolute reference with F4 you can also manually type in the '$' signs. To change an absolute reference back to a relative reference, activate the cell with the formula and either click behind the reference or highlight it before you press F4. In Figure 2.17 you see the formulas of Figure 2.16 again, first with relative and then with absolute references.

	A	B	C	D	E
1				Discount	
2		Qty	<10	● 5%	
3		Qty	>10	● 10%	
4				●	
5	ID	Qty	Unit Rate	Discount	Total
6	A110		3	● £3.00 £0.15	£8.55
7	B123		7	● £4.00 £0.40	£25.20
8	C198		3	● £5.00 =C8*D4	£15.00
9					£40.20
10					

	A	B	C	D	E
1				Discount	
2		Qty	<10	● 5%	
3		Qty	>10	10%	
4					
5	ID	Qty	Unit Rate	Discount	Total
6	A110		3	● £3.00 £0.15	£8.55
7	B123		7	● £4.00 £0.20	£26.60
8	C198		3	● £5.00 =C8*$D$2	£14.25
9					£40.85
10					

Fig. 2.17:   Relative and absolute references compared

Mixed References

Apart from relative references and absolute references you can also create mixed references. They contain either one absolute column part or one absolute row part:

- Absolute column in a mixed reference: $D1

- Absolute row in a mixed reference: D$1

Only the relative part changes

In a mixed reference, only the relative part changes when it is copied, while the absolute part remains unchanged. You can toggle through the various reference possibilities using the F4 key:

- Relative reference → absolute reference → mixed reference, absolute row reference → mixed reference, absolute column reference.

The mixed references have one part of each reference type:

- either an absolute reference to the row and a relative reference to the column,

- or an absolute reference to the column and a relative reference to the row.

Changing the reference type

You can create the right type of reference when you press the F4 key two or three times right after clicking the cell or selecting the cell range. Pressing once inserts an absolute reference, pressing twice inserts a mixed reference with absolute row and pressing three times inserts the mixed reference with absolute column. During copying, the relative part will be adjusted to the new position and the absolute part will remain unaltered.

Fig. 2.18:   Relative and absolute references

=$F4   =F$4

Fig. 2.19:   Mixed references

Using Names and Titles as References

As long as your sheet is small enough to fit onto your screen and you can see all the cells at once, it is easy to create the references by simply typing in or selecting the respective cells.

However, when the worksheet size increases, or if you want to make references to other worksheets or even other workbooks, this procedure becomes more and more tedious. Then it is easier to use column or row labels or just names of cells. Names are always treated like absolute references, so you do not have to convert them with the F4 key.

You can name cells or cell ranges as you like but it would be more meaningful to name them according to the labels you've already given to the rows or columns. These names would be easy for you to remember, since you see the worksheet every day.

Naming Cells

Instead of using cell references like A15 or $G$4 you can now create references in a much simpler way, by just typing in the names of the cells and cell ranges.

In a formula you can use these names of cells or cell ranges as references instead of the actual cell addresses. Names like *Annual_Turnover* or *VAT* can be remembered more easily than K12 or $C$14.

These user-defined names for cells or cell ranges can consist of up to 255 characters but they have to start with either a letter or an underscore character.

In order to define a name for a cell or a cell range, select this cell or cell range and choose *Insert/Name/Define*.

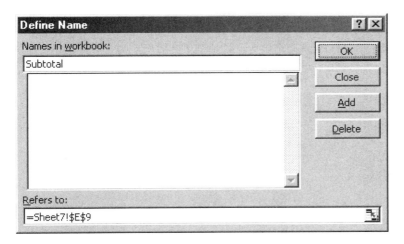

Fig. 2.20: The *Define Name* dialog box

Enter a name of your choice into the *Names in workbook* text box. In the *Refers to* text box *Excel* shows the address of the cell to be named. Inspect this reference and if it is correct, close the dialog with the *OK* button.

Fig. 2.21: Defining and selecting names in the *Name* box

A faster and more convenient method of naming a cell is by clicking into the *Name* box at the left end of the *Formula* bar, typing in a name, and confirming with ⏎.

99

References to Row and Column Labels

Excel 97 recognizes row labels and column labels in most cases, so they can be used immediately in formulas without the need to define an extra name.

You can use labels straightaway without further preparation, instead of the cell addresses. Up to the next blank row/column or up to the next cell that contains text, *Excel* automatically assigns the cells below or beside a label to a row label or column label. Use these row or column labels instead of the usual references.

F2	▼	=	=SUM(India north:India south Monday)			
	A	B	C	D	E	F	G
1		Monday	Tuesday	Wednesday		Sum	
2	India north	123.45	124.56	98.50		249.45	
3	India south	126.00	115.90	135.45			
4	Mexico	98.00	111.00	102.35			
5	Kenya	231.45	212.43	198.95			
6	Jamaica	87.50	98.98	101.50			
7							

Fig. 2.22: Sheet with row and column labels

In the table in Figure 2.22 you can immediately use the following labels:

- *India north* to *Jamaica*:
  to refer to the cell ranges from B2:D2 up to B6:D6 in a formula.

- *Monday* to *Wednesday*:
  to insert references for the cell ranges from B2:B6 up to D2:D6 into a formula.

- *India north Monday* to *Jamaica Wednesday*
  or *Monday India north* to *Wednesday Jamaica*:
  to create references to the single cells B2 to D6.

100

If you insert such a reference into a formula and copy this formula, the reference will be automatically adjusted to the new cell position and the row/column labels will be replaced by the correct new labels. If, for example, you create in E2 the formula:

```
=SUM(India north)
```

and you copy it to E3, the formula will automatically be changed to:

```
=SUM(India south)
```

Accepting Row and Column Labels as Names

Additionally *Excel* offers a very convenient way to accept names automatically from a selected cell range. You can use *Insert/Name/Create* to define names out of already existing row and column labels.

In order to accept row and column labels as valid names, select the cell range containing the row and/or column labels and the cells to be named. Choose then *Insert/ Name/Create* and select the check boxes for the rows or columns you want to pick the names from. Close by clicking the *OK* button.

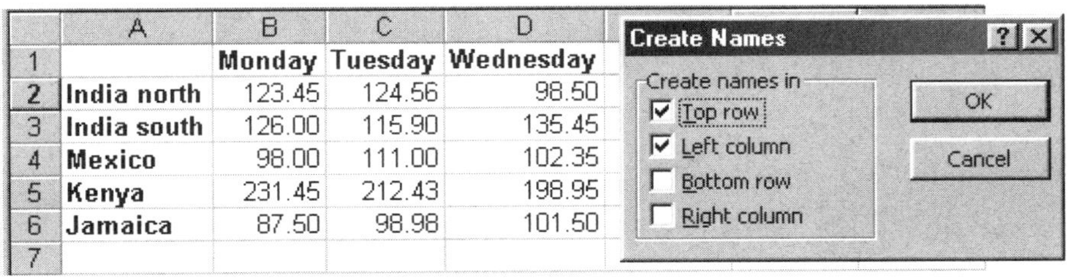

	A	B	C	D
1		Monday	Tuesday	Wednesday
2	India north	123.45	124.56	98.50
3	India south	126.00	115.90	135.45
4	Mexico	98.00	111.00	102.35
5	Kenya	231.45	212.43	198.95
6	Jamaica	87.50	98.98	101.50
7				

Create Names — Create names in: ☑ Top row ☑ Left column ☐ Bottom row ☐ Right column — OK — Cancel

Fig. 2.23: Accepting names

Inserting names

In the sheet in Figure 2.23 the top row and the left column supply the names. To insert names created in such a way into formulas, either type them in or choose *Insert/Name/Paste*, select the name and click the *OK* button.

When accepting names, *Excel* automatically replaces spaces in the cells by underscores, because spaces are not allowed in cell names, just like in the old DOS convention. Therefore, 'India north' becomes 'India_north'.

The following names have been automatically created for the worksheet in Figure 2.23 and can be used while creating formulas.

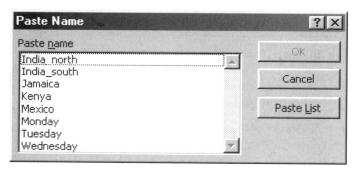

Fig. 2.24: Automatically accepted names

The top two row sums in the sheet can now be calculated with the following formulas:

```
=SUM(India_north)
```

```
=SUM(India_south)
```

The first two column sums can be calculated by the following formulas:

```
=SUM(Monday)
```

```
=SUM(Tuesday)
```

Inserting and Printing a List of Names

If you are editing an extensive sheet and you have named a lot of cells in order to enter references easily and to create formulas that are comprehensible, you may need to display a list of those names. You may even want to make a printout to give to somebody else, who is working on that sheet, or for your personal use.

Display the full list of names

If you only want to display the names contained in the worksheet choose *Insert/Name/Define*. The complete list of names appears. Scroll through the list using the scroll bar. When you select a name in the list, the respective reference is displayed in the *Refers to* text box. Close the dialog box by clicking the *OK* button.

To insert a list of all available names into the worksheet, click into a blank area of the table where you want the list to appear and choose *Insert/Name/Paste*. In the *Paste Name* dialog box click the *Paste List* button.

Excel then pastes into the worksheet all cell names and in an additional column all the respective cell references. You may need to double-click the right boundary of the column heading in order to *AutoFit* the column width.

Fig. 2.25:   The *Paste Name* dialog box

To print the list of names, select the area with the names and references and choose *File/Print*. In the *Print what* option group choose the *Selection* radio button and start the printout by clicking *OK*.

10	India_north	=Sheet3!$B$2:$D$2
11	India_south	=Sheet3!$B$3:$D$3
12	Jamaica	=Sheet3!$B$6:$D$6
13	Kenya	=Sheet3!$B$5:$D$5
14	Mexico	=Sheet3!$B$4:$D$4
15	Monday	=Sheet3!$B$2:$B$6
16	Subtotal	=Sheet3!$A$8
17	Support	=Sheet3!$A$10
18	Tuesday	=Sheet3!$C$2:$C$6
19	VAT	=Sheet3!$A$9
20	Wednesday	=Sheet3!$D$2:$D$6

Fig. 2.26: The pasted name list

Tip! You can also use the *Name* box to move to a named cell or cell range. Open the list, and click the name to which you want to move. *Excel* will automatically select the cell or cell range and display it highlighted.

Linking Worksheets with References

If you use your PC effectively, all data that you type in will be entered only once. This principle is of particular importance when working with tables.

What is a link?

If you need the data in more than one worksheet, you have to create a link. Links can exist to cells within the same worksheet, or from one worksheet to another within the same workbook, or to cells in a worksheet of another workbook. You supply, for example, to your current worksheet the content of a cell of another worksheet, or include cells of another worksheet in the calculations.

Link types

Links can be created to a cell, a cell range or cells in a different worksheet. A link to more than one worksheet is called a 3-D reference or a 3-D link. You can find more information on this topic in 'Inserting 3-D links'.

When you link two workbooks, the workbook from where the data comes is called *source* file and the receiving workbook is called *destination* file.

Source file   Destination file

Fig. 2.27:   Source and destination of a link

If the data of the source file changes, these changes are automatically transferred to the destination file. Links are always created by a formula. The simplest link shows the content of one cell in another cell.

Links are
automatically
updated

If you get, for example, in Sheet1 a subtotal in cell D25 and you want to display this subtotal in Sheet2, you have to enter the following formula:

```
=Sheet1!D25
```

In order to create this link formula, click the cell in Sheet2 where the results of the link should appear; in our example, the subtotal. Enter the equal sign and click the worksheet tab of Sheet1. In the now active Sheet1, click the cell D25 and finish the entry of the formula with *Enter*.

External links

Links that refer to a single cell or a cell range in worksheets of different workbooks are called external links.

External links

In order to create a link to a cell of another workbook, you have to open both the source workbook as well as the destination workbook. Arrange the windows with the *Window/Arrange* command in such a way that you can conveniently edit both workbooks.

You can open several workbooks in one go by selecting them in the *Open* dialog box while holding down the Ctrl key.

Creating the link

Click the cell in which the link should be displayed. Here too, begin by typing the equal sign. Then activate the source workbook with a click on the tab of the correct worksheet, and after that click the cell that should be displayed in the destination workbook. As usual, finish the procedure by pressing the *Enter* key ↵.

A simple link formula to a cell in another workbook will look something like this:

```
='C:\My Documents\[Countries.xls]Sheet3'!$E$2
```

The structure of this path is as follows:

File name in [ ]

The formula starts with the complete MS-DOS path. However, the name of the workbook has to appear in square brackets.

! following the table

This is followed by the name of the worksheet and the cell reference, which are separated from each other by an exclamation mark.

If the path, the file name, or the table name contains spaces or symbols, you have to enclose the path, file name, and table name in single quotation marks.

Cell reference as
absolute reference

The last information is the cell reference, which is always an absolute reference.

In many cases you do not obtain proper results with a link formula. Or rather, the link should be part of a calculation in order to be effective. In principle the creation of such a formula containing one or more links does not vary from the procedure described above.

Calculating
with links

The starting point is, again, the cell in which the result will be displayed. Start the entry of the formula with an equal sign and enter the formula up to the point where you need data from the linked table. Insert the link in the above described manner and complete the formula in the same way as you would complete one without links. Finish by pressing the *Enter* key ⏎.

```
=SUM('C:\My Documents\[Countries.xls]Sheet3'!
$E$2:$E$3)*85%
```

In this formula, the sum of a link is calculated and multiplied by 85% The linked data originates from the *Countries.xls* workbook. The workbook is located in the *My Documents* folder in the *C:* drive. The data covers the cell range $E$2:$E$3 in Sheet3.

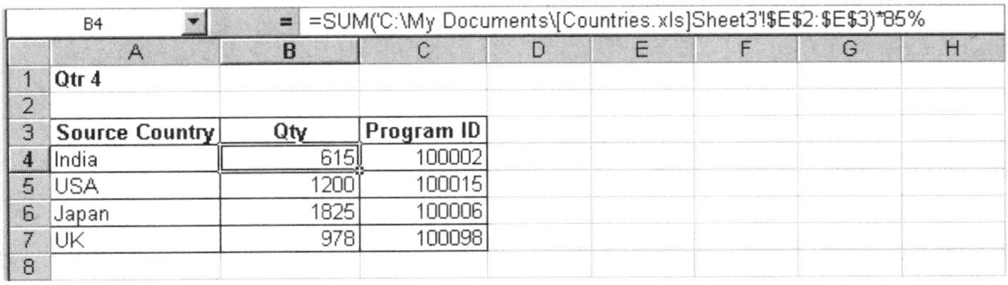

B4	▼	=	=SUM('C:\My Documents\[Countries.xls]Sheet3'!$E$2:$E$3)*85%				
	A	B	C	D	E	F	G	H
1	Qtr 4							
2								
3	Source Country	Qty	Program ID					
4	India	615	100002					
5	USA	1200	100015					
6	Japan	1825	100006					
7	UK	978	100098					
8								

Fig. 2.28: Link formula and result

You can save a workbook that contains linked data just like any other file. If you open a workbook that contains linked data, you will be prompted to update the linked data.

Confirm the update by clicking the *Yes* button in order to automatically transfer data that might have changed from the source file to your workbook.

If you cancel the update by clicking the *No* button, *Excel* will open the workbook keeping the existing information.

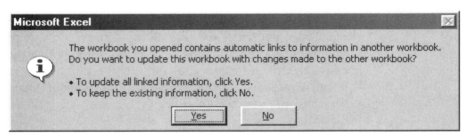

Fig. 2.29:   Update your workbook

In a workbook that contains links, you can open the *Links* dialog box with the *Edit/Links* command. This dialog box shows all links and allows you edit them.

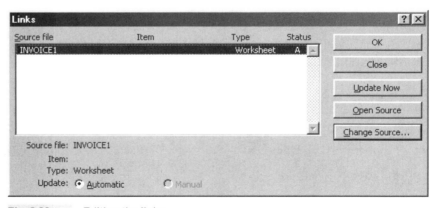

Fig. 2.30:   Editing the links

If you want to update the links manually and not automatically, select the *Manual* radio button in this dialog box. You can then update the workbook in this particular dialog box at any time with a click on the *Update Now* button.

3-D References

A 3-D reference connects the result cell with a single cell or a cell range in more than one source table. A good example of this is a workbook that contains one worksheet for each month and calculates the sum on another worksheet.

When creating a 3-D reference it is important that all worksheets in the 3-D reference are stacked immediately one after the other. In addition, you should respect the following rules for the creation of a three-dimensional reference:

- You can use 3-D references to create formulas by using the following functions: SUM(), AVERAGE(), AVERAGEA(), COUNT(), COUNTA(), MAX(), MAXA(), MIN(), MINA(), PRODUCT(), STDEV(), STDEVA(), STDEVP(), STDEVPA(), VAR(), VARA(), VARP(), and VARPA().

No array formulas
- Array formulas cannot contain 3-D references.

No intersection
- In connection with 3-D references you cannot use intersections.

Fortunately, you can drag-and-drop the worksheets into the right position before you start creating the 3D-reference. To do so, drag the worksheet tab with the left mouse button along the row of sheet tabs.

Arrange
worksheets by
drag-and-drop

Above the mouse cursor a sheet symbol appears and a little triangle is indicating the current worksheet's position. Drag it to the new position and release the mouse button when the insertion point appears right in front of the tab to which you want to insert your worksheet.

Once you have arranged all your sheets with this procedure, activate the worksheet on which the result should be displayed and click the cell where you want to enter the 3-D reference.

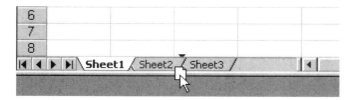

Fig. 2.31:   Arranging worksheets

Creating 3-D links

Start the formula with an equal sign and type the formula to the point where you want to insert the 3-D reference. Click the tab of the first worksheet in the 3-D reference and activate the cell or cell range to which you want to refer. Then click the last worksheet in the 3-D reference, while holding down the ⌘ key. Type whatever is needed to complete the formula and finish the procedure with the *Enter* key ⏎.

For example, if you want to calculate the sum of the cells B4:B7 on worksheet 1 through worksheet 3, start by entering:

=Sum(

After that, click the tab of worksheet 1 and select the cells B4:B7. While holding down the ⌘ key, click the tab of worksheet 3 and press *Enter* ⏎ to close the formula. The closing parenthesis is supplemented by *Excel* automatically.

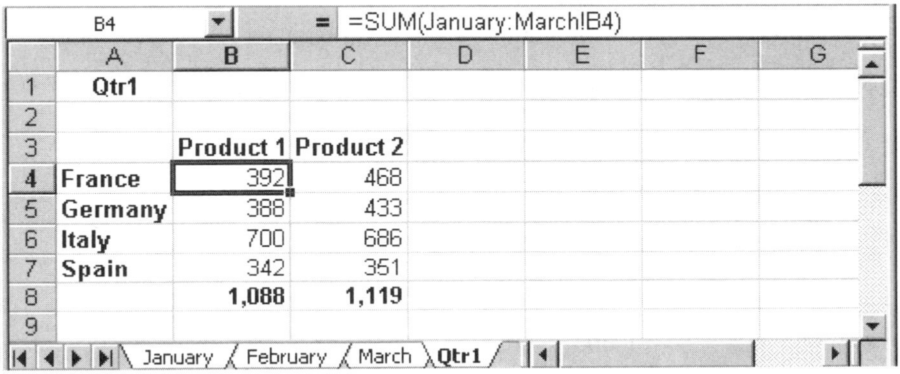

B4	▼	**=**	=SUM(January:March!B4)				
	A	B	C	D	E	F	G
1	Qtr1						
2							
3		Product 1	Product 2				
4	France	392	468				
5	Germany	388	433				
6	Italy	700	686				
7	Spain	342	351				
8		1,088	1,119				
9							

January / February / March \ Qtr1 /

Fig. 2.32: A three-dimensional reference

Preparing a 3-D reference by grouping

A 3-D reference always addresses the same cells in the worksheets involved. You can save a lot of time and at the same time guarantee an identical worksheet structure by grouping the worksheets prior to editing them. *Excel* then applies all entries and commands that you make in one worksheet to all grouped worksheets.

To group a number of worksheets, click the first and the last worksheet in your group while holding down the ⬙ key. The grouping can be cancelled via the shortcut menu. To do so, right-click one of the grouped sheet tabs and choose *Ungroup Sheets*.

Consolidating and Connecting Worksheets

Consolidate

In order to put together data from different worksheets or from different areas of a worksheet, you can also use the consolidation procedure.

111

Consolidating and linking

By consolidating you can also insert a link to the source areas so that the data in the consolidation sheet will be updated automatically.

Possible functions

The following functions can be used for consolidation:

- Sum()
- Count()
- Average()
- Max and Min()
- Product()
- Count Nums()
- StdDev() (Standard Deviation)
- Var() (Variance)

To be able to consolidate data, *Excel* needs the same structure in the different worksheets. To consolidate data in a consolidation function, on the consolidation worksheet select the cell that you want to contain consolidated data and choose *Data/Consolidate*.

Open the *Function* drop-down list and choose the required function to consolidate the data. Subsequently click the *Reference* box and select the first reference in the worksheet. On the right-hand side of the text box you find the *Collapse Dialog* button to minimize the *Consolidate* dialog box.

Reference to other worksheets

If you want to refer to another worksheet, first click the tab for the worksheet, and then drag to select the cell range for the consolidation.

External reference

In order to create a reference to another workbook which is not open, you can choose the *Browse* button. Open the folder that contains the required workbook, select the workbook file and click the *OK* button.

Once you have selected the first reference, click the *Add* button. The first reference will be added to the *All references* list box.

Select the next reference in the worksheet whose data you want to include in the consolidation. Again click the *Add* button and repeat these steps until you have included all desired data ranges.

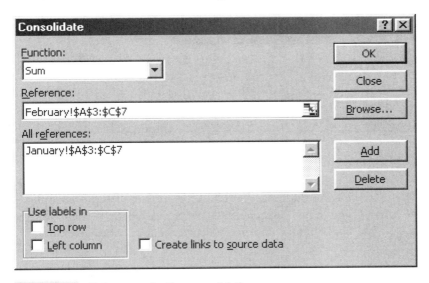

Fig. 2.33: References for the consolidation

Labelling   If *Excel* should use the labels of the top row or the labels of the left column for the consolidated area, check the *Top row* and/or *Left column* check boxes in the *Use labels in* group box.

If the consolidated data should be linked with the source data, select the *Create links to source data* check box.

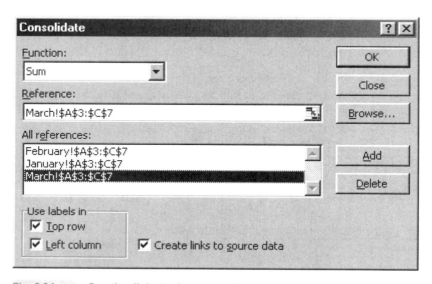

Creating links to the source data

Close the dialog box by clicking the *OK* button. *Excel* inserts the data you chose, combines it with the options you have selected into the specified cell range for the consolidated data on the consolidation worksheet.

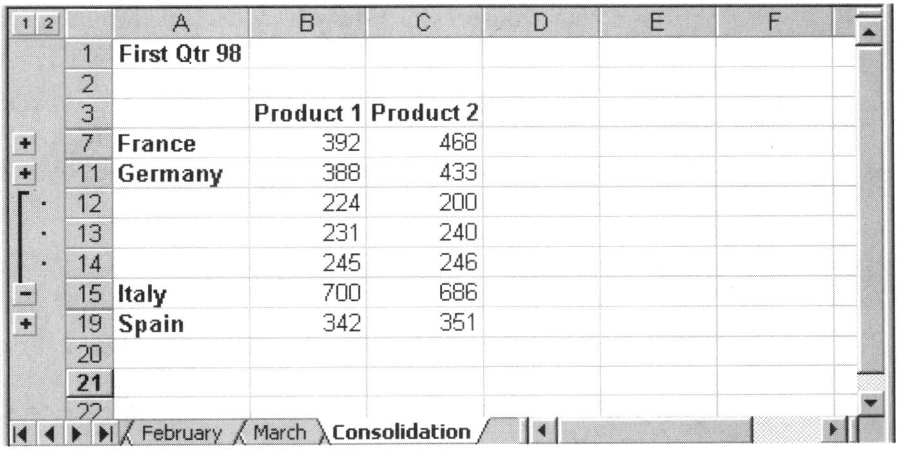

1 2		A	B	C	D	E	F	
	1	First Qtr 98						
	2							
	3		Product 1	Product 2				
+	7	France	392	468				
+	11	Germany	388	433				
	12		224	200				
·	13		231	240				
·	14		245	246				
−	15	Italy	700	686				
+	19	Spain	342	351				
	20							
	21							
	22							

February / March \ Consolidation /

Fig. 2.35:   The result of a consolidation

As you can see in Figure 2.35, the data automatically show a hierarchical structure. Use the buttons before or above the row headings to expand or collapse the display.

▪ 1 2

Using these buttons above the row headings you can display or hide data up to the level on the corresponding button.

▪ +

This button is displayed if there are further levels below this level that are hidden. Click the button if you want to display them.

▪ −

This button shows that all sublevels are visible. Click this button to hide them.

Deleting references

In order to change or delete the references for the consolidated table, click the top-left cell of the consolidated table and choose *Data/Consolidate*. Select the reference in the *All references* list and click the *Delete* button.

Replacing references

If you do not want to delete the reference but only to change it, choose at this point the *Add* button instead of *Delete*. Click the *OK* button to close the dialog box and transfer the changes to the worksheet.

Making References Visible

When you start using a worksheet again after a long break, or if you are using a table created by someone else, it will be difficult to reconstruct all the references and formulas contained in it.

Also, when your worksheet displays ugly errors like #NUM or #REF, you have to be able to see the structure of the worksheet in order to find and correct the mistakes.

The formulas of a worksheet consist partly of references and partly of references that build upon these references, in such a way that many cells have precedent and dependent cells.

A dependent cell is a cell containing a formula that refers to an active cell. A precedent cell is a cell that provides data to a formula contained in another cell.

Auditing

The cell references to precedent and dependent cells can be made visible in the worksheet with the help of the *Auditing* feature. This feature offers commands on a special toolbar to show the references in the form of colored arrows.

Trace precedents

To show these arrows in the worksheet, choose *Tools/ Auditing/Trace Precedents*. Each time you repeat this command the cells will be marked one reference further back.

116

	A	B	C	D	E	F
1		Monday	Tuesday	Wednesday	Thursday	
2	Machine1	34	44	32	43	153
3	Machine2	32	29	24	22	107
4	Machine3	23	32	33	43	131
5	Machine4	32	23	23	27	105
6		121	128	112	135	496
7						
8	Target	133				
9	Difference	-12	-5	-21	2	
10						
11	Target all	532			Delayed	36

Fig. 2.36:   Traces to the precedents of cell F11

To show those cells whose values depend on an active cell, choose *Tools/Auditing/Trace Dependents*. Likewise, you have to repeat the command each time you want to see one more level of dependents, i.e. another set of arrows.

C4		=	32			
	A	B	C	D	E	F
1		Monday	Tuesday	Wednesday	Thursday	
2	Machine1	34	44	32	43	153
3	Machine2	32	29	24	22	107
4	Machine3	23	32	33	43	131
5	Machine4	32	23	23	27	105
6		121	128	112	135	496
7						
8	Target	133				
9	Difference	-12	-5	-21	2	
10						
11	Target all	532			Delayed	36

Fig. 2.37:   Traces to the dependents of C4

Use the arrows

A double-click on the trace arrow between two related cells toggles between highlighting the precedent and the dependent cells. With the *Tools/Auditing/Remove all Arrows* command you can hide all traces from the worksheet.

Tracing a mistake

If your worksheet contains mistakes, you can use this feature to trace them. Click a cell with an error value and choose *Tools/Auditing/Trace Error.*

Auditing toolbar

Instead of choosing the commands from the menu you can also call up the *Auditing* toolbar. You can move this toolbar around or dock it like other toolbars, either on top or to one side of your workspace.

Fig. 2.38:   The *Auditing* toolbar

In order to display the *Auditing* toolbar choose *Tools/ Auditing/Show Auditing Toolbar.* The buttons on the toolbar are:

- *Trace Precendents*
  Click this button to display the traces of the precedent cells.

- *Remove Precedent Arrows*
  This button removes the traces of the precedent cells.

- *Trace Dependents*
  With this button you can display the traces to the dependent cells.

- *Remove Dependent Arrows*
  This button removes the traces to the dependent cells.

- *Remove All Arrows*
  Click this button to remove all traces in one step.

- *Trace Error*
  This button will trace the errors in your worksheet.

Hide the
***Auditing* toolbar**

You can close the *Auditing* toolbar any time with a click on the *Close* button ⊠ or by choosing the *Tools/Auditing/ Show Auditing Toolbar* command again. The little check mark in the menu indicates that the menu item works more or less like a switch that you can put off or on.

Functions

In many spreadsheets the same kind of calculations, comparisons and evaluations have to be performed over and over again. *Excel* offers different kinds of standardized formulas, which are functions that you can use instead of creating every little formula from scratch.

One example of such a function is the SUM() function. If you want to calculate the sum of the cells B5:E5, you can develop the formula yourself.

Sum without
a function

Click the result cell, enter an equal sign and click the first cell that should be contained in the sum. Subsequently enter a plus sign, select the next cell or cell range and repeat this procedure until you have chosen all the desired cells.

Sum with
a function

A quick way to go about this would be to click the cell which should display the result, insert the SUM() function and then, while pressing down the Ctrl key, select all cells to be included in one go.

Creating a Function from Scratch

In order to create an *Excel* function in a formula, start with the equal sign. If you forget to insert the equal sign, *Excel* will format the intended formula as left-aligned text. The content of the cell will not work as a function because *Excel* will not be able to recognize it as a formula.

Functions are always inserted into formulas. The formula can consist only of the function name followed by the parentheses.

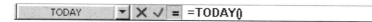

Fig. 2.39:   A simple function without arguments

You can enter the function directly into the formula or with the help of the *Paste Function* button 𝑓ₓ. *Excel 97* also provides you with the *Formula Palette* and the *Function* box.

The *Function* Box

The *Function* box at the left end of the *Formula* bar can be used in different ways.

▪ Click the button to choose and insert a function. The button text will always show the name of the last function used.

▪ Click the drop-down button to display the list of functions and select the required function.

▪ Click the drop-down button to expand the list of functions and select the *More Functions* entry in order to open the *Paste Function* dialog box.

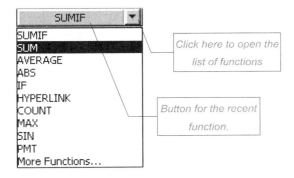

The *Function* list

In *Excel 97* the *Paste Function* dialog box closes auto-matically after selecting a function with a double-click or by selecting a function with a single click and confirming with *OK*.

The Construction of a Function

If you want to work with a function in a formula, you have to construct this function correctly. This means not only writing the function name in a proper way but also using the correct order and the right type of arguments.

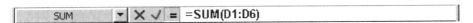

Fig. 2.41: The SUM() function

A function can consist of the following elements:

- Function name
- Function parentheses
- Arguments
- Comma separators, if the function has more than one argument.

Arguments

Functions handle values which are called arguments. However, not every function needs arguments. Also, some functions require certain arguments and have additional optional arguments.

Rules for the Creation of Functions

Here are some rules to follow during the construction of functions:

- The parentheses for the arguments follow the function name immediately and without a space.

- The arguments, which are the values and references the function deals with, are enclosed by parentheses.

- There are required and optional arguments. Without the required arguments, the function will not work. The optional arguments can be omitted.

- Arguments are separated by a comma.

- Respect the particular function syntax. The syntax dictates the order and data type of the arguments in each function. If you are not precise, the function will not yield a proper result.

- Arguments that are character sequences have to be entered within quotation marks.

- Functions can be used as arguments for other functions. These functions are then called nested functions. In order to have such a function, at least one argument of the first-level function is also a function. In *Excel* a formula can contain up to seven levels of nested functions.

- In a nested function, make sure that every opening parenthesis has its closing parenthesis.

Using the *Paste Function* Dialog Box

If you are new to creating functions, it is easier to take the help of the *Paste Function* dialog box.

Paste function

Any of the following steps will call up the *Paste Function* dialog box and start the formula in one go:

- Click the *Paste Function* button **f∗** on the *Standard* toolbar.

- Choose the *Function* command from the *Insert* menu.

- Press the ⟨⇧⟩+⟨F3⟩ key combination.

Category

The *Paste Function* dialog box displays a list of all available functions. The functions are sorted by category. Make your selection in the *Function category* list box, and the *Function name* list box will immediately display all functions available in that category. If the required function is listed here, select it and close the dialog box by clicking the *OK* button.

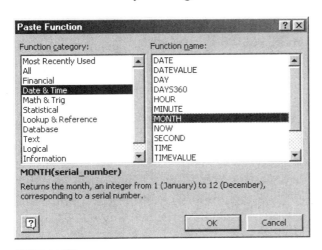

Fig. 2.42:   The *Paste Function* dialog box

Now, as a rule, enter the various arguments the function requires into the *Formula Palette*. Arguments are the values a function uses. There are certain functions that do not need any arguments, like for example the TODAY() function.

The Formula Palette

The *Formula Palette* opens automatically after selecting a function. You can enter the function arguments into text boxes and thus you do not have to worry about the order in which you enter them. The *Formula Palette* displays additional information for each argument and shows the value that the function returns.

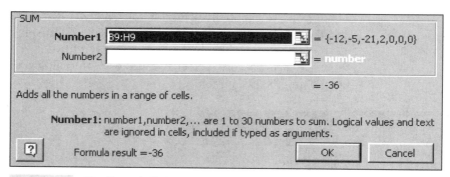

Fig. 2.43:   The Formula Palette

Entering
arguments

In order to enter arguments, click into the text box of an argument and subsequently select the cell or cell range in your worksheet that contains the value or values for the argument.

Collapse Dialog
button

Next to the text box you will find the *Collapse Dialog* button . Use it to minimize the *Formula Palette* so that it does not disturb the process of selecting cells on your worksheet.

D3:E11	

Fig. 2.44: The minimized Formula Palette

Restore Dialog
button ⬚

When the *Formula Palette* is minimized, the button displays the *Restore Dialog* icon ⬚ and can be used to restore the *Formula Palette* to its original size.

As an alternative to selecting the cells you can also manually type in the respective cell references. After entering all arguments close the *Formula Palette* by clicking the *OK* button.

Formula result =

At the right-hand side of the text box and the *Collapse Dialog* button, the current value of the argument is displayed. At the bottom of the *Formula Palette*, right to the *Formula Result* = label, the return value of the function is displayed.

The *Formula Palette* is also useful for editing existing functions in formulas.

Editing Functions

After you have inserted a function into a cell, you can still edit it, if you want to replace certain arguments or to correct wrong references.

You can manually edit it directly within the cell, or you can make use of the *Formula Palette* once again with its special text boxes.

Editing functions
within the cell

To edit the function within the cell, double-click on the cell or press the ⬚F2 key and then click into the exact position in the cell where you want to make your changes.

Editing functions
in the *Formula* bar

To edit the function within the *Formula* bar, click on the cell and then in the *Formula* bar at the point where you want to change the data.

Execute your changes by deleting arguments with the [Del] key or by highlighting and then overwriting them with new ones.

Edit Formula button =

To edit the function with the *Formula Palette*, click the cell that contains the function and then open the *Formula Palette* by clicking either the *Paste Function* button *fx* or the *Edit Formula* button =.

In both cases the *Formula Palette* will open and display the text boxes for the arguments. You can then make your changes.

Changing cell references

Existing cell references can be selected in the text boxes in order to replace them with new ones. Right after the *Formula Palette* appears, the first argument is automatically selected.

Close the *Formula Palette* with the *OK* button.

Nested Functions

A function can contain another function as an argument, for example when you use the ROUNDDOWN() function as an argument to the SUM() function in order to calculate with rounded values.

```
=SUM(ROUNDDOWN(A3,2),ROUNDDOWN(A5,2))
```

Seven levels

In *Excel* a formula can contain up to seven levels of nested functions. The nested functions can be entered manually. To do this, instead of the argument, type the function name of the second-level function, followed by the opening parenthesis. Enter the arguments of the second-level function followed by the closing parenthesis and enter the remaining arguments of the first-level function. Do not forget to finish the first-level function with a closing parenthesis, too.

It is easier to create nested functions using the *Formula Palette*. Since the *Formula Palette* only shows the text boxes for the arguments of the current function, the entry procedure remains always clear. Select the text box of the argument that should contain another function, click the drop-down button of the *Function* box and choose the second-level function from the list.

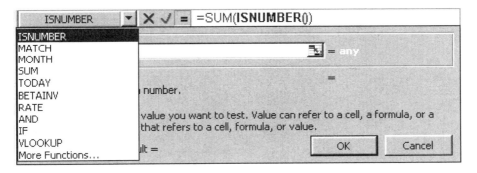

Selecting a second-level function

If you are somewhat familiar with the structure of formulas you can bypass these procedures and enter the second-level formula directly without using the *Formula Palette*.

Entering functions manually

Just enter the function at the right point in the formula followed by the opening parenthesis. Enter all required function arguments either by typing in or by selecting the respective cell references.

Separate arguments by a comma

After the entry of an argument, enter a comma. Then select the next range for the next argument.

Finish the function with the closing parenthesis. *Excel* will try to do this in any case, but sometimes it does not work.

The SUM() Function

In *Excel* you can add up numbers one by one with the '+ ' addition operator or you can add up several numbers with the SUM() function.

Sum Σ

To add numbers in a range of adjacent cells above or left of the cell that should display the result, use the SUM() function, since this yields the fastest results. To do so, click the result cell and double-click the *AutoSum* button Σ on the *Standard* toolbar.

Excel automatically adds up the cells above or to the left of the result cell up to the first empty cell.

You can also use the *AutoSum* button Σ to add up the contents of cell ranges that *Excel* does not automatically recognize, for example, because they contain empty cells. In this case click the *AutoSum* button Σ only once.

'Marching Ants' frame

Drag the 'marching ants' frame that pops up across the desired range of cells and confirm by clicking the *Enter* button ✓ on the *Formula* bar, or by clicking the SUM() button Σ again, or by pressing ↵ on the keyboard.

Adding non-adjacent cells

In order to find the sum of non-adjacent cells or cell ranges, first click the cell that should return the result. Then click the *AutoSum* button Σ.

Now, while pressing down the Ctrl key, select all cells or cell ranges that should be included in the sum and finish the creation of the function by clicking the *AutoSum* button Σ again.

The *AutoSum* button Σ calls the SUM() function to calculate the result. The function has a simple syntax:

```
SUM(number1,number2,...number n)
```

Of course you can also type the function into the *Formula* bar yourself or assemble it with the *Formula Palette*. However, both procedures are more tedious than using the buttons.

The *Maximum* and *Minimum* Functions

Part of the basic statistical functions are the functions that determine the minimum and the maximum values in a worksheet. In addition to these statistical functions, *Excel 97* offers more commands to get information on maximum and minimum values in a worksheet.

AutoCalculate

If you do not want to perform calculations with these values, but you just want to see them, you do not need to go through the complicated process of using a formula: You can use the *AutoCalculate* feature instead to display the values.

Select the worksheet area you want to investigate. By default, the status bar immediately displays the sum of all selected values. If you right-click this sum on the status bar, a shortcut menu pops up. It offers you several options to determine what is displayed on the status bar. Choose the *Max* or *Min* entry to display the respective values.

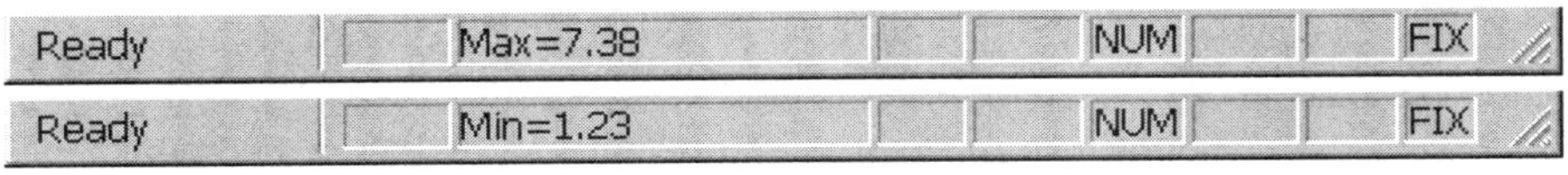

| Ready | | Max=7.38 | | NUM | | FIX |
| Ready | | Min=1.23 | | NUM | | FIX |

Fig. 2.46:   Maximum and minimum value

To display *Max* and *Min*, it is not worth the trouble to create real formulas, since the syntax is too simple. But if you are using them, within a more complicated formula for example, you will find the functions in the *Statistical* category in the *Paste Function* dialog box.

129

In the *Function name* list box, scroll down to the letter
'M', and select the desired function before closing the
dialog box with the *OK* button.

Entering arguments

Select the first worksheet range or the first cell you want
to include in the search for the maximum value. To include the next range or single cell, click into the *Number2*
text box and select another cell in your worksheet. In this
manner, proceed until all necessary cells are included and
finish the function with a click on the *OK* button.

Max and Min manually

It would be faster if you inserted the function name followed by an opening parenthesis and then, using multiple
selection, selected all the cells from which you want to
find the maximum. Finish the formula by typing the
closing parenthesis and pressing the *Enter* key ⏎.

```
=Max(
=Min(
```

Top 10 for minimum and maximum

To determine a certain number of maximum or minimum
values, create *AutoFilters* with *Data/Filter/AutoFilter*
and choose *Top 10* from the filter lists. Read more about
the *Top 10* in chapter 7.

The *Average* Function

The arithmetic mean, or statistical average, belongs to the
basic statistical functions, like the maximum, the minimum and the sum. You can calculate the average for at
least two values by taking the sum of all values and
dividing it by the number of values.

For all basic statistical functions *Excel* offers the appropriate function which is easy to use and will make your
calculations fast.

AutoCalculate

First, get an idea of the average of a cell area. Basically,
all you have to do is to select the cell range to be

calculated. The status bar will automatically display the results, but it will display the sum of the range and not the average. Right-click on this value and choose the *Average* entry from the shortcut menu.

The *AutoCalculate* feature with the *Average* function

The average value for the selected area will be displayed.

If the average should not only be displayed on-screen but also printed, use the AVERAGE() function in a cell. The function uses the following arguments:

```
Average(number1,number2,...number 30)
```

The AVERAGE() function calculates the statistical average from the constant values or from cell references, formula results and calculated values. You can transfer up to 30 values as arguments.

If you use cell ranges that contain blank cells as arguments, these empty cells will be ignored. However, cells containing a zero will be taken into account.

To insert the function choose *Insert/Function* or open the *Paste Function* dialog box by clicking the respective button f_x on the *Standard* toolbar.

Select the *Statistical* entry in the *Function category* list box and choose *AVERAGE* in the *Function name* list box. Confirm with *OK*.

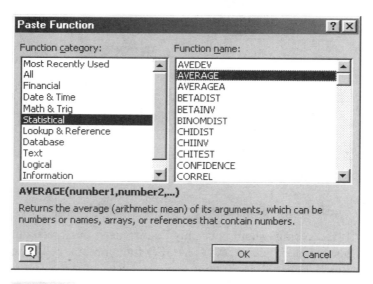

Fig. 2.48: The AVERAGE() function

Next, transfer the function arguments. Click into the *Number1* text box and then, on the worksheet, in the first cell. If you want to obtain the average of adjacent cells, drag to select the range. If you want to calculate the average of a number of non-adjacent single cells, then after selecting the first cell, click into the *Number2* text box, select the second cell and repeat this procedure until you have selected all required cells.

Close the *Formula Palette* after entering all arguments by clicking the *OK* button.

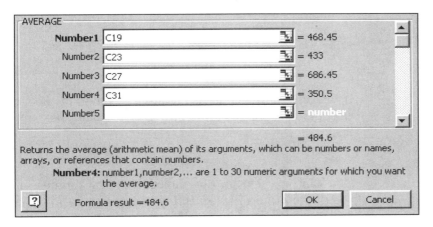

Fig. 2.49:   The function arguments

Exponentiations

Exponentiation is a type of calculation that returns the result of a number raised to a power. The '^' (caret) operator can be used to indicate to what power the base number is to be raised.

Exponentiation operator

To calculate, for example, 2 raised to the power of 3 you would type the following formula:

```
=2^3
```

The formula returns '8'. The actual calculation performed is shown below:

```
=2*2*2
```

Power()

Instead of the operator you can as well use the POWER() function. The function works with the syntax:

```
=POWER(number,power)
```

■ *Number* is the base number and can be any real number.

■ *Power* is the exponent to which the base number is raised – which indicates how often the base number has to be multiplied by itself.

If you use the function in the proper syntax, the above example of 2 raised to the power of 3 would look like this:

```
=Power(2,3)
```

You can type the function directly into the formula, or you can use the *Paste Function* dialog box by clicking the *Paste Function* button ✔ on the *Standard* toolbar. Select the *Math & Trig* category and, in the *Function name* list box, select the *POWER* function. Click the *OK* button to open the *Formula Palette*.

Enter the base number in the *Number* text box or select the cell the data of which you want to raise to a power. Enter the exponent to which the base number is raised into the *Power* box and close the *Formula Palette* with *OK*.

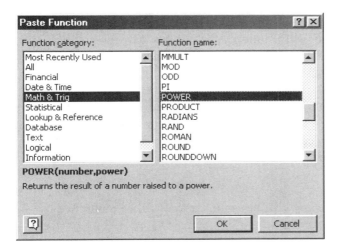

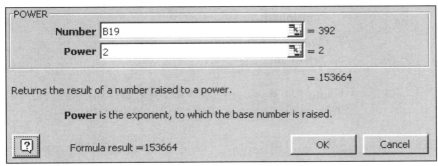

Fig. 2.50: The POWER() function

Products

A product is the result of multiplication. *Excel* supports this calculation by an arithmetic operator and by the PRODUCT() function. For special product calculations, *Excel*, additionally, offers other functions, for example SUMPRODUCT() or DPRODUCT().

Operator for
multiplication

The arithmetic operator for multiplication is the '*' (asterisk) sign. To multiply the number 4 by the number 5 you would create the following formula:

```
=4*5
```

PRODUCT()
function

Instead of the '*' arithmetic operator you can use the PRODUCT() function. The function returns the product of all entered arguments and works with the following syntax:

```
PRODUCT(number1,number2,...number30)
```

▨ *Number1*: is any number that will be multiplied by *Number2*.

▨ *Number2*: is any number by which *Number1* is multiplied.

▨ *Number30*: the function can handle up to 30 arguments.

Using the syntax of the PRODUCT() function, the formula in the above example will look like this:

```
=PRODUCT(4,5)
```

You can type the function directly into the formula or you can use the *Paste Function* feature. Click the *Paste Function* button *f∗* on the *Standard* toolbar to open the corresponding dialog box. Select the *Math & Trig* category and in the list to the right select the *PRODUCT* function.

In the *Formula Palette*, enter the first number or the first reference of the product into the *Number1* text box and repeat this for every number that has to be incorporated into the multiplication. Close the *Formula Palette* by clicking the *OK* button.

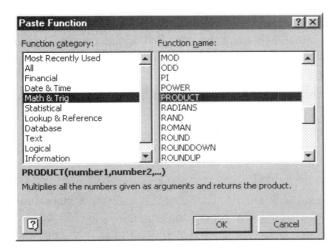

Fig. 2.51:   The PRODUCT() function

IF() Conditions

A condition needs to be used when you want *Excel* to execute a calculation or any other command only under particular circumstances.

A condition in its basic form is:

```
IF...THEN
```

If

For *IF* you insert the condition, and for *THEN* you insert the command that is to be executed or the value that is to be calculated if the condition you specify evaluates to TRUE.

A condition can also be formulated in such a way that a different command is executed or another value is returned if the condition you specify evaluates to FALSE. Such a condition can be reduced to the simple basic form:

```
IF...THEN...ELSE
```

Then

Here again, *IF* stands for the condition, *THEN* stands for the command if the condition evaluates to TRUE and *ELSE* stands for the case that the condition evaluates to FALSE.

In *Excel*, you use the IF() function to formulate a condition. Click at the point in the formula where you need to put the condition. Open the *Paste Function* dialog box by clicking the *Paste Function* button  on the *Standard* toolbar. Select the *Logical* entry in the *Function category* list box and in the *Function Name* list choose the *IF* function. Close the dialog box by clicking the *OK* button.

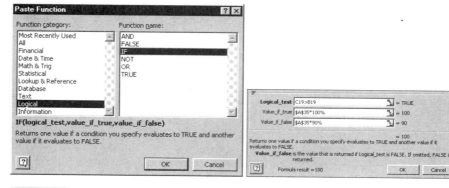

Fig. 2.52:   The IF() function

138

In the *Formula Palette*, the next step is to enter the condition into the *Logical_test* box. For example, to test whether the value in the cell C19 is greater than the value in cell B19, you would type the following entry into the *Logical_test* box:

```
C19>B19
```

Value_if_true
Value_if_false

Subsequently, click into the *Value_if_true* box and enter the formula or the numeric constant or text constant that should be returned if the condition evaluates to TRUE. Into the *Value_if_false* box, enter the return value or command for the case that the condition you specified evaluates to FALSE.

If you require another function for the formulation of the condition in the *Logical_test* box or for one of the commands in the *Value_if_true* box or the *Value_if_false* box, open the *Function* box and choose the necessary function.

OK

After entering the condition, the *Value_if_true* value and the *Value_if_false* value, close the *Formula Palette* by clicking the *OK* button.

Minimizing the
Formula Palette

In order to create cell references by selecting cells or cell ranges in the worksheet, you may need to first click the *Collapse Dialog* button ⊞ next to the *Logical_test* box or one of the other boxes to minimize the *Formula Palette*. After selecting the required cells, maximize the *Formula Palette* again by clicking the *Restore Dialog* button ⊞. If this is not sufficient, you can freely drag around the *Formula Palette* to move it out of the way.

If you are familiar with *Excel* you can also enter the IF() function into the formula manually. The syntax is as follows:

```
IF(logical_test,value_if_true,value_if_false)
```

139

Using Operators for Comparisons

If you perform a comparison, for example in a logical test, you can transfer one or more comparison values that should be compared with the content of cells.

Comparison value

The simplest comparison value is a constant value or a constant character sequence that has to be contained in a cell in order for the condition to evaluate to TRUE .

Several
comparison values

Other comparisons are performed with more than one criterion, for example to determine values within specified limits.

Operator

In both cases, you will use at least one operator that determines the type of comparison between comparison criteria and cell contents.

Comparison
operators

Comparison operators return the value TRUE if the comparison gives a positive result and they return FALSE if the result is not true. *Excel* supports the following comparison operators:

▓ =

The *Equal to* operator is used to compare for identical values.

▓ >

The *Greater than* operator tests whether the value being compared is greater than the comparison value.

▓ <

The *Less than* operator tests whether the value being compared is less than the comparison value.

▓ >=

The *Greater than or equal to* operator tests whether the value being compared is greater than or equal to the comparison value.

■ <=

The *Less than or equal to* operator tests whether the value being compared is less than or equal to the comparison value.

■ <>

The *Not equal to* operator is used to test whether the value being compared and the comparison value are not identical.

Enclose any character sequences that you want to compare in quotation marks.

Determining the Order of Operators

In order for a formula to return the correct result, it is imperative that all components that you enter conform to the rules for formula creation.

Correct order

Part of this is making sure that you stick to the correct order when working with calculation operators and comparison operators. You probably still remember the 'multiplication before addition' rule.

This is the rule for *Excel* as well. To give calculation priority to particular parts of the formula, enclose these parts in parentheses.

This means that it is not only the order of the arithmetic operators that is important, but also the priority of comparison operators in relation to each other and in relation to other operators.

Excel works with operators in the following order:

■ Reference operators:
  Colon, space, comma

- Negation
  to indicate negative values

- %
  Percentage

- ^
  Exponentiation

- * and /
  Multiplication and division

- + and -
  Addition and subtraction

- &
  Text operator, to combine several text values to produce one single piece of text

- = < > <= >= <>
  Comparison operators

Conditions with AND()

If you want *Excel* to perform a calculation or some other action only when more than one condition evaluates to TRUE, use the AND() function. This function belongs to the logical functions and links criteria in such a way that all criteria have to be true in order for the condition to evaluate to TRUE.

FALSE

TRUE

If any argument is not true the function returns FALSE. To link several conditions so that only one of the conditions has to be true in order for the function to return TRUE, use the OR() function instead of the AND() function. More about that in the next section.

Syntax

The AND() function works with the following syntax:

```
AND(logical1,logical2,logical30)
```

142

In order to use this function so that a certain action is performed if the TRUE value is returned by the function and another action is performed if the FALSE value is returned, you have to use the AND() function as an argument for the IF() function, or nested.

```
IF(AND(logical1,logical2,...logical30),
Value_if_true,Value_if_false)
```

For example, if you want to test whether a customer placed more than three orders (in cell A10) and if the total value of the orders equals or exceeds 1,000 (B10), and calculate a discount of 3% if those conditions evaluate to TRUE, then use the following formula:

```
=IF(AND(A10>3,B10>=1000),B20*3%,"")
```

Selecting the IF() function

To create such a function with the *Formula Palette* and the *Paste Function* dialog box, click the *Paste Function* button ![fx], select the *Logical* entry in the *Function category* list box and choose *IF* in the *Function name* list box. Then click the *OK* button.

Logical test

Then click into the *Logical_test* box and click the drop-down button on the *Function* box. Then select *More functions* from the list. Now select the *AND* item from the *Function name* list box, and click *OK*.

TRUE value

Now enter the first value that should be TRUE into the *Logical1* text box. In our example this would be 'A-10>3'. Next, enter the second condition in the *Logical2* text box, in our example this would be 'B10>=1000'.

You can enter up to 30 logical tests. When you have completed entering the logical values, you can finish the entry of the AND() function which is here a second-level function. To do this and get back to the first-level function, click on the *IF* entry in the *Formula* bar.

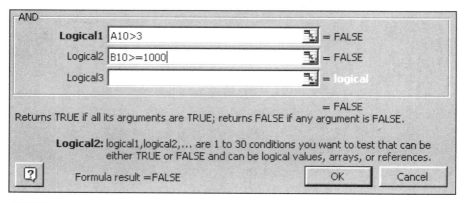

The arguments of the AND() function

Value_if_true

Value_if_false

The *Formula Palette* will display the IF() function again. Now enter into the *Value_if_true* and *Value_if_false* text boxes, the commands if the condition is TRUE and if it evaluates to FALSE. In the example, when the condition is true *Excel* will execute the calculation 'B20*3%', while in the event that it is false, it will blank the cell. Close the dialog box by clicking the *OK* button.

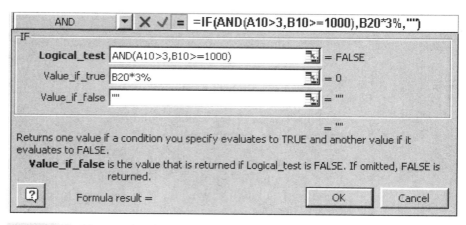

Fig. 2.54: The complete function

The OR() Function

The OR() function is used in connection with the IF() function to create a condition with more than one logical test, when not all criteria need to be true. The OR() function tests several conditions and returns TRUE if any of the conditions are true. It returns FALSE if all arguments evaluate to FALSE . The function works with following syntax:

```
Or(logical1,logical 2,...logical 30)
```

Alternative conditions

To create a condition with alternative criteria, click the *Paste Function* button 𝑓ₓ at the point in the formula where you want to insert the function.

In the *Paste Function* dialog box, select the *Logical* category, choose the *IF* function and close the dialog by clicking the *OK* button.

In the *Formula Palette*, the cursor will blink in the *Logical_test* box. Now click the drop-down button of the *Function* box and select *More Functions*. Choose the *OR* entry and click *OK*.

The *Formula Palette* now shows the syntax for the nested OR() function, a description and the text boxes for the first two logical values. Despite the fact that the second argument is optional, the use of the OR() function only makes sense if there are at least two alternative possibilities. Single conditions can anyway be tested with the IF() function.

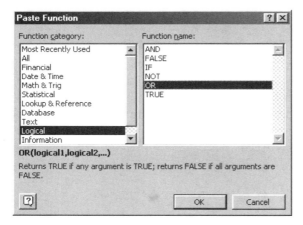

Fig. 2.55: The OR() function

Value_if_true 1

Enter the logical condition in the first text box. Supposing you want to test whether one cell content is larger than another, enter:

```
A10>B10
```

Then click into the second text box and create the next condition. Automatically, a third text box will be displayed as soon as the second condition is entered. You can enter a maximum of thirty conditions. To get back to the first-level function, click on the *IF* entry in the *Formula* bar.

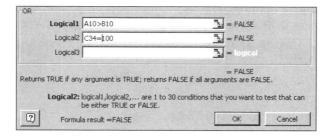

Fig. 2.56: Entering arguments for the OR() function

Value_if_true

Now complete the *Value_if_true* and *Value_if_false*. In the *Value_if_true* box you have to enter the formula, text or function that has to be executed if any of the conditions evaluates to TRUE.

Value_if_false

In the *Value_if_false* box enter the operation that is to be executed if all conditions formulated in the OR() function evaluate to FALSE. Close the dialog box by clicking the *OK* button.

The following formula executes the calculation of F3*G4 only if A10 is greater than B10 or if C34 contains the value 100.

```
If(OR(A10>B10,C34=100),F3*G4,"")
```

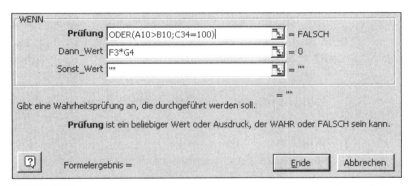

Fig. 2.57:   The second-level OR() function as an argument of the IF() function

Calculating with Date and Time Values

Internally, *Excel* treats date and time values as serial numbers. The date 31/12/99 represents for example the serial number:

```
36525
```

147

Time is administered as a serial decimal number. 12:00 corresponds to the decimal number:

`0.5`

Date and time as
serial numbers

Because *Excel* treats date and time values as numbers, calculating with these values is no problem. The result of a calculation with two date and time values is a serial number.

You should be aware of the fact that no negative date and time values are possible. *Excel* displays an error message in this case:

`#####`

Normally, certain functions are used in dealing with date and time values to isolate the required elements of a date or to render the serial number in the required date and time format. Here are a couple of examples of date and time functions:

- NOW()
  Supplies the serial number for the current date and time.

- TODAY ()
  Supplies the serial number for the current date.

- YEAR(number), MONTH(number), DAY(number)
  Converts the serial number to a year, a month or a day.

- DAY360(start date,end date,method)
  Calculates the difference between a starting date and an ending date on the base of a year with 360 days.

To use date and time functions in a formula, start as usual with an equal sign and choose *Insert/Function* or click the *Paste Function* button ![f*] at the point where you want the date value or the time value to be inserted.

Date & Time
category

Choose the *Date & Time* entry in the *Function category* list and in the *Function name* list box select the required function. Close the dialog box by clicking the *OK* button. If the function needs arguments, either enter them manually or create the cell references by clicking the respective cells.

Minimize the
Formula Palette

Use the *Collapse Dialog* ![icon] and *Restore Dialog* ![icon] buttons, to minimize and maximize the *Formula Palette*, so as to have better access to all cells when creating cell references. Finish the formula with a click on the *OK* button.

In the following figure, you see an example of the calculation of a date for a reminder based on the current date. The current date is inserted into the formula with the TODAY() function.

	B3	▼	=	=TODAY()+14			
	A	B	C	D	E	F	G
1							
2	Today	24-Nov-98					
3	Reminder	08-Dec-98					
4							

Fig. 2.58:   Calculating with dates

3. Formats

Changing Fonts, Font Size and Font Color

When you start a new worksheet *Excel* uses the default font and font size. This is the *Arial* font in the 10 point size.

Font attributes can be assigned to parts of a cell or to entire cells or even to cell areas. Highlight the cell area to which you want to assign a font style or click the individual cell for which you want to assign a new font format.

If you want to assign a new font format to only part of a cell, double-click on the cell to put it into edit mode. Then drag the mouse to select the part of the cell contents that you would like to format.

Using the *Formatting* Toolbar

The *Formatting* toolbar offers you a feature whereby you can change the font and font size using drop-down lists. Additionally you will find buttons for special formatting to visually enhance the text and numbers in cells.

Fig. 3.1:   The *Formatting* toolbar

When you've started *Excel 97*, all the drop-down boxes on the *Formatting* toolbar will display the default settings. Following any changes you make, these boxes will reflect the formatting of the selected cell,

In order to manipulate fonts with the tools on the *Formatting* toolbar, you can:

Arial

open the *Font* drop-down list by clicking the drop-down button and subsequently choosing the font you like.

10

open the *Font Size* drop-down box in the same way and choose the desired font size. If the particular size is not available in the list you can also type it into the text box and confirm it with the *Enter* key ↵.

A ▾

click the *Font Color* button to apply the displayed color to the font in a cell. If you open the drop-down list by clicking on the drop-down button, you can choose a different color from the color palette.

Additional buttons enable you to apply special font formatting to certain cells:

This button will make the font in a cell bold.

Use this button to italicize the cell contents.

Click the *Underline* button to underline the selected text.

Changing Fonts with the Dialog Box

There are even more font attributes, such as the double underline style, but to use them you will have to bring up

the *Font* tab page. To do so, choose *Format/Cells* and activate the *Font* tab page.

Here you will find the same lists as on the *Formatting*
toolbar for choosing the font, the font size, the font color
and the font attributes, such as *Italic*, **Bold**, ***Bold Italic*** or
Regular.

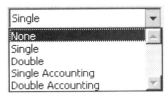

Fig. 3.2:   Underline types

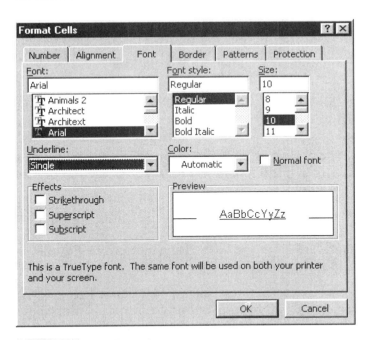

Fig. 3.3:   The *Font* tab page

Underline

Additionally, the dialog box offers the *Underline* drop-down box that lets you choose from four different types of underlining.

Effects

The *Effects* option group contains three check boxes to display the text in *Subscript*, *Superscript* or *Strikethrough*.

After you've chosen from the various options, close the dialog box by clicking the *OK* button.

Resetting the Font Format to Default

To remove all assigned font formatting from formatted cells and restore the default settings for font and font size, select the cells in question and choose *Format/Cells*. Activate the *Font* tab page and select the *Normal font* check box. Then close the dialog box with *OK*.

Excel will remove from the selection all the alterations to the formatting and restore the default settings.

Changing a Default Font in a Workbook

The default font in a workbook will display all the new entries in that font until the cells are assigned a different formatting.

The default settings are easy to see. Immediately after starting *Excel* or after creating a new workbook the, defaults are displayed in the list boxes on the *Formatting* toolbar.

All properties of this default font are controlled by a style called *Normal*. In order to change the default settings for the whole workbook, you will have to change this style.

Change

Choose *Format/Style*, and from the *Style name* drop-down list select the *Normal* entry. Click the *Modify* button and on the *Font* tab page, make all necessary changes for your new default settings. Then close the dialog box by clicking the *OK* button.

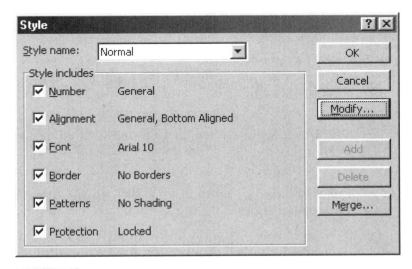

Style

| Style name: | Normal ▼ | | OK |

Style includes

☑ Number   General

☑ Alignment   General, Bottom Aligned

☑ Font   Arial 10

☑ Border   No Borders

☑ Patterns   No Shading

☑ Protection   Locked

OK   Cancel   Modify...   Add   Delete   Merge...

Fig. 3.4:   Changing the *Normal* style

In the *Style* dialog box, next to the various check boxes, all settings on the new *Normal* style are reflected. Click on the *OK* button to close this dialog box as well.

You can see the changes immediately in any worksheet based on the *Normal* style. This means that every worksheet in your workbook and all cells the *Normal* style is applied to will be affected by these changes.

Changing the Default Font Settings for all Workbooks

By default *Excel* uses the *Arial* font in 10 point size. When you change font, font size or font color on the *Formatting* toolbar or on the *Font* tab page in the *Format Cells* dialog box, this change will always affect only the highlighted cell areas.

Changing the font in the *Normal* style, however, will result in a change of font in all existing and new worksheets in the currently active workbook.

If you want to change the default font for *Excel* in general, choose *Tools/Options*. The *Options* dialog box has eight tab pages. For now you only need to activate the *General* tab page.

Standard font

The *Standard font* list box displays the standard font and the *Size* list determines the size of the font.

Font size

Open the *Standard font* drop-down list box and from among the available fonts, choose the one you want to use from now on as your standard font. Subsequently, *Excel* will always start with this font as the default one. Of course you can undo your changes any time you like. If you are not happy with the *Excel* default size of 10 point, open the *Size* drop-down list and choose the appropriate size. Intermediate sizes have to be typed in manually. Once you've finished making your changes, press the *Enter* key ⏎.

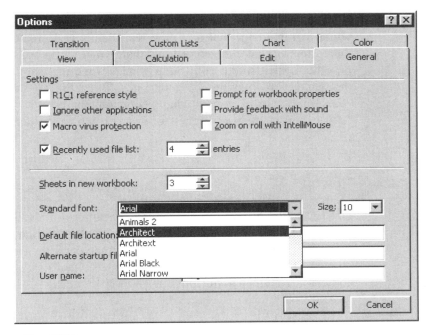

Fig. 3.5: Changing the standard font

When you close the dialog box with the *OK* button a message box pops up to remind you that the above changes become effective only after you restart the program. *Excel* has to reload and read the initialization files again in order to display the alteration in the standard settings.

Fig. 3.6: Message informing you that Excel has to restart

Click the *OK* button and restart *Excel*. It would be worth-while to remember that any new workbooks you create thereafter will have different fonts than *Excel* workbooks on other systems, and you might want to give this some thought before making these changes. Even the *Office Assistant* begins to wonder what's happening and pops up to ask you whether you really want to do what you just did.

Aligning the Cell Content

One of the things that can change the appearance of a cell is the alignment of the cell contents. The horizontal align-ment determines on which side of the cell the contents are aligned. The vertical alignment determines whether the contents are aligned to the top or the bottom of a cell.

Aligning Horizontally

In *Excel* cells that have the default *General* format, text data is left-aligned, and numbers, dates, and times are right-aligned. Therefore, just by looking at the alignment you can immediately spot if there is a mistake in the entry of any values.

Alignment buttons   The *Formatting* toolbar provides some buttons for the horizontal alignment of selected cell areas:

▦ *Align Left*
Click this button to align the cell contents to the left edge of the cell.

▦ *Center*
With this button you can display the cell contents centered in between the left and the right edges of the cell.

■ ▤ *Align Right*
  Use this button to align the cell contents to the right edge of the cell.

■ ▦ *Merge and Center*
  Click this button to merge the selected cells into one cell and align the contents of the upper-left cell to the center of the new merged cell.

If the choice of buttons on the *Formatting* toolbar is not sufficient, open the *Format Cells* dialog box, choosing *Format/Cells*. You can also reach this dialog box by right-clicking and choosing *Format Cells* from the context menu. In the *Format Cells* dialog box, activate the *Alignment* tab page.

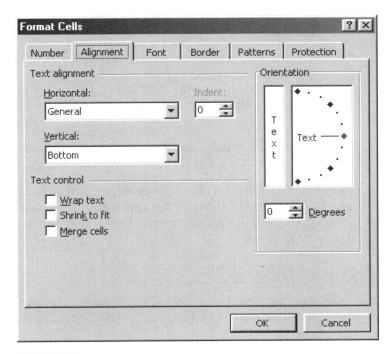

Fig. 3.7:   The *Alignment* tab page

The text alignments are displayed in the *Horizontal* and *Vertical* drop-down boxes. Apart from the already described options, the *Horizontal* drop-down list also contains the *General*, *Justify*, *Fill* and *Center Across Selection* alignments. *General* is the default setting which aligns text to the left and numbers to the right.

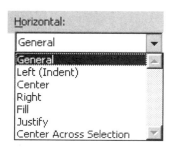

Justify

Justify aligns the text to both horizontal edges of the cell by uniformly increasing the spacing and automatically inserting line breaks.

Fill

Fill fills all selected cells with the contents of the upper-left cell of the selected area.

Center Across Selection

Center Across Selection does the same thing as the *Merge and Center* button. It merges the selected cells into one cell and aligns the contents of the upper-left cell to the center of the new cell.

Centering a Title Across a Worksheet

A common method of constructing a worksheet is to place the column labels in one of the top rows and the data in the rows below it.

If the table has a title, it usually appears on top of the column labels, preferably centered right across the top row of cells.

The *Center* alignment is not useful here because it centers text within one cell only and not across several columns as required.

Excel therefore offers another alignment called *Merge and Center* to do this particular job. You can select this alignment using a button on the *Formatting* toolbar or from the *Format Cells* dialog box.

Highlight the cell whose contents you want to align. Then additionally select its adjacent cells. Click the *Merge and Center* button ⊞ to merge the selected cell area and center the data of the first cell in the new cell area.

Only the first
cell remains

The functionality of this button has been extended in *Excel 97*. The command merges the cells into one cell and centers the contents. The cells can be selected either vertically or horizontally. Remember that only the contents of the top-left cell will remain, while the other cell contents, if any, will be lost.

Of course you can also use the dialog box to merge cells. Choose *Format/Cells* and click the *Alignment* tab.

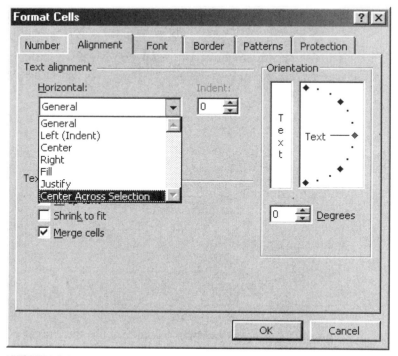

Center across selection in the horizontal drop-down list

On the *Alignment* tab page of the *Format Cells* dialog box, select the *Merge cells* check box and choose the *Center Accross Selection* entry from the *Horizontal* drop-down list to produce the same results as with the button.

	A	B	C	D	E
1		daily acceleration			
2		Monday	Tuesday	Wednesday	Thursday
3	Machine1	1.50%	3%	1.50%	0%
4	Machine2	2%	1.50%	0%	0%
5	Machine3	0%	4%	3.50%	1.50%
6	Machine4				

Fig. 3.9: The cell content of B1 was merged and centered in B1:E1

Apart from the normal horizontal alignment, in *Excel 97* there is also a vertical alignment. The default setting of the vertical alignment is *Bottom*, which means that the text is located at the lower edge of the cell. The vertical alignment determines the placement of text between the top and bottom edges of a cell.

The choices for vertical alignment are *Bottom*, *Top*, *Center* and *Justify*. The vertical alignment *Justify* distributes the cell contents evenly within the cell.

To change the vertical alignment select *Format/Cells* and activate the *Alignment* tab page.

Vertical

Open the *Vertical* drop-down list. Choose the required entry and close the dialog box by clicking the *OK* button.

Inserting a Line Break

When you enter character sequences, it is sometimes easier to read them if you break the text up into several lines rather than increasing the width of the column. To be able to distribute text over several lines you have to insert line breaks. You can do this either manually or automatically.

Automatic Line Breaks

Automatic line breaks can be inserted by *Excel* after any space. This can have some undesirable side effects but it does have the advantage that the line wrap will be automatically updated if the column width or the cell content is modified later on.

An automatic line wrap can be specified for a cell by selecting the *Wrap text* check box. This check box is located in the *Text control* option group on the *Alignment* tab page in the *Format Cells* dialog box. After confirming with *OK*, the text will automatically wrap in the selected cells.

Inserting Manual Line Breaks

If you want to define the line breaks yourself, for example to write an address into a single cell, you should insert the line breaks during the data entry.

To insert a forced line break within a cell, press the `Alt`+`↵` key combination.

Defining an Indent for the Cell Contents

You probably know about indents from word processing programs, where they are used to emphasize certain paragraphs. The indent in *Excel* sets off the cell contents from the left side of the cell.

In *Excel 97* you can, for example, visually group certain categories of data by assigning them a uniform indent.

1	Income	
2	concerts	£250.00
3	recordings	£135.00
4	teaching	£260.00
5	sales	£120.00
6	sum	**£765.00**
7		
8	**Expenses**	
9	travel	£83.00
10	instruments	£1,000.00
11	promotion	£60.00
12	studio rent	£340.00
13	sum	**£1,483.00**

Fig. 3.10: Indents

You can organize and apply indents in steps, and assign them either by buttons on the *Formatting* toolbar or with the *Format Cells* dialog box. *Excel* views indents as a kind of alignment, and that's why you will find the control for the indentation on the *Alignment* tab page.

	A	B	C	D
1	**Income**			
2	concerts			£250.00
3	townhall, 2.3.99	£150.00		
4	music school 4.3.99	£80.00		
5	birthday party 9.3.99	£20.00		
6	recordings			£135.00
7	teaching			£260.00
8	sales			£120.00
9	sum			**£765.00**
10				
11	**Expenses**			
12	travel			£83.00
13	instruments			£1,000.00
14	promotion			£60.00
15	studio rent			£340.00
16	sum			**£1,483.00**

Fig. 3.11:   Stepped indents in Worksheet cells

To quickly change the indentation in steps, select the respective cells and click on one of the following buttons:

Decrease Indent   A click on this button decreases the indent of the cell.

Increase Indent   Click this button to assign a left indent or to increase an assigned left indent.

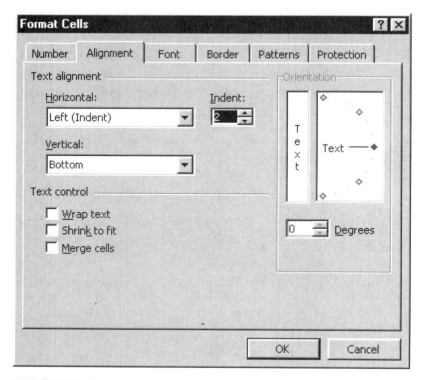

Fig. 3.12: Defining the indent in the dialog box

In order to define the indent in the dialog box, select the cells and choose *Format/Cells*. Open the *Horizontal* drop-down list in the *Text alignment* option group and choose the *Left(Indent)* entry.

In the *Indent* box increase the value point by point using the spin buttons, or just type in the number of indent steps you want. Each increment in the *Indent* box is equivalent to the width of one character. Close the dialog box by clicking the *OK* button.

Changing the Text Orientation

Earlier versions of *Excel* already had the option to change the orientation of the text from horizontal to vertical and to decide whether it runs from top to bottom or vice versa.

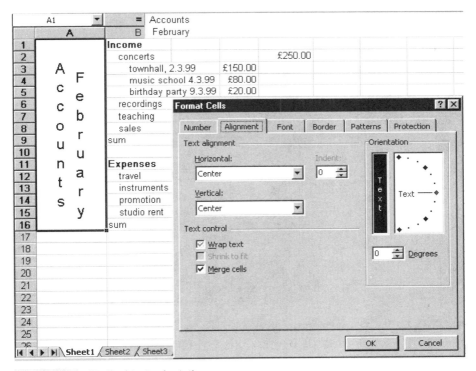

To change the text orientation from horizontal to vertical, click the long button in the option group that reads 'Text' in a vertical orientation.

In *Excel 97* you have, additionally, the possibility to rotate the text within the cell.

Degrees

To specify the degree of rotation for a horizontally oriented text, either manipulate the 'hand' in the semicircle by
dragging it with the mouse cursor, or change the value in
the *Degrees* box.

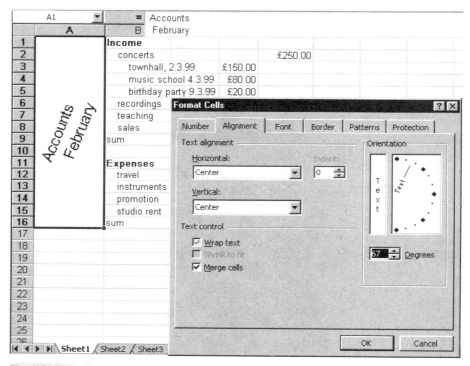

Fig. 3.14: Rotating text in a cell

Rotations between -90 and +90 degrees are possible.
Minus 90° corresponds to a text orientation from top to
bottom, while plus 90° corresponds to a text orientation
from bottom to top.

Restore default
orientation

In order to display rotated text horizontally once again,
select the cell or cell area, call up the *Format Cells* dialog

box and set the value in the *Degrees* box in the *Orientation* option group to zero.

Row Height and Column Width

When you create a new worksheet or switch to a blank worksheet in your workbook you will find the rows and columns formatted according to the default row height and column width.

If you enter more data than the current cell can display, the cell size does not automatically change. If the cell next to the active one is empty, it will display the data that does not fit into the current cell.

If the cell to the right of the active cell already contains data, then only the data that fits into the active cell will be displayed, or an error message will appear.

To adjust the cell size for the entered data, change the row height and the column width.

Adjusting the Column Width with the Mouse

The default column width in every new table is exactly 8.43 characters in a cell formatted with the standard font. If you enter data that requires more space than that, *Excel* automatically cuts off the display, or it displays numbers as exponential values, or even displays the error message #####. In this case, increase the column width to display the content of a cell properly.

If you are creating a worksheet with many columns and relatively short entries, you can also reduce the column size in order to fit more columns onto one page.

You can change the column width either with the mouse or by using a dialog box. To do the job with the mouse, point to the right boundary of the column heading. The mouse cursor becomes a split pointer ✛. Drag the boundary on the right side of the column heading to change the column width to accommodate your data. While dragging, a dashed line is displayed across the entire worksheet. This is useful for determining the point at which the appropriate column width is reached.

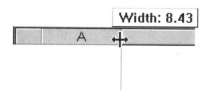

Fig. 3.15:   Split pointer on the right boundary of column heading A

Excel 97 displays the current column width in a *ScreenTip* if you click on the line between two column headings. While dragging the column, this information is updated so that you have a fairly good control over the width of the column.

Adjusting the Column Width in the Dialog Box

If you want to change the width by typing in the exact width or if you want to change the width of several columns in one go, highlight all that columns that you want to change.

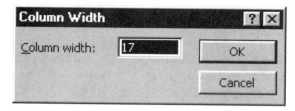

Fig. 3.16:   Changing the column width

Subsequently choose the *Format/Column/Width* item and enter the desired column width into the *Column width* box. Confirm your choice with the *OK* button.

The default for the row height is 12.75 pt. The row height is automatically adjusted to the size of the font used in the row. If there are different font sizes, *Excel* adjusts the row height so as to accommodate the largest font used.

Of course you can also change the row height manually by using the mouse or a dialog box.

To change the row height with the mouse, point to the lower boundary of a row heading. Here too, the pointer changes into a split pointer ✛.

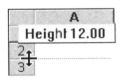

Fig. 3.17:   The split pointer at the lower boundary of the row heading

Drag the boundary below the row heading with the split pointer until the row is the height you want. While dragging, a dashed line across the worksheet displays the new position of the lower boundary of the row. Release the mouse button when you have reached the desired height.

Excel 97 displays the current row height in a *ScreenTip* when you click on the line between two row headings. While dragging, this information is updated so that you have quite a bit of control over the height of the row.

Adjusting the Cell Contents to the Cell Size

With a new formatting method in *Excel 97* you can adjust cell contents to the column width automatically. This has the advantage that it will be adjusted automatically should you make any further changes to the column width. This adjustment is made by reducing the apparent size of font characters so that all data in a selected cell fits within the column. The character size is adjusted automatically if you change the column width. The applied font size is not changed.

To automatically adjust the cell content to the available column width, select the cells to be adjusted. Subsequently choose *Format/Cells* and activate the *Alignment* tab page.

Check the *Shrink to fit* check box and click on the *OK* button to close the dialog box.

Adjusting the Row Height in the Dialog Box

If you want to change the height by typing in the exact number, or if you want to change the height of several rows in one go, select all the rows that have to be changed.

Fig. 3.18:   Changing the cell height

Then choose *Format/Cells/Height* and enter the required height into the *Row height* box. The height is entered in points and can vary between 0 and 409.5 points. Close the dialog box by clicking the *OK* button.

AutoFit Row Height and Column Width with the Mouse

Excel cells have a default height and a default width. These depend on the specified default row height and default column width. The default is a height of *12.75 pt* and a width of *8.43* characters of the standard font. If one of your prime interests is to save space, then you should leave the adjustments of the row height and column width to *Excel*.

However, even though the row height is automatically adjusted to the cell content, you might have to set the column width yourself.

The fastest way to automatically size a cell height is to double-click on the lower boundary of a row heading. Likewise, the fastest way to automatically fit the column width to the size of the cell is to double-click on the right boundary of a column heading.

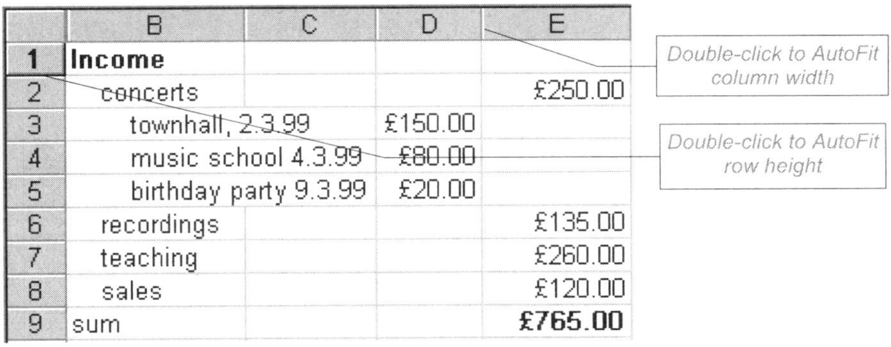

	B	C	D	E
1	**Income**			
2	concerts			£250.00
3	townhall, 2.3.99		£150.00	
4	music school 4.3.99		£80.00	
5	birthday party 9.3.99		£20.00	
6	recordings			£135.00
7	teaching			£260.00
8	sales			£120.00
9	sum			**£765.00**

Double-click to AutoFit column width

Double-click to AutoFit row height

Fig. 3.19: Automatically fitting height and width

Fitting several rows or columns

You can also select multiple rows or columns before automatically fitting them to the cell width by double-clicking on any line between column headings or row headings. To size the whole worksheet, highlight the entire worksheet by clicking on the intersection of the column and row headings, or by pressing the Ctrl+A key combination and subsequently double-clicking on one of the lines, either between row headings or between column headings.

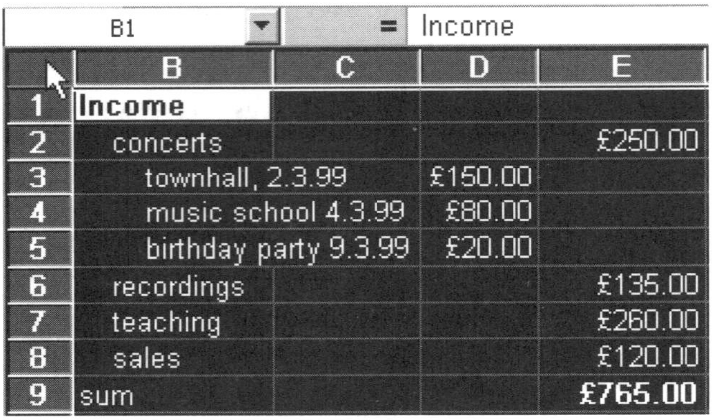
B1
= Income
B
C
D
E
1 Income
2 concerts £250.00
3 townhall, 2.3.99 £150.00
4 music school 4.3.99 £80.00
5 birthday party 9.3.99 £20.00
6 recordings £135.00
7 teaching £260.00
8 sales £120.00
9 sum £765.00

Fig. 3.19a: The *Select All* button

AutoFit Height and Width by Menu Command

If you prefer working with menus rather than the mouse, you can enter the values for height and width by typing them into the respective boxes. The *Format/Rows/Height* and *Format/Column/Width* commands will call up the respective dialog boxes.

AutoFit height

The *Format/Row/AutoFit* menu command fits a row height automatically to the optimal value.

The *Format/Column/AutoFit Selection* menu command fits a column width to the optimal value.

Changing the Default Column Width

When you open a new worksheet you will always find that the columns are 8.43 characters wide in the standard font spacing.

Of course, you can adjust the column width to the cell sizes by either entering a particular value by dragging the boundary of the column heading or by using the *AutoFit* command.

However, if you frequently work with larger or smaller column widths, it is a nuisance to have to do this every time. In that case it is better to change the *Standard Width*.

Standard: 8.43

Excel can have only one standard column width. For your new default, define the width that you use most of the time when you want to minimize the use of *AutoFit* procedures.

Choose *Format/Column/Standard Width*. In the dialog box enter the new standard. Values between *0* and *255* are allowed. Close the dialog box by clicking the *OK* button.

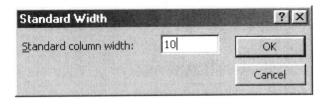

Fig. 3.20:   Changing the standard column width

Excel changes the column width for all columns that are still formatted with the *Standard Width*, that is, for all columns that have not been changed yet.

Merging and Splitting Cells

Excel 97 offers a new formatting feature to merge cells, which you can use for the cells of a row as well as for the cells of a column.

As mentioned above, you can use this formatting feature to merge and center the title of a table within your worksheet. But you can also merge cells without centering their contents.

Advantage of
merging cells

The advantage of merging cells, as opposed to adjusting the column width, is that you do not have to adjust the whole column by the longest cell in the column. This way, in some cases you can save a lot of space without sacrificing clarity.

Remember that only the contents of the upper-left cell will remain. To avoid loss of data, you will be given the option to cancel the procedure if *Excel* detects data in more than one selected cell.

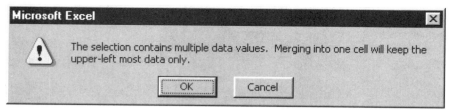

Fig. 3.21:   Warning message prior to merging

It is helpful to have a rough idea of the structure of the worksheet before you start entering data. Then you can merge cells before you enter the information.

Merging Cells

To merge cells first select them and then choose *Format/ Cells*. On the *Alignment* tab page in the *Text control* option group, select the *Merge cells* check box.

If your motivation for merging cells in a column is to save space, you can also try rotating the text if you want to save even more space.

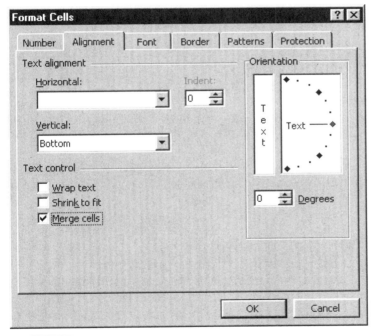

Fig. 3.22:   Merging cells

In Figure 3.23 you see the cells A1:A9 merged. The text in these cells has been rotated by +90 degrees and vertically centered.

	A	B	C	D	E
1		**Income**			
2		concerts			£250.00
3	**INCOME**	townhall, 2.3.99		£150.00	
4		music school 4.3.99		£80.00	
5		birthday party 9.3.99		£20.00	
6		recordings			£135.00
7		teaching			£260.00
8		sales			£120.00
9		sum			**£765.00**

Fig. 3.23:   Merged cells

Splitting Merged Cells

If you have already joined cells and you want to split them again, select the cells and choose *Format/Cells*.

Uncheck the *Merge cells* check box on the *Alignment* tab page. The cell will revert to its original condition, and the original number of cells will be restored. Text will be displayed only in the first cell, and the cell height of vertically merged cells will be automatically adjusted if necessary.

Borders for Cells, Rows and Columns

The grid is the main means of visually orienting yourself in an *Excel* worksheet. However, by default it is not printed out. But in a table you often need frames and borders to heighten the visual clarity of the contents.

You can emphasize one or several highlighted cells using lines or a full frame, a border that will be printed out as well. Design your worksheet in such a way that:

- borders and lines emphasize important cell areas.

- borders join related cell areas.

- lines separate different cell areas.

With the *Borders* button on the *Formatting* toolbar *Excel* offers a palette of borders for quick access. It also provides a tab page in the *Format Cells* dialog box which can be used for this purpose.

Borders and Lines on the Palette

A very quick method of adding and removing borders and lines is by using the border palette. Open the border palette by clicking the drop-down button and choose what you want from among the various possibilities. If you use this palette a lot, you can 'undock' the drop-down list and drag the floating toolbar to wherever you need it.

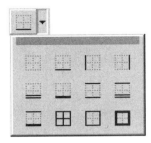

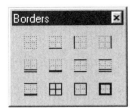

Fig. 3.24:   The *Borders* palette

On this palette you will find buttons for all kinds of single lines, for a simple or a thick cell border or for a printable grid that will frame every cell of the selected area.

The button for the *Borders* palette on the *Formatting* toolbar shows the last used border or line. A single click on this button is enough to reassign this border or line.

Borders and Lines in the Dialog Box

Select the worksheet or part of the table you want to embellish with borders and lines and then choose *Format/ Cells* and activate the *Border* tab page.

The appearance of the *Border* tab page has changed a bit, but its basic functioning and method of handling remain the same in *Excel 97*. Now, on the *Border* tab page in the *Format Cells* dialog box, you can assign lines and borders by clicking the same buttons that appear on the *Borders* palette. In addition, you can assign lines that diagonally connect opposite corners.

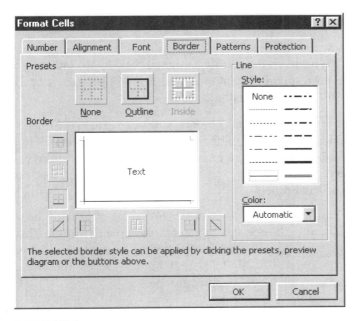

Fig. 3.25: The *Border* tab page

To assign a complete border to a selected area, click the *Outline* button. If you want to insert lines on particular edges, click the respective buttons. The style of the lines can be selected from the *Style* list box in the *Line* option group.

If you work with a color printer, or if your worksheet is only meant for screen display, you can specify lines and border colors in the *Color* drop-down list. Open the *Color* drop-down box, choose a color and then select the lines and borders you want to color. You will immediately be given a preview so that you can evaluate the effects of your choices. Close the dialog box by clicking the *OK* button.

Removing Lines and Borders

You can individually remove every single line or border that you have previously assigned. To do so, either use the corresponding button on the *Borders* palette or open the *Format Cells* dialog box.

Removing lines

To remove lines and borders you can open the *Borders* palette with a click on the drop-down button and click the first button in the upper-left corner, which displays a very thin dotted grid. The *None* button stands for 'no lines and borders'.

If you prefer to work with the *Format Cells* dialog box, go to the *Border* tab page and click on a button that represents exactly the line you want to remove. If you want to remove all lines and borders, click the *None* button in the *Presets* option group.

Assigning Shading and Patterns

There are a number of other ways to enhance cells that contain important data or formulas, as well as row or column labels. You can apply background colors, shading and patterns to any cell or cell area.

Using these tools you can, for example show the integrity of non-adjacent cells or parts of the worksheet. You could also permanently highlight cell areas that contain very good or very unsatisfactory results in business events. Background color, shading and patterns can be used as backgrounds for cells or cell areas but not for parts of the cell contents.

Background color different from font color

Use patterns and background colors carefully so as not to disturb the readability of your data. The font color and the background color should be clearly different from one another. When you assign a pattern to the background, choose a font size big enough to not impair the readability.

Assigning Colors Using the *Fill Color* Palette

To enhance cells by using a particular background color, select the cell and open the *Fill Color* palette. Choose a color by clicking the respective color button.

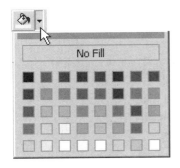
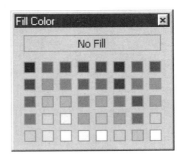

Fig. 3.26:   The *Fill Color* palette

No Fill

Later you can remove assigned colors by clicking the *No Fill* button on the *Fill Color* palette.

Patterns and Shading in the Dialog Box

To use the *Format Cells* dialog box instead of the *Fill Color* palette, choose *Format/Cells* and activate the *Patterns* tab page. In addition to the colors you can also choose patterns for the background by opening the *Pattern* drop-down list.

No Color

The *No Color* button clears all patterns and colors. You will find this button above the color buttons in the dialog box.

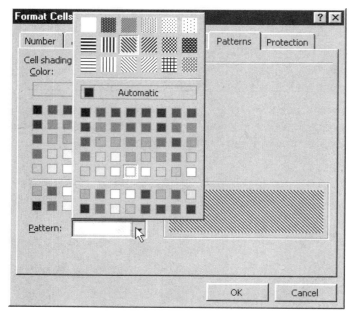

Fig. 3.27:   The *Pattern* drop-down list on the *Patterns* tab page

Formatting with Keyboard Shortcuts

If you create worksheets under severe time pressure, you will want to have quick access to all the necessary functions. Unlike the process of entering data where it is possible to save a lot of time by copying constants and formulas, the process of formatting and visual enhancement takes a lot of time.

Many formatting commands can be accessed with the buttons on the *Formatting* toolbar, which already speeds up the process.

`Ctrl`+`1`

Alternatively, you can work with keyboard shortcuts to select the most important formatting commands. You can open the *Format Cells* dialog box more quickly with the `Ctrl`+`1` key combination than with the menu command.

Given below is a list of key combinations for quick formatting of cells.

Character Formatting and Outline

▦ Bold	`Ctrl`+`B`
▦ Italic	`Ctrl`+`I`
▦ Underline	`Ctrl`+`U`
▦ Strikethrough	`Ctrl`+`5`
▦ Outline	`Ctrl`+`⇧`+`&`

Number Formats

▦ General number format	`Ctrl`+`⇧`+`~`
▦ Currency format	`Ctrl`+`⇧`+`$`
▦ Percentage format	`Ctrl`+`⇧`+`%`
▦ Exponential number format	`Ctrl`+`⇧`+`^`
▦ Date format	`Ctrl`+`⇧`+`#`
▦ Time format	`Ctrl`+`⇧`+`@`
▦ 1000 separator	`Ctrl`+`⇧`+`!`

Copying Formatting

If some cells in your worksheet contain formatting that you would like to use in other cells, you can copy this formatting to the destination cells, with or without the data.

Copy 🗈

Select the cell that contains the formatting you want to transfer and choose *Edit/Copy* or click the *Copy* button 🗈.

Paste Special

Then select the cell to which you want to transfer the formatting and choose *Edit/Paste Special.* The *Paste Special* dialog box allows you to specify which data you want to include in the paste process.

	A	B	C	D	E	F
1		Monday	Tuesday	Wednesday	Thursday	
2	Machine1	34	44	32	43	153
3	Machine2	32	29	24	22	107
4	Machine3	23	32	33	43	131
5	Machine4	32	23	23	27	105
6		121	128	112	135	496

Fig. 3.28:   To copy the format from B1 to F6 ...

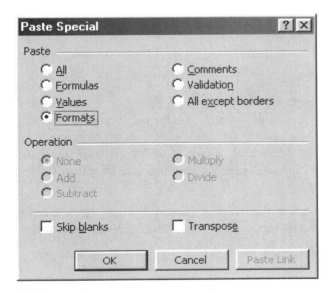

Fig. 3.29:   Copying formats

Select the *Formats* radio button and close the dialog box by clicking the *OK* button.

	A	B	C	D	E	F
1		Monday	Tuesday	Wednesday	Thursday	
2	Machine1	34	44	32	43	153
3	Machine2	32	29	24	22	107
4	Machine3	23	32	33	43	131
5	Machine4	32	23	23	27	105
6		121	128	112	135	496

Fig. 3.30:   The formatting was transferred to F6

The next section will show how to use the *Format Painter* to transfer formatting quickly and easily.

To copy and paste formats you can also use the shortcut menu commands instead of the menu commands. This context-sensitive menu pops up when you click the right mouse button.

Paint Formatting

If you want to give a uniform format to your worksheet, you do not have to activate the formatting commands for each and every cell. *Excel* provides a button to easily transfer formats only, without the data contained in the cells.

Format Painter

You can use the *Format Painter* button 🖌 to transfer formats with the mouse. This *Format Painter* button can:

- transfer formats from a source cell to a destination cell.

- transfer formats from a source cell to a destination cell area.

- transfer formats from a source cell to several destination cell areas.

- transfer formats from a source cell area to one or more destination cell areas.

Single click to copy

Select the cell or cell area containing the format and click the *Format Painter* button 🖌, to transfer the format to a destination cell or cell area. This is like taking the brush of the *Format Painter*. Now click the cell or wipe the brush over the cell area to be formatted.

Double-click for several copies

In order to 'paint' the format of the selected cell to more than one cell area, double-click the *Format Painter* button 🖌 and subsequently drag the mouse over all the required cell areas. To exit this mode either click the *Format Painter* button again or press [Esc].

When you transfer more than one format to a destination cell area, the format is transferred in the same order in which it appears in the source area.

How to save formats that you need all the time as a style is discussed in the next section.

Styles

Even if you've never heard the term *Styles* until now, you have already been using them! Formatting is saved in styles. Formatting such as the font, font style, borders, alignment, and number format are all stored in a style.

What is a style?

Styles can store particular formatting information under a name so that when you select that name, all the formatting attached to it will be applied in one go.

Built-in styles

Excel provides built-in styles that you use when you click on one of the number format buttons on the *Formatting* toolbar or when you choose these formats in the *Format Cells* dialog box.

User-defined styles

In addition to these integrated styles, you can create your own user-defined styles. Both types of styles, the custom ones as well as the built-in ones, can be modified.

Every style receives a name under which all formatting of that style is stored and saved.

You can modify the preset styles that are used to display cells in the *General*, in the *Currency* and in the *Percentage* formats. You can also add new styles.

Creating a New Style

To create a new custom style, choose *Format/Style*. The name of the style with which the active cell is formatted will be displayed in the *Style name* box within the *Style* dialog box.

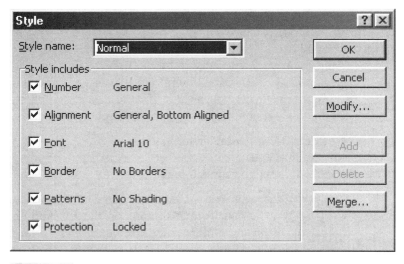

Fig. 3.31:   The *Style* dialog box

If you have not assigned any other format, this will be the *Normal* style. Type a name for your new style into the *Style name* box and click the *Add* button.

Modify

The new style is then included in the list of styles. Click the *Modify* button to start assembling the style. The *Format Cells* dialog box will appear. Choose from the various tab pages the formatting you want to include in your new style, and close the dialog box by clicking the *OK* button.

As an example, we will go through all the steps needed in order to create a user-defined style that formats all cells with totals, so that the numbers will appear in bold and with double underline, and the cells are in *Currency* format and shaded. Start by typing 'Totals' over the entry in the *Style name* box.

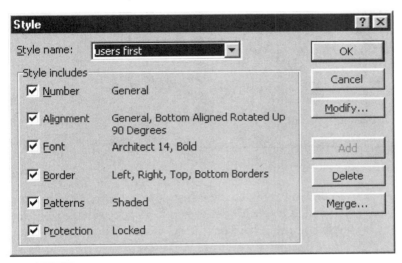

Style

Style name: users first

Style includes
- ☑ Number   General
- ☑ Alignment   General, Bottom Aligned Rotated Up 90 Degrees
- ☑ Font   Architect 14, Bold
- ☑ Border   Left, Right, Top, Bottom Borders
- ☑ Patterns   Shaded
- ☑ Protection Locked

OK
Cancel
Modify...
Add
Delete
Merge...

Fig. 3.32:   A user-defined style

Click the *Add* button and then the *Modify* button. In the *Format Cells* dialog box, activate the *Number* tab page. Choose the *Currency* entry in the *Category* list box. Change to the *Font* tab page and choose *Bold* and in the *Underline* drop-down list choose the *Double* item. Change to the *Patterns* tab page and choose a color or pattern for the background of the cell. Then close the dialog box by clicking the *OK* button.

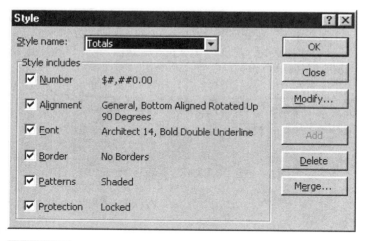

Fig. 3.32:   The new user-defined style

To directly apply the new format to the selected cell, close the dialog box with *OK*, whereas if you want to store the style and use it later on, then close the dialog box with the *Close* button.

Designing Cells Using Styles

To apply the style, choose *Format/Style*, open the *Style name* drop-down box and select from the list the name of the required style. Then close the dialog box by clicking the *OK* button.

You can assign styles more quickly by displaying the list of styles on the *Formatting* toolbar. Choose *View/Tool-bars/Customize*. Since you have this book you can safely send the *Office Assistant* home for now, if it pops up. Click the *Commands* tab page and choose the *Format* entry from the *Categories* list. Then drag the *Style* drop-down list onto the *Formatting* toolbar. Close the dialog box by clicking the *Close* button.

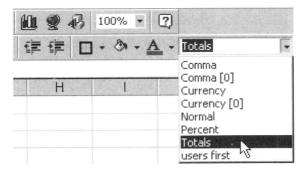

Fig. 3.33:   The *Style* list on the *Formatting* toolbar

If you want to transfer only parts of a style to the selected cells, clear those check boxes in the *Style* dialog box that represent the formatting you do **not** want to transfer. In the following figure, the number format is not transferred, because the existing number format needs to be retained.

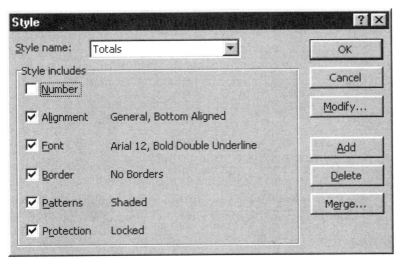

Fig. 3.34:   Transferring parts of a style

Changing Styles

You can change the preset styles as well as the user-defined styles if the formatting does not correspond to your needs anymore.

To change a style, choose *Format/Style* and select the name of the style to be changed in the *Style name* drop-down box.

Change

The *Style* dialog box will then display the properties of the selected style. Click the *Modify* button.

The *Format Cells* dialog box will be displayed, allowing you to disable certain formatting or activate additional formatting. After you have chosen all the formatting you need, close the dialog box by clicking the *OK* button.

You can then view all the properties of the style at a glance in the *Style* dialog box. Close this dialog box by clicking the *OK* button in order to immediately apply the modified style to the selected cells.

Close

If you do not want to apply the style right away, for example because you want to select other cell areas first, then close the dialog box with the *Close* button.

Deleting Styles

If you do not need a style any more and it's just taking up space in your style list, you can delete it. The style will then be removed from the current workbook.

To delete a style, choose *Format/Style* and in the *Style name* drop-down list, select the name of the style to be deleted.

Normal

The *Normal* style cannot be deleted because it is the basis for all standard cell formatting prior to any other formatting in other styles.

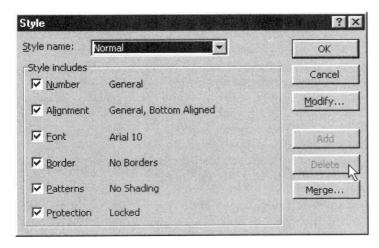

Fig. 3.35:   The *Normal* style cannot be deleted

Therefore, as soon as you select the *Normal* style in the *Style name* drop-down list, the *Delete* button will appear disabled and cannot be selected.

After you have selected a style that can be deleted, click the *Delete* button to remove it.

When you have cleaned up your list and all unnecessary styles have been deleted, close the dialog box by clicking the *OK* button.

Copying Styles from Workbook to Workbook

The best way to give a comprehensive and uniform look to your worksheets is by using styles. Working with styles is simple and does not pose many problems, as you will have noticed from the previous sections.

Once you've begun to work with custom styles, you will not want to do without them in the next workbook you create. You also will not want to waste time recreating them all over again, but would like to transfer them right away to the new workbook instead.

To transfer styles between workbooks, both the source workbook as well as the destination workbook have to be open. The source is the workbook that contains the styles to be transferred, and the destination is the new and empty workbook or any workbook where you want to use the styles.

Merge

Select *File/Open* and, while holding down the ⌨Ctrl key, click on the names of the source workbook and the destination workbook in order to select both of them. Then click the *Open* button. Select the destination workbook from the *Window* menu and choose *Format/Style*. Finally, click the *Merge* button.

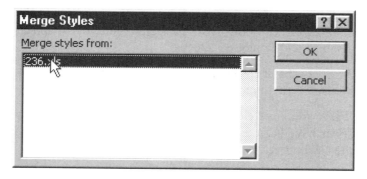

Fig. 3.36:   Transferring styles from the 236.xls workbook

In the *Merge Styles* dialog box all open workbooks except the one you are currently in are listed. Select the name of the workbook from which you want to import the styles and confirm your choice with *OK*.

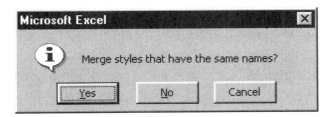

Fig. 3.37: Transferring styles with the same name

If there are styles with the same name in both workbooks, a dialog box pops up asking you if you want to merge these styles. Merging in this case, however, means actually overwriting and discarding the current one. Therefore, only click the default *Yes* button if you are ready to lose the style of the same name from your current workbook. Choose *No* to keep the style in your current workbook.

After transferring the styles, close the dialog box by clicking the *Cancel* button.

Changing the *Normal* Style

New entries in a worksheet are automatically designed with a particular formatting:

- Arial 10 font

- Text left aligned

- Numbers right aligned with the *General* number format

You can design the visual appearance of your worksheet by using various formatting, such as font, alignment, number formats and shading. Often such formatting is done after the data has been entered. The creation and use of formatting styles can speed up the process of worksheet design tremendously.

Read the above sections for detailed information on how to work with styles.

Standard

You can change the standard format of a workbook. All cells will be automatically formatted with this style upon the creation of a new workbook. The standard format is also a style that exists in every workbook and is called the *Normal* style.

Format/Style

To change the *Normal* style in a workbook, choose *Format/Style* and select the *Normal* style in the *Style name* drop-down list. Then click the *Modify* button. The *Format Cells* dialog box will appear. Use the various tab pages to modify the style to accommodate your future 'normal' needs. Supposing you usually need all numeric values to be shown in pounds: then on the *Number* tab page, select the *Currency* item from the the *Category* list box, and in the *Symbol* drop-down list select *£ English (United Kingdom)*. Close the dialog box by clicking the *OK* button.

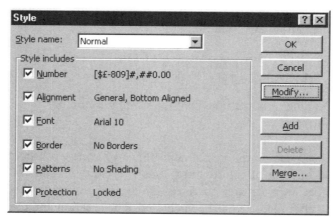

Fig. 3.38:   The modified *Normal* style

Number Formats

While the power and appearance of word processing programs depends largely on the formatting options for characters, the number formats are of more importance when you want to work quickly and comfortably in spreadsheet programs.

Why number
formats?

The number formats are there to help you concentrate on the main facts during data entry. You should not be distracted by the superfluous and repetitive parts of the formatting, like having to set currency symbols or non-significant decimal places.

Display precision

Number formats determine how values are displayed in a worksheet. They do not change the value, they just change the way it is displayed. The precision with which *Excel* can calculate depends on the data stored in a cell and not on the way it is displayed.

Generally you will prefer number formats instead of entering measurement units, special characters and currency symbols manually. If you enter data into formatted cells, you save time, the worksheets get a uniform look and the display is more flexible. *Excel* offers a good quantity of ready-made number formats. If you do not find what you are looking for, you can also create you own number format and use it in the same way as you use the preset ones. More about the creation of user-defined number formats is given in the next section.

The number format determines how data is displayed in a cell. The number format regulates, for example:

- The number of decimal places.

- Thousands separator

- Currency symbols

- Percentage symbol

- Quantity indications and other measurement units.

- Font color for positive/negative numbers

The number format is, however, responsible only for the precision of the display and not for the precision of the calculations. Calculation takes place using the precision of your entries, even if the number format shown on the screen has fewer decimal places.

Assigning Currency Formats

Naturally, in a spreadsheet program you will perform calculations relating to money sooner or later. For *Excel* to display the data precisely, the cells should be formatted with the correct currency format. Part of the formatting includes the thousands separator, two decimal places and the currency symbol £ before or after the numeric value, but that's up to you.

During data entry you do not have to worry about these elements any more. You just need to enter raw numbers. Even the non-significant zeros after the point can be omitted, since *Excel* will not make use of them anyway.

Standard currency format

After entering the data, you can assign the currency format to the required cells. You can assign the standard currency format by clicking a button. Other choices can be made on the *Number* tab page in the *Format Cells* dialog box.

Currency 🖳

Select the cells to be formatted in the currency format and click the *Currency* button 🖳 to apply the standard currency format.

####

If, after assigning a format the error message #### is displayed in the cells, it means that the column width is now too small. Double-click on the right boundary of the column heading to automatically *AutoFit* the column width to the cell width.

To determine the currency format more precisely, choose the *Format/Cells* command instead of the *Currency* button. Activate the *Number* tab and select *Currency* in the *Category* list.

Choosing the
currency symbol

You can change the number of decimal places in the *Decimal places* text box on the same tab page by using the spin buttons. If you want the numbers to appear without the currency symbol, open the *Symbol* drop-down list and select *None*.

In the same list you can also choose among many other symbols, if you have to deal with foreign currency, for example 'F' for France and '$' for the USA.

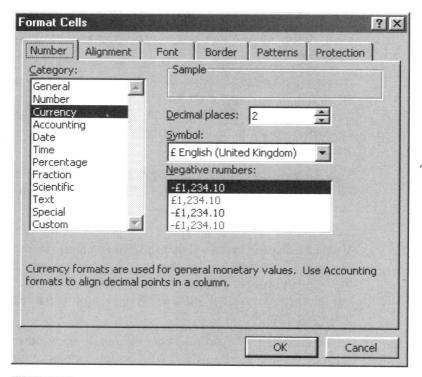

Fig. 3.39: Designing the currency format

Negative numbers In the *Negative numbers* list you can select in which way negative numbers will be displayed. After you have made your choices, close the dialog box by clicking the *OK* button.

Assigning the Percent Style

Percentage is another frequently used number format, and it has its own button on the *Formatting* toolbar.

This button multiplies a value by 100 and subsequently places the percentage symbol right after the number.

Therefore, you have to enter values that you want to have displayed as percentages as decimal numbers, for example: 0,15.

If you want to calculate the VAT and display it as

```
15%
```

Entering percentages

or you enter the number directly as a percentage

```
15%
```

then *Excel* will automatically assign the percentage format to this particular cell.

Percentage format with space

If you want to display the percentage symbol separated from the numeric value by a space, as is in fact correct, you have to create a user-defined number format.

User-defined

Choose *Format/Cells* and activate the *Number* tab page. In the *Category* list, select the *Custom* entry located at the end of the list. Overwrite the entry in the *Type* box with the following line:

```
0.00 %
```

Or, if you need a percentage format without decimal places,

```
0 %
```

After confirming with the *OK* button, the percentage format is created and can be assigned and used exactly like any other preset format.

Using User-Defined Formats and Preset Formats

You can assign the most important number formats with the simple click of a button on the *Formatting* toolbar or by using certain key combinations. A complete list of formats is given on the *Number* tab page in the *Format Cells* dialog box.

Fig. 3.40: The number format buttons

You can select the number formats for currency, percentage, and comma style with the respective buttons on the *Formatting* toolbar. Additionally, you will find two buttons to increase and decrease the number of decimal places.

- *Currency £ 1,200.00*
  Formats the cells with a thousands separator, £ sign and two decimal places.

- *Percent Style 15%*
  Formats the cells in the percentage format. Multiplies the cell content by 100 and adds the percentage symbol. This button adds the percentage symbol without any space between the number and the symbol. If you want 15 %, that is, with a space, you have to create a user-defined format.

- *Comma Style 1,000.00*
  Formats the cell with a comma to separate the thousands and a point for the decimal places.

- *Increase Decimal*
  Displays one decimal place more.

- *Decrease Decimal*
  Displays one decimal place less.

In order to choose other number format presets or user-defined number formats, choose *Format/Cells* and activate the *Number* tab page. You can assign or change preset number formats by selecting them in the *Category* list and modifying them with the check boxes and list boxes.

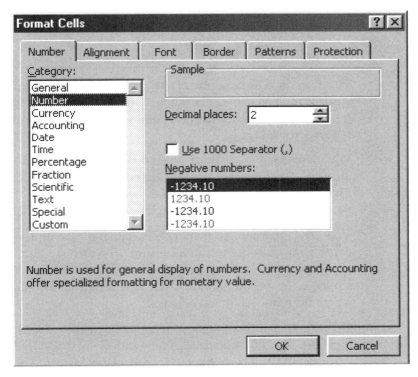

Fig. 3.41:   Preset formats

Certain categories such as *Special* or *Fraction* need to be further selected in a list box. Choose the required item by selecting it.

User-defined   Most items in the *Category* list show preset formats. To select a user-defined format, choose *Custom* from the *Category* list. Again, a long list of presets are displayed as a basis for your new formats.

205

Once you have designed a new number format you will find it at the bottom of the list. Select the entry for your new user-defined format and close the dialog box by clicking the *OK* button.

Showing and Hiding Decimal Places

The way in which numbers are displayed in an *Excel* worksheet depends on the number format. Among other things, the number format determines how many decimal places are displayed.

Provided that you did not change the format of a cell already, *Excel* will not display the non-significant zeros. That means that even if you enter extra zeros after the decimal point, *Excel* will not display them.

You can determine the number of decimal places by for-matting the cells in the correct manner. To assign a num-ber format, choose *Format/Cells* and activate the *Number* tab page. In the *Category* list box select the category to which the required format belongs.

For example, choose the *Number* category to format numbers with a thousands separator and decimal point, or *Currency* if the number should be displayed as a mone-tary value.

Most number formats allow you to specify the number of decimal places in a text box. There you can change the number of decimal places of the preset format.

Increase or decrease the number in the *Decimal places* box using the spin buttons to the right of the text box, or directly type in the number and close the dialog box by clicking the *OK* button.

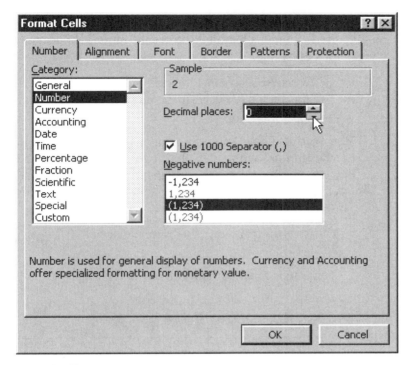

Excel provides a number of buttons on the *Formatting* toolbar to insert number formats with two decimal places, or to increase or decrease decimal places:

Currency
Use this button to display the cell as currency with two decimal places.

Comma Style
This button displays the cell with a comma as a thousands separator, with two decimal places and without currency symbol.

■ :⁺⁰⁸ *Increase Decimal*
A click on this button increases the number of decimal places by one.

■ ⁺⁰⁸ *Decrease Decimal*
Use this button to decrease the number of decimal places by one.

Key combination
You can also use key combinations to quickly assign number formats with a default of two decimal places, and then change these numbers with the *Increase Decimal* and *Decrease Decimal* buttons.

■ `Ctrl`+`⇧`+`$`
Currency format with two decimal places

■ `Ctrl`+`⇧`+`!`
Thousands separator and two decimal places

Creating User-Defined Number Formats

One of the commodities offered by a spreadsheet program such as *Excel* is the option to enter the data raw, with the minimum entry of values only. Any additional elements such as commas, currency symbols, non-significant decimal places, or units of measurements, can automatically be assigned by *Excel* using number formats.

The moment you enter data into a cell it is displayed in the standard format. This only happens with data that you do not enter in a particular way so that *Excel* can automatically detect the data format, such as with date and time values. If, for example, you were to enter the percentage symbol or a currency symbol after the numeric value, the cell would automatically be formatted using one of the preset formats.

Automatic formatting

If *Excel* recognizes that the characters attached to a value correspond to a number format, the cell will be immediately formatted in the respective number format.

If *Excel* does not recognize these characters as attributes of a number format, the whole entry is classified and formatted as text and not as a number format. You will immediately see this, because text is automatically left-aligned while numbers are right-aligned. When data is formatted as text you cannot perform calculations on it anymore. Therefore, if your data is meant to be used for calculations, you will have to create a user-defined number format for it.

Number tab page

To format cells with a number format, first open the *Format Cells* dialog box. On the *Number* tab page you have a choice of number formats listed in categories. Almost all items provide you with further lists and boxes to accommodate your needs.

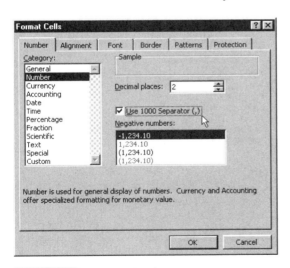

Fig. 3.43:   The number format presets

If you do not find the formatting that you need, this is the right place to develop it. You can either develop a completely new format or modify an existing one.

Custom item in
Category list

In order to create a new number format, choose *Format/ Cells* and select the *Custom* entry in the *Category* list box. You will find this item at the bottom of the list. After choosing this item, a list box and a text box are displayed on the right hand side of the dialog box.

Formats

You can then select one of the displayed formats and modify it according to your requirements, or overwrite the entry with a completely new format. During the creation of number formats you can use placeholders for future values, to be able to determine the exact order and to specify where additional symbols have to be inserted.

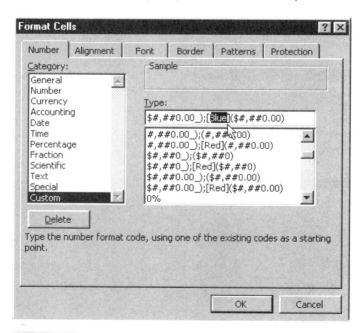

Fig. 3.44:   User-defined number format

■ *0*

Use this placeholder for numbers. Non-significant
zeros are displayed.

```
Number format : 0000
Entry: 1
Display: 0001
```

■ *#*

Use this placeholder for numbers. Non-significant
zeros are not displayed.

```
Number format: #,##0
Entry: 1,200.00
Display: 1,200
```

■ *?*

Placeholder for numbers. Non-significant zeros are
displayed as spaces. Numbers are aligned to the
decimal point, fractions are aligned to the fraction
stroke.

```
Number format: ??/??
Entry: 1/3 and 1/10
Display: 1/3 1/10
```

■ *'.' and ','*

The comma is used as a thousands separator, the point
as decimal separator.

```
Number format: #,##0.00
Entry: 1201
Display: 1,201.00
```

■ %

Specifies a percentage symbol and will be displayed in the correct position in the format code.

```
Number format: 0.00 %
Entry: 3
Display: 3.00 %
```

■ [Color]

In square brackets you can specify a color to be used to display the cell contents.

```
[Red]-#,##0.00
```

Text entered together with values will be handled as follows:

■ "Text"

Enclose units of measurements that should be displayed after a value, such as "meter" or "inch" or "buckets of water", in quotation marks.

```
Number format: 0 "meters"
Entry: 12
Display: 12 meters
```

■ "Text"@ "Text"

The text in quotation marks is displayed as a constant in the cell. The @ symbol signifies the position of the data within the constant.

```
Number format: "commission from "@
Entry: Benson
Display: commission from Benson
```

For the display of the $ - + / () characters, quotation marks are not required.

When assembling number formats, use different formats for the four different types shown below:

- Positive value
- Negative value
- Zero value
- Text

Stick to the order in the following picture. The different formats are separated by a semicolon.

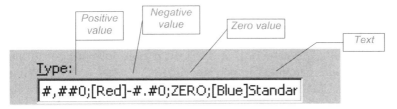

Fig. 3.45:   A user-defined number format

The user-defined number formats always appear at the bottom of the *Type* list box.

Removing User-Defined Number Formats

If you have already created a lot of user-defined number formats and your list gets too full of formats that you do not need anymore, you can delete the unnecessary number formats. To do so, choose *Format/Cells* and click the *Number* tab to activate the *Number* tab page. Select the *Custom* item in the *Category* list box. Choose the format to be deleted in the *Type* list box. Then click the *Delete* button and after you have made all your changes, close the dialog box by clicking *OK*.

Formatting Date and Time Values

Excel deals with date and time values internally as serial values. How these type of data is displayed depends on the formatting of the cell into which you have entered the data. Date and time values that *Excel* recognizes as such will be automatically displayed in the current date and time format.

Date and time categories

If you want to display a date in a different way than the one which is displayed by default, use a number format. The list of number formats available are listed in the *Format Cells* dialog box. Choose *Format/Cells* and activate the *Number* tab page. To edit a date format, choose the *Date* category, and to edit a time format choose the *Time* category. If you do not find what you are looking for, select the *Custom* item and create a new user-defined time format.

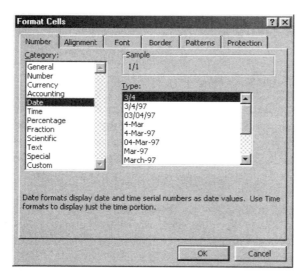

Fig. 3.46:   Date and time values

When you create user-defined number formats for date and time values, use the following placeholders:

- *D*

  Type this character as placeholder in date formats for the day.

- *M*

  Use this character in date formats for the position of the month.

- *Y*

  Use this character in date formats for the position of the year.

- *h*

  This is the placeholder for the hour.

- *m*

  Type this character in time formats for the minute.

- *s*

  Enter this character as a placeholder for the seconds.

- :

  The colon is used as a separator in connection with time values.

- / or - or .

  Use the slash, dash or point as a separator in date formats.

- AM and PM

  If you want to display the time in the 12-hour format, enter the characters 'AM' and 'PM' as placeholders.

Formats

In order to assemble a date or time format, click into the *Type* box and insert the placeholders for the respective elements separated by the correct separators. Close the dialog box by clicking the *OK* button.

215

Sample

You can preview the formatting effects on your data in the *Sample* box. In the following figure you see a user-defined number format for a new date format and the respective result.

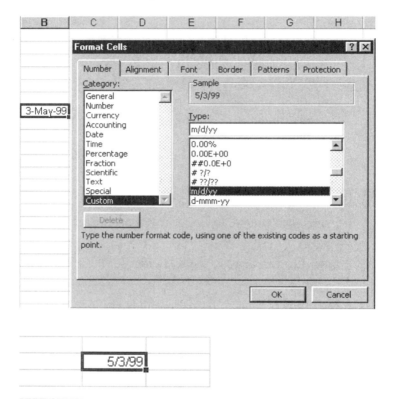

Fig. 3.47:   A user-defined date format

After creating the user-defined number format you can choose this format from the list just like any preset format. You will find it at the bottom of the *Type* list box when the *Custom* option is selected.

Conditional Formatting

If you have already worked with the IF() function, you will probably know that under this function different commands can be given for a cell. Using this feature you can, for example, display different text in a cell depending on the value in the cell. You could display the 'discount' message in a cell once a certain sum is exceeded, and no message or the message 'no discount' if this sum has not yet been reached.

What is conditional formatting

This type of conditional assignment can be used not only with formulas but also in connection with formatting. This function allows you to specify that a certain formatting, such as a red background, is only displayed if certain conditions are true, like for example when there is absolutely no money in the bank account. You can add a second and third condition in the dialog box, which *Excel* checks if the first condition is not met.

Assigning Conditional Formatting

In order to assign one or more formats, depending on a certain condition, choose *Format/Conditional Formatting*. The first drop-down box displays the *Cell Value Is* entry, which makes the formatting dependent on the cell contents.

Comparison operators

In the next drop-down list, choose the operator. This operator determines what the relation between the cell contents and the comparison value has to be in order for the condition to apply. Choose for example *greater than*, if the cell content should be greater than the comparison value.

Fig. 3.48:   A conditional formatting

The entry box, or for certain operators the entry boxes, are on the right-hand side of the *Conditional Formatting* dialog box. There you have to enter the comparison value or values. This can be a numeric constant, a text constant, a cell reference or a formula.

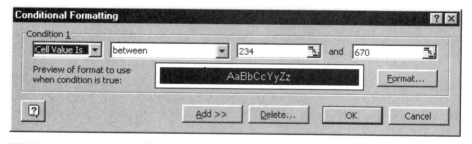

Fig. 3.49:   A value range

If you want to use a cell reference, click the *Collapse Dialog* button ⬛ next to the text box to minimize the dialog box so you can select the correct cell. This procedure is the same as the one you probably know from the *Formula Palette*. Here too, you maximize the dialog box after selecting the cell by clicking the maximize button ⬛.

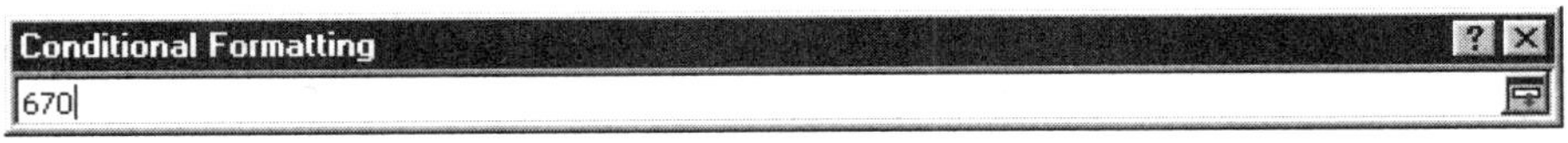

Fig. 3.50:   The minimized *Conditional Formatting* dialog box

After formulating the condition, click the *Format* button. The *Format Cells* dialog box appears containing only the *Font*, *Border*, and *Pattern* tab pages. Assemble the formatting of your choice, which will be applied whenever the condition becomes true. Close the *Format Cells* dialog box and the *Conditional Formatting* dialog box by clicking the *OK* button.

If you organize the food supply or a company's stock with *Excel*, you can use the conditional formatting to automatically show when a particular value, say 560, has been reached. Enter the following conditions:

```
Cell Value Is     less than or equal to     560
```

You can now assign the conditional formatting to the cell. The cell could become red or get a blue border as soon as the minimum value is reached. As an alternative to selecting the *Cell Value Is* entry in the first box you can also choose *Formula Is* from the drop-down list in order to enter a formula whose return value will determine the format of the cell. The formula has to be formulated in such a way that it can return only TRUE or FALSE.

If you want to formulate a second or third condition, if the first condition is not true, then after the entry of the first condition and the selection of the formatting, click on the *Add* button.

Immediately the dialog box is enlarged by the text boxes for the second condition. Formulate the second condition following the above procedure and here, too, choose the formatting by clicking on the *Format* button. You can enter a third condition in the same way, after clicking the *Add* button again.

Since a condition is either *True* or *False*, at least in a spreadsheet, you can format the cell so that it displays the cell contents in either one way or the other. This gives you quick information at a glance.

Deleting Conditional Formatting

In order to remove one or more conditional formatting entries at a later time, select the respective cell and choose *Format/Conditional Formatting*. Then click the *Delete* button. A dialog box pops up which gives you the choice to delete one, two or all of the conditions for the selected cell. Select the desired check boxes and close the dialog box by clicking the *OK* button.

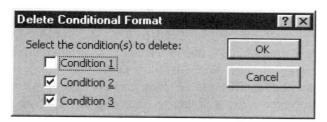

Fig. 3.51:   Deleting conditional formatting

4. Page Layout and Printing

If you are printing out your workbooks, worksheets and charts will be printed using the default page margins unless you change them. Changing the page margins with the mouse is possible in the *Print Preview*, in the new *Page Break Preview* or in the *Page Setup* dialog box.

Setting Page Margins and Paper Format

If you are satisfied with the default margins, you do not have to change them and you can start printing right away. But it is advisable to have a peek at the *Print Preview* to see how the table or chart will look when it is printed.

The Default Settings for Margins and Paper Format

You can find the default settings for paper size, margins and orientation of *Excel* in the *Page Setup* dialog box. *Excel* works with the default you define during the installation of the program. You can print in either *Portrait* or *Landscape* orientation. The default orientation is *Portrait*, which means that the page will be longer than it is wide. The default settings of the page margins are:

- Top: 2.5 cm
- Bottom: 2.5 cm
- Left: 1.9 cm
- Right: 1.9 cm

Headers and footers are printed in the top and bottom margins at a distance of 1.3 cm from the edge of the printed page.

You can change the page margins in the *Print Preview* or in the *Page Setup* dialog box.

Changing the Page Margins

If you want to change these page margins by entering new values into a dialog box, choose *File/Page Setup* and click the *Margins* tab if the *Margins* tab page is not already activated.

The boxes for the adjustment of the page margins are designed as spin boxes, so that you can increase the value with a click on the arrow which points upward and decrease the value with a click on the downward-pointing spin button. Every click on a spin button changes the value by 0.5 cm. If you need to work with greater precision, you will have to enter the values directly via the keyboard.

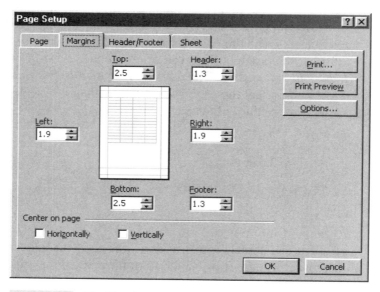

Fig. 4.1:   The *Margins* tab page

Type the values you require into the *Top*, *Bottom*, *Left* and *Right* boxes.

The *Header* and *Footer* boxes in *Excel 97* are not grouped along with the other margins anymore. Now they are placed right next to the preview at the respective positions on the page. The values refer to the distance between the paper edge and the top edge of the header, and between the bottom edge of the paper and the bottom edge of the footer respectively.

Print Preview and Page Setup

After changing the page margins, you can switch from the *Page Setup* to the *Print Preview* by clicking the *Print Preview* button on the right-hand side of the *Page Setup* dialog box. You can later switch back using the *Setup* button on the toolbar of the *Print Preview* window. The *Page Setup* dialog box will not show the *Print Preview* button anymore in this case, since the *Print Preview* does not really close when the dialog is called up in this way. To preview your changes then you will need to close the dialog box by clicking the *OK* button.

Changing the Page Layout of a Worksheet

After entering the data and formulas, you probably made use of the font, color, borders and line formatting features to present the data in your worksheet in the most appealing or practical way possible.

What the Page Setup does

An important factor in the overall impression of a worksheet is the page layout. This should not be ignored. The page layout controls the order, the alignment, the size and the page margins with which tables are printed.

All settings for the page layout are grouped together in the *Page Setup* dialog box. The following section describes how you change paper margins and paper format.

Size and alignment

In order to control the size and alignment of the printout of a worksheet, choose *File/Page Setup* and activate the *Margins* tab page. Here you can adjust the table in relation to the left and right edges of the paper.

Centering horizontally and vertically

By default, a worksheet is aligned to the top left margin. In order to center the table, select the *Horizontally* check box in the *Center on page* option group. Similarly, select the *Vertically* check box in the same option group to center the table between the top and the bottom margins.

Page tab page

On the *Page* tab page you can determine the size of the printout of your worksheet. To print the table in such a way that it fits onto a specified number of pages, click the *Fit to* radio button and enter the required values into the *page(s) wide* box and the *tall* box. By typing a value into the *Adjust to X % normal size* text box you can scale the table in relation to its original size. Select the *Adjust to* radio button if you want to do this.

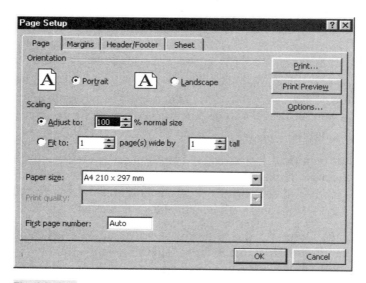

Fig. 4.2:   Page layout

The *Orientation* option group determines whether the worksheet is printed in *Portrait* (with Letter 8 ½ x 11 in 4: 29,7 x 21) or *Landscape* (with Letter 11 in x 8 ½ in A4: 21 x 29,7).

Sheet tab page

On the *Sheet* tab page you can decide which elements of the worksheet should be printed. Select the check boxes for *Row and column headings* or *Gridlines* if you want to include them in your printout.

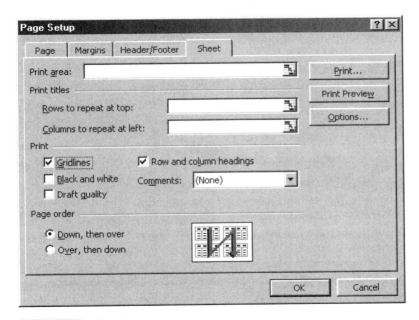

Fig. 4.3:   The *Sheet* tab page

Page order

The *Page order* option group decides upon the print order. The arrow in the iconized pages shows in which order the worksheet pages will be printed. This option is only important if your worksheet is larger than one page.

In this case, by selecting the *Down, then over* radio button, *Excel* first prints the pages that lie on top of each other. On the other hand, by selecting the *Over, then down* radio button, the iconized pages will change to illustrate that *Excel* first prints the pages that sit next to each other.

After changing the page layout, check the result in the print preview. To call up the print preview click the *Print Preview* button.

Choosing *Landscape* Format

An A4 page has a length of 29,7 cm and a width of 21 cm. Therefore, an *Excel* worksheet in this format has more length than width. Since tables regularly do not conform to this format, it is often advisable to switch from *Portrait* format to *Landscape* format. Then the paper will provide 29,7 cm for the table width.

Tables that contain more columns than rows and worksheets that are wider than the width of an A4 page should be printed in *Landscape* format so as to try and print all necessary columns on one page.

You do not have to go to the setup of the printer to change the orientation, since *Excel* takes care of this irrespective of the connected printer. You can determine the orientation in the *Page Setup* dialog box.

Page tab page

Choose *File/Page Setup* and activate the *Page* tab page.

Orientation

Select the *Landscape* radio button in the *Orientation* option group. Subsequently adjust the page margins on the *Margins* tab page to the new alignment.

Check the results of the change of orientation in the *Print Preview*. The button with the same name will bring you to the *Print Preview*. If you are satisfied with the result of your changes, click the *Print* button.

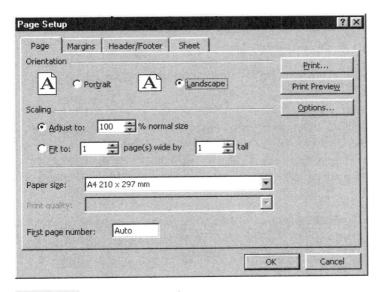

Fig. 4.4: Changing to Landscape

Landscape only for current worksheet

The change in the orientation applies only to the current worksheet. The other worksheets remain in the default *Portrait* format.

Back to portrait

To change back to *Portrait* orientation at a later time, choose *File/Page Setup* and select the *Portrait* radio button on the *Page* tab page. Then close the dialog box by clicking the *OK* button.

Print Preview

Before you print a worksheet or a chart, click the *Print Preview* button to see how the sheet will look when you print it.

To view the current worksheet or the current chart in the *Print Preview*, apply one of the following methods:

■ Click the *Print Preview* button 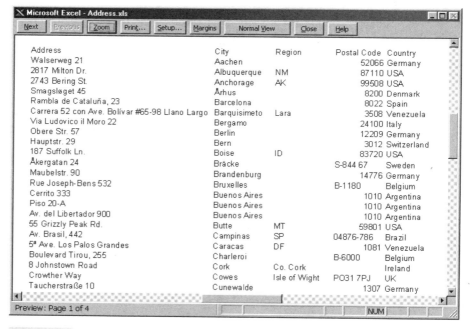.

■ Select *File/Print Preview*.

■ Activate the *PrintPreview* button in either the *Page Setup* or *Print* dialog boxes.

The mouse pointer changes into a magnifying glass in the *Print Preview* as soon as you point to the sheet. With this *Magnifier* click on any position on the worksheet that you want to magnify. Another click will reduce the display to its former size again.

Fig. 4.5: Print Preview

Zoom

You can also click the *Zoom* button to magnify the display. The *Zoom* feature gives you the option to either magnify the display or to return to the full-page view.

Margins

By clicking the *Margins* button you can display page margins and boundaries for columns. You can drag the margins to different positions. If you activate the margin feature, the boundaries between the individual columns appear as dotted lines. Drag the margin handles to change the column widths in the *Print Preview*.

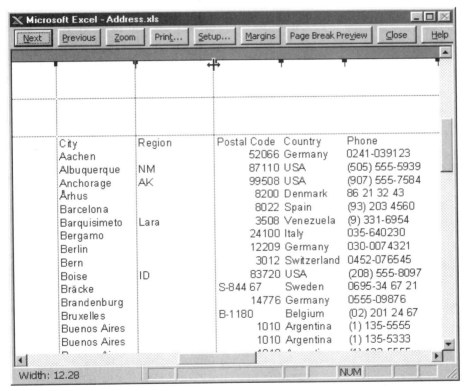

Fig. 4.6:   The mouse pointer on a margin handle for columns

Print

You can start your printing directly by clicking the *Print* button. This will open the *Print* dialog box, enabling you to set the options for the printout, such as the number of copies.

By clicking the *Close* button you will return to the *Normal* view. Alternatively you can also close the *Print Preview* by:

▪ pressing the Esc key, or

▪ clicking the *Page Break Preview* button.

If you want to print more than one page or if the table consists of more than one page, you can go backwards and forwards between the pages by pressing the *Previous* and *Next* buttons.

Setup

By clicking the *Setup* button you can access the *Page Setup* dialog box in which you can make any necessary modifications.

Changing Page Margins in Print Preview

In the *Print Preview* it is possible to adjust top and bottom page margins and header and footer margins to suit the size of your worksheet.

Unlike in the *Normal* view, in *Print Preview* you can view the worksheet in the way it will actually be printed. In order to display the entire page on-screen, it is accordingly reduced. Therefore, the *Print Preview* is eminently suitable for setting page layout and margins.

To activate the *Print Preview* select *File/Print Preview* or simply click the *Print Preview* button ▨.

Margins

Click the *Margins* button if the page margins are not displayed.

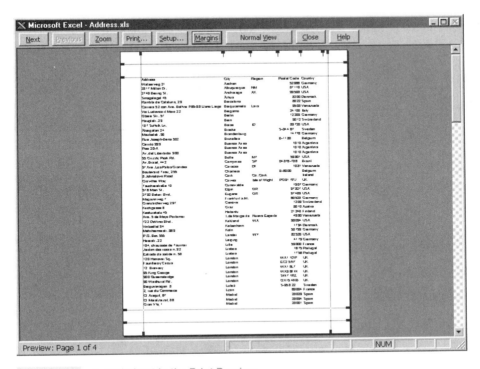

Fig. 4.7:   A worksheet in the Print Preview

Position display in
the status bar

As soon as you point the mouse at the margins the mouse pointer becomes a double-headed arrow. Click and drag the margin handle to the position you want. If you click on a margin or if you drag a margin handle with the split pointer, the status bar displays the current position of the margin.

Fig. 4.8:   The position for the left margin on the status bar

Changing Page Margins in the Page Break Preview

Page Break Preview is a new feature in *Excel 97*. Unlike in the ordinary view, now known as the *Normal* view, the *Page Break Preview* displays all the pages of a worksheet.

Of course, the worksheet has to be reduced accordingly in order to do this. But you can also magnify the display by selecting or entering a value in the *Zoom* drop-down box. It is not possible to use *Page Break Preview* for chart sheets.

Activating Page Break Preview

To activate the *Page Break Preview* select the *Page Break Preview* command on the *View* menu or click the *Page Break Preview* button in the *Print Preview*.

Page breaks as lines

Page breaks are indicated in the *Page Break Preview* by thick dashed lines. If you rest the mouse pointer over such a line, the mouse pointer becomes a double-headed arrow.

Using this resize pointer you can drag the page breaks to another position. In addition, you can enlarge or reduce the print area of the worksheet by dragging the margins.

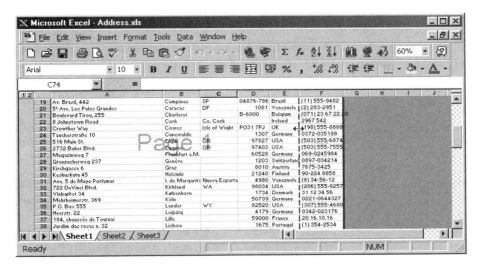

Page

Fig. 4.9: A worksheet in the Page Break Preview

If you move a horizontal page break downward or a vertical page break to the right, *Excel* scales the contents of the worksheet in such a way that the enlarged worksheet will still fit onto the page.

Normal view

To return to *Normal* view from *Page Break Preview* select the *Normal* command on the *View* menu.

Displaying Page Breaks in the *Normal* View

The page breaks that you manually insert in a worksheet or that *Excel* inserts automatically because a page is completely filled, are not normally displayed in all views. You can determine whether these page breaks are to be displayed or not. To do so, use the *View* tab page in the *Options* dialog box.

Options

Select *Tools/Options* and activate the *View* tab page. Check the *Page breaks* check box to always display the page breaks and close the dialog box by clicking *OK*.

233

Inserting Page Breaks in Tables

Automatic page
break

Excel automatically inserts a page break if the worksheet is wider or longer than the print page. *Excel* bases its calculations of the page break on the paper size and the margin settings.

If you want to insert a page break before reaching a page margin, select the position at which you want to start printing the new page.

Horizontal page
break

A horizontal page break inserts a page break between two rows. To insert a horizontal page break in a worksheet, position the cell cursor in the first cell of the row in front of which you want to insert the horizontal page break.

Vertical page
break

A vertical page break separates a worksheet between two columns. To insert a vertical page break position the cell cursor in the first cell of the column in front of which you want to insert the page break.

Horizontal and
vertical page break

You also have the possibility to insert a horizontal and a vertical page break simultaneously. To do so, select the cell before which you want the two page breaks to cross.

After selecting the cell, choose *Insert/Page Break*. A page break will be indicated by a dashed line if you have activated the option to display page breaks. Close the dialog box by clicking the *OK* button.

	A	B	C	D	E	F	G	H	I	J
1	Income and Expenses 1998									
2										
3			Q1			Q2			Q3	
4	Income	Jan	Feb	Mar	Apr	May	Jun	Jul	Aug	Sep
5	concerts	£250.00	£280.00	£100.00	£180.00	£300.00	£320.00	£0.00	£180.00	£180.00
6	recordings	£135.00	£0.00	£210.00	£190.00	£0.00	£110.00	£0.00	£0.00	£190.00
7	teaching	£260.00	£260.00	£260.00	£260.00	£260.00	£260.00	£0.00	£260.00	£260.00
8	sales	£120.00	£0.00	£0.00	£120.00	£120.00	£60.00	£0.00	£0.00	£60.00
9		£765.00	£540.00	£570.00	£750.00	£680.00	£750.00	£0.00	£440.00	£690.00
10	Expenses									
11	travel	£83.00	£90.00	£50.00	£60.00	£110.00	£100.00	£0.00	£85.00	£90.00
12	instruments	£1,000.00	£0.00	£0.00	£0.00	£0.00	£0.00	£0.00	£0.00	£600.00
13	promotion	£60.00	£60.00	£60.00	£60.00	£60.00	£60.00	£60.00	£60.00	£60.00
14	studio rent	£340.00	£340.00	£200.00	£0.00	£0.00	£300.00	£0.00	£0.00	£300.00
15		£1,483.00	£490.00	£310.00	£120.00	£170.00	£460.00	£60.00	£145.00	£1,050.00
16										

Sheet1 / Sheet2 / Sheet3 /

Fig. 4.10:   A vertical or a horizontal page break

In the following section you will learn about how to move or remove inserted page breaks.

Moving and Removing Page Breaks

Page breaks are displayed only when the relevant option has been activated in the *Options* dialog box. Page breaks appear as dashed lines.

Insert page break

If *Excel 97* does not display page breaks, select *Tools/Options* and activate the *View* tab page. Select the *Page breaks* check box and close the dialog box by clicking the *OK* button.

Remove horizontal page break

To remove a manually inserted horizontal page break, select the cell directly below the page break and click *Insert/Remove Page Break*.

Remove vertical page break

To remove a manually inserted vertical page break, select the cell directly to the right of the page break and click *Insert/Remove Page Break*.

Manually inserted page breaks, i.e., user-defined page breaks, can be moved by deleting them from their former position and inserting them again in a new position.

Automatic page breaks are page breaks that *Excel* inserts when you reach the end of a page. This type of page break cannot be removed, it can only be moved.

Remove automatic page break

To remove an automatic horizontal page break, insert a manual page break above the automatic horizontal page break. To remove an automatic vertical page break insert a manual page break on the left side next to the automatic vertical page break.

Page Break Preview

Open a new *Excel 97* feature which is very handy for this purpose by clicking the *Page Break Preview* command on the *View* menu. In the *Page Break Preview* you can change the page margins and page breaks by dragging them with the mouse.

Headers and Footers

Headers or footers that you have inserted yourself as well as built-in headers or footers that you have chosen are printed at the top or bottom of a worksheet or chart sheet.

Setting Headers and Footers

In order to change the position of a header and footer, you can either open the *Page Setup* dialog box or change the position directly in the *Print Preview*.

Default position

By default, *Excel* prints headers at a distance of 1.3 cm from the top edge of the page, while footers are printed at a distance of 1.3 cm from the bottom edge of the page.

Changes in Print Preview

In *Print Preview* you can change headers and footers in steps of 0.1 cm. It is possible to enter values in the *Page Setup* dialog box. To do this select *File/Page Setup* and click the *Margins* tab.

Change distance

Click the up-arrow button ▲ in the *Header* or *Footer* spin box to increase the distance between the header or footer and the top or bottom of the page respectively. To decrease the distance click the down arrow ▼. Each click changes the value by 0.5 cm.

Intermediate values

To enter intermediate values click into either the *Header* or *Footer* text box and overwrite or change the number manually. Once you have changed the distance according to your requirements, close the *Page Setup* dialog box by clicking the *OK* button.

You can also alter the position of headers and footers in the *Print Preview*. In this view you can drag the header and footer positions with the mouse.

Change distance in Print Preview

To do this, select either *File/Print Preview* or click the *Print Preview* button. If you are in the *Page Setup* dialog box, you can directly change to this view by clicking the *Print Preview* button after creating the header/footer.

Page margins

In the *Print Preview* you can show and hide the margins by clicking the *Margin* button. If the margins are not displayed, click the *Margins* button. The top horizontal margin indicates the distance from the top edge of the page to the header.

Distance

The bottom horizontal margin indicates the distance from the bottom edge to the footer. This margin defines the bottom edge of the footer. If you click on one of these margins with the mouse the status bar will display the current distance to the edge of the page.

Position indicator

header/footer

Drag these margins to change the distance from the top edge to the header or from the bottom edge to the footer respectively. While dragging, you can simultaneously see the new distance in the status bar.

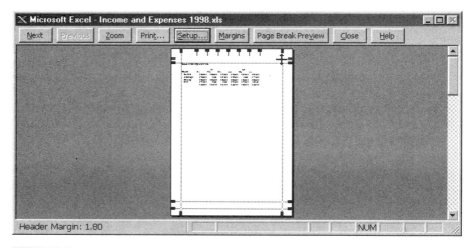

Fig. 4.11: The status bar indicates the distance between the header and the top of the page when the split pointer drags the header margin

Zoom

You can also click the *Zoom* button to magnify the display and to be able to more precisely move the margins in it.

Print

Once you have changed the page margins to the positions you want, you can print the modified worksheet directly from the *Print Preview* by clicking the *Print* button, or you can close the *Print Preview* by clicking the *Close* button or pressing [Esc].

Using Default Headers and Footers

Unlike with earlier *Excel* versions, *Excel 97* does not automatically print a default header and footer.

But this program version disposes of numerous integrated headers and footers which you are able to print:

■ the page number, with or without the total page number.

■ the name of the workbook and/or table.

■ the author with or without date.

You can also use different combinations of this information. To print one of the integrated default headers or footers, select *File/Page Setup* and activate the *Header/ Footer* tab page. Alternatively, you can activate the *Header/Footer* tab page by selecting *View/Header and Footer*.

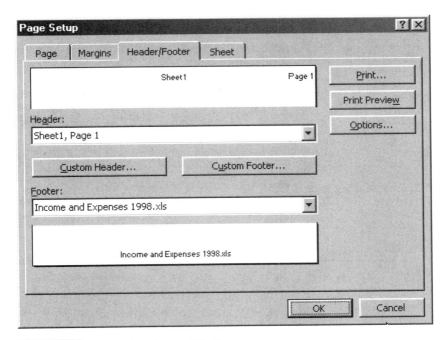

Fig.4.12:   Built-in headers and footers

Built-in headers and footers

To use one of the built-in headers open the *Header* drop-down list and select one of the items. To apply a built-in footer, open the *Footer* drop-down list and select one of the items. Scroll through the list using the scroll bar. Once you have completed your selection close the *Page Setup* dialog box by clicking the *OK* button.

Setting Default Headers

Headers contain information that is printed at the top margin of every page. As already mentioned before, *Excel 97* no longer prints default headers.

However, the default headers in the *Header* list still exist. To define a different header from the default header, select *View/Header and Footer*.

Click on *Custom Header* in order to create your own header and, if necessary, remove the code that is displayed in the *Center section* box.

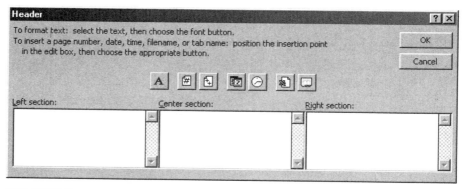

Fig. 4.13:   Empty text edit boxes for creating headers

The dialog box contains three text boxes. Everything you enter in the *Left section* text box will be displayed at the top left corner of the worksheet page.

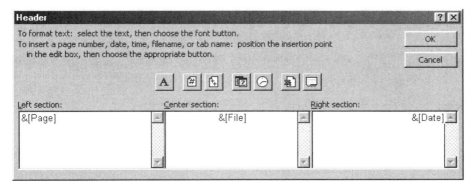

Fig. 4.14: Creating a user-defined header

The text entered in the *Center section* edit box will be displayed centered at the top, while the text entered in the *Right section* box will be displayed at the top right corner of the worksheet.

In order to enter particular information, such as the page number, the total number of worksheet pages or sheet and workbook names, *Excel* offers you the following options:

A		Opens the *Font* dialog box
	&[Page]	page number
	&[Pages]	total number of pages
	&[Date]	date
	&[Time]	time
	&[File]	file name
	&[Tab]	name of the worksheet

To create a custom header, enter the text you want into the edit boxes and click on the relevant buttons in order to apply the features.

Setting fonts

To set the fonts for the header open the *Font* dialog box by clicking the **A** button.

Close the *Font* dialog box by clicking the *OK* button and click *OK* again to close the *Header* dialog box.

| 1 | Income and Expenses 1998.xls | 11/11/98 |

Fig. 4.15: The header as it will be printed

If you are able to remember the codes that you insert using the buttons, then you could also enter them directly into the text boxes.

Creating Custom Footers

Headers and footers are printed in the margin area of each page beyond the actual worksheet area. The margin areas accommodate, for example, page numbers, file names, date and time information as well as text.

To set the position of headers and footers, open the *Page Setup* dialog box and activate the *Margins* tab page. Then insert the values into the *Header* and *Footer* text boxes.

In addition to the header, you can apply further default footers or you can create your own footers.

To create a custom footer select *View/Header and Footer*. The *Header/Footer* tab page will be automatically activated.

Custom defined footer

Click the *Custom Footer* button if you want to create your own footer. A dialog box appears with three edit boxes and various buttons. Everything that you insert in the *Left section* text box will be displayed in the lower left corner of the worksheet.

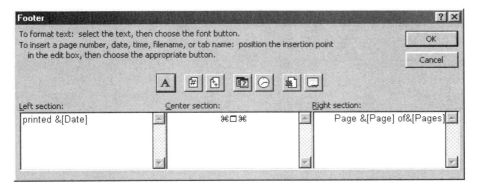

Create a custom footer

The text entered into the *Center section* edit box will be displayed centered at the bottom of the page, while the text entered into the *Right section* text box will be displayed in the lower right corner of the worksheet page.

Buttons and codes *Excel* offers you a number of buttons to insert information. Read about the function of these buttons and the code that they insert in the previous section.

Insert the text you want, and click the relevant buttons to insert the corresponding functions.

Close the dialog box by clicking the *OK* button and click *OK* again to also close the *Page Setup* dialog box.

Removing Headers and Footers

After having selected one of the built-in headers or footers for a worksheet or a chart, these will appear henceforth at the top and bottom of every printout. If you do not want them any more, you can remove the default header and footer or you can replace them by another built-in or custom header and footer. If you have already created a custom header or footer and want to remove it you can apply the same procedure.

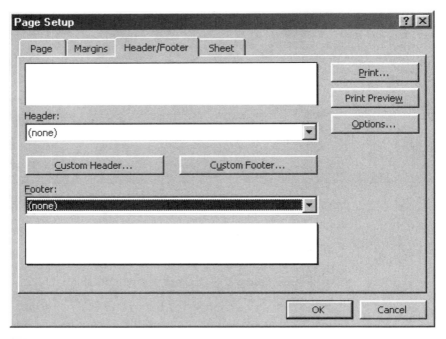

Fig. 4.17: Remove header and footer

Select *File/Page Setup* and activate the *Header/Footer* tab page or select *View/Header and Footer* directly. Open the *Header* drop-down list which contains the integrated as well as the custom headers.

Select (none)   With the help of the scroll bars scroll to the very beginning of the list and select *(none)*. Do the same for the footer.

Click the *OK* button to close the *Page Setup* dialog box. Check the worksheet without header and footer in the *Print Preview*.

Page Numbers

Since *Excel 97* does not print default headers and footers, the pages are not automatically numbered anymore. Nevertheless, now as before, you can apply page numbers by either activating one of the built-in headers or footers that contains a page number, or by creating a custom header or footer with a page number yourself.

Inserting Page Numbers

Selecting built-in page numbers

If you want to print a header or footer that contains a page number in *Excel 97*, select *File/Page Setup* and click the *Header/Footer* tab. You can also directly activate the *Page Setup* dialog box by clicking *View/Header and Footer*.

There are a number of options for page numbering in the *Header* and *Footer* drop-down lists. For example, you can select the page number separately or together with the name of the worksheet or the name of the workbook.

Custom page numbers

If you cannot find a suitable format in the drop-down list, click on the *Custom Header* or the *Custom Footer* button.

Then define how you want to number and arrange your pages yourself.

- To display the page number in the right corner of the worksheet page, enter it in the *Right section* text box.

- To display the page number in the left corner of the worksheet page, enter it in the *Left section* text box.

- To display the page number centered on the worksheet page, enter it in the *Center section* edit box.

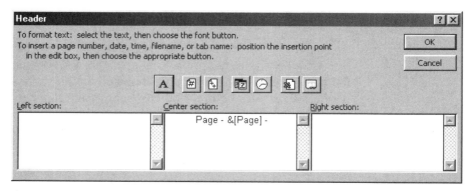

Centered page numbers

To insert the page number, click the *Page Number* button ⊞ . If you want to enter any text after the page number, type it in after the code for the page number. Do not forget the spaces necessary to separate the page number from the surrounding text. The entry in Figure 4.18 will insert the page numbers in the following manner:

```
Page - 1 -, Page - 2 - , Page - 3 -
```

In the next section you will learn how to print the total number of pages in the header or footer.

Inserting Page Number and the Total Number of Pages

You should always insert page numbers in a header and footer but never directly into the worksheet. If you were to insert a number on every page it would be too difficult to maintain, since a page break in a worksheet changes frequently and you would have to continuously have go back and check and perhaps correct the position of the page number.

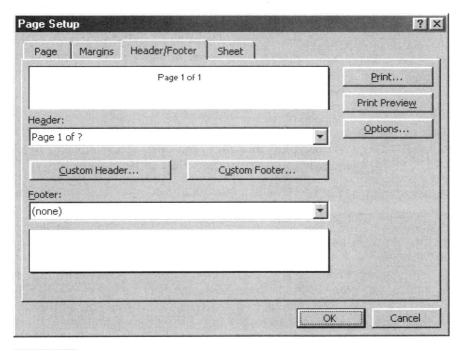

Fig. 4.19:   The built-in header with total number of pages

Total number
of pages

To print the total number of pages in a header or footer select *View/Header and Footer*.

You can either apply one of the built-in headers or footers in *Excel* to insert the total number of pages, or you can create a custom header or footer of your own.

Built-in header
or footer

In order to apply a built-in header or footer, open the *Header* or *Footer* drop-down list and select the item:

```
Page 1 of ?
```

Then close the dialog box by clicking the *OK* button.

To create your own header or footer, which you might do if you wanted to write additional information in the header or footer for instance, activate the *Header/Footer* tab page in the *Page Setup* dialog box. Then click either the *Custom Header* or *Custom Footer* button, depending on whether you want to print the total number of pages in the header or the footer.

Total pages number in the left corner

If necessary, delete any custom entries in the *Center section* text box by selecting the text and pressing the Del key. If you want to print the total number of pages in the left corner, click into the *Left section* text box.

Total pages number centered or in the right corner

If you want to print the total number of pages in the center of the page, continue working in the *Center section* edit box. If you want to print the total number of pages in the right corner, click into the *Right section* text box. By clicking the A button you can open the *Font* dialog box to set the font and the other attributes you want to use for the header or footer. Close the *Font* dialog box by clicking the *OK* button. In most cases, the total number of pages is printed as follows:

```
Page 1 of 21
```

Here the number '1' indicates the page number of the current page and the number '21', the total number of pages. To create an entry like this, first enter the word 'Page' followed by a space. Next, click the *Page Number* button 🔢. *Excel* then inserts the code for the current page:

```
Page &[Page]
```

Next insert a space, then type in 'of' followed by a space, and finally click on the *Total Pages* button 🔢 so that *Excel* can insert the code for the total number of pages.

```
Page &[Page] of &[Pages]
```

If you want to insert additional text into the area to the left or right, you can do so now. Close the *Header* or *Footer* dialog box by clicking the *OK* button, then click it again to also close the *Page Setup* dialog box.

Neither headers or footers, nor the total number of pages, are displayed on the worksheet. You can only view the headers and footers in the *Print Preview*.

Removing Page Numbers

If you want to remove any numbering that you have inserted by means of one of the built-in headers or footers or a custom header or footer, select *View/Header and Footer*.

If you want to completely remove the header or footer that contains the page number, open the *Header* or *Footer* drop-down list respectively and select the *(none)* item.

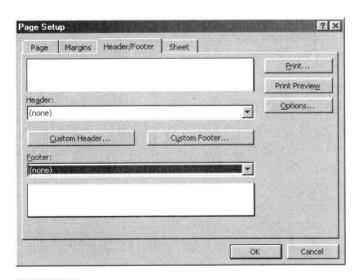

Fig. 4.20:   No page number

If, on the other hand, you want to remove only the page number itself but not the remaining content of the header or footer, click the *Custom Header* or *Custom Footer* buttons, as the case may be.

Remove the page
number only

Remove the code for the page number in the *Left section*, the *Center section* or the *Right section* text box. The code for the page number is:

`&[Page]`

If the page number is printed along with the total number of pages and if you want to remove them both, then you can also delete the code:

`&[Pages]`

Close the *Header* or *Footer* dialog boxes by clicking the *OK* button and do the same to close the *Page Setup* dialog box.

Quick Printing

Print 🖨

If you want to print only one copy of the active worksheet in its entirety, you can quickly print it by either clicking the *Print* button 🖨 on the *Standard* toolbar or pressing the ⌈Ctrl⌉+⌈P⌉ key combination.

Print dialog box

If you want to select an area of a worksheet or a special worksheet of a workbook that you want to print or if you want to determine the number of copies you need, you should open the *Print* dialog box.

Setting Print Options

In the *Print* dialog box you can set exactly how and what you want *Excel* to print. If you want to print only a certain area, you should select it before calling up the *Print* dialog box. Open the *Print* dialog box via the *File/Print* command.

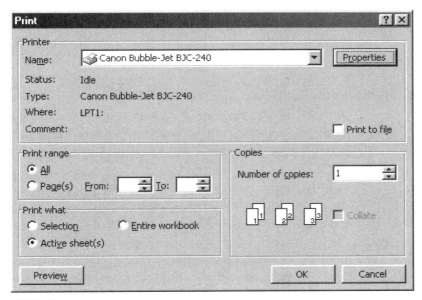

Fig. 4.21:   The *Print* dialog box

You can also access the *Print* dialog box from all the tab pages on the *Page Setup* dialog box and from the *Print Preview*, also by clicking the *Print* button.

The name of the selected printer is displayed under the *Printer* option group in the *Print* dialog box. If you have access to more than one printer you can select a different printer from the *Name* drop-down list.

Properties

The properties of the selected printer can be viewed and modified by clicking the *Properties* button. The options in the dialog box that you can access through this button are dependent on the printer.

Print range and print what

In the *Print range* and *Print what* option groups you have the possibility to restrict the printout to particular areas of a worksheet or to extend the printout to all sheets in the workbook.

Preview

By clicking the *Preview* button in the *Print* dialog box you can change to the *Print Preview* to see the worksheet in full-page view before printing it.

Printing Single Pages

As soon as you click the *Print* button ▣ or choose the *File/Print* command, *Excel* generally prints out the entire active worksheet once.

If your worksheet consists of more than one page, you may want to print only single pages or a part of a page. This is possible in *Excel* if you enter the page numbers of the pages that you want to print. If you are not so sure of the sequence in which the single pages of your worksheet will be printed, select *File/Page Setup* and activate the *Sheet* tab page prior to activating the *Print* command.

View page order

In the *Page order* option group you can view the sequence in which the pages are printed. Either the pages that are next to one another are printed first and then the pages that are underneath them, or vice versa. Afterwards you can directly change to the *Print* dialog box by clicking the *Print* button in the *Page Setup* dialog box.

In *Excel 97* you have another possible way of viewing the sequence of the pages prior to printing by selecting *View/ Page Break Preview*.

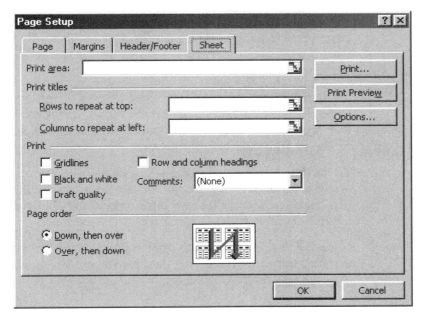

Viewing the order of printing in the *Page order* option group

If you did not open the *Print* dialog box from the *Page Setup* dialog box, then choose *File/Print* and select the *Page(s)* radio button in the *Page range* option group.

Click into the *From* spin box and enter the number of the first page that you want to print, or set it with the help of the spin buttons.

Printing single pages

Click into the *To* box and enter the number of the last page that you want to print. Start the printout by clicking the *OK* button.

Printing Several Worksheets

In *Excel* it is also possible to simultaneously print areas that are not displayed on the same worksheet without having to print the whole workbook.

To do this, select all tabs that you want to print prior to printing. If the sheets are adjacent, click the tab for the first sheet and then hold down the ⬦ key, and click the tabs for the other sheets.

If the sheets that you want to print are not adjacent, click the tab for the first sheet and then hold down Ctrl and click the tabs for the other sheets.

Fig. 4.24:   Printing several worksheets

Selected
worksheets

After you have done this, select *File/Print*. If the *Active sheet(s)* radio button in the *Print what* option group is not selected automatically, select it before beginning the printing.

By selecting the tabs, you group the relevant sheets. You can cancel the group by either clicking a sheet tab that does not belong to the group or by right-clicking a grouped tab and selecting the *Ungroup Sheets* command.

Printing a Selection

You can print single ranges in a worksheet without printing the rest of the worksheet. If the selected ranges are not adjacent to each other, each range will be printed on a separate page.

Selecting

To print single areas of a worksheet, select the range of cells before activating the *Print* command. To print a non-adjacent range of cell areas, make a multiple selection. To do this select the first range of cells, then hold down [Ctrl] and select all the additional ranges.

Selection

Next, select *File/Print* and click the *Selection* radio button in the *Print what* option group.

Fig. 4.25:   Printing a selection

Preview

You should view how the selected ranges of cells will be printed by clicking on the *Preview* button, since the position of the selected cells deviates from their actual position on the sheet. All selected ranges of cells are printed on separate sheets, left-aligned, starting from the top edge of the sheet. Furthermore the selected ranges of cells are printed in the sequence in which they were selected and not in the sequence in which they are displayed on the worksheet.

You can go back and forth through the pages that contain the selected ranges of cells with the help of the *Next* and *Previous* buttons, and start the printing directly from the *Print Preview* by clicking the *Print* button.

Printing the Entire Workbook

As already mentioned above, *Excel* prints only the worksheet of the active tab by default. If your workbook contains adjacent worksheets you may want to frequently
print them in one go without having to activate the print
command for each page individually.

Fig. 4.26:   Printing the entire workbook

To print the entire workbook choose *File/Print* and select
the *Entire workbook* radio button in the *Print what* option
group. Then start the printing by clicking the *OK* button.

Selecting the Print Area in Page Setup

If you click the *Print* button or if you start a default
printout from the *Print* dialog box, *Excel* will consistently
print the entire active worksheet once.

If you only want to print a certain area of a worksheet,
select the relevant range prior to opening the dialog box,
as described above, or define a print area.

Print area in
Page Setup

You can define a print area in the *Page Setup* dialog box.
To do this select *File/Page Setup* and click the *Sheet* tab.

Click the *Print area* text box and select the worksheet
range you want to print. Next to the text box you will see
the *Collapse Dialog* button 🔲 which reduces the size of
the dialog box. To display the *Page Setup* dialog box
again in full size, click 🔲.

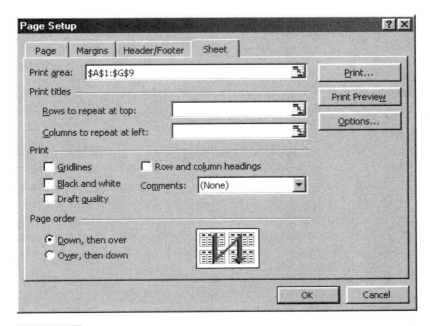

Print Preview

Click *Print Preview* and view your settings before prin-ting.

Excel now inserts manual page breaks in such a way that the selected area is on a page of its own. By clicking the *Print* button you can print the selected print area directly from this dialog box. To cancel the print area again, select *File/Page Setup* and delete the entry in the *Print area* box.

Selecting a Print Area Quickly

There is a much faster way of selecting a print area: Select the area that you want to print and choose *File/ Print Area/Set Print Area*. Later you can cancel the area by activating *File/Print Area/Clear Print Area*.

Printing Cell Gridlines and Row and Column Headings

The display and the printout of the gridlines of a work-sheet and its row and column headings, are controlled independent of each other.

Elements are
not printed

Gridlines as well as row and column headings are displayed on the screen by default, but they are not printed.

You can determine whether you want to print the row and column headings of the worksheets or whether you want to hide them. If you want to view formulas in worksheets, or if you want to create them exclusively for inter-office use, you will probably want to print them along with the row and column headings. If you have an invoice that you want to send to a client, it will, of course, be printed without these elements.

Check in the *Print Preview* whether the gridlines and the row and column headings are visible on the printout or not. The worksheet will be printed exactly as it is shown there.

Gridlines and row
and column
headings

The printing of gridlines and row and column headings, as well as the position of the table on the sheet is controlled through the *Page Setup* dialog box.

Sheet tab page

To display or hide gridlines or row and column headings select *File/Page Setup* and click the *Sheet* tab.

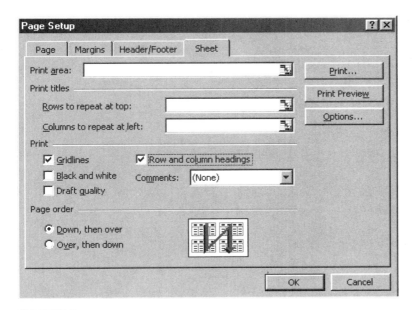

Fig. 4.28: Printing gridlines as well as row and column headings

Check or clear the *Gridlines* and the *Row and column headings* check boxes under the *Print* option group and close the dialog box by clicking the *OK* button.

Printing a Worksheet with Formulas

By default *Excel* displays the values produced by a formula, but not the formula itself, in the cells of a worksheet. Since *Excel* always prints a document as it is displayed, the formulas do not appear on the printout in this case.

To print the formula itself but not the resulting values, you need to display the formulas on the worksheets themselves. To do this select *Tools/Options* and click the *View* tab page.

259

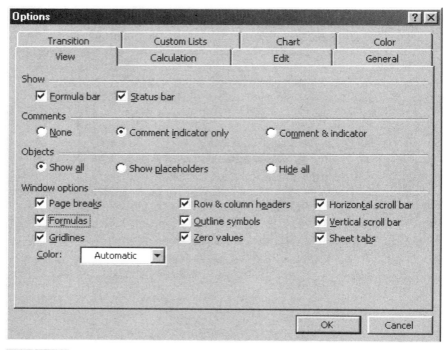

The *Formulas* check box in the *Windos options* group

Select the *Formulas* check box under *Window options* and close the dialog box by clicking the *OK* button.

Adjust the width of the column to the width of the formula by double-clicking the right boundary of the column heading and start the printout either by clicking on the *Print* button on the *Standard* toolbar or by selecting *File/Print*.

By clearing the *Formulas* check box in the *Options* dialog box you can return to the display of the values produced by formulas.

Tip!
It is faster to switch between formulas and values pro-duced by formulas by pressing *CTRL* plus *SINGLE LEFT QUOTATION MARK*.

Defining Print Titles

If you frequently edit and print extensive worksheets you will know how difficult it is to interpret the rows and columns of a worksheet if they have not been given an appropriate title.

What is a
print title?

This can be avoided by printing row and/or column titles on each sheet. Row and column headings are called *Print titles* in *Excel*. You can choose a print title that is larger than one row or column.

To select print titles for your worksheets select *File/Page Setup* and activate the *Sheet* tab page. Click into the *Rows to repeat at top* text box and then select the rows on your worksheet that you want to print out on each sheet.

Click the *Columns to repeat at left* text box and then select the column that you want to print out on each sheet. The print title of the column may also be comprised of more than one column.

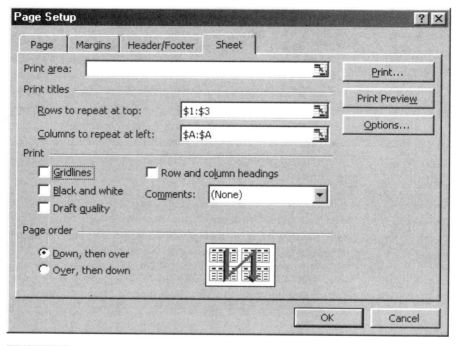

Fig. 4.30: Defining print titles

Next to the text boxes for row and column titles you will find the *Collapse Dialog* buttons 🔲 to reduce the size of the dialog box. After selecting the print titles click the 🔲 button to restore the dialog box to its full size and confirm your selection by clicking the *OK* button.

Remove print title

To remove the print titles again, select *File/Page Setup* and activate the *Sheet* tab page again. Delete all items in the *Rows to repeat at top* and *Columns to repeat at left* text boxes.

Changing the Printing Sequence

If your worksheet is wider and longer than a single print page, it will be printed on several pages. Either *Excel* will insert the page breaks automatically or you can insert them yourself by selecting *Insert/Page Break*.

Unless you select a different order, *Excel* automatically defines the order in which the individual page sheets will be printed. *Excel* first prints the pages that are below each other in one column and then the data in the columns to the right.

Select *View/Page Break Preview* to view the order in which the pages will be printed. The pages will be printed in the order of the page numbers shown there.

Open *File/Page Setup* and activate the *Sheet* tab page to select a different print order.

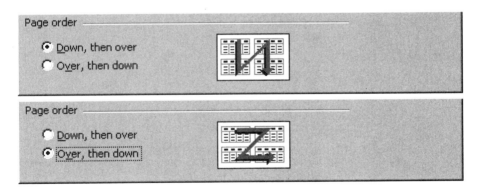

Fig. 4.31:   Page order options

In the *Page order* option group select the *Over, then down* radio button if you first want to print the worksheets that are next to each other. Now click the *Print* button in the *Page Setup* dialog box to start printing.

Printing Several Copies of a Worksheet

If you click the *Print* button on the *Standard* toolbar or choose the *File/Print* command, the current worksheet, the workbook, the pages, the selection or the chosen print area will be printed only once by default.

If you want to print more than one copy of the selected worksheets or worksheet areas, determine the number of copies you want in the *Print* dialog box. Select *File/Print* to open the dialog box and enter the number of copies you want to print in the *Number of copies* spin box in the *Copies* option group.

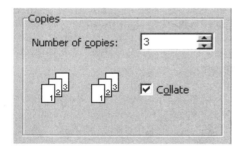

Fig. 4.32:   Printing several copies

If you are printing more than one page, check the *Collate* check box in order to print the sheets in the correct order – always every sheet once – prior to beginning the next printout so that it will not be necessary for you to manually collate the printed sheets.

Start printing by clicking the *OK* button.

5. Managing Sheets and Files

An *Excel* workbook corresponds to a file. Each workbook can contain several worksheets or chart sheets. The worksheets and chart sheets are managed by the sheet tabs.

Managing
workbooks

You can manage workbooks within *Excel* in the dialog boxes for the saving, opening, and finding of files.

Templates

If you frequently use the contents of a workbook in similar ways, such as a workbook for the completion of an order, the confirmation of order, or an invoice and delivery note, you can create a template.

The *Save* dialog box enables you to create new files that are either workbooks or templates.

Managing Worksheets

In *Excel 97*, each new workbook contains no longer 16, but only three empty worksheets. If you need more, you can increase the number of the sheets contained by default in the workbook. You can insert additional worksheets or other objects like charts, put the sheets in any order you like, and copy them, or move them into another workbook.

Fig. 5.1: The sheet tabs

You can use the sheet tabs together with the shortcut menu in order to easily rename, move, copy, group, and delete tables.

Each worksheet in each new workbook automatically gets a default name which you can then replace with another name of your own choosing.

In order to keep your workbook clear, you can delete worksheets you no longer need.

Rename Sheets

Excel automatically gives a default name to every sheet which remains valid until you give it another name. The default name consists of the expression 'Sheet' and a sequential number.

Rules for table names

Instead of the default names, you can use any names as long as they abide by the following rules:

- They can have a length of up to 31 characters.

- They can consist of digits, letters, special characters, and empty spaces.

- They must not start with the [character nor end with the] character.

- None of the following characters must be used: ? / \ : *.

In order to rename a worksheet which still has a default name, either click with the right mouse button onto the corresponding sheet tab to call up the shortcut menu and select the *Rename* command, or double-click onto the sheet tab.

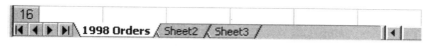

Fig. 5.2:   Renaming sheets

In *Excel 97*, after double-clicking or selecting the *Rename* command from the shortcut menu, a dialog box is not opened anymore. Instead, the sheet tab itself is activated, and you can overwrite the old name with the new one right away. Confirm the entry of the new name by pressing the *Enter* key ⏎.

Menu command to rename

If you do not feel so comfortable working with the mouse, you can just as easily use the menu to activate the *Rename* command. In this case, choose *Format/Sheet/Rename*.

Moving and Copying Sheets with Drag-and-Drop

If you want to arrange the worksheets which are contained in a workbook in a specific order, for example, because you want to group them, you can do so by using drag-and-drop. Likewise, you can use drag-and-drop when you want to duplicate a worksheet.

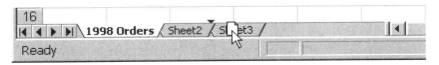

Fig. 5.3:   Move with Drag-and-Drop

In order to move a worksheet of a workbook to another position in the sheet tab bar, activate it by clicking on the sheet tab, and drag it with the mouse to the desired new position.

In order to copy a worksheet within the current workbook, drag it to the new position while holding down the Ctrl key.

Moving and Copying Sheets by Using the Menu or Shortcut Menu

Instead of drag-and-drop, you can also use a command on the *Edit* menu or on the shortcut menu in order to move or copy worksheets.

Choose the *Edit/Move or Copy Sheet* command or use the shortcut menu of the sheet tab. In order to open the dialog box via the shortcut menu, click on a tab with the right mouse button and select *Move or Copy*.

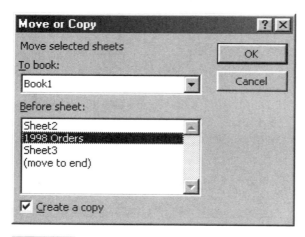

Fig. 5.4: Move or copy sheets

Create a Copy

In order to move the sheet, in the *Move or Copy* dialog box, select the sheet before which the current sheet is to be inserted. In order to copy the sheet, in addition select the *Create a copy* check box. Confirm the selection by clicking *OK*.

Move or copy into another workbook

If you want to move or copy a sheet into another workbook, open both the source as well as the destination workbook. Activate the workbook containing the sheet which you want to copy, and choose *Edit/Move or Copy Sheet*. The *Move or Copy* dialog box appears. Open the

To book drop-down list and there select the name of the destination workbook. In the *Before sheet* list box, select the name of the sheet before which you want to insert the sheet. Do not forget to select the *Create a copy* check box if you want to copy the sheet.

New workbook

If the sheet is not to be copied into an existing workbook, but into a new one, select the *(new book)* item in the *To book* drop-down list. Finish the *Move or Copy* command by clicking *OK*.

Creating a New Sheet

You can insert additional sheets if you want to create a table on a new worksheet, and all the existing worksheets are already in use.

Default workbook

There can be many worksheets in a workbook. By default a new workbook has three empty sheets. A default workbook is a workbook that you create by clicking the *New* button, or by choosing the *File/New* command, and then selecting the *Workbook* template. This workbook can contain up to 255 sheets. The number of sheets in open workbooks is limited only by the capacity of your physical memory.

New sheets

New sheets are always inserted before the active worksheet. Therefore in order to insert a new worksheet into a workbook you need to activate the sheet before which you want to insert the new worksheet.

Then choose *Insert/Worksheet*. After the insertion, you can, however, drag the sheet to another position in the sheet tab bar by using drag-and-drop.

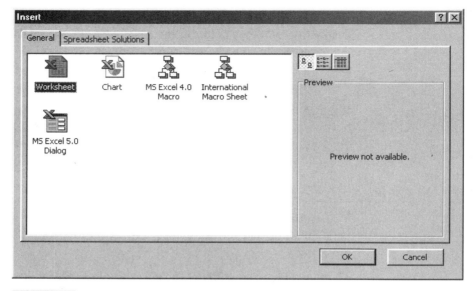

Fig. 5.5: Inserting a new worksheet

You can also use the shortcut menu in order to insert new worksheets. To do this, click on the sheet tab with the right mouse button and, from the shortcut menu, choose the *Insert* command.

Select the icon with the *Worksheet* label and confirm with *OK*.

Copying a worksheet

If you want to insert a new worksheet as a copy of another worksheet already existing in the workbook, press and hold down the [Ctrl] key, and drag the sheet to the desired insertion position.

If the default number of sheets in the workbook does not suit your needs, you can change it by choosing *Tools/ Options* and activating the *General* tab page. Change the number in the *Sheets in new workbook* spin box and confirm with *OK*.

Deleting Worksheets

When you realize that you do not need a worksheet in your workbook, or if a worksheet contained in it has some mistakes and rather than correcting those mistakes you would prefer to create the worksheet again from scratch, you can remove the worksheet from the workbook.

Delete Sheet

To delete worksheets, use either a menu command or the shortcut menu. In order to remove a sheet from the workbook, first activate it by clicking on its tab. Choose *Edit/ Delete Sheet*, or right-click on the tab and select the *Delete* command from the shortcut menu.

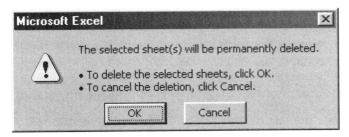

Fig. 5.6:   Confirming the deletion

Undo is not

possible

No matter how you activate the delete command, you need to confirm the deletion before the sheet is finally removed. A deletion is permanent and cannot be undone by choosing the *Edit/Undo* command or the corresponding button!

Saving Files

You should save a workbook that you've created to be used more than just once, and that you also want to use when you start *Excel* again later on. Save your workbook on the hard disk or a floppy.

First saving

When you save a workbook for the first time, you give it a name and determine the drive and the folder in which you want to save the file. If you later save the workbook again, these steps are not necessary anymore. It will then be enough to click on the *Save* button on the *Standard* toolbar.

The First Saving

When you want to save a workbook for the first time, no matter how you call up the *Save* command, *Excel* will always open the *Save As* dialog box so that you can define a name and the location of the workbook to be saved.

Therefore you can use any of the following procedures:

- Choose the *File/Save* command.
- Choose the *File/Save As* command.
- Click onto the *Save* button 🔲.
- Press the ⌈Ctrl⌋+⌈S⌋ shortcut key combination.

Close and save

Choose the *File/Close* command if you want to close the file at the same time, and confirm the saving with *Yes*. In the *Save As* dialog box, select the desired drive, and open the desired folder by double-clicking it.

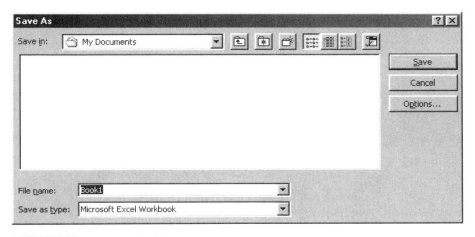

The *Save As* dialog box

Overwrite the default name in the *File name* box with a name of your choice, and click the *Save* button. For more details on the rules for file names read the next section.

Saving Changes

In order to save changes to a workbook which you have previously saved, choose an accelerated procedure so that the *Save As* dialog box is not opened anymore.

- Choose the *File/Save* command.

- Click on the *Save* button ▣.

- Press the Ctrl+S shortcut keys.

In each of the three cases, none of which will open the *Save As* dialog box, the saving process is very fast.

Naming Workbooks

If you save a workbook for the first time, give it a name. Of course, you could leave it with the name *Excel* gives it, but this is not recommended, since this name is not very meaningful and will make any subsequent search for the workbook rather difficult.

Long file names

With the long file names that you've been able to use ever since *Windows 95* first appeared, you have the opportunity to give your workbook an unambiguous name.

You can use the same name within a folder only once.

Rules for

file names

When you are naming a workbook, keep in mind the general rules that Windows sets for file names:

▦ A file name may be as long as 255 characters, including the path.

▦ It can contain empty spaces, digits, letters and special characters.

▦ It should not contain any of the following characters: :\|<>?*/

File name

In order to give a new file name to a workbook, you need to save it. Choose *File/Save As* and enter the file name in the *File name* text box. *Excel* suggests a default name consisting of 'Book' and a sequential number.

Title bar shows

file name

After the dialog box opens, the name is automatically selected. You can then overwrite the name with one of your choice. After you have entered the new name, select the folder and start the saving with the *Save* button, after which *Excel* closes the *Save As* dialog box. In the title bar of the *Excel* workbook, the name you've given will be displayed.

Save the workbook under different name

If later on you want to save the workbook under a different name, you always need to choose the *Save As* command. Then you can enter the new name into the *File name* text box.

Rename workbook

You can rename a workbook by right-clicking onto the file name in the *Open* or *Save* dialog box and then selecting the *Rename* command. Then overwrite the selected workbook name, and confirm the action by clicking *OK*.

Creating Backup Copies

When you save a workbook for the first time, *Excel* saves it under the name you give it, and in the folder you determined.

Repeated saving

When you save a workbook a second time, you normally do not give it a new name, nor do you give it another location in a different folder. That is why in the saving process the old version is overwritten by the current one.

Saving the last version as a backup copy

If you are working on workbooks that contain information that should never be lost no matter what happens, you should save it in such a way that apart from the original, you still have the previous version in a backup copy. Already from the very first save onwards you can have *Excel* create backup copies.

Low capacity

If the capacity of your hard disk is small, you should not activate this option. In this case, save a second copy of the workbook on a floppy disk, and get into the habit of updating it every time you save.

Options

In order to arrange for the automatic saving of backup copies, choose *File/Save As*, and click on the *Options* button.

Always create
backup

Select the *Always create backup* check box, and close the dialog box by clicking *OK*.

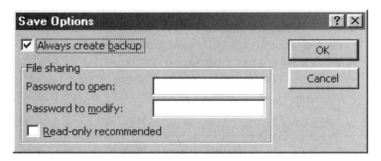

Fig. 5.8:   Creating backup copies

Next, save the file. If the workbook is being saved for the first time, give it a name of your choice in the *File name* text box, and open the folder in which you want it to be saved. Then save the workbook by clicking on the *Save* button.

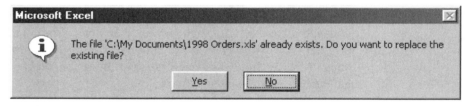

Fig. 5.9:   Saving replaces the original file

If you have saved the file before, *Excel* will now display a message asking you whether you want to overwrite the existing file. Confirm the replacement by clicking the *Yes* button.

In the next section, read how in the case of an emergency you can access the backup copy.

Open Backup Copy

XLK

If the *Always create backup* saving option is activated, *Excel* keeps the previous version of a workbook in addition to the current version. These file versions are saved in the same folder as the original versions. While *Excel* saves the normal workbook under the *XLS* extension, the backup copies are saved under the *XLK* extension.

Show extension

Since the applications under *Windows 98* do not necessarily need this suffix for identification anymore, the extension is displayed only if in Windows the *Hide file extensions for known file types* check box is cleared.

Backup copy of

As an additional means of identification, backup copies are prefixed with *Backup of*. For an *Excel* workbook that is originally called:

```
Turnover 98
```

you would have a backup copy called:

```
Backup of Turnover 98
```

In order to open a backup copy, either choose *File/Open* or click the *Open* button. In both cases, the *Open* dialog box is displayed. In the dialog box, the files in the current folder are displayed.

Files of type

as filter

Which files are displayed in the current folder depends on the selection in the *Files of type* drop-down box. The selection in this list works like a filter. Only file extensions that match the specified filter criterion are displayed. In *Excel*, the file type is by default set to *Excel* files, i.e., files with the **.XL** extension. This setting displays all of the following:

- Excel workbooks (XLS)
- Excel templates (XLT)

277

- Excel backup copies (XLK)

- Excel Workspaces (XLW)

Display only
backup files

If the display is too unclear due to the volume of files, open the *Files of type* drop-down list and choose the *Backup Files* item. *Excel* will then filter only the backup copies of the current and the previous versions. Select the file you want, and confirm by clicking *OK*.

Automatic Saving

Excel is equipped with an automatic saving function which makes sure that workbooks containing important data are automatically saved at regular intervals.

Install add-in

This automatic saving function is an *Add-In*, that is, an additional program function. If the function is not yet installed on your computer, read in Chapter 11 how you can install and use this Add-In.

In order to check whether the function is activated, open the *Tools* menu. If you find a check mark in front of the *AutoSave* command, the function is active.

By choosing the *Tools/AutoSave* command, you open the dialog box to set the saving interval.

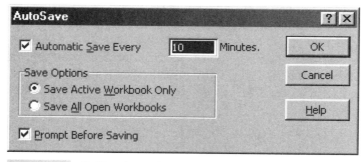

Fig. 5.10:   Setting the saving interval

Overwrite the value in the *Minutes* text box with the desired saving interval. You can choose intervals between 1 and 120 minutes. The interval recommended depends on your data or on the speed of changes respectively.

Save Options

In the *Save Options* options group, you can determine whether only the active workbook or all open workbooks are to be saved.

If you do not want to automatically save all changes, for example because you want to first try out certain formulas, you should select the *Prompt Before Saving* check box. Then every time when the saving interval comes up, a dialog box appears to let you confirm with click on *Save* or *Skip* the saving.

Keep in mind that the combination of the save confirmation and the automatic saving of all open workbooks together with a comparatively narrow saving interval can hinder your work, since you will have to confirm the saving of each of the open workbooks separately.

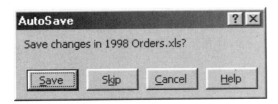

Fig. 5.11:   Confirming the AutoSave

Click the *Skip* button, if you do not want to save the changes.

279

Define the Properties of a Workbook

An *Excel* workbook is saved in a file for which you can define certain properties in order to be able to search for and organize the workbook according to these properties later on.

In order to display the properties of a workbook, it does not necessarily need to be open. In the *Save As* and *Open* dialog boxes you will find buttons to display the properties of the saved files.

Display properties

In order to display the properties of an open workbook, choose *File/Properties*. The *Properties* dialog box contains several tab pages which display the properties organized in categories.

General and
Statistics tab
pages

Windows can display most of the properties only after a file has been saved for the first time, and can update them only after changes have been saved. On the *General* and *Statistics* tab pages, autmatically generated properties are displayed.

 ▥ Date of creation, saving, opening, and printing

 ▥ Windows file name und MS-DOS file name

 ▥ Location and size

 ▥ Last saved by

Contents tab page

On the *Contents* tab page, *Excel* shows the names of the sheets, charts, tables, etc. contained in the workbook.

Summary tab page

On the *Summary* tab page you have the possibility to enter some information about the file organization. You can overwrite the entries suggested by *Excel* in the text boxes.

Save preview picture

If you select the *Save preview picture* check box, you can see a preview of the workbook contents even from outside *Excel* in the Windows *Open* dialog box.

Custom tab page

The *Custom* tab page can be used to set additional predefined file properties or properties which you can create yourself. In order to set an additional preset property, choose its name from the *Name* list box, and in the *Type* drop-down list select the type of data which you want to save in this property. You can use text, date, numbers, or logical (Yes/No) types.

Value

Enter the value which is to be saved in the property into the *Value* text box. The value must correspond to the selected type. Then click the *Add* button.

Name and Type

In order to define a new customized property, enter a new name into the *Name* text box. In the *Type* list select the type of data and enter the value which is to be saved in this property of the workbook.

Add

Click the *Add* button in order to include the new property in the list box. Close the dialog box by clicking *OK*. After defining new properties, you need to save the workbook.

The properties of unopened workbooks can be viewed in the *Open* or *Save As* dialog boxes, as well as in the *Explorer* window by clicking with the right mouse button on a file and then selecting the *Properties* item from the shortcut menu.

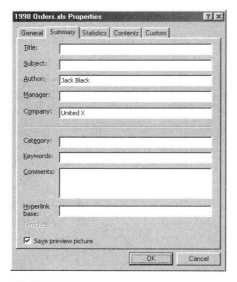

Fig. 5.12: The *Summary* and *Custom* tab pages

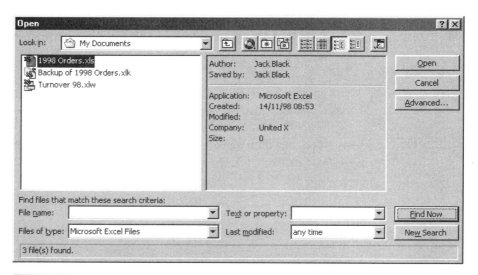

Fig. 5.13: The properties in the *Open* dialog box

Managing Folders

Excel, like all *Office* applications, saves all the user-created files in a folder that Windows offers under the default name of:

```
My Documents
```

You can create folders of your own, to save and organize your workbooks, in order to group them together according to certain criteria.

Also the templates, meaning the workbooks which you create as samples to be used over and over again, are saved in a certain location. The folder is called:

```
Templates
```

It is found in the *Office* folder and contains several subfolders in which the templates of certain categories are saved. You can, however, also choose any other saving location for the templates. Since *Excel*, however, looks for templates by default in this folder, you should, in this case, make the corresponding change to the folder in the *Options* dialog box as well (*Alternate startup file location*).

Changing the Location of Workbooks

When you save a workbook for the first time, in addition to its name, you also need to select its folder. Later, when you save it again by using the *File/Save* command or clicking the *Save* button 🖫, the workbook will be saved at the same location under the same name. In such cases, the previous version will be overwritten by the current one, unless you chose to enable the creation of automatic backup copies.

If you want to change the folder in which you keep a workbook, choose the *File/Save As* command in order to open the *Save As* dialog box. In *Excel*, this is the only way to change the saving location.

Windows Explorer

You can, however, use the *Windows Explorer* to move or copy files among folders. If you are working on several files at once, you might prefer this alternative, since the windows display is much clearer.

Default folder

In order to choose a different folder for a workbook, select the *File/Save As* command. You can see in which folder the workbook is presently stored from the entry in the *Save in* drop-down box. The default folder for Office files is the *My Documents* folder. It is located directly in the root directory of the hard disk.

Fig. 5.14:   The *Save in* drop-down box

Save in

In order to save a file in another drive, open the *Save in* drop-down list and select the desired drive letter, for example, *A* to save it on a floppy disk which is in drive *A*.

Up One Level

In order to move into another folder, open it by double-clicking it. If the folder is not displayed, change to the next higher level by clicking the *Up One Level* button , or open one of the folders that is displayed. If the desired folder is contained in a subfolder, it will be displayed only after opening the subfolder.

Create New Folder

If you want to create a new folder specifically for your workbook, click the *Create New Folder* button . Overwrite the preset name with a new name, and confirm the entry by clicking *OK*. Double-click on the new folder in order to define it as the folder in which you want to save

284

your workbook. It will then appear in the *Save in* drop-down box.

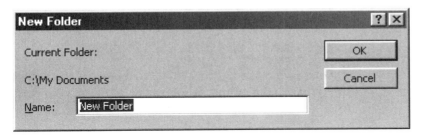

Fig. 5.15:   The default name for new folders

After you have selected the correct folder, click the *Save* button.

Second version in new folder

With the procedure we described, the workbook is now saved in the new folder, while the old version at the old location is preserved.

Alternatively, you can move a workbook between saving folders in such a way that the workbook is saved exclusively in the new saving folder. To do this, the workbook should be closed. Choose *File/Open* or *File/Save As*, and open the current folder of the workbook by double-clicking it.

Move by using the shortcut menu

With the right mouse button, click on the name of the workbook which you want to move to another folder, and select the *Cut* item.

Paste into the target folder

Move the folder into which you want to move the workbook by opening the folder in which it is contained, and right-click on the desired target folder. Choose the *Paste* command from the shortcut menu. The workbook is then taken from the clipboard and inserted into the target folder; in *Excel 97* this is accompanied by a little animation. Close the *Open* or *Save As* dialog box by clicking on the

Cancel button. The first time you open the workbooks you moved, do not use the entries at the bottom of the *File* menu, but rather the *File/Open* command instead, since otherwise *Excel* will not find the file.

Determine the Saving Location of Templates

If you have already worked with templates, you will surely have noticed that while saving a file of this type, *Excel* opens a certain folder in the *Save in* drop-down box after you have selected the file type.

Default saving
folder for
templates

This is the *Templates* default saving folder in which all customized templates are saved.

You can also save templates in a different folder if that folder is within the *Templates* folder. Folders not contained in this folder will not be displayed in the *Open* or *New* dialog boxes.

Tab pages of
your own

Create a new folder of your own within the *Templates* folder in order to save any customized templates in it. Your own templates are then displayed in the *New* dialog box on a tab page of their own.

In order to create a folder for templates of your own, choose *File/Save As* and open the *Templates* folder. You find this folder in the directory:

```
C:\Program Files\Microsoft Office
```

Create New Folder

If you did not buy *Excel* as part of the *Office Suite*, you will find the *Templates* folder in the *Excel* program directory. Click the *Create New Folder* button. Overwrite the default name of the new folder with a name of your own and confirm by clicking *OK*.

Open folder by
double-clicking

Now open the new folder by double-clicking it, and save the newly created templates in this folder.

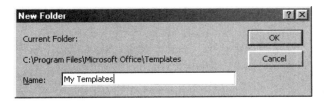

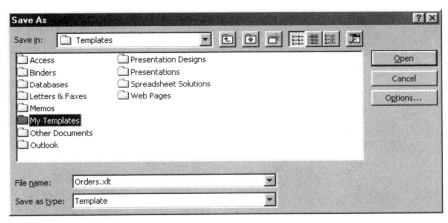

Fig. 5.16:   The new folder

After you have saved the first template in the new folder, it will be displayed in the *New* dialog box on a separate tab page which contains as its label the name of the folder.

Changing the Default Folder

The default working folder is the folder in which *Excel* searches automatically for saved workbooks, and *Excel* will suggest this as a saving folder for workbooks. This folder is automatically opened and displayed, as soon as you open the *Open* or *Save* dialog boxes for the first time after starting *Excel*.

287

Even if you open a different folder at this point, it will only be open for the duration of the current *Excel* session. The next time you start *Excel*, the default folder will again be opened and displayed.

My Documents

Immediately after the installation of Office, the *My Documents* folder is set as the default saving or working folder for all Office applications. You can change these settings in the general options.

Options/General

To change the preset default working and saving folder, choose *Tools/Options* and activate the *General* tab page. In the *Default file location* text box the *My Documents* working folder is displayed.

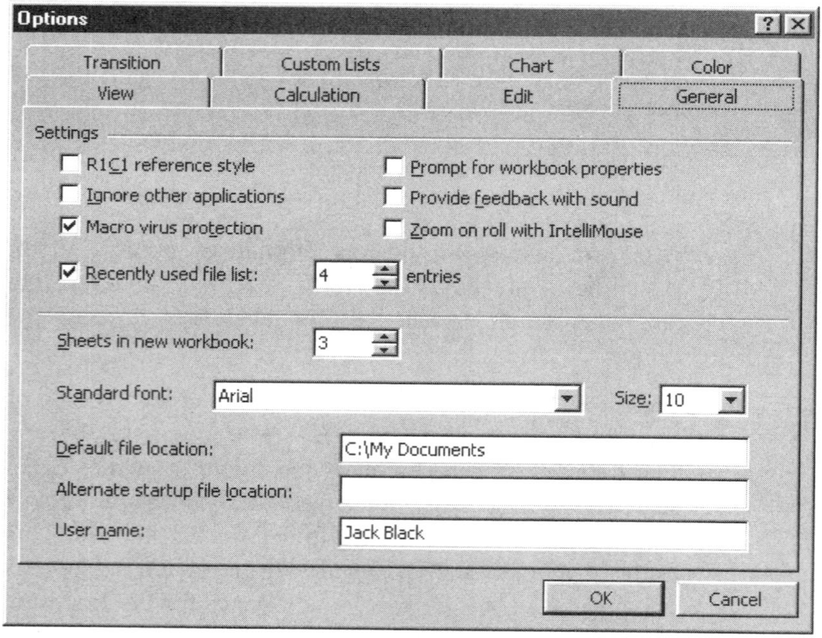

Fig. 5.17: The preset default working folder

Indicate path

Delete this and add the path to the folder which you want to use as the new default working folder. By path is meant the folder hierarchy which leads to the respective folder. For example, a folder with the name of *Excel Data* which is saved directly in the root directory, would have the following path:

```
C:\Excel Data
```

The path of the same folder which you created within the *My Documents* folder, however, would be:

```
C:\My Documents\Excel Data
```

Close the dialog box by clicking *OK*. If you then choose the *File/Open* or the *File/Save As* command, the new default working folder will be automatically opened in the dialog boxes.

Saving Workspace

If you are working on a certain project over a longer period of time, and you always need to display several workbooks in different windows, it will take some time before you have adjusted and organized the workbooks in a way that makes working with them ideal.

Creating

Workspace file

But then after you close *Excel*, the next time you want to work on the project you normally need to adjust the working space again. You will have to open all the workbooks again, and you will have to organize them all over again. In order to spare yourself this trouble, you can create a *Workspace* file. In such a file, *Excel* saves the following items:

▪ The names and the saving locations of the open workbooks

- The window arranging

- The window sizes

- The window positions

If you work with several workbooks at the same time, it is worthwhile in any case to create a workspace file, because then you can open and organize all the project workbooks with a single command.

File/
Save Workspace

In order to save a workspace file, open all the workbooks which are to be contained in the saved workspace, and organize them in the way you want them to be displayed when you reopen the workspace. Then choose the *File/ Save Workspace* command and enter a name for the workspace file into the *File name* text box.

Resume

As a name for the workspace, *Excel* automatically suggests *resume*. Overwrite this suggestion with a name of your own. Then open the desired saving folder for the new workspace, and click the *OK* button.

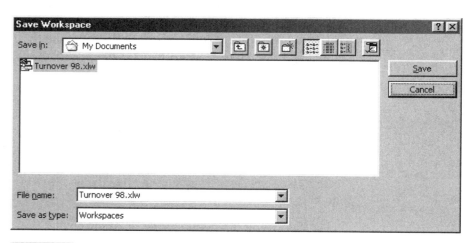

Fig. 5.18: Saving a workspace file

You can open a workspace file – along with all the work-books saved therein – by using the *File/Open* command, selecting the name of the workspace file and clicking the *Open* button.

Creating New Excel Files

If you merely want to create a new table, you do not necessarily have to create a new workbook. You can place several tables in a worksheet, or you can insert a new worksheet into a workbook, if the new table does not fit on the existing ones.

Creating Default Workbooks

In order to save new data in a file of its own, create a new workbook. The term 'workbook' corresponds to an *Excel* file.

Create default
workbook

Workbooks are either created as a default workbook, or on the basis of a certain template, like for example a template for invoices. In order to create a simple default workbook, use one of the following procedures:

- Click onto the *New* button ▫ .

- Press the Ctrl+N shortcut keys.

- Choose *File/New*, then on the *General* tab page select the *Workbook* icon, and confirm the action by clicking *OK*.

Creating Other Workbooks

A click on the *New* button ▫ always creates a new default workbook. *Excel* offers you additional templates, for example for the creation of invoices, or for claiming travelling expenses. Moreover, you can create templates for new workbooks yourself.

New dialog box

If you want to create a new workbook on the basis of a certain template, use the *New* dialog box. The templates are grouped together by their contents and displayed on separate tab pages. These tab pages correspond to the subfolders of the *Templates* saving folder.

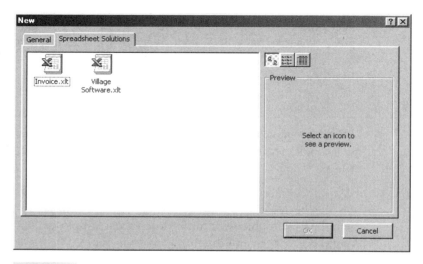

Fig. 5.19: Templates on the *Spreadsheet Solutions* tab page

Choose *File/New* and activate the tab page which contains the desired template. Select the name of the template with which you want to create a new workbook, and click the *OK* button.

Templates of your own

In the section after the next one, you will learn how to create templates of your own. Templates which you create yourself are always displayed on the *General* tab page unless, instead of using the default location, you chose a different one.

Opening Saved Files

A file which you saved on the hard disk or on a floppy disk can be loaded into the active memory in order to be further worked upon. This procedure is called *Opening* a file.

Excel makes a distinction between the files which are simple workbooks and those which are samples of workbooks, i.e., their templates. When you select the *Open* command, the contents of the default saving folder or the saving folder which was last used are displayed.

If you want to open a workbook in a different folder, or if you want to open a template, you first need to open the corresponding folder in order to access the file.

Opening Workbooks

A workbook which has already been saved earlier can be opened with the *File/Open* command or by using the *Open* button ☒ on the toolbar.

Open dialog box

In the *Open* dialog box, either type the file name in the *File name* text box (you need not type the *XLS* extension) or select it from the list box.

If you want to load a file from a floppy disk or from a location other than the current folder, select the drive in the *Look in* drop-down list.

In the list box below, you can select a folder. Double-click on this folder to open it. Then select the desired file name, and click on the *Open* button.

Open

If you want to open more than one workbook, select all of the desired workbooks before you click the *Open* button. Workbooks which are next to each other in the list can be selected by dragging with the mouse. Non-adjacent workbooks can be selected in the list by clicking on them while and holding down the Ctrl key.

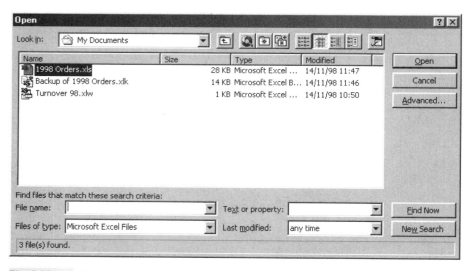

Fig. 5.20:   The *Open* dialog box

Open the last
four files

The four files you last worked on are displayed at the bottom of the commands on the *File* menu. You can open them by clicking on the file name.

Open with the
Documents menu

You can also click the *Start* button on the *Windows* taskbar and choose the *Documents* command in order to open the workbooks you worked on last. In this case, *Windows* starts *Excel* and loads the workbook automatically.

In Chapter 1 you read about how you can put the workbooks into the *XLSTART* folder so that they will be automatically loaded when you start *Excel*.

Opening Templates

Templates serve as a sample for new workbooks. They contain all settings and elements needed in a certain category of workbooks so that these elements do not have to be created from scratch every time.

When to open a template

You open a template only if you want to change its contents, not when you want to create a workbook based on it. In order to create a workbook on the basis of a template, use the *File/New* command.

Excel has a preset default folder for templates so that it can automatically save and reuse the different templates.

In the *Open* dialog box *Excel* displays only the files in the current folder. Therefore, first open the template folder in order to display the templates.

Templates

Choose the *File/Open* command or click the *Open* button. Open the *Look in* drop-down list and select the drive. By double-clicking, open the *Program Files* folder, *Microsoft Office* and then *Templates*. You will find the spreadsheet templates either in the *Templates* folder itself or in one of its subfolders. Predefined templates can be found in the *Spreadsheet Solutions* folder.

If you have already created a customized default workbook, you will find it in the *XLStart* folder which is located in the ...*Program Files\Microsoft Office\Office* folder.

If the file list already shows a multitude of items, and if your templates are saved together with other files, you can display just the templates by selecting the *Templates* item in the *Files of type* drop-down list box at the bottom of the *Open* dialog box. In the large list box, select the name of the desired template, and click the *Open* button.

Searching for *Excel* Files

In order to search for certain files, in *Excel 97* you can use the search functions which you find directly in the *Open* dialog box.

In addition, you can use the *Windows* or *Outlook* search functions, in order to quickly find certain workbooks.

Searching for Workbooks in the *Open* Dialog Box

Excel automatically saves certain file properties for each workbook. You can search for the workbooks with the help of these properties.

If you have assigned certain properties to the *Excel* workbooks yourself, you can use these for the search as well.

The search in the
Open dialog box

In order to search for files, choose *File/Open*. In the *Open* dialog box, you can already carry out a simple search. Enter the name of the workbook you are searching for into the *File name* text box, and click the *Find Now* button. *Excel* then searches the workbooks in the current folder. The result of the search is displayed in the large list box.

Contents or
properties

In order to search workbooks according to their contents or to their properties, enter the text or property into the *Text or property* text box. If you are searching for a character chain containing empty spaces, enter the character chain in full and put it in quotation marks.

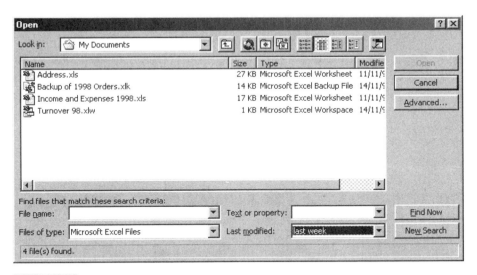

Fig. 5.21:   A search in the *Open* dialog box

New search

With the *Find Now* button you can start a search. With the *New Search* button you clear all previously entered search criteria and begin a new search.

The Advanced Search

Advanced

If you want to search through entire drives or enter specific properties for the search criteria, click the *Advanced* button in the *Open* dialog box.

Property and
Condition

In order to search for workbooks that contain certain properties, open the *Property* drop-down list and either enter or select the name of the property. In the *Condition* drop-down list select a comparison operator. The items in this list differ according to the respective property selected.

Value

Enter the compared value which is to serve as the search criteria into the *Value* text box. Once you have completed entering a search criterion, click the *Add to* list button. The search criterion is inserted into the list of criteria.

297

And

If you want to define further search criteria, you can link these by clicking the *And* radio button so that both conditions need to be met in order for the workbook to be found. Click instead the *Or* radio button if you want to select a search criterion as an alternative criterion for the search. By clicking the *Delete* button, you can remove an already defined search criterion from the list.

Match case

If, in your search, the specification of upper or lower case letters plays a role, select the *Match case* check box.

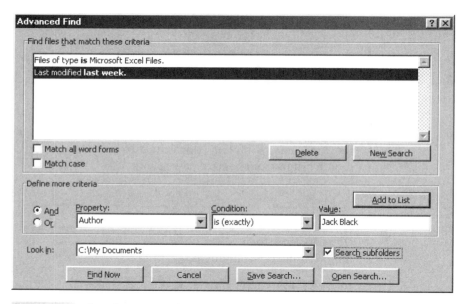

Fig. 5.22:   Carrying out an advanced search

Search subfolders

In the *Look in* drop-down box, you can name the folder or the drive which is to be searched. Select the *Search subfolders* check box if you want all subfolders contained in the selected folder to be searched as well. Click the *Find Now* button to start the search using the search criteria you have defined.

Save Search

In order to reuse a saved search, in the *Advanced Find* dialog box click the *Save Search* button. Give this search a name so that you can load it later when you click the *Open Search* button in order to reuse the saved criteria in a new search. For more on the saving and reusing of search criteria, see further down in this section.

Searching Workbooks with the Windows *Find* Function

The kinds of search which you can activate by using the *Open* dialog box are already quite convenient. You can search for files even more quickly, however, by using the Windows search function.

Start/Find

In order to activate the Windows *Find* function, click on the *Start* button on the taskbar and select the *Find* item from the *Start* menu. In the overlapping menu, click *Files or Folders*.

Include subfolders

In order to search for files with a certain name or a certain part of a name, enter the name into the *Named* text box on the *Name & Location* tab page. In the *Look in* drop-down list, select the location in which you want to search.

If you want to search all the subfolders contained in the selected drive or folder, check the *Include subfolders* check box. You can also click the *Browse* button and select a specific folder. If you want to search for specific text contained in a file, enter the text into the *Containing text* text box. Click the *Find Now* button to start the search.

299

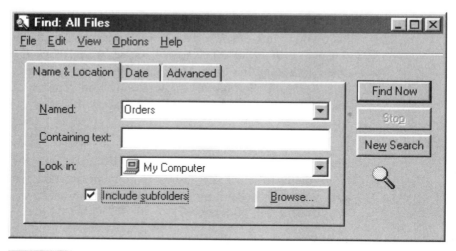

Fig. 5.23:   Searching according to name and location

Date tab page

On the *Date* tab page, you can search for workbooks according to a certain date of creation or saving respectively. Delimit a certain period of time by clicking the *between* radio button and entering the period at which the search should start into the first text box and end into the second text box, respectively.

During the

previous ...

As an alternative, you can select either the *during the previous x month(s)* or the *during the previous x day(s)* radio button, and enter the desired months or days using the spin buttons.

Advanced

tab page

On the *Advanced* tab page you can, using the *Of type* drop-down list, search for a certain type of file or for all files of a certain size.

Of type

Open the *Of type* drop-down list, and select the *Microsoft Excel Worksheet* item if you want to search exclusively for *Excel* workbooks.

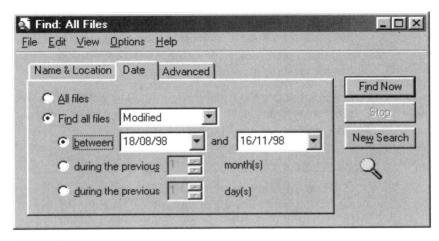

Fig. 5.24:   Search according to date

At least, at most   In the *Size is* drop-down list box, choose either the *At least* or the *At most* item. In the *KB* spin box to the right, enter the limit which is to serve as the value for the minimum or maximum size of the workbook for which you are searching.

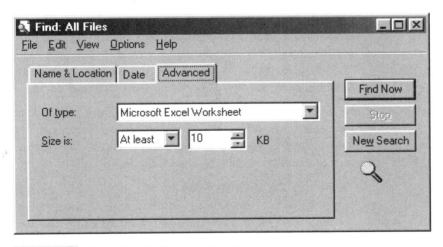

Fig. 5.25:   Searching for Excel workbooks

Stop

You start the search, like in all earlier cases, by clicking the *Find Now* button. You can cancel the search by clicking the *Stop* button, for example if the workbook you were searching for is already found.

New Search

If you click the *New Search* button, all search criteria you previously entered will be deleted so that you can enter new ones and start a new search.

Saving and Reusing Search

If you use the search function of the *Open* dialog box or the dialog boxes for the advanced search rather frequently to look for workbooks that have been created during the previous month for instance, or those which have been worked on by specific persons, and if you always use the same search criteria for the search, then you should save these search criteria so you can spare yourself the trouble of setting it up again each time.

Why save search?

Even if you only use a search with certain criteria once in a while, you should save it if the search contains many or complex search criteria.

This way, instead of composing and entering all the properties, values and comparison operators again, you will only need to select the name of the search in order to have all the saved search criteria at your disposal again.

Advanced Find

In order to save a search to reuse it again later, choose *File/Open* and click the *Advanced* button. Enter all the search criteria you want into the *Advanced Find* dialog box, and select the path to be searched.

Save Search

Then click the *Save Search* button. Enter a name for the composition of the search criteria, and confirm it by clicking *OK*. Then, if you do not want to carry out any more searches, close both dialog boxes by clicking *Cancel*.

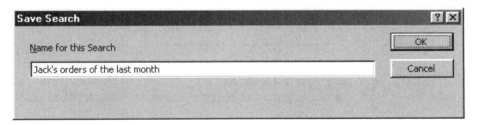

Fig. 5.26:   Naming a search

Open search

In order to carry out a search with the saved search criteria, choose *File/Open* and click the *Advanced* button. Click on the *Open Search* button, and select the name of the saved search.

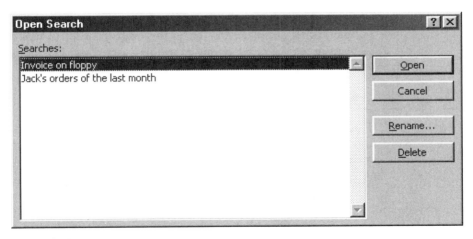

Fig. 5.27:   Activating a saved search

Click the *Open* button, and start the search with the saved search criteria by clicking the *Find Now* button.

Templates

If you need the data contained in a table more than once, copy the tables which you want to use again. You can create copies either by grouping the worksheets before or by duplicating them after they have been created.

Likewise, you can save a whole workbook with all the worksheets it contains in such a way that the worksheets can serve as templates for new workbooks. For example, you could create a workbook for the creation of invoices, with a template for the invoices, for the first and second reminders, etc.

Then you can, by choosing the *New* command, select a workbook template created in this way in order to make new workbooks based on it. In this case, *Excel* produces the new workbook as a copy of your template workbook.

Saving a File as a Template

Excel is already equipped with some template workbooks. You can access these template workbooks on the different tab pages of the *New* dialog box. Before you create a template workbook of your own, you should find out whether the use of a new template workbook is really necessary, or whether the existing ones *Excel* has to offer can be changed and adjusted in such a way that a new template would be superfluous.

Create template
workbook

In order to create a template workbook of your own, create a workbook with worksheets which you then want to save in the template workbook.

■ Enter the formulas and constant values as well as text which you will always need in this workbook.

- Format the tables in the way they will be used later. If several variations are possible, you should always decide upon the one which you will need most often.

- Do not enter data into the workbooks which will later differ in the various applications, because then you will have to delete this data every time.

Naming the template workbook

After you have composed all the elements you need, choose *File/Save As* and enter a name for the template workbook in the *File name* text box.

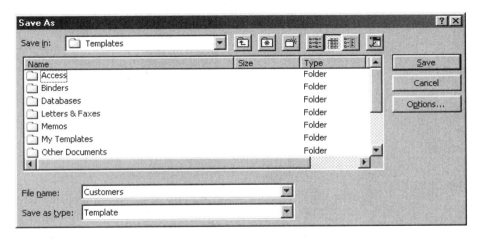

Fig. 5.28:   Saving a workbook as a template

Then open the *Save as type* drop-down list, and select the *Template* item. If you leave the preset template folder unchanged, the workbook will later be displayed on the *General* tab page in the *New* dialog box.

Spreadsheet Solutions

In order to display the workbook on the *Spreadsheet Solutions* tab page, or on any other tab page, open the corresponding folder by double-clicking it. Click the *Save* button in order to save the workbook.

Do not forget to close the template workbook by choosing *File/Close* or by clicking the *Close* button, since for
the entry of data, the template is not used, but only a copy
of the template.

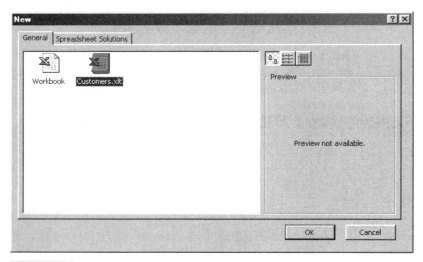

The new template workbook in the *New* dialog box

You can create a new workbook as a copy of a previously
created template workbook using the *New* dialog box. By
default, the dialog box contains tab pages for *General*
templates and *Spreadsheet Solutions*.

Using Your Own Templates

When you click the *New* button, normally a new file is
created on the basis of the default workbook. In order to
create a workbook on the basis of your own template,
choose *File/New* and activate the tab page with the name
of the folder in which you saved the template.

Select the name of the template you want to use as the
basis of the new workbook, and click the *OK* button.

Changing the Default Workbook

New workbooks are always created on the basis of a template. A template is a sample workbook which is saved in a special way, and of which *Excel* makes a copy each time you select the *File/New* command and choose the sample.

You do not have to create the default template because it's already there automatically. Each time you create a new workbook by clicking on the *New* button, a copy of the default template is made. In this default template, all basic settings for the new workbooks are saved. The following settings belong to the basic settings:

- Number formats, column width and row height

- Number of worksheets, and other sheets

- Page layout, settings of the print area

- Text, values, and formulas in worksheets

- Customized toolbars, protection settings

- View options and calculation/formula options

- Macros, Hyperlinks, ActiveX controls, etc.

Defining a workbook as a new default workbook template

In order to change the settings of the default workbook, create a new template workbook into which you enter all formatting, constants, formulas, settings, etc. in the way you want them to be for your new default workbook. Then choose *File/Save As*, and enter the file name:

```
Workbook
```

Save in XLSTART

In the *Save as type* drop-down list, choose the *Template* item and open the *XLSTART* folder. If you use *Excel* within the *Microsoft Office Suite*, the folder is contained in the following folder:

C:\PROGRAM FILES\MICROSOFT OFFICE\OFFICE

Save the workbook by clicking on the *Save* button, and then close the workbook. In order to activate the new default workbook template, you need to restart *Excel*.

Returning to the Built-in Default Workbook Template

Move the *WORKBOOK.XLT* file from the *XLSTART* folder into another folder or delete it in order to return to the built-in default settings. You could alternatively re-name the workbook.

If you rename the workbook, it will be automatically opened at the start of *Excel*, but it will no longer be the basis for new workbooks.

6. Excel Views

Various Views

You can display your *Excel* tables in various ways, depending on what kind of work you want to do. For example, if you want to view it in its totality, you can display the table in a reduced size. Or, you can enlarge it to view inserted objects.

Print Preview

In the *Print Preview*, you can see the table the way it will later be printed. Here you can adjust the margins and the column width to the desired size.

Page Break
Preview

In a new display, the *Page Break Preview*, you can view and format the page breaks, the printing order, and the print area.

Depending on the respective work steps, you can also show or hide individual screen elements, tables, or workbooks.

Print Preview

Use the *Print Preview* in order to check the worksheet one last time before you print it. Only in this view can you see the headers and footers in the positions they will actually be printed. Besides this, you can use the *Print Preview* in order to:

- leaf through the worksheet page by page

- view how a certain print area, for example a selected area or selected sheets of a workbook, will later be printed

- change the margins and/or the position of the headers and footers visually using the mouse

Start

You can activate or deactivate the *Print Preview* in diffe-rent ways. In the *Print* and *Page Setup* dialog boxes, you will find buttons to call up the *Print Preview*, without having to close the dialog box and choose an additional command, so that you can quickly check what a worksheet looks like after you have changed it or give it a final once-over before printing. In order to call up the *Print Preview*, choose:

- the *Print Preview* button 🔍 on the *Standard* toolbar.

- the *file/Print Preview* command.

- the *Preview* button in the *Print* dialog box.

- the *Print Preview* button in the *Page Setup* dialog box.

Zoom

After you have activated the *Print Preview*, the current worksheet is displayed in a reduced size to display a full printing page. The worksheet will be printed out exactly as you see it here. Click onto the *Zoom* button or directly onto a certain part in the worksheet in order to enlarge the display. Click once more onto the button or into the worksheet in order to return to the original size.

Next
Previous

On the toolbar, you will find the *Next* and *Previous* buttons which allow you to leaf through the different printing pages. If the buttons are displayed in light grey, this means that either there is only one page to be printed or only one page has been selected for printing.

Margins

On the status bar, the page number of the current page as well as the total number of pages is displayed. Click the *Margins* button to view the margins. You can then drag the markers of the margins as well as those of the headers and footers in order to change their position. For further details on this topic refer to Chapter 4.

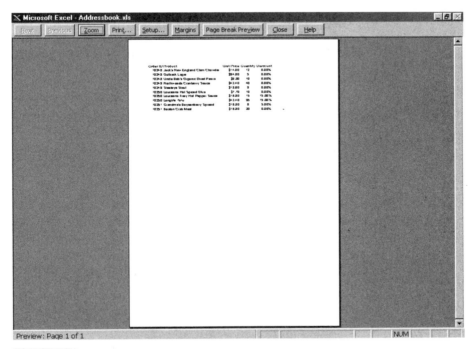

You can close the *Print Preview* in one of the following ways:

Page Break
Preview

- Click the *Page Break Preview* button, or the *Normal* button. The label of the button depends on the previous view from which you originally switched to the *Print Preview*

- Click the *Close* button

- Press the Esc key

Normal View

The normal view is the basic presentation for *Excel* worksheets. It is displayed as soon as you start *Excel*. From the

Print Preview, you can switch to the *Normal View* if you were last in *Page Break Preview* by clicking the *Normal* button. Otherwise, you can return to *Normal View* by clicking *Close*.

The *Normal View* shows the worksheet in the size you selected without headers and footers.

From the *Page Break Preview*, you can return to the *Normal View* by selecting the *View/Normal* command.

The *View/Normal* command cannot be used in order to return from any zoomed display to the 100% view.

Page Break Preview

In *Excel 97,* there is a new view called the *Page Break Preview*, in which the active worksheet is shown in a reduced size. The page breaks, the print area, and the print order are emphasized in a special way.

From the normal view, you can switch to the *Page Break Preview* by selecting the *View/Page Break Preview* command. From the *Print Preview*, you can get there by clicking the *Page Break Preview* button. When you start the *Page Break Preview* for the first time, a *Welcome* window is displayed. Read the message, and then select the *Do not show this dialog again* check box in order to hide the message in future.

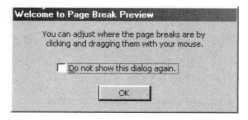

Fig. 6.2:   The Welcome message

In the *Page Break Preview*, the margins are depicted by dashed lines and the print area by a thick line. You can drag these lines to a different position in order to change the margins or the print area.

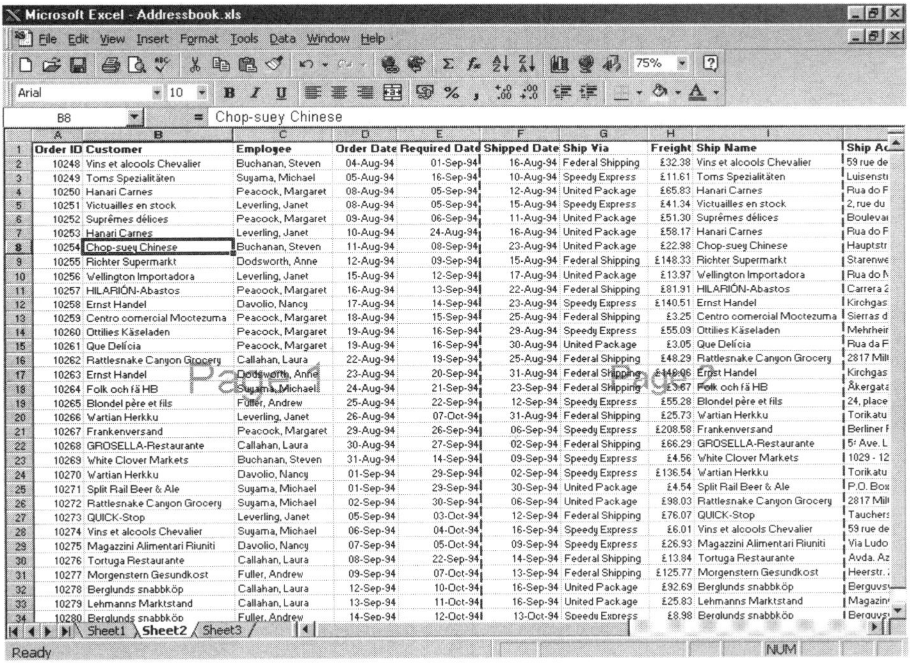

Fig. 6.3: The *Page Break Preview*

You can use the commands on the shortcut menu in order to set or reset page breaks or the print area.

Insert Page Break

With the right mouse button, click onto one of the cells at the beginning of a row or column in order to insert a horizontal or vertical page break respectively, and choose the *Insert Page Break* command from the shortcut menu. Click onto any cell in order to insert both a horizontal as well as a vertical page break at the same time.

Remove Page Break	With the right mouse button, click onto a cell below or to the right of a page break, and choose the *Remove Page Break* command from the shortcut menu in order to delete the page break.
Reset All Page Breaks	Choose *Reset All Page Breaks* in order to remove all user-defined page breaks from the worksheet and to activate the automatic page breaks instead.
Set Print Area	Select a certain table area, click with the right mouse button on the selected area, and choose *Set Print Area* in the shortcut menu in order to define a print area. *Excel* then inserts page breaks above and next to the selected area.
Exclude From Print Area	Select a certain area, right-click on the selection, and in the shortcut menu choose *Exclude From Print Area* in order to print the contents of the table except for the selected area. The *Exclude From Print Area* command is only available after choosing *Set Print Area*.
Reset Print Area	With the right mouse button, click into the worksheet, and choose the *Reset Print Area* in order to reset a previously selected print area.

Full Screen

If you want to display a worksheet without any additional elements disturbing you, in order to see as much as possible of the worksheet, choose the *Full Screen* view. Select the *Full Screen* view by choosing the *View/Full Screen* command.

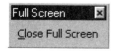

Fig. 6.4: The *Full Screen* toolbar

314

In this view, all superfluous screen elements such as the title bar, the formula bar, and the status bar are hidden. Instead, an additional *Full Screen* toolbar is displayed. In order to close this view, click the *Close Full Screen* button on the toolbar, or press the ⌈Esc⌋ key.

Setting Basic View Options

The screen elements which surround the entry area are supposed to help you with your data entry and formatting of the *Excel* tables or charts. Each screen element, however, takes up a certain amount of space which is then no longer available for other elements, such as the actual data in the table. Therefore you have the opportunity to specify which elements you want to use in general while working on a worksheet, and which elements you want to display in the application and workbook window. In order to define the basic display options, choose the *Tools/Options* command and activate the *View* tab page.

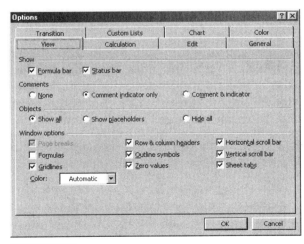

Fig. 6.5: The *View* tab page

Formula bar and Status bar

In the upper area of the dialog box, you can set whether or not you want to show the *Formula* bar and the *Status Bar*, by selecting or clearing the appropriate check boxes. If you prefer, for example, to work directly in the cells instead of using the *Formula Bar*, then clear the *Formula Bar* check box.

Indicators comments

In the *Comments* option group, you can define how you want to show the comments (which formerly used to be called notes) contained in the worksheet. You can choose to display only the indicator, that is, the little red triangle that marks a cell containing a comment. The proper comment is then displayed only when the mouse pointer is directly above the cell containing the comment. You can also show both indicators and comments permanently, or you can keep them hidden.

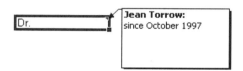

Fig. 6.6:   Indicator and comment

Show placeholders

In the *Objects* option group, you decide in what way pictures, embedded charts or other graphic objects are displayed in a worksheet. Select the *Show placeholders* radio button in order to display embedded charts as grey frames, thus increasing the speed of display.

Hide all

Select the *Hide all* radio button if you want to hide all graphic objects such as charts, AutoShapes, pictures, etc.

Window options

In the *Window options* option group, you can determine the view options of the current window. Select the check boxes for the window elements that you want to show in general. The view options are saved together with the workbook, and will be loaded again automatically the next time you start *Excel*.

Formulas

You can determine whether the formulas or the results of formulas are to be displayed in the cells. If you want to print out the actual formulas, select the *Formulas* check box before printing.

Furthermore, in the *Window options*, you can define whether or not the following elements are to be displayed in the window:

▧ Row and column headings

▧ Gridlines

▧ Vertical and horizontal scroll bars

▧ Sheet tabs

In the *Color* list box, you can choose a color other than the default color for the gridlines.

Scroll bars
Sheet tabs

If you normally use the keyboard to work with your tables, you can hide the horizontal and the vertical scroll bars as well as the sheet tabs, and use the shortcut keys instead to move within the workbook and/or among the different workbooks.

Zero values

If you clear the *Zero values* check box, those cells which contain the constant value of '0' or a formula with the result of '0', appear empty.

Show or Hide Screen Elements

If you accidentally or consciously removed screen elements from the screen and want to show them again, you will find the corresponding commands either in the *View* menu or in the *Tools/Options* command.

317

Formula Bar

The *View* menu with the *Formula Bar* command shows or hides the bar just above the worksheet. On this bar, you can, as an alternative to working in a cell, edit the data of a selected cell.

Status Bar

The *View/Status Bar* command activates or deactivates the *Status Bar* at the bottom of the window. Here you find the status of certain functions and keys, such as NUM for an activated number pad, and EXT if the extended selection is activated.

Toolbars

If certain toolbars are not visible, choose *View/Toolbars* and click on the name of the respective toolbar in the overlapping menu in order to display it. You can also right-click onto a toolbar which is already displayed, and then click on the name of the toolbar which you want to show in the popup menu.

Open, Arrange and Close Windows

In *Excel*, you can work on several worksheets and workbooks at the same time in order to, for example, link worksheets, or copy data from one table into another. By means of the *Window* menu, you can create new windows, arrange and close open windows.

New Window

In order to open a new window for a worksheet in the current workbook, choose the *Window/New Window* command. In the new window, the name of the workbook is shown with a colon and the window number, for example: Turnover: 1, Turnover: 2, etc.

Window/Arrange

In order to arrange both windows in such a way that you can see both worksheets at the same time, choose the *Window/Arrange* command. *Excel* opens a dialog box so that you can choose how you want to arrange the windows.

▣ *Tiled*
Choose this window arrangement in order to show the windows evenly split on the screen. If you had, for example, four windows, the screen would be divided into four quarters with one worksheet displayed in each quarter.

▣ *Horizontal*
With this option button, you arrange the worksheets in several horizontal windows.

▣ *Vertical*
This arrangement shows the windows in vertical order next to each other.

▣ *Cascade*
Arranges the windows in a way that they lie on top of each other and overlap for the most part. However, the title bar is visible so that you can activate whichever window you currently need.

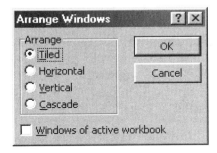

Fig. 6.7:   Arranging windows

Changing the size
of the windows

You can change the size of the windows by using the window frame. As soon as you move over the window frame, the mouse pointer changes into a double-headed arrow. With this double-headed arrow, drag the window to the desired size. At the right side of the window title bar you also find buttons which you can use to set the window to the smallest or biggest size possible.

■ ⬜ *Maximize*
  Click this button in order to enlarge the active window to the largest size possible. It will then cover all the other workbook windows

■ ⬛ *Minimize*
  This button reduces the window to the size of a toolbar button

■ ⬛ *Restore*
  By clicking this button you return to the previous window size

Split and Arrange Windows

If you want to look at different areas of a worksheet at the same time and they are not displayed completely on the screen, you can split the worksheet window into several window sections.

You can then scroll each window section separately so that you can look, for example, at the beginning and the end of a table at the same time. In order to divide a window, click into the desired dividing position, and then choose the *Window/Split* command. Or, drag the window's split bar out of the horizontal or vertical scroll bar to the desired splitting position.

Fig. 6.8:   The split bar

You find split bars at the top of the vertical scroll bar, above the scroll bar arrow which you use to scroll the worksheet downwards, and in the right corner of the horizontal scroll bar.

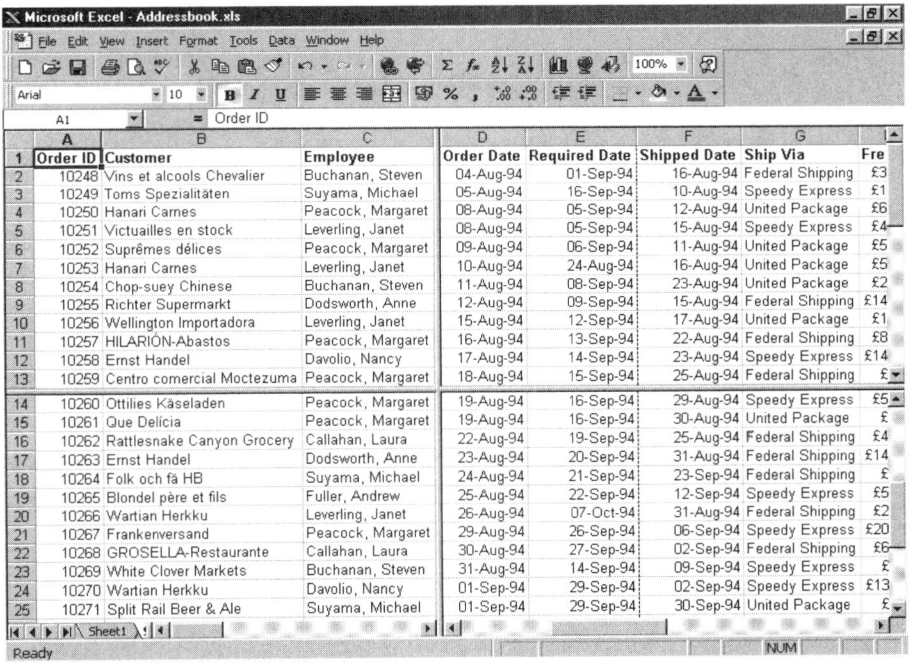

	A	B	C	D	E	F	G	
1	Order ID	Customer	Employee	Order Date	Required Date	Shipped Date	Ship Via	Fre
2	10248	Vins et alcools Chevalier	Buchanan, Steven	04-Aug-94	01-Sep-94	16-Aug-94	Federal Shipping	£3
3	10249	Toms Spezialitäten	Suyama, Michael	05-Aug-94	16-Sep-94	10-Aug-94	Speedy Express	£1
4	10250	Hanari Carnes	Peacock, Margaret	08-Aug-94	05-Sep-94	12-Aug-94	United Package	£6
5	10251	Victuailles en stock	Leverling, Janet	08-Aug-94	05-Sep-94	15-Aug-94	Speedy Express	£4
6	10252	Suprêmes délices	Peacock, Margaret	09-Aug-94	06-Sep-94	11-Aug-94	United Package	£5
7	10253	Hanari Carnes	Leverling, Janet	10-Aug-94	24-Aug-94	16-Aug-94	United Package	£5
8	10254	Chop-suey Chinese	Buchanan, Steven	11-Aug-94	08-Sep-94	23-Aug-94	United Package	£2
9	10255	Richter Supermarkt	Dodsworth, Anne	12-Aug-94	09-Sep-94	15-Aug-94	Federal Shipping	£14
10	10256	Wellington Importadora	Leverling, Janet	15-Aug-94	12-Sep-94	17-Aug-94	United Package	£1
11	10257	HILARIÓN-Abastos	Peacock, Margaret	16-Aug-94	13-Sep-94	22-Aug-94	Federal Shipping	£8
12	10258	Ernst Handel	Davolio, Nancy	17-Aug-94	14-Sep-94	23-Aug-94	Speedy Express	£14
13	10259	Centro comercial Moctezuma	Peacock, Margaret	18-Aug-94	15-Sep-94	25-Aug-94	Federal Shipping	£
14	10260	Ottilies Käseladen	Peacock, Margaret	19-Aug-94	16-Sep-94	29-Aug-94	Speedy Express	£5
15	10261	Que Delícia	Peacock, Margaret	19-Aug-94	16-Sep-94	30-Aug-94	United Package	£
16	10262	Rattlesnake Canyon Grocery	Callahan, Laura	22-Aug-94	19-Sep-94	25-Aug-94	Federal Shipping	£4
17	10263	Ernst Handel	Dodsworth, Anne	23-Aug-94	20-Sep-94	31-Aug-94	Federal Shipping	£14
18	10264	Folk och fä HB	Suyama, Michael	24-Aug-94	21-Sep-94	23-Sep-94	Federal Shipping	£
19	10265	Blondel père et fils	Fuller, Andrew	25-Aug-94	22-Sep-94	12-Sep-94	Speedy Express	£5
20	10266	Wartian Herkku	Leverling, Janet	26-Aug-94	07-Oct-94	31-Aug-94	Federal Shipping	£2
21	10267	Frankenversand	Peacock, Margaret	29-Aug-94	26-Sep-94	06-Sep-94	Speedy Express	£20
22	10268	GROSELLA-Restaurante	Callahan, Laura	30-Aug-94	27-Sep-94	02-Sep-94	Federal Shipping	£6
23	10269	White Clover Markets	Buchanan, Steven	31-Aug-94	14-Sep-94	09-Sep-94	Speedy Express	£
24	10270	Wartian Herkku	Davolio, Nancy	01-Sep-94	29-Sep-94	02-Sep-94	Speedy Express	£13
25	10271	Split Rail Beer & Ale	Suyama, Michael	01-Sep-94	29-Sep-94	30-Sep-94	United Package	£

Fig. 6.9: A split window

Window/ Remove Split

In order to reset a split window, either choose the *Remove Split* command from the *Window* menu, or double-click onto the split bar, or just drag the split bar out of the window.

Displaying Several Workbooks at the Same Time

If you want to work on several workbooks at the same time, first choose *File/Open*, select all the desired workbook names by clicking them while holding down the Ctrl key, and then click the *Open* command.

Windows of
active workbook

Next, choose *Window/Arrange* and proceed as described above. If you have opened several workbooks, but want to display only the worksheets of the current workbook, select the *Windows of active workbook* check box in the *Arrange Windows* dialog box.

Windows/Hide or
Windows/Unhide

Use the *Windows/Hide* or *Windows/Unhide* commands in order to hide workbooks which you do not need at present so that, by using the *Windows/Arrange* command, you can display only the workbooks now required.

Switch between
windows

In order to switch between open windows, either click into the desired window, or press the shortcut key Ctrl+F6. In order to close an open window, click on the *Close* button ☒ in the window's title bar.

Show or Hide Rows, Columns, Tables, and Workbooks

If you are working on extensive tables, it is helpful to hide certain areas which you do not need at the moment. The same is true for worksheets and workbooks. If you have several worksheets of one or more workbooks in several windows, you can hide those worksheets which you are not working on at present. This way you get more space for the rest of the worksheets.

Show or Hide Columns

In order to hide certain columns in a table, select them. Click onto an individual column, or drag the mouse across several column headings. Then choose *Format/Column/ Hide*. You can recognize hidden columns by the missing column headings.

Later, select the column heading to the right and to the left of the hidden column, and choose *Format/Column/ Unhide* in order to display the hidden columns again. Likewise, you can open the column heading shortcut menu by clicking with the right mouse button on the column heading, and then select *Unhide* or *Hide*.

	A	D	E	F
1	Order ID	Order Date	Required Date	Shipped Date
2	10248	04-Aug-94	01-Sep-94	16-Aug-94
3	10249	05-Aug-94	16-Sep-94	10-Aug-94
4	10250	08-Aug-94	05-Sep-94	12-Aug-94
5	10251	08-Aug-94	05-Sep-94	15-Aug-94
6	10252	09-Aug-94	06-Sep-94	11-Aug-94
7	10253	10-Aug-94	24-Aug-94	16-Aug-94
8	10254	11-Aug-94	08-Sep-94	23-Aug-94

Fig. 6.10:   Columns B and C are hidden

Hide or Unhide Rows

In order to hide one or more rows, select the row headings and choose the *Format/Row/Hide* command.

	A	B	C
1	Order ID	Customer	Employee
5	10251	Victuailles en stock	Leverling, Janet
6	10252	Suprêmes délices	Peacock, Margaret
7	10253	Hanari Carnes	Leverling, Janet
8	10254	Chop-suey Chinese	Buchanan, Steven
9	10255	Richter Supermarkt	Dodsworth, Anne
10	10256	Wellington Importadora	Leverling, Janet
11	10257	HILARIÓN-Abastos	Peacock, Margaret

Fig. 6.11:   Rows 2 to 4 are hidden

In order to later show the hidden rows again, select the row headings above and below the hidden rows, and choose the *Format/Row/Unhide* command. Like with the columns, here too you can use the shortcut menu by clicking on the row heading with the right mouse button, and then selecting the *Hide* or *Unhide* commands.

Hide and Unhide Sheets

In order to hide a worksheet, select it by clicking onto its sheet tab. Then select *Format/Sheet/Hide*. If the workbook contains hidden sheets, a dialog box with a list of all hidden worksheets is displayed as soon as you select the *Format/Sheet/Unhide* command.

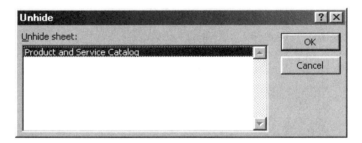

Fig. 6.12:   Hidden worksheets

Select the name of the sheet which you want to show again, and click the *OK* button, or double-click on the name.

Hide and Unhide Workbooks

In the same way as worksheets, whole workbooks can also be hidden or unhidden. Activate the workbook in question, and choose the *Window/Hide* command. By choosing the *Window/Unhide* command, a dialog box is opened listing all the hidden workbooks. Double-click on the workbook which you want to display again.

Show or Hide Gridlines, Row Headings and Column Headings

By default, *Excel* tables contain gridlines so as to label the cells using letters for the columns and numbers for the rows. As long as you create references, type in entries and assign data, having these elements displayed is very helpful. But when you create an order which you want to print out later on, you may want to do this without the disturbing gridlines and column and row headings, so that you can judge the visual effect more easily.

You can choose whether or not to show the gridlines. The same is true for the column and row headings.

When you hide the column and row headings, keep in mind that important information will then only be displayed via the position of the cell in the name box.

The selection of column and row headings is also not possible in this case.

B3	▾	➡	Outback Lager			
Order ID	**Product**			**Unit Price**	**Quantity**	**Discount**
10248	Jack's New England Clam Chowder			$14.00	12	0.00%
10248	Outback Lager			$34.80	5	0.00%
10248	Uncle Bob's Organic Dried Pears			$9.80	10	0.00%
10249	Northwoods Cranberry Sauce			$42.40	40	0.00%
10249	Steeleye Stout			$18.60	9	0.00%
10250	Louisiana Hot Spiced Okra			$7.70	10	0.00%
10250	Louisiana Fiery Hot Pepper Sauce			$16.80	15	15.00%
10250	Longlife Tofu			$42.40	35	15.00%
10251	Grandma's Boysenberry Spread			$16.80	6	5.00%
10251	Boston Crab Meat			$16.80	20	0.00%

Fig. 6.13: Table with hidden gridlines and row/column headings

In order to hide gridlines and/or column and row headings, choose the *Tools/Options* command and open the *View* tab page. In the *Window Options* options group, clear the *Gridlines* and/or *Row & column headers* check boxes.

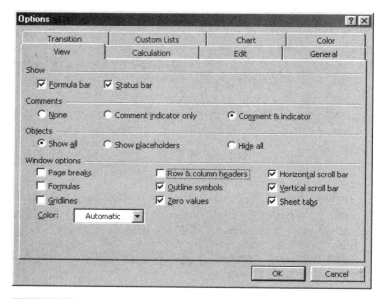

Fig. 6.14:   Hide gridlines and headings

Showing or hiding the gridlines as well as the column and row headings has nothing to do with the printing of these elements.

Zooming the Display

If you work on large tables, or if you want to check certain table areas, it is helpful to be able to enlarge or reduce the display on the screen.

In *Excel*, you can adjust the size of the display to the size of a table by either using preset default values or custom values. You can also automatically adjust the view to the size of a selected cell area.

Zoom

drop-down list

All the changes of these settings can be implemented either via the *Zoom* drop-down list on the *Standard* toolbar, or in the corresponding dialog box. In order to change the view from the toolbar, click on the *Zoom* drop-down button and select one of the preset zoom values.

Fig. 6.15: The Zoom list

In order to use a value of your own that is not shown in the list, click into the *Zoom* text box and overwrite the given value with the one you want. Confirm the entry by pressing the *Enter* key ⏎.

Selection

In order to automatically adjust the display size of *Excel* to a certain cell area, first select this area and then open the *Zoom* drop-down list. Choose the *Selection* item. This selection only changes your view if you had activated at least two cells before choosing the *Zoom* command.

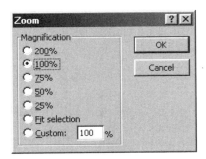

Fig. 6.16: The *Zoom* dialog box

Zoom dialog box

In order to set the display size using a dialog box, choose the *View/Zoom* command. The *Zoom* dialog box opens, with various options for the magnification. This dialog contains the same values that are displayed in the *Zoom* drop-down list. If you want to use values of your own, type them into the *Custom* text box.

The *Fit selection* radio button corresponds to the *Selection* item in the *Zoom* drop-down list. It magnifies, or reduces respectively, the active window in such a way that the selected area is fully displayed.

Adjusting and Saving a View

If you are working with several windows, or if you have hidden part of an extensive table, you can save the current settings in order to return to them later on. In this way, you can save a series of different views of a project so that, according to the working situation, they can be displayed again.

Custom Views

In *Excel 95*, the views were managed by the *View Manager*. In *Excel 97*, instead of choosing *View/View Manager*, you now choose the *View/Custom Views* command. The way the dialog box works, however, remains unchanged. Before you open the dialog box, arrange the screen as you want to have it displayed again later when calling up the saved view. A view saves:

- Shown or hidden columns

- Activated filters

- The arrangement of the displayed worksheets

- The splitting or freezing of a window

- Set print areas

328

In order to create a new view, choose *View/Custom View* command and click the *Add* button. In the *Add View* dialog box, decide which settings you want to save in the new view by clicking or clearing the appropriate check boxes. Enter a name for the new view into the text box, and confirm by clicking *OK*.

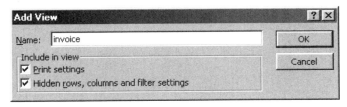

Fig. 6.17:   The *Add View* dialog box

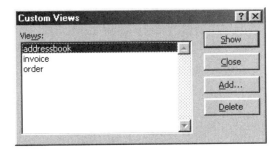

Fig. 6.18:   Views in the *View Manager*

Show

In this way, you can create several custom views. In order to call up a saved view, choose the *View/Custom Views* command, select a view in the *Custom Views* dialog list box, and click *Show* in order to activate the particular settings saved in the view again.

Delete

When you do not need a saved custom view any longer, select the name of the corresponding view in the *Custom View* dialog box, and click the *Delete* button in order to remove this view from the dialog box.

329

7. Database Functions

If you use *Excel* to create lists or databases, *Excel* supports you with comfortable functions. In order to make good use of them, however, you have to enter the database in such a way that *Excel* can recognize and distinguish it from the rest of the data.

- Leave at least one empty row or column between the last data row/column and the rest of the table.

- Do not use empty rows or columns within the list.

Using Databases – an Overview

Here you find a summary of the most important functions which can be used in the context of databases. Regarding the editing of databases, the following functions will be of interest to you:

- Data form

- AutoFilter and special filter

- Find and Replace

- Sort

- Subtotals

With the help of the data form you can carry out changes to the database, search for records, or remove records from the database.

Database functions

In the list of functions, *Excel* offers you a special category for the manipulation of a database. To use these functions, choose *Insert/Function* and in the *Function category* list, select the *Database* item.

Data form

For the entry and editing of records, the data form is particularly helpful. The data form is a dialog box in which records can be displayed, edited, searched for, and removed individually. *Excel* recognizes a database which you created according to certain rules, and automatically displays the entry fields with their corresponding field contents.

In order to insert records into a database, or to edit or remove them, click into the database range and choose *Data/Form*. In the *Sheet1* dialog box, you will find several buttons with which to edit the records.

New

In order to add a record, click the *New* button and enter the record into the empty form boxes. New records are always inserted at the end of the table. You will learn how to insert new records with the help of the data form in the following section.

Scroll bar

In order to change an already existing record, display it with the help of the scroll bar in the dialog box, and click into the appropriate text box.

Restore

If while making changes you realize that you made a mistake, click the *Restore* button. This button resets the changes in the current record as long as the record is still displayed.

Find Next
Find Prev

With the help of the *Find Next* and *Find Prev* buttons, you can move among the records. On top of the buttons for manipulating the database, a text displays the number of the current record and the total number of records.

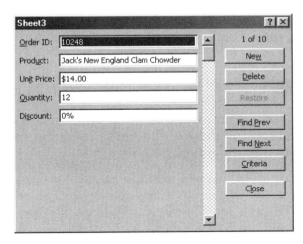

Fig. 7.1: Running a database using the form

Criteria

By clicking the *Criteria* button you can display a form with the help of which you can search for certain records.

AutoFilter

With the help of the *AutoFilter* function you can select a database according to certain criteria. You can activate an *AutoFilter* by clicking into the database range and then choosing *Data/Filter/AutoFilter*.

Find and replace
function

In databases, use the *Find and Replace* function to search for certain field contents in the database, or to replace certain field contents automatically. To activate the *Find* function, choose *Edit/Find*, while for the *Replace* function choose the *Edit/Replace* command.

Sort

In order to sort your database, choose *Data/Sort*. In the *Sort* dialog box, you can determine up to three sorting keys.

Subtotals

With the *Subtotals* function, you can sum up the list entries according to certain column contents and calculate totals or other statistic functions for the individual groups that you have formed this way. In order to be able to use the *Subtotals* function, the table first needs to be sorted.

Using the Data Form for the Entry of Records

Excel not only supports tables in which calculations are carried out, but it is also extraordinarily well suited for smaller data arranged in the form of lists.

What are fields?

In a database or a list similar to a database, the individual entries are called fields, and the related individual entries are called records. For example, in an address file *Name* or *First Name* would be a field, and an address would be a record.

In order to use *Excel* functions for databases, the fields and records of a table should be structured in the following way:

- The data fields are arranged in columns next to each other.

- The records are arranged in rows underneath each other.

- The column labels are found in the first row.

You can use the *Excel* database functions in each table that is arranged in this way. A data form for the entry and editing of database records is also part of the database support. The advantage of entering data in the data form is that it has a very clear presentation. Besides, in a form it is much easier to jump from one field to the next and from one record to another.

In order to insert table data with the help of the data form, all you need is existing column labels. You can even enter the first record with the help of the form.

Select the column labels, or click into the records already created, and choose *Data/Form*. In the data form *Excel* displays a text box for each column label. Columns in which *Excel* found formulas are not displayed as text boxes, but instead as calculated fields.

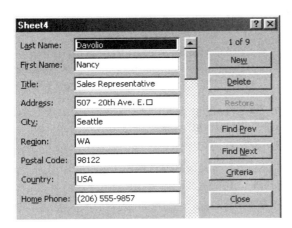

Fig. 7.2:   The data form

Adding Records

It is easier to add new records by means of the form rather than directly into the table, because in the form you cannot make the mistake of entering data into a wrong row or column.

Add

Click on the *Add* button in order to display an empty form. Then click into the first text box, and there enter the first field's content.

You can use the following keys and buttons for the entry and editing:

▪ With a mouse click, or by pressing the tab ⌷ key you jump to the next field.

■ In order to display an empty form, click on the *New* button, or in the last field of the last record press ⏎.

■ Press the shortcut key ⧉+⇆ in order to move backwards from text box to text box.

■ In order to remove already inserted characters, use the Del key or the ← key.

■ To display the next existing record in order to check it, click on the *Find Next* button, press ↓, or click on the scroll bar arrow in the scroll bar of the dialog box.

■ In order to display the previous existing record, click on the *Find Prev* button, press ↑, or click on the scroll bar arrow at the top of the scroll bar.

■ In order to jump to a record further away, drag the scroll bar box until the record number appears in the record display.

■ After you have entered all records, close the data form by clicking the *Close* button.

After having entered the records, copy with the help of the fill handle, if need be, the formulas which cannot be entered in the form into the fields of the corresponding columns.

Filtering the Database with AutoFilter

When editing lists or databases, once a certain scale has been reached it becomes more difficult to maintain the overview. When you search for one or more records or list entries, the search may take quite some time, and you cannot, in any case, be sure that you did not overlook a list entry.

In a database program, in such a situation you would create a query and determine one or several criteria that are/should be contained in the searched for records. As a result, only the records that contain the specified criteria are displayed.

When can
AutoFilter
be used?

Although *Excel* is not a database program, it offers you a similar function which can be used with all databases or lists. For *Excel*, each table that contains the column labels in the first column and underneath arranges the data in rows is a database.

What is
AutoFilter?

For a table arranged in this way you can use the *AutoFilter* funtion that helps you select the required list entries. The function is called *AutoFilter* because you do not need to create the filter yourself, but can choose it from a list of predetermined entries.

Default-AutoFilter

In order to activate the *AutoFilter* function, click into the table area containing the list or database, and choose *Data/ Filter/AutoFilter*.

	B	C	D	H	I	J
1	Last Na ⯆	First Nar ⯆	Title ⯆	Address ⯆	City ⯆	Regi ⯆
2	Davolio	Nancy	Sales Representative	507 - 20th Ave. E.□	Sea (All)
3	Fuller	Andrew	Vice President, Sales	908 W. Capital Way	Tac (Top 10...) (Custom...)
4	Leverling	Janet	Sales Representative	722 Moss Bay Blvd.	Kirk WA
5	Peacock	Margaret	Sales Representative	4110 Old Redmond Rd.	Red (Blanks)
6	Buchanan	Steven	Sales Manager	14 Garrett Hill	Lor (NonBlanks)
7	Suyama	Michael	Sales Representative	Coventry House□	London
8	King	Robert	Sales Representative	Edgeham Hollow□	London
9	Callahan	Laura	Inside Sales Coordinator	4726 - 11th Ave. N.E.	Seattle	WA
10	Dodsworth	Anne	Sales Representative	7 Houndstooth Rd.	London

Fig. 7.3:   AutoFilter in a database

Filter criteria

In the first row of the table or the list, drop-down buttons are displayed next to the column labels. Click on these buttons in order to show a list of all possible filter criteria. The list contains all entries contained in the column plus some additional default entries:

- *(All)*
  This selection cancels a filter and displays all records again

- *(Top 10...)*
  Opens a dialog box to display the top ten values

- *(Custom...)*
  Opens a dialog box for the creation of a user-defined filter

- *(Blanks)*
  Filters all records in this column which have no entry

- *(NonBlanks)*
  Filters all records in this column which are not blank

Blanks and NonBlanks

The *Blanks* and *NonBlanks* list items are only contained in the AutoFilter list if there are blank entries in the table or list.

Using an AutoFilter

In order to use an *AutoFilter*, open the *AutoFilter* list of the column you want to filter, and choose one of the list entries. In an address list, for example, in the *City* column choose the *London* entry in order to display only the records with the address 'London'.

Combine filters

You can also combine several filters by opening additional *AutoFilter* lists in an already filtered list and then selecting the corresponding entry.

Display all records

In order to display all records again, choose from each *AutoFilter* list in which you activated a filter the *All* entry. In order to cancel all filters in one go, choose *Data/Filter/Show All*.

Filter Top 10 Values

The *AutoFilter* function is the fastest method of filtering data. The command with which you activate the *AutoFilter* inserts a drop-down list at the top of each column from which can choose the filter criteria.

Top 10

One of the list entries is called *Top 10* and it opens a dialog box which you can use to easily find out the highest and lowest values in a list. Unlike the MIN() and MAX() functions, with this filter you can see more than one minimum or maximum value.

Maximum and
Minimum values
with Top 10

You can decide how many top values you want to filter and specify this either by item or by percentage. In the dialog box you have the choice of displaying either the *Top* or the *Bottom* values.

Items or Percent

In the text box in the middle, enter how many list entries are to be displayed. In the list to the right, choose the *Items* entry if the middle value contains the number of the list entries to be displayed. Select *Percent* if the value contains a percentage instead.

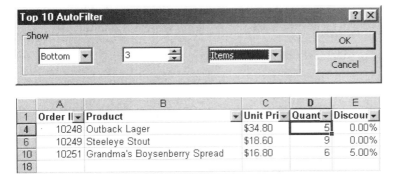

Fig. 7.4:   AutoFilter in a database and the result

If you want *Excel* to display, for example, the rows with the three lowest quantity in stock, in the first list choose *Bottom*, in the middle list '3', and in the last drop-down list choose *Items*.

Like all the other filters, you can also reset a *Top 10* filter by selecting the *All* entry. In order to close the *AutoFilter* function altogether, choose again *Data/Filter/AutoFilter*.

If you want to use several filter criteria as alternative filters, use a customized *AutoFilter*.

If you are searching for one or more specific records, you can sometimes achieve your goal faster if instead of the *AutoFilter* function you use the *Find* function which you can activate by choosing *Edit/Find*.

Customized AutoFilters

If you select lists with the help of default *AutoFilters*, only simple selections with AND links for several columns are possible. That means that all selected filter criteria must apply in order for a list entry to be displayed. More specific filters are not possible with this method.

For example, you cannot:

- establish an OR link to a column. You cannot select two or more alternative filters for one single column to filter, for example, all persons from London or Cambridge.

- use an AND link for a single column in order to filter a value range.

- use wildcards for characters in order to filter list entries which match only part of the search criteria.

In all these cases, instead of the default *AutoFilter* entries use a custom filter. If you have not activated *AutoFilter*, click into the list and then choose *Data/Filter/AutoFilter*.

Custom

Open the *AutoFilter* drop-down list in the column you want to filter, and choose the *Custom* entry. In the *Custom AutoFilter* dialog box, the column label is shown above the first drop-down list.

In the drop-down list, choose the comparison operator. Choose for example the *is greater than* entry in order to filter all rows whose contents are greater than the comparison value which you either enter in the box to the right or select from the drop-down list that contains all entries in the current column.

If you want to use more than one filter criteria, select the *And* radio button so that the first and the second filter criteria will be fulfilled before a list entry is displayed.

Choose *Or* in order to display a list entry where either the first or the second filter criteria is fulfilled. Then select the second comparison operator and either enter the second comparison value or choose it from the list.

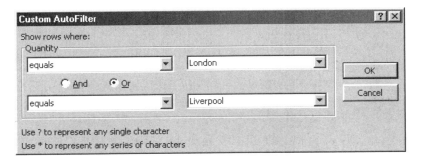

Fig. 7.5:   An OR link

In order to filter all persons from London or Liverpool with the help of an 'Or' link, in the first list select the *equals* entry and select 'London'. Then select the *Or* radio button. In the second list select the *equals* entry as well and in the list next to it, choose the 'Liverpool' entry.

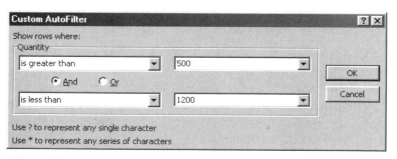

Fig. 7.6:   An AND link

In order to filter all customers having bill amounts of between £500 and £1200 with the help of an *And* link, in the first list choose the *is greater than* entry, and into the box to the right, enter 500. In the second list, choose the *is less than* entry, and in the list box to the right, enter 1200 or select it from the list.

Wildcards in AutoFilters

If you search a list for records containing certain series of characters, and if you do not know the entire column entry, or if only a part of the field content is relevant for the search, then use wildcards for the unknown or irrelevant parts. In *AutoFilters*, use:

- ?

  For any single character which is to be replaced

- *

  For any series of characters which is to be replaced

With the '*ton' entry, for example, you can search for all towns ending with the 'ton', regardless of how they begin. Use the 'Sm?th' entry, if you do not know whether the name is 'Smith' or 'Smyth'.

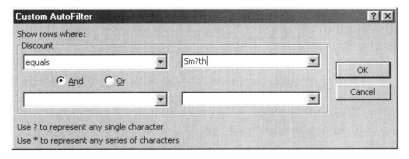

Fig. 7.7: Wildcard in a filter

The operators displayed in the drop-down list boxes can be used as follows:

- *equals*
  Lists entries with identical field contents

- *does not equal*
  Lists entries with different field contents

- *is greater than*
  Lists entries with larger values

- *is greater than or equal to*
  Lists entries with larger or equal values

- *is less than*
  Lists entries with smaller values

- *is less than or equal to*
  Lists entries with smaller or equal values

Furthermore, the lists contain additional operators: *begins with, does not begin with, ends with, does not end with, contains*, *does not contain*. Use these operators to filter series of characters for the first or last characters respectively, or to search for parts of a series of characters without using a wildcard.

Advanced Filter

To quickly filter tables, databases and lists you use the entries of the *AutoFilter* drop-down lists. In order to define several filter criteria for a column, or to create filter criteria with an OR link, select a custom filter, also through the *AutoFilter* function.

Why advanced
filter?

If you want to create filters that go beyond these conditions in order to link more than two filter criteria, for example, or filter value ranges or copy the filtered list entries in one step, then create an advanced filter.

In order to filter a list with an advanced filter, you should create one or two additional ranges outside the area containing the list. This means that altogether you will work with two or even three table ranges.

- *List range*
  This range indicates the cells containing the list to be filtered. If *Excel* does not automatically recognize the list, select this range.

- *Criteria range*
  This first row of this range contains the column labels of the list range as well. In this criteria range, the filter criteria are entered. Use it to define the criteria range before creating an advanced filter.

- *Copy to*
  This range is needed only if the list entries are to be filtered and copied in one go.

Creating a Customized Advanced Filter

In order to create a customized advanced filter, you first need to create the additional ranges for the entry of the filter criteria and for the display of the filtered records, as described above.

Copy 📋

As a first step, copy the labels of your list. Click the *Copy* button 📋, or select *Edit/Copy*, and click into the first cell of the table range which is supposed to serve as the criteria range.

Paste 📋

Keep a distance of at least one blank row between the list range and the criteria range. Click the *Paste* button 📋, or select the *Edit/Paste* command in order to insert the copied column labels from the clipboard. Now enter the filter criteria with which you want to filter the list. Maintain the following rules:

▦ Filter criteria entered in the same row are always linked by AND.

	A	B	C	D	E	F	G	H
1	ID	Name	First Name	Address	City	Region	Postal Code	Country
2	>10010				= London			

Fig. 7.8: An AND link

▦ Filter criteria in different rows are linked by OR.

	A	B	C	D	E	F	G	H
1	ID	Name	First Name	Address	City	Region	Postal Code	Country
2						WA		
3						WY		

Fig. 7.9: An OR link

345

- In order to filter text, in the search for matching entries use the following expression:

```
= character sequence
```

- In order to search parts of a character sequence, you can use the following wildcards: '*' for a character sequence of any length, and '?' for a single character.

- In order to search for identical values it is sufficient to enter the value into the corresponding column in the search criteria range.

- In order to search for value ranges, use the comparison operators *is greater than* and *is less than or equal to*. The following expression searches for all values between 10 and 20:

```
>10      <20
```

Filter a

value range

In order to be able to filter a value range, you need to include the column label in the criteria range a second time so that the lower and upper limits can be linked by AND.

6	ID	ID
7	>10001	<10020

Fig. 7.10:   Filtering a value range

List range

After you have entered the filter criteria, click into the table or list and choose *Data/Filter/Advanced Filter*.

If *Excel* has not entered the list reference correctly into the *List range* box, select the correct range.

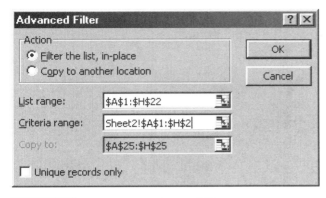

Creating the advanced filter

Criteria range

Then click into the *Criteria range* box and select the rows with the copied column labels and the entered search criteria.

Note that you should not include any blank rows in the selection, since this may lead to mistakes. Confirm with *OK*.

Show All

The list is filtered according to the advanced filter criteria. The filter process can be cancelled by using the *Data/ Filter/Show All* command.

Copy to another location

In order to copy the filtered records of a list to another location in one go, after entering the filter conditions choose *Data/Filter/Advanced Filter*, and click the *Copy to another location* radio button.

Click into the *Copy to* text box, and select the table range into which you want to insert the filtered records. If you select only one row, *Excel* copies the column labels into this row and all records below the row.

Select a range of more than one row in order to limit the number of items copied.

Unique records
only

If your list contains the same entry more than once, and if each entry is to be copied only once, select into the *Unique records only* check box.

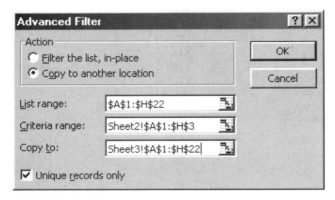

Fig. 7.12:   Filtering and copying in one step

Click the *OK* button to close the dialog box. The records are copied into the new location. If as a paste area you select a range that is smaller than the number of the list entries found, *Excel* displays a message to this effect before copying.

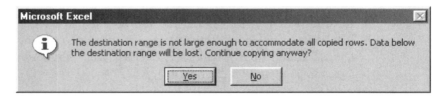

Fig. 7.13:   The paste area is smaller than the number of copies

Click the *Yes* button in order to copy all records anyway. In this case the area below the defined paste area must be blank! Click the *No* button in order to limit the records to the selected range.

If you give the range you are using as the criteria range the name 'Criteria' using *Insert/Name/Define*, it will be automatically displayed in the *Criteria range* box in the *Advanced Filter* dialog box without any further selection being necessary.

Searching for Records

Once your database or list has reached a certain size, it is rather laborious to use the scroll bar to find a particular entry in your table.

Neither does browsing in the data form quickly lead you to the searched record. You can, however, make the data form only show filtered data, and in this way search for records more effectively.

Searching in the Data Form Using Search Criteria

To search databases and database-like lists, *Excel* offers you a special form, the search criteria form. It is actually a part of the data form and can take one or more search criteria.

Search criteria form

In order to specify search criteria for the data form, first click into the table range containing your database, and select *Data/Form*. *Excel* then displays the data in the data form. In this form, you will see the *Find Prev* and *Find Next* buttons which you can use to browse your database records.

In order to not have to search through all records this way, you can limit the search by entering search criteria. A search criterion defines which field content is to be contained in a certain column. A typical example for a search criterion is a name. If you are looking for a customer called Jackson, the search criterion for the *Name* column is then Jackson.

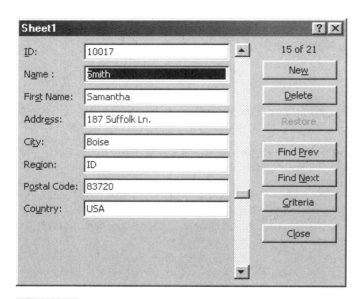

The data form

In the data form, click the *Criteria* button. The entry boxes now are cleared, above the buttons the label *Criteria* appears, and the label of the *Criteria* button is replaced with *Form*.

Now enter the search criteria into the corresponding text boxes. If you enter more than one search criterion, they are linked with an AND link. That means that all entered search criteria have to be fulfilled in order for a record to be found. While searching for records you can use the following comparison operators:

- =
- <
- >
- =>
- <=
- <>

Sheet1	? X
ID: [ ] ▲	Criteria
Name : [Jackson]	New
First Name: [ ]	Clear
Address: [ ]	Restore
City: [ ]	Find Prev
Region: [ ]	Find Next
Postal Code: [ ]	Form
Country: [ ] ▼	Close

Fig. 7.15:   The Criteria form

If, for example, in an inventory you are looking for items whose stock is less 20, in the *Stock* text box you would enter:

```
<20
```

Using wildcards in the search

You can use wildcards in order to look for character sequences which you do not use completely, or which you do not know completely.

■ ?

Use the question mark for single unknown characters. 'Ba?er' finds 'Baker' and 'Baler' and 'Bater',etc.

■ *

Use the asterisk for several unknown characters. '*man' finds 'Newman', 'Merryman' and other names that end with 'man'.

If you are searching for the beginning of a word, you can drop the asterisk at the end. 'New' is the same as 'New*' and finds 'Newman', 'Newlander' or 'Newton'.

Find Next
After entering the search criteria, click the *Find Next* button to move towards the end of the list and to display the next record which fulfills the search criteria.

Find Prev
Click the *Find Prev* button in order to search the database moving backwards towards the beginning of the list. You can use both buttons until the searched for record is displayed, or until the end or beginning respectively of the database is reached.

Excel gives an audible signal if no further records that fulfill the entered search criteria are available.

Clear
With the *Criteria* button you can again display the criteria form and remove the field contents entered there by clicking the *Clear* button.

Form
Later on, you can start a new search or, by clicking the *Form* button, display the data form again. Then close the form by clicking *Close*.

Lookup and Reference Functions for the Automatic Search

If you manage data in the form of lists, such as an address database, a CD library, or an inventory, you can search these lists with certain functions of *Excel*, and with the search result you could then fill a form, or display all the searched information.

The functions that are in charge of the search and of the search results are called lookup and reference functions and are searching in a rectangular cell range in which the information is arranged in rows and columns.

According to the arrangement of the data, you can use three different lookup functions:

- VLOOKUP
  This function searches the first column of an array and returns the value of the row in which the search criteria was found

- HLOOKUP
  This function searches the first row of an array and returns the value of the column in which the search criteria was found

- LOOKUP
  This function searches the values of an array or a search vector

When to use a
VLOOKUP?

Lists that are arranged in the form of a database containing the column labels in the first row and the records in the rows below, can be searched with the VLOOKUP function. In order to search through the table shown below, enter the number of the customer, after which the first name, the last name, and the phone number will all be shown using the VLOOKUP.

	A	B	C	D	E	F	G
1	Number	Name	First Name	Address	Zip	City	Tel
2	10001	Blomberg	Charly	44A Port Avenue	67L182	Portsmouth	5002369
3	10002	Brown	Chester	89 Illworth Lane	S7818D1	Inverness	7531598
4	10003	Farlow	Gene	23 Ansilact Road	73HAD2B	Manchster	3579512
5	10004	Frazer	Bob	90 Wadhurst Rd.	OX15 4NB	London	7762847
6	10005	Jackson	Freddy	35 King George	WX3 6FW	London	5279301
7	10006	Jordan	Mike	12 Milky way	PW81LB	Salisburry	2244557
8	10007	Miller	Jack	120 Hanover Sq.	WA1 1DP	London	8853100
9	10008	Smith	Samantha	13, Belly Lane	A44W12	Dublin	3012597
10	10009	Springsteen	Eric	76 M.C. Square	IT78S12	London	4561203

Fig. 7.16:   The search range

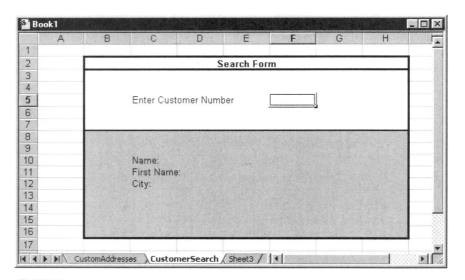

Fig. 7.17:   The form

```
VLOOKUP(lookup_value,table_array,col_index_num,range
lookup)
```

■ *Lookup_value*

Here you enter the field contents which VLOOKUP is
supposed to search for. In our example, this is F5, the
cell in which the customer's number is entered

■ *Table_array*
The table array is the range containing the table which is to be searched; in our case A1:G10

■ *Col_index_num*
The number of the column from which the matching value is to be returned; in our case column 2, because the names are found in the second column of the table

■ *Range_lookup*
An optional argument which may be TRUE or FALSE. TRUE means that the list is sorted in ascending order.

In order to automatically display the name of the customer after entering the customer's number, the following arguments would be placed in the E10 cell:

```
=VLOOKUP($F$5,CustomAddresses!$A$1:$G$10,2,True)
```

```
┌──────────────────────────────────────────────────┐
│                    Search Form                     │
├──────────────────────────────────────────────────┤
│                                                    │
│     Enter Customer Number      ┌──────────┐        │
│                                │   10002  │        │
│                                └──────────┘        │
│                                                    │
├──────────────────────────────────────────────────┤
│                                                    │
│     Name:              Brown                        │
│     First Name:        Chester                      │
│     City:              Portsmouth                   │
│                                                    │
│                                                    │
└──────────────────────────────────────────────────┘
```

Fig. 7.18:   A Lookup result after the entry of the customer's number

Search array range and column index   As soon as the customer number 10002 is entered into cell F5 in the *CustomerSearch* form, the name 'Brown' is displayed. In order to be able to create the rest of the formulas from copies which use the same cell as well as the

355

same search array range for the search criteria, the arguments are taken over as absolute references. The column index is accordingly adjusted in the copied formulas:

```
=VLOOKUP($F$5,CustomAddresses!$A$1:$G$10,3,TRUE)
=VLOOKUP($F$5,CustomAddresses!$A$1:$G$10,6,TRUE)
```

Finding and Replacing Records with the General Find Function

Find what

In order to search a database with the help of the *Find* function, select the *Edit/Find* command, or press the shortcut keys Ctrl+F. In the *Find* dialog box, enter the information into the *Find what* text box.

Search

Select the *By Rows* entry in the *Search* list box so that *Excel* will first search through the rows of the database.

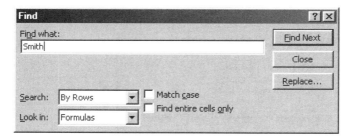

Bild 7.19:   Searching a table

Values

If you want to search the database for values, in the *Look in* drop-down list box define what elements you are looking for. Choose *Values* in order to search for the entry as a constant value or as the result of a formula.

Formulas

Choose *Formulas* instead if you want to search for the entry merely as a constant value directly in the cell or as part of a formula, but not as a formula result.

Match case

Select the *Match case* check box if the search criteria must correspond exactly with the upper and lower case letters of the cell contents. Select the *Find entire cells only* check box if you want to search only for cells in which the search criteria forms the complete cell contents.

Find next

Start the search by clicking on the *Find Next* button. If you are looking not just for one record, but for all records fulfilling the search condition, click the *Find Next* button repeatedly until you have found all the records for which you are looking.

Replace

You can click the *Replace* button in order to automatically replace the cell contents in the records found with another value. Finish the search by clicking the *Close* button.

Sorting

In order to display the entries of a table, list or database in a clear way, and to make the search for the individual cell contents easier, you usually display the tables in a sorted manner.

Excel puts various possibilities at your disposal for sorting the databases or database-like lists according to one or more criteria. An easy way to sort is by using two buttons on the *Standard* toolbar.

If you want to regulate the sort order in greater detail, or if you want to use more than one sorting criterion, instead of the buttons there use the *Sort* dialog box. Basically, you can arrange the data in any of the following ways:

- Ascending
- Descending
- By rows

- By columns

- Case sensitive or not

- By one to three sort keys

The Sort Buttons

If you want to arrange a table by only one sort key, click into the column containing the sort key and then on one of the following buttons:

- 🔲 *Sort Ascending*
  Click this button in order to arrange the table in ascending order. *Excel* then sorts it from A to Z and from 0 to 9

- 🔲 *Sort Descending*
  Click this button in order to arrange the table in descending order. *Excel* then sorts it from Z to A and from 9 to 0

Undo sort

Immediately after the sorting, you can reset the table to the previous sort order, if the sorting does not yield the desired result. To do this, click the *Edit/Undo Sort* command from the menu, or click on the *Undo* button on the toolbar.

Sort by Several Sort Keys

A sort key is the column by which the table is sorted. *Excel* supports the sorting of tables with up to three sort keys.

More than one
sort key

Sorting by more than one sort key is useful if there are identical cell entries in the first sort column. You could then define a second column as an additional sort key.

If, for example, a database contains two identical entries of 'Miller', the first name can used as an additional sort key.

Should there be any identical entries in the second sort key as well, you can select a third sort column as a sort key. When sorting names this might be, for example, the place of residence.

Sort by
In order to sort data by more than one column, click into the list and select the *Data/Sort* command. *Excel* recognizes the column headers automatically if they are formatted differently than the rest of the table rows.

If *Excel* has recognized the headers, they are displayed as sort keys in the *Sort by*, the first *Then by*, and the second *Then by* drop-down list boxes.

My list has
Apart from this the *Header row* radio button in the *My list has* option group is selected.

You can verify whether *Excel* has recognized the headers correctly by looking to see if it takes the first row to be a header or not.

If your table does not contain any headers, make sure you select the *No header row* radio button.

Recognized headers are automatically excluded from the sorting, while non-recognized headers are included in the sorting and will afterwards be found within the table, placed according to their value.

Then open the *Sort by* drop-down list and select the column header, or, if your table does not contain headers, the column letter by which you want the table to be sorted.

Fig. 7.20: The *Sort* dialog box with three sort keys

Excel always suggests the first column for the first sort key. You can choose the second sort key only after having selected the first, and the third one can be selected after having determined the second.

For every sort key, choose the sort order, and finally start the sort process by clicking *OK*.

	A	B	C	D	E	F	G
1	Number	Name	First Name	Address	Zip	City	Tel
2	10001	Blomberg	Charly	44A Port Avenue	67L182	Portsmouth	5002369
3	10002	Brown	Chester	89 Illworth Lane	S7818D1	Inverness	7531598
4	10003	Farlow	Gene	23 Ansilact Road	73HAD2B	Manchester	3579512
5	10004	Frazer	Bob	90 Wadhurts Road	OX15 4NB	London	7762847
6	10005	Jackson	Freddy	35 King George Road	WX3 6FW	London	5279301
7	10006	Jordan	Mike	12 Milky Way	PW81LB	Salisbury	2244557
8	10007	Miller	Jack	120 Hanover Square	WA1 1DP	London	8853100
9	10008	Smith	Samantha	13, Belly Lane	A44W12	Dublin	3012597
10	10009	Springsteen	Eric	76 M. C. Square	IT78S12	London	4561203

Fig. 7.21: A list sorted by name

Sort by Column

As a rule, an *Excel* table is arranged in such a way that the column headers are entered into the first row, and the various records or list entries follow in the rows below. When a table is sorted, it is usually arranged in this manner.

Sort options

In addition to this scheme you have other sort options. You can specify that instead of the rows, you want to sort the columns of a list. Furthermore, you can decide that the sort process is to be case-sensitive – which it normally is not. In order to choose any of these sort options before sorting your table, in the *Sort* dialog box click the *Options* button.

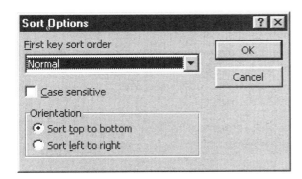

Fig. 7.22:   Defining the sort options

Sort columns

In order to sort the columns of a table, instead of the rows as is normally the case, in the *Orientation* option group select the *Sort left to right* button. If you want the use of capitalization and lower case letters to play a role, click the *Case sensitive* check box.

Close the dialog box by clicking *OK*, and start the sort process by closing the *Sort* dialog box by clicking *OK* as well.

	A	B	C	D	E	F	G
1	**Address**	**City**	**First Name**	**Name**	**Number**	**Tel**	**Zip**
2	44A Port Avenue	Portsmouth	Charly	Blomberg	10001	5002369	67L182
3	89 Illworth Lane	Inverness	Chester	Brown	10002	7531598	S7818D1
4	23 Ansilact Road	Manchester	Gene	Farlow	10003	3579512	73HAD2B
5	90 Wadhurts Road	London	Bob	Frazer	10004	7762847	OX15 4NB
6	35 King George Road	London	Freddy	Jackson	10005	5279301	WX3 6FW
7	12 Milky Way	Salisbury	Mike	Jordan	10006	2244557	PW81LB
8	120 Hanover Square	London	Jack	Miller	10007	8853100	WA1 1DP
9	13, Belly Lane	Dublin	Samantha	Smith	10008	3012597	A44W12
10	76 M. C. Square	London	Eric	Springsteen	10009	4561203	IT78S12

Fig. 7.23: The list sorted by columns

Defining sort orders of your own

When sorting tables with the help of the sort buttons or by means of the *Data/Sort* command, *Excel* uses a default sort order. As an alternative, you can use your own order to sort your table. You can do this with the help of the entries in the *Custom lists*. When you choose an ascending sort order, *Excel* sorts the data in the way shown below. When you choose a descending sort order, *Excel* sorts the data in the reverse order.

▪ Numeric values from the smallest to the largest value, that is, first negative, then positive numbers

▪ Series of characters, digits and special signs

```
0 1 2 3 4 5 6 7 8 9
' - (Space) ! " # $ % & ( ) * , . / : ; ? @ [ \ ] ^ _
` { | } ~ + < = >
A B C D E F G H I J K L M N O P Q R S T U V W X Y Z
```

▪ FALSE before TRUE for logical values

▪ Error values are all equal

▪ Blanks

Blanks are always sorted last, regardless of the chosen sort order.

Custom lists

To sort a table in your own order, do the following: choose *Tools/Options*, and in the *Custom Lists* tab page create a new list in which you type the entries in the desired sort order. In order to define a sort order deviating from the default sort order, choose *Data/Sort* and in the *Sort* dialog box click the *Options* button.

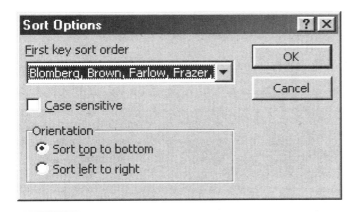

Fig. 7.24: A customized sort order

Open the *First key sort order* drop-down list box and select the new list entry. Close the *Options* dialog box by clicking *OK*, and start the sort by clicking *OK* as well.

Even a sort you carried out through the *Sort* dialog box can be returned to the previous state if its result does not show the desired result. To do this, click the *Undo* button or use the *Edit/Undo* command immediately after the sort process has been completed.

The Subtotals Function

Data/Subtotals

If you are working on a list or a database in which you want to sum up certain list entries in order to calculate a total result from these grouped data, you can use an *Excel* function. For each group of records the *Data/Subtotals* command creates a total with a function you defined for it, and then inserts a subtotal.

Sort first!

In order to use the *Subtotals* function, you first need to sort the list by the criterion according to which you want to summarize the list entries. You can do this with the *Data/Sort* command.

At each

change in

Then choose *Data/Sutotals*. Open the *At each change in* drop-down list box, and select the column by which the table is sorted and by which you now want the subtotals to be grouped. In the *Use function* drop-down list box, select the function you want for the summary. For the summary of text you can only use the *Count* function.

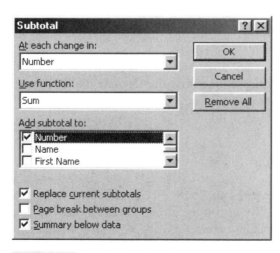

Fig. 7.25: Calculate subtotals

Add subtotal to   In the *Add subtotal to* list box, click the check box for the column or columns which are to be summarized, and then click *OK*.

1 2 3		A	B	C	D	E
	1	Order ID	Product	Unit Price	Quantity	Discount
	2	10871	Pavlova	$17.45	12	5.00%
	3	10871	Alice Mutton	$39.00	16	5.00%
	4	10872	Pâté chinois	$24.00	10	5.00%
	5	10872	Tarte au sucre	$49.30	20	5.00%
	6				5.00% Count	4
	7	10823	Original Frankfurter grüne Soße	$13.00	15	10.00%
	8	10833	Uncle Bob's Organic Dried Pears	$30.00	20	10.00%
	9	10833	Gorgonzola Telino	$12.50	9	10.00%
	10	10833	Perth Pasties	$32.80	9	10.00%
	11	10839	Escargots de Bourgogne	$13.25	30	10.00%
	12	10839	Mozzarella di Giovanni	$34.80	15	10.00%
	13				10.00% Count	6
	14	10664	Louisiana Fiery Hot Pepper Sauce	$21.05	15	15.00%
	15	10677	Gumbär Gummibärchen	$31.23	30	15.00%
	16	10677	Geitost	$2.50	8	15.00%
	17	10693	Tourtière	$7.45	60	15.00%
	18	10693	Gudbrandsdalost	$36.00	30	15.00%
	19	10693	Röd Kaviar	$15.00	15	15.00%
	20				15.00% Count	6

Fig. 7.26:   Subtotals

The subtotals are inserted in a structure. With the help of the buttons displayed in front of the row headers, you can show or hide the subtotals. In the following section you can read about how to work with structured tables.

Remove all   In order to remove the subtotals, choose the *Data/Sub-totals* command and click the *Remove All* button.

Group and Outline

With extensive tables and lists it is easy to loose the view if they are not particularly well structured.

Group and Outline

One way to structure extensive tables is by using the outline. In *Excel*, this is contained in the *Group and Outline* command, since an outline is built upon the summing up of rows and columns into groups.

Establish a group hierarchy

By building groups, a hierarchical structure is established. Once the lowest level of data has been summarized.

The summaries are again summarized in groups and hence form the second level, and so forth.

After you have grouped the data, you can show or hide the data groups up to a certain level.

Sort first!

Before you can create an outline, you first need to sort the table into a sort order in which equivalent entries that can be summarized in groups are arranged underneath each other.

In *Excel*, you can arrange selected table ranges in the desired sort order by using the *Data/Sort* command, as described above in more detail.

Auto Outline

You can sum up the columns as well as the rows of a table.

If the table already contains summarizing formulas beneath the individual summarizing data rows and columns, the outline can be created automatically.

In order to outline the table entries automatically, select the corresponding table range and choose *Data/Group and Outline/Auto Outline*.

Income and Expenses 1998

	A	B	C	D	E	F	G	H
3			Q1			Q2		TOTAL
4	Income	Jan	Feb	Mar	Apr	May	Jun	
5	concerts	£250.00	£280.00	£100.00	£180.00	£300.00	£320.00	
6	recordings	£135.00	£0.00	£210.00	£190.00	£0.00	£110.00	
7	teaching	£260.00	£260.00	£260.00	£260.00	£260.00	£260.00	
8	sales	£120.00	£0.00	£0.00	£120.00	£120.00	£60.00	
9		£765.00	£540.00	£570.00	£750.00	£680.00	£750.00	£4,055.00
10								
11	Expenses							
12	travel	£83.00	£90.00	£50.00	£60.00	£110.00	£100.00	
13	instruments	£1,000.00	£0.00	£0.00	£0.00	£0.00	£0.00	
14	promotion	£60.00	£60.00	£60.00	£60.00	£60.00	£60.00	
15	studio rent	£340.00	£340.00	£200.00	£0.00	£0.00	£300.00	
16		£1,483.00	£490.00	£310.00	£120.00	£170.00	£460.00	£3,033.00
17								
18	Income		Q3			Q4		
19	concerts	Jul	Aug	Sep	Oct	Nov	Dec	
20	recordings	£0.00	£180.00	£180.00	£320.00	£320.00	£500.00	
21	teaching	£0.00	£0.00	£190.00	£250.00	£80.00	£0.00	
22	sales	£0.00	£260.00	£260.00	£260.00	£260.00	£260.00	
23		£0.00	£0.00	£60.00	£120.00	£0.00	£0.00	
24		£0.00	£440.00	£690.00	£950.00	£660.00	£760.00	£3,500.00

Fig. 7.27: A table which can be outlined automatically

Income and Expenses 1998

	A	B	C	D	E	F	G	H
3			Q1			Q2		TOTAL
4	Income	Jan	Feb	Mar	Apr	May	Jun	
5	concerts	£250.00	£280.00	£100.00	£180.00	£300.00	£320.00	
6	recordings	£135.00	£0.00	£210.00	£190.00	£0.00	£110.00	
7	teaching	£260.00	£260.00	£260.00	£260.00	£260.00	£260.00	
8	sales	£120.00	£0.00	£0.00	£120.00	£120.00	£60.00	
9		£765.00	£540.00	£570.00	£750.00	£680.00	£750.00	£4,055.00
10								
11	Expenses							
12	travel	£83.00	£90.00	£50.00	£60.00	£110.00	£100.00	
13	instruments	£1,000.00	£0.00	£0.00	£0.00	£0.00	£0.00	
14	promotion	£60.00	£60.00	£60.00	£60.00	£60.00	£60.00	
15	studio rent	£340.00	£340.00	£200.00	£0.00	£0.00	£300.00	
16		£1,483.00	£490.00	£310.00	£120.00	£170.00	£460.00	£3,033.00

Fig. 7.28: The table after Auto Outline

367

Group level

Excel sums up the table rows for which a unifying formula is found in horizontal groups, and the table columns for which a unifying formula is found in vertical groups. In Figure 7.28, the row subtotals are given in rows 9 and 16. Therefore these data are summed up at the first group level.

Show and hide

After activating the *Auto Outline*, in front of and above the table, marks and symbols are displayed to indicate the groups and to show or hide them. The lines indicate a group. You use the buttons in order to show or hide the subordinate data of a group or of all groups.

▪ ⊞

Click on this button in order to show the subordinate rows or columns in a group. This button is only displayed if there are any subordinate table rows which are presently hidden

▪ ⊟

Click on this button in order to hide the subordinate rows or columns of a group

▪ 1 2 3

With the help of these buttons you can show or hide all subordinate data rows or columns up to the group level displayed on the button

Manual Grouping

Tables which do not contain matching summaries, or the summary of which *Excel* does not recognize correctly, can be grouped manually.

Group and ungroup

To do this, select the records which are to be summarized in a group by dragging the mouse across the row or column headings of the respective rows and columns. Then choose *Data/Group and Outline/Group*. An incorrectly summarized group can be reset by choosing the *Data/ Group and Outline/Ungroup* command.

Show or Hide Details

You can show or hide subordinate row and/or column levels by using the *Data/Group and Outline/Show Detail* or *Hide Detail* commands.

You can hide the data of an outlined table up to a certain level and then print the table with only the outline you specified.

	A	B	C	D	E	F	G	H
1	**Income and Expenses 1998**							
2								
3			Q1			Q2		TOTAL
4	Income	Jan	Feb	Mar	Apr	May	Jun	
9		£765.00	£540.00	£570.00	£750.00	£680.00	£750.00	£4,055.00
10								
11	Expenses							
16		£1,483.00	£490.00	£310.00	£120.00	£170.00	£460.00	£3,033.00
17								
18			Q3			Q4		
19	Income	Jul	Aug	Sep	Oct	Nov	Dec	
24		£0.00	£440.00	£690.00	£950.00	£660.00	£760.00	£3,500.00
25								
26	Expenses							
31		£60.00	£145.00	£1,050.00	£500.00	£155.00	£170.00	£2,080.00

Fig. 7.29: The table of Figure 7.28 with hidden detail data

Using a Toolbar to Edit an Outline

Instead of the commands described above, you can also use a toolbar to group and outline your data more quickly. By choosing *View/Toolbars/PivotTable* you display buttons that help you to form groups more quickly. Besides, you can use these buttons to show or hide details.

Fig. 7.30: The toolbar with buttons to show or hide the data details

Primarily this toolbar is used for the creation and editing of Pivot tables.

However, it also contains four buttons which you can use to influence the display of an outline.

■ ➡ *Group*
Drag the mouse across the row or column headings of the rows or columns you want to group. Then click on this button in order to unite the selected data

■ ⬅ *Ungroup*
Click into a group and then on this button in order to dissolve the group and display the data once again as individual rows or columns

■ ▭ *Hide detail*
Click this button in order to hide the lower levels of the outline

■ ▭ *Show detail*
Click this button in order to display the hidden outline levels

Removing an Outline

By choosing the *Data/Group and Outline* command and clicking *Clear Outline* you can remove outlines and display the table in its normal view again.

Showing Row and Column Headings Permanently

In an extensive table, your row and column headings will disappear as you move down the table. It is not very convenient to have to go back up to the beginning of the table just to find out where you are and to assign data to the correct rows and columns.

Since this is a situation which arises frequently, *Excel* offers you various ways of displaying the row and column headings while the rest of the table moves down the screen.

Fixing the Database Window by Splitting the Window

You can split a window horizontally and in the upper section display the column headings while moving the list entries in the lower part.

You can also split the screen vertically and display the row headings in the left half of the pane while scrolling through the list entries in the right part of the pane. There are two ways to split a window. One is to drag the split box to the point where you want to divide it.

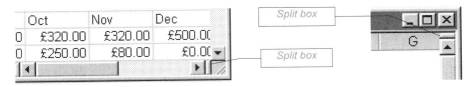

Fig. 7.31:   The split boxes

You will find a split box above the upper scroll arrow button on the vertical scroll bar, and to the right of the right scroll arrow button on the horizontal scroll bar.

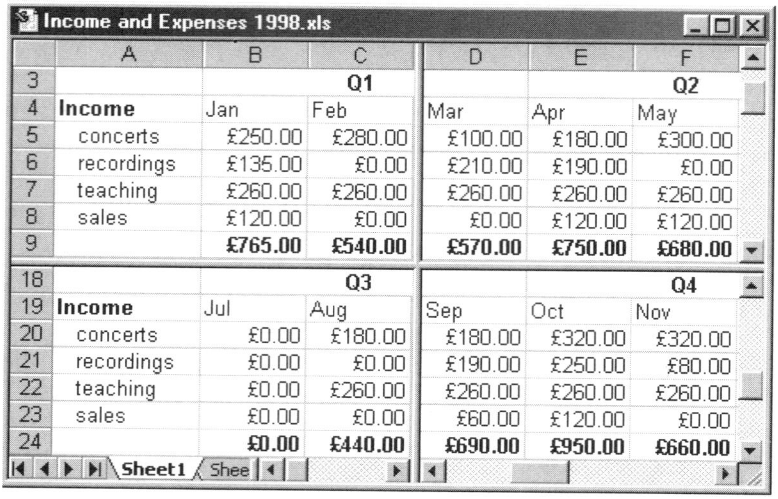

Income and Expenses 1998.xls

	A	B	C	D	E	F
3			Q1			Q2
4	**Income**	Jan	Feb	Mar	Apr	May
5	concerts	£250.00	£280.00	£100.00	£180.00	£300.00
6	recordings	£135.00	£0.00	£210.00	£190.00	£0.00
7	teaching	£260.00	£260.00	£260.00	£260.00	£260.00
8	sales	£120.00	£0.00	£0.00	£120.00	£120.00
9		**£765.00**	**£540.00**	**£570.00**	**£750.00**	**£680.00**
18			Q3			Q4
19	**Income**	Jul	Aug	Sep	Oct	Nov
20	concerts	£0.00	£180.00	£180.00	£320.00	£320.00
21	recordings	£0.00	£0.00	£190.00	£250.00	£80.00
22	teaching	£0.00	£260.00	£260.00	£260.00	£260.00
23	sales	£0.00	£0.00	£60.00	£120.00	£0.00
24		**£0.00**	**£440.00**	**£690.00**	**£950.00**	**£660.00**

Sheet1 / Shee

Fig. 7.32: The window of Figure 7.31 split into four panes

Split and remove split

The second method works as follows: click into the first cell of the row where you want to split the screen horizontally into two panes, and choose *Window/Split*.

Or, for a vertical split, click onto the first cell of the column where you want to split the window. You will then get two panes next to each other. If you want to split the window horizontally as well as vertically, click into the cell at which the row and column should be split. In order to reset the split, either double-click onto the split separator bar, or choose *Window/Remove Split*.

Display Cells Permanently by Freezing Panes

Instead of splitting a window, you can also fix row and column headers by freezing them in the same pane section while you scroll through other rows or columns.

Window/Freeze Panes

To do this, click to the right of the row heading or below the column heading that you want to freeze, and choose the *Freeze Panes* command from the *Window* menu. You can then scroll through the rest of the table while the frozen cells remain fixed in their positions.

	A	B	C	D
1	Customer	Company Name	Contact Name	Contact Title
56	OLDWO	Old World Delicatessen	Rene Phillips	Sales Representative
57	OTTIK	Ottilies Käseladen	Henriette Pfalzheim	Owner
58	PARIS	Paris spécialités	Marie Bertrand	Owner
59	PERIC	Pericles Comidas clásicas	Guillermo Fernández	Sales Representative
60	PICCO	Piccolo und mehr	Georg Pipps	Sales Manager
61	PRINI	Princesa Isabel Vinhos	Isabel de Castro	Sales Representative
62	QUEDE	Que Delícia	Bernardo Batista	Accounting Manager
63	QUEEN	Queen Cozinha	Lúcia Carvalho	Marketing Assistant
64	QUICK	QUICK-Stop	Horst Kloss	Accounting Manager
65	RANCH	Rancho grande	Sergio Gutiérrez	Sales Representative
66	RATTC	Rattlesnake Canyon Grocery	Paula Wilson	Assistant Sales Representative
67	REGGC	Reggiani Caseifici	Maurizio Moroni	Sales Associate
68	RICAR	Ricardo Adocicados	Janete Limeira	Assistant Sales Agent
69	RICSU	Richter Supermarkt	Michael Holz	Sales Manager
70	ROMEY	Romero y tomillo	Alejandra Camino	Accounting Manager
71	SANTG	Santé Gourmet	Jonas Bergulfsen	Owner
72	SAVEA	Save-a-lot Markets	Jose Pavarotti	Sales Representative

Fig. 7.33:   Frozen column headings

In Figure 7.33 you see a table with column headers that have been frozen up to row 1. You can see that the window was scrolled by the row headings: row 56 is displayed immediately underneath the first row.

Unfreeze Panes

In order to display the table in its original view, choose the *Window/Unfreeze Panes* command.

Print Field Names on Each Page

With the help of freezing panes you can make sure that the field names are permanently displayed on the screen. By setting the field names as a print title, you can also have them printed on each page.

In order to specify print titles for your table, choose *File/Page Setup* and open the *Sheet* tab page.

Rows to repeat
at top

In the *Print title* option group, click into the *Rows to repeat at top* box and then, in the worksheet, into the row which you want to print on each page. You can also select more than one row to be repeatedly printed.

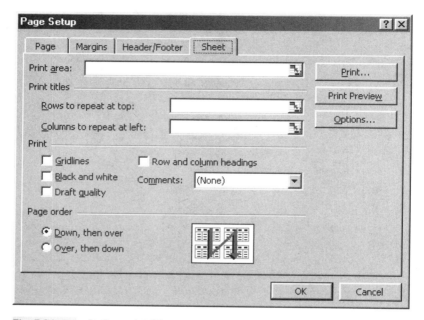

Fig. 7.34:   Define print titles

Use the button ⬚ next to the entry box for the row title to reduce the dialog box. After selecting your row, click on the 🗗 button to enlarge the dialog box again, and then confirm by clicking *OK*.

Delete print title

In order to delete the selected print title, choose *File/ Page Setup* once more and activate the *Sheet* tab page again. Select the entries in the *Rows to repeat at top* box and press the Delete key ⌊Del⌋. For more information on working with print titles, see Chapter 4.

8. Charts

Excel is not only the specialist in making formulas and calculations of all sorts, but *Excel* is also capable of displaying all the calculated data in the form of charts. A multitude of different types of charts is available, such as column, bar, line, area charts, as well as unusual shapes, like for example pie and radar charts.

Creating Charts

In the *97* version, the chart function of *Excel* has been simplified and equipped with some new features. There are two different kinds of charts in *Excel*:

- *Chart Sheets*
  This kind of chart is created on a separate worksheet which can be displayed and managed just like the table sheets in the workbook.

- *Embedded Charts*
  Embedded charts are inserted and displayed within a table sheet. They are run just like all the other embedded objects.

When you create a new chart, you have to decide upon one of the two kinds of charts. You can, however, change from one kind to the other at any time, i.e., you can turn an embedded chart into a separate chart sheet, or vice versa.

Creating a Chart Sheet

In *Excel 97*, the creation of a chart has become even more convenient. Now you can select the data which will become the basis of the new chart with the wizard, either before you start or while you are working on it. Moreover, you can alternate between the kind of chart, either an embedded chart or a chart on a separate chart sheet, any time.

Chart Wizard 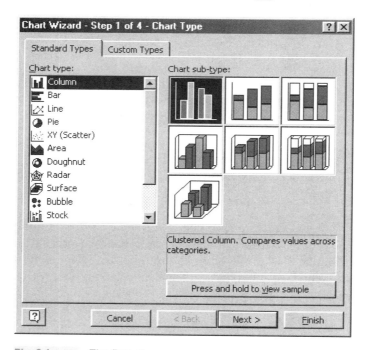   In addition, the variety of chart types has been extended. Before you activate the *Chart Wizard*, you should mark the data range for the chart. This will enable you to preview your chart with the selected formats in the dialog boxes of the *Chart Wizard*. In order to create a new chart on a separate chart sheet, choose *Insert/Chart* or click the *Chart Wizard* button.

Fig. 8.1:   The first step

The first step   In the first dialog box, choose the kind of chart you want to create from the *Chart Type* list. Depending on which category you select, its respective sub-types will be displayed on the right side. Click the button of the *Chart sub-type* you want.

If you had selected a data range before activating the assistant, you can now click the *Press and hold to view sample* button and keep the left mouse button pressed down in order to display a preview of the selected chart type with your data.

After you have selected the main and sub-type of your chart, click on *Next*.

The second step

In the second step you need to verify that *Excel* has correctly recognized the data range.

If necessary, switch from *Columns* to *Rows* or vice versa, if one type of presentation displays the data more clearly than the other.

In this dialog box you have the opportunity to select a (further) data range as source data for the chart by clicking on the 🖳 button, selecting the range, and then extending the dialog box again by clicking on the 🖼 button.

Tab page *Series*

In the *Series* tab page you can add data from other table ranges, or delete already displayed data series by using the *Add* and *Remove* buttons.

Click on *Add*, and into the *Name* and *Values* text boxes establish a reference by selecting those cells from which you want to take the name of an additional data series.

Name

If in your chart you want to use a name for your data series which differs from that in the table, overwrite the cell reference in the *Name* box with the name you want. In order to delete an already inserted data series, select it in the *Series* list box and press *Remove*.

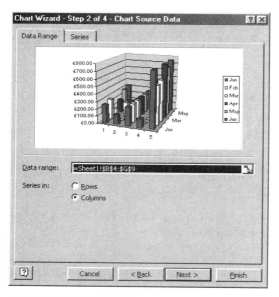

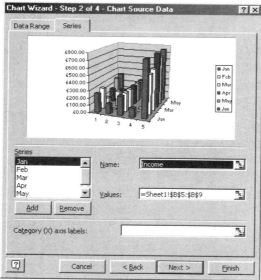

Fig. 8.2: The second step

When you have completed putting all your data together, click on the *Next* button. The following dialog box allows you to give a specific setting to all the elements of your new chart.

Titles tab page

On the *Titles* tab page, you can enter a title for the chart and, if your chart contains axes, enter individual labels for the axes into the corresponding text boxes.

Axes tab page

On the *Axes* tab page, you determine which axes are to be displayed.

Gridlines tab page

On the *Gridlines* tab page, you can modify the scale of the primary and secondary axes with gridlines.

Legend tab page

On the *Legend* tab page, you determine the placement of the legend. If you do not want a legend, clear the *Show Legend* check box.

Data Labels

tab page

Whether and which labels of the data series are to be displayed is determined on the *Data Labels* tab page.

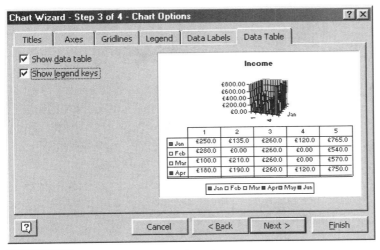

Fig. 8.3:   Data table to be displayed

379

Data Table tab
page

On the *Data Table* tab page, you can choose whether the underlying data is to be shown or not. Check the *Show Data Table* check box if you want the data to be displayed underneath the chart.

Chart Options

All the settings that you choose are only provisional and may be modified later on by using the *Chart/Chart Options* command. After you have made your selection from the chart options, click on the *Next >* button.

As new sheet

As a last step you have to decide whether you want to insert the data as an embedded object in your worksheet or as a new sheet. Click on the *As new sheet* radio button to create the chart on a separate chart sheet.

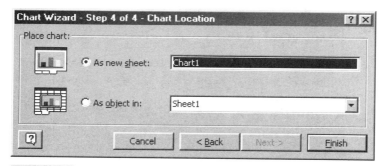

Fig. 8.4:   The last step for a chart sheet

The chart sheet is inserted into the workbook in front of the current worksheet. The name you gave in the dialog box of step 4 of the *Chart Wizard* is immediately displayed in the sheet tab.

You can move the chart sheet using drag-and-drop to another position in the sheet tab and edit it by using the commands already explained in the context of table worksheets.

Creating an Embedded Chart

If you do not want to give a chart its own chart sheet in the workbook, but rather to display it within a worksheet, you create the chart as an embedded object.

Chart Wizard 📖   To do this, select the relevant table range containing the data from which you want to create the chart and then select either *Insert/Chart* or click the *Chart Wizard* button 📖.

Then choose in the next steps the main type and the sub-types of your embedded chart. Check whether *Excel* has correctly recognized the assignment of the data series as well as the labels of the axes.

In the preview, you can check the effects a change has on the chart. As a third step type a chart title and enter labels for the axes, if there are any axes in your chart.

After you have completed this procedure in the chart options dialog, click again on the *Next* button. Finally, select the *As Object in* radio button, and select the worksheet in which the chart is to be embedded from the drop-down list box to the right of it.

After you have done this, close the *Chart Wizard* by clicking on the *Finish* button. In order to change the size of the embedded chart, first click anywhere within the chart.

Then drag the border of the chart using one of the selection handles which you see at the sides and in the corners, until you have the size you want.

An embedded chart has to be selected in order to change its position. Click on the chart and while holding down the mouse drag it to another position in the worksheet.

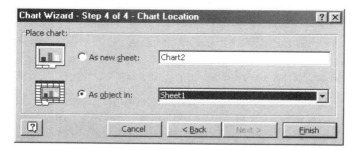

Fig. 8.5: Fig. 8.5:   The last step for an embedded chart

Transferring an Embedded Chart onto a Separate Chart Sheet

Even if you originally decided upon an embedded chart while creating it, this does not mean that you cannot change your mind later on. You can at any time transform an embedded chart into a separate chart sheet and vice versa.

In *Excel 97*, it's child's play to transform an embedded chart into a new chart sheet or vice versa. First, select the embedded chart by clicking on it.

Location

As new sheet

Select *Chart/Location*, and choose the *As new sheet* radio button. If you want to give a name to the new chart sheet right now, overwrite the entry in the text box to the right with the desired name. Close the dialog box by clicking on the *OK* button.

As object in

You can change the chart on its own chart sheet back into an embedded object. Choose *Chart/Location*. This time click the *As object in* radio button.

Select the sheet in which you want to place the embedded chart from the drop-down list box to the right, and click on *OK*.

Defining the Properties of an Embedded Chart

Like any other embedded object, an embedded chart's size and position can be edited. The positioning and any change in its size can be done using the mouse. The size and position can be determined either according to, or independently of, the cell.

After activating the chart, choose *Format/Selected Chart Area*. To position the object, display the *Properties* tab page in order to make the position of the chart dependent on a certain cell.

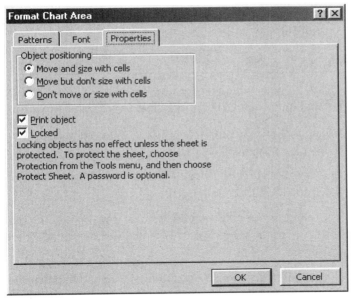

Fig. 8.6:   Setting the object positioning

In the *Object Positioning* option group box you can choose from three different options:

▪ *Move and size with cells*
Select this option in order to move the embedded chart together with the cells below and to adjust the chart automatically to their change of size.

▪ *Move but don't size with cells*
With this option you can associate the position of an embedded chart with the cells below. If you move these cells, the chart will automatically be moved along with it.

▪ *Don't move or size with cells*
Click this radio button in order to fix the size and the position of the embedded chart independently of the cells below.

Changing the Size of an Embedded Chart

Chart objects which are embedded in a worksheet are printed in the same size in which they are displayed.

Changing their size on the worksheet therefore immediately affects the size of the printout.

In order to change the size of an embedded chart, click on the embedded chart to select it.

The chart is now displayed with a thin border. On all sides and at the corners of this frame resizing handles are displayed.

If you point the mouse on one of the resize handles, the mouse pointer changes into a double-headed arrow ↔.

Press and hold down the mouse button and drag the chart with this double-headed arrow to the desired size.

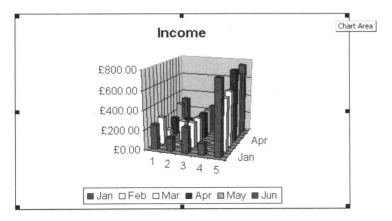

The selection handles

Changing the Position of an Embedded Chart

In order to change the position of an embedded chart, point onto the selected chart. Make sure that the *ScreenTip* shows *Chart Area* as a description so that you do not accidentally move a single element of the chart within the chart.

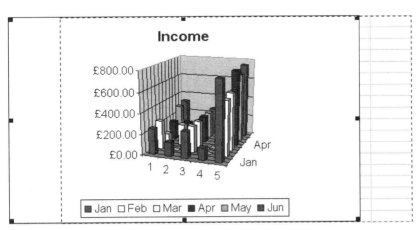

Changing the position of an embedded chart

385

Press and hold the mouse button down. The mouse cursor turns into a four-headed arrow. Now drag the embedded chart to the desired position, and release the mouse button.

Changing the Display Size of Chart Sheets

You can change the display size of a chart sheet by selecting a different zoom value in the zoom drop-down list, or via the *Zoom* dialog box on the *View* menu, following the same procedure which you use for a table worksheet. For further details see Chapter 6.

Sized with window

Alternatively, you can click the *View/Sized with window* command so that the chart size is always adjusted to the respective window size. A chart sized with the window cannot be zoomed.

Printing the Chart

A chart sheet is printed out on a separate page. An embedded chart is normally printed within the table worksheet in which it is displayed. In *Excel 97* you can, however, print out an embedded chart on a separate sheet as well.

Deciding the Size of the Printout

The print size of chart sheets can be selected from a special tab in the *Page Setup* dialog box. Select the chart sheet by clicking its sheet tab. Then select *File/Page Setup*. In the dialog box, activate the *Chart* tab page. This tab page is only available if you have selected a chart sheet or an embedded chart beforehand.

In the *Printed Chart Size* option group you can determine the size of the chart which will be printed.

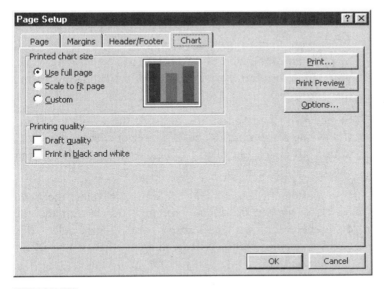

▣ Select the *Use full page* option, if you want the chart to fill the entire page. This selection may distort the proportions of the chart.

▣ Click the *Scale to fit page* radio button, if you want to adjust the chart to the page size you are using, yet want to maintain the proportions of height and width. With this selection, the chart does not necessarily fill the entire page.

▣ Select *Custom* if you want to decide upon the size of the printout by setting the size of the chart in the window.

Via window size

Should you choose the latter option, you can size the chart in the chart sheet itself. If you select the chart and change its size, you can view the resulting printout in the *Print Preview*.

Printing Options for Charts

When you want to print out a chart sheet, or if you want to print an embedded chart on a separate printing page, you can determine the printing quality of the chart using the *Chart* tab.

Printing quality

Select *File/Page Setup*, and activate the *Chart* tab page. Check the *Draft quality* check box in the *Printing quality* option group if you need a quick draft printout of your chart.

Print in

black and white

If you are using a black and white printer, select the *Print in black and white* check box in order to replace the different colors with patterns. If you do not select this check box, the colors will be displayed in a variety of shades of grey.

Print Preview

From the *Page Setup* dialog box, you can, with a click, move directly to the *Print Preview* in order to check the effects of changing the printing quality.

Printing an Embedded Chart on a Separate Chart Sheet

In *Excel 97,* you can print an embedded chart within a table worksheet or alternatively on a separate page. How it is printed out depends on whether or not it has been selected before you give the print command.

Select/

Deselect

Click into the worksheet to deselect an embedded chart. A deselected chart will be printed within the worksheet. If you click onto the chart to select it, the chart will be printed as a separate page.

Editing the Chart Source Data

While creating a new chart, in the *Chart Wizard* dialog box you will find a tab page on which you decide from which cells the data is to be taken and how the data series as well as the chart titles are to be displayed. In order to change the references to the source data after you have completed the new chart, select *Chart/Source Data*. The *Source Data* dialog box contains two tabs, *Data Range* and *Series*.

Arranging the data range

In the *Data Range* tab, you can change the reference to the cell range of the table from which the values and labels for the chart are being taken. Here you can also determine whether the data series are to be taken from the *rows* or from the *columns* of the cell range.

Series tab

In the *Series* tab, you can select more detailed options for the display of the labels and the data series. You can:

- Add or remove dependent or independent series.
- Change the reference for the label of a data series.
- Change the reference for the values of the data series.
- Rename a data series.
- Change the label of the data series in the category axis.

Add

The names of existing data series are displayed in the *Data Series* list box. In order to add a new data series, click the *Add* button. In the *Name*, *Values*, and *Labels* text boxes, you can now enter the references to those cells from which *Excel* is supposed to take the values and labels for the new data series.

Independent *Name* and *Values*

Likewise, if you want to insert the new data row into the chart independent of its basic table, you can, as an alternative, enter a name directly into the *Name* text box. In the *Values* box, matrix parentheses will automatically appear. Type the respective values into these parentheses and separate them by commas.

Remove

In order to remove an already existing data series from the chart, select its name in the *Data series* list and click the *Remove* button.

Add or Delete Chart Elements

Already while creating a new chart you have the opportunity to decide whether or not you want to show certain elements in the chart, such as gridlines for example, or a title or a legend.

The settings you specify while creating the chart are not final. At any time later on you can change your mind and decide to display an additional element in the chart or remove an already existing one.

Insert Labels into a Chart

While making a new chart, you can decide whether you want to insert a chart title or axes labels. You have the opportunity to enter the corresponding text.

Should you have decided against inserting these labels while creating the chart, or if you have removed them from the chart, you can still put them back in again later on.

Title and
free text

Regarding the labels of a chart you have to distinguish between text which are assigned to a chart element, like for example the chart title or the labels of the value axis on the one hand, and any free text on the other.

Insert Titles

In order to insert a title for a chart element, choose *Chart/ Chart Options* for a selected chart, and activate the *Titles* tab.

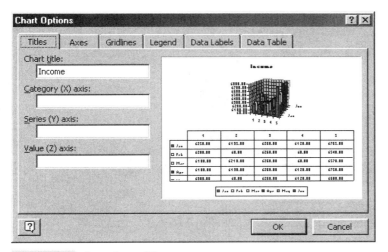

Fig. 8.10: Inserting a title

Now type the desired text for the title directly into the appropriate text box.

▦ Text which you enter into the *Chart Title* text box will be displayed centered above the chart.

▦ Titles that you enter into the *Category Axis* text box will be shown underneath, or next to, the category axis respectively.

▦ A title which you type into the *Value Axis* text box will be inserted next to, or underneath, the value axis respectively.

▦ In a 3-D chart with several series, you can also label the series axis. The title which you type into the *Series Axis* text box will appear to the right of the series axis.

After you have closed the dialog box by clicking on *OK*, *Excel* will insert text boxes for the titles of the corresponding elements at the standard positions.

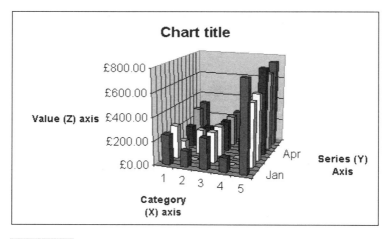

Fig. 8.11: The titles in the chart

If you want to edit the text in a text box later on, first click on the text in order to display the editing border of the text box, then click into the text box itself.

Formatting the
chart title

You can edit the text of a title with the normal commands and buttons for the formatting of fonts. With a double-click on a title you can open the *Format Chart Title* dialog box, or the *Format Axis Title* dialog box respectively, and then change the appearance by giving shadows, a background, or changing the alignment of the text.

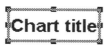

Fig. 8.12: A selected title

Instead of double-clicking you can just as well choose the *Format/Selected Chart Title*, or *Format/Selected Axis Title* command respectively. You can move a title to another position in the chart with the mouse by dragging the text box to where you want it to appear.

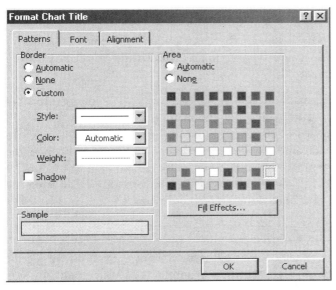

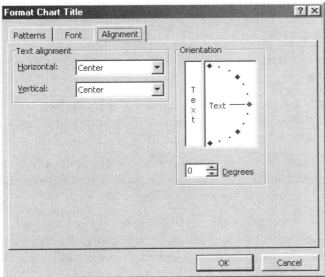

Inserting Free Text

In order to insert free text, click in the chart selected for editing, and type your text. Finish the entry by pressing Enter ⏎.

The text will first be displayed in the editing box, but after confirming the action by pressing Enter ⏎ it will appear in a text box. Point at the text box and move it to the desired position in the chart. You can change the alignment, frame, patterns, color, etc. of the text by double-clicking on the frame of the text box or by choosing the *Format/Selected XY Title* command.

Inserting and Deleting Axes in the Chart

Charts can contain either no axis or a changing variety of axes. A circle chart, for example, does not contain any axis at all, since its values do not scale in proportion to an axis, but instead in proportion to each segment of the whole circle.

In a two-dimensional chart, there is normally a value axis and a category axis.

A three-dimensional chart with more than one data series contains an additional series axis. Each of these axes can be shown or hidden.

Additional axis

In charts in which you want to display values whose ranges differ greatly, you can insert an additional axis for the differing row (or rows) of data.

To show or hide axes, select the chart or click on the tab of the chart sheet and select *Chart/Chart Options*. In the *Axes* tab then check or clear the corresponding check boxes in order to show or hide the axes. In *Excel 97* you can enter a label for a newly dubbed axis directly on the *Titles* tab.

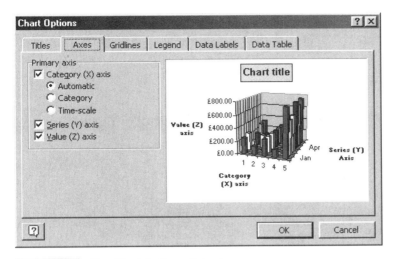

Insert an Additional Secondary Axis

When you create a chart containing a data series of greatly differing value ranges, you should insert an additional axis for the deviating data row (or rows) to facilitate the interpretation.

Secondary axis

The first value axis is called the primary axis, while the additional value axis is termed the secondary axis. Secondary axes can only be established for two-dimensional charts.

Composite chart

In the first step, make a composite chart. Select the deviating data row (or rows). Then select a presentation style for the deviating series in the *Chart* toolbar drop-down list. For example, choose the line chart type, if the other data rows are currently displayed as columns.

Primary axis

After this procedure, all data series are automatically assigned to the primary axis, with the additional axis therefore not yet visible.The moment you assign the first data row to the secondary axis, it will appear on the screen. Now click on the data series and select *Format/Selected Data Series*. Activate the *Axis* tab and in the *Plot series on* option group box, select the *Secondary Axis* radio button.

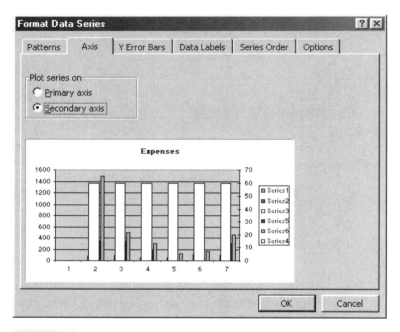

Fig. 8.15:   The additional secondary axis

You can check the effect of the change immediately in the dialog box. The new axis is now inserted. If you agree with the displayed result, close the dialog box by clicking *OK*.

Insert Data Series into a Chart

When you make a chart, you determine from which table cells the data for the new chart is going to be taken, by selecting the cell range, or by stating the cell references.

Excel then automatically builds the data series from the values given there.

Series from rows or columns

If the data table contains more rows than columns, the series will be made from the columns. If the table contains more columns than rows, *Excel* will make the series from rows.

If you add data to the worksheet area your chart is based upon, you do not need to remake the chart, but can instead transfer the values added to the table into the chart. The easiest way to expand your chart is to insert a new data series between the existing ones. In this case, *Excel* extends the chart automatically with the inserted series.

Insert/rows

In order to include an additional row into the table, activate the row on top of which you want to insert the new data series. Then choose *Insert/Rows* or *Insert/Columns*. *Excel* moves the existing data in the table in a way that gives space for the series to be inserted.

Copy

Alternatively, you can attach new data at the end of the existing table and then copy it into the chart. To do this, select the cells containing the label and the values of the data series.

Then click the button or choose the *Edit/Copy* command, and select the embedded chart or the separate chart sheet by clicking once.

Paste

Now choose *Edit/Paste Special*. Select the *New Series* radio button in the *Add cells as* group box. If the label for the data series is given in the first line of the selected range, check the *Series Names in first line* box.

If you selected more than one row or column, you should now state in the *Values in* option group box whether the series values are taken from the selected columns or rows.

397

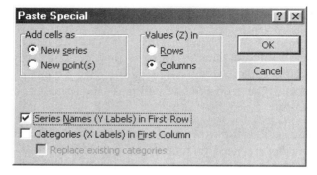

Fig. 8.16: Inserting data series

After you have closed the dialog box by clicking *OK*, the new data series is inserted.

Drag-and-drop   In many cases, it is also possible to add data series to a chart by using drag-and-drop. Select the data series and drag it into the chart.

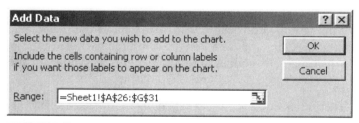

Fig. 8.17:   Adding new data

Adding new data   In addition, *Excel 97* is equipped with a new command which you can use to transfer additional data series from the table into the chart. Choose *Chart/Add Data* in order to open the *Add Data* dialog box.

Next to the entry box there is the ⬛ button which minimizes the dialog box. Click this button and then the tab page of the table.

Select the data row(s) you want to add. By later clicking on the ▣ button you can restore the dialog box to its original size. Select your cell range and confirm with *OK*.

Delete Data Rows

If you want to delete a data row from the chart, you need not go into its basic table. You can delete it independently of the table.

To delete data series from a chart, select the embedded chart for editing by clicking on any point inside. A separate chart sheet can be selected by clicking on the sheet tab.

Undo: Clear

Then click on the data series you want to remove and press the ⌈Del⌉ key. The data series in the chart is deleted. Should you have accidentally deleted the wrong data series, choose *Edit/Undo:Clear*.

If this is not possible anymore because you did too many other operations after the deletion, then select the corresponding column or row in the basic table, copy the data, and insert it once again into the chart by using the *Edit/Paste Special* command.

Delete series

Instead of pressing the ⌈Del⌉ key, you can also use the *Edit/Clear/Series* command in order to remove selected data rows from the chart.

Changing the Assignment of Values to Data Rows

In the *Chart* toolbar, you will find two new buttons. With their help you can quickly change the assignment of values of the basic table to the data series. Click the *By Row* button ▣, in order to build the data series from the table cells of the underlying table. Click the *By Column* button ▣, in order to build the data series from the table columns of the underlying basic table.

Inserting Gridlines into the Chart

Charts which contain axes are often easier to read if you insert gridlines which facilitate the assignment of the respective data to the axes for the viewer. The assignment to the category axis is important; more important though is the assignment to the value axis which, as a reference point for the values of the data series, displays a scale. This scale may consist of main and also additional supporting lines.

Major and minor gridlines

The gridlines into which you insert a chart further extend the main and the supporting lines of the axis. You can assign a gridline to the main lines as well as to the supporting ones.

The gridline you assign to the main lines is called a major gridline, while the other one is termed a minor gridline. The minor gridlines will be inserted only to the extent that the supporting lines are shown on the axis.

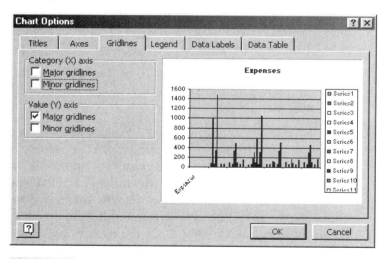

Fig. 8.18:   Inserting gridlines

Many charts are already equipped with gridlines by default. As for the other charts, you can show or hide the gridlines later on by using the chart options. Select *Chart/Chart Options*, and click the *Gridlines* tab.

Select the check boxes for the gridlines you want to show, and clear the check boxes for the gridlines you do not want to be displayed.

Close the dialog box by clicking *OK*. You can change the setting of the gridlines anytime.

With a double-click onto one of the inserted gridlines you can open the *Format Gridlines* dialog box, and therein change the scale as well as the patterns of the gridlines.

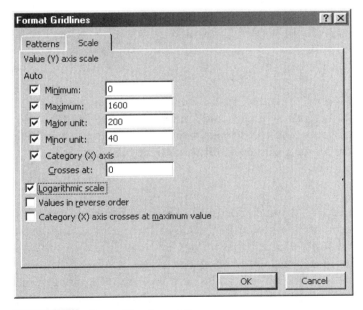

Fig. 8.19: Formatting the gridlines

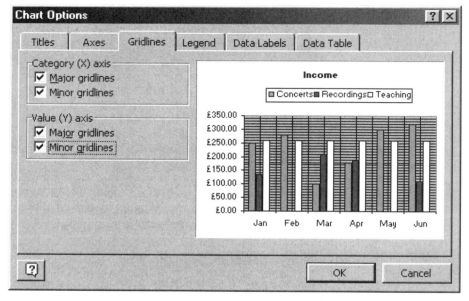

Fig. 8.20:   A chart with minor gridlines

Figure 8.20 shows a chart which contains vertical as well as horizontal major and minor gridlines. In this case, however, the chart looks rather confusing, and therefore the minor gridlines could better have been hidden.

In *Excel 97*, the button for gridlines contained in the earlier versions is missing in the *Chart* toolbar. You can insert the *Category Axis Gridlines* and *Value Axis Gridlines* buttons by using the *Tools/Customize* command. Activate the *Commands* tab and select the *Charting* category in order to display the list of available buttons. Drag the buttons onto a toolbar. Use the two buttons to show or hide the gridlines more quickly.

Show or Hide the Legend

A legend explains the data series on a chart. For each data series, in a circular chart, a column chart or a bar chart, with only one row of data respectively, it shows the data points and their corresponding pattern or colors. If the data series or the data points are satisfactorily labelled, you can hide the legend.

When to show a legend?

If there is not enough space for a label for the data points or the data series, or if for any other reason you do not want to display any labels, you should show a legend in the chart.

When you create a chart with the *Chart Wizard*, you can determine whether or not the chart should contain a legend. You can also add or remove a legend at any time later on. In order to add a legend to your chart, choose *Chart/Chart Options* and open the *Legend* tab. Select the *Show Legend* check box.

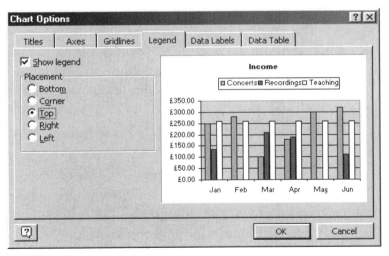

Fig. 8.21: Inserting and placing a legend

Placement

When you check the check box, the option radio buttons of the *Placement* option group are enabled. Click one of the radio buttons to determine where you want the legend to be displayed, and close by clicking *OK*.

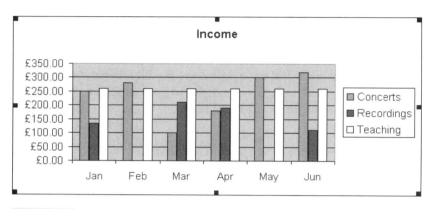

Fig. 8.22:   Chart with a legend

You can remove a legend from your chart by clicking on the legend and pressing the ⌈Del⌉ key.

Showing or Hiding a Data Table

A new feature in *Excel 97* is the option to display a chart along with the basic table containing the data from which the chart is made.

Already while creating the chart, you can decide upon a chart type which contains this data table.

Show data table

In order to show or hide the data table later on, choose *Chart/Chart Options* and open the *Data Table* tab.

Select the *Show Data Table* check box to show the data table, or clear the check box in order to hide it.

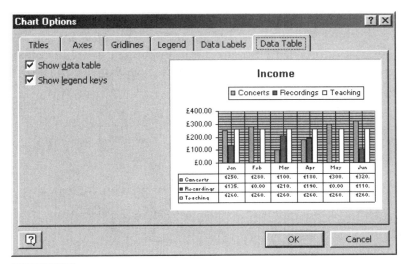

Fig. 8.23:   Show data table

Show legend keys   If in your chart you already have a legend, you can suppress the pattern or color keys in the data table by clearing the *Show Legend Keys* check box. After you click *OK*, the data table can be formatted by using the usual formatting commands.

Instead of using the *Chart/Chart Options* command and then clicking the check box on the *Data Table* tab, you can also just click the *Data Table* button in the *Chart* toolbar in order to show or hide a data table.

Formatting Chart Elements

When you want to format a chart element, the first step is to select the chart. After the chart is selected, you have to select the chart element to be formatted. To do this in *Excel 97*, a simple click on the element is sufficient. A chart sheet is selected by clicking on its sheet tab.

The number and type of chart elements which are displayed in a chart depends on the selected chart type. A circular chart for example has no axes, but a 3-D chart may contain the series axis as a third axis. A chart consists of the following main elements:

- *Chart Title* (the headline of the chart)

- *Chart Area* (the area within the chart frame)

- *Drawing Area* (the area among the axes)

- *Data Series* (e.g., a column series, a line series)

- *Data Points* (the value of a cell in the data series)

- *Y-Axis* (contains as default the units of measurement)

- *X-Axis* (contains as default the categories)

- *Z-Axis* (the series axis, only in a 3-D chart)

- *Gridlines* (major and minor gridlines)

- *Legend* (contains the reference of the descriptions to the data series)

- *Data table*

To get an overview of the respective components of a chart simply point to a certain element after selecting the chart.

In *Excel 97*, it is enough to point with the mouse pointer at a chart element. A *ScreenTip* will automatically be displayed, giving the name and, for some elements like data series and points, additional information on its background.

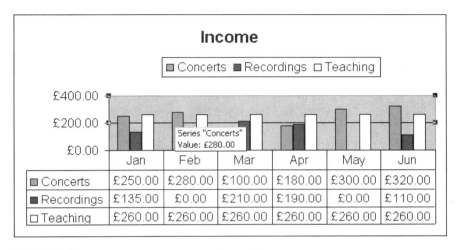

Income

Legend: □ Concerts ■ Recordings □ Teaching

	Jan	Feb	Mar	Apr	May	Jun
■ Concerts	£250.00	£280.00	£100.00	£180.00	£300.00	£320.00
■ Recordings	£135.00	£0.00	£210.00	£190.00	£0.00	£110.00
□ Teaching	£260.00	£260.00	£260.00	£260.00	£260.00	£260.00

Fig. 8.24:   Chart with data table and *ScreenTip*

In order to format an element, double-click on the element. The formatting command changes according to which element is selected.

Select for example the chart area and choose *Format/ Selected Chart Area*. Or double-click on the chart area. Or just click the right mouse button, and then choose the command to format the object from the shortcut menu. For further information read the topics on the respective chart elements.

Format Labels

For chart titles, free text or chart elements like data tables, axes or legends, all of which contain labels, you can determine the font, the size and other text formatting options.

If you select a chart element and choose the *Format/ Selected 'Object'* command, or if you click the *Format 'Object'* button on the *Chart* toolbar, the dialog box for the respective element will be displayed, containing the

Font tab. There you will find the usual list boxes for the choice of font, style, size, color, underlining and other effects.

Auto Scale

Normally, *Excel 97* scales the size of the labels in proportion to the size of the chart, or with respect to the object to which the label belongs. Clear the *Auto Scale* check box in order to deactivate this automatic calibration and instead set the formatting yourself.

Background

In the *Background* drop-down list box you can determine whether the background of the text should be chosen automatically by *Excel* depending on the font color, or whether it should be transparent or opaque.

Format Axes

Each axis in a chart can be changed and adapted precisely to the specific requirements of the user. *Excel* automatically takes the labels from the data table which forms the basis of the chart. The scale of an axis can be changed, as can the other chart elements in order to make the visual appearance of the chart more clear, for example by showing or hiding intermediate values.

In order to change an axis, select the chart for editing. If the chart is embedded, a simple click is sufficient. A separate chart sheet can be selected by clicking its sheet tab.

Format Axis

Then double-click on the axis you want to change. The *Format Axis* dialog box will be called up. In order to change the scale of the selected axis, activate the *Scale* tab.

Minimum and
Maximum

Now you can change the various elements of the selected axis. The beginning and end points of the axis are determined by the values given in the *Minimum* and *Maximum* box. The distance between the values displayed on the axis is determined by the major tick marks. In order to change the space between the values, increase or decrease the the values in the *Major unit* text box. These values are oriented along with the values of the table.

Minor Tick Mark

In addition to the major tick marks, a minor tick mark can be displayed for the value axis. For a minor tick mark, the distance can be changed in the *Minor unit* text box.

In order to display the minor tick marks, activate the *Pattern* tab page and in the *Tick Mark Labels* option group box, change from *None* to the desired position of the tick marks.

Value axis
crosses
category axis

For the value axis, you can also decide at which value the category axis is to cross the value axis. Only in exceptional cases will you need to define a value other than zero. For the category axis, you can decide at which category the value axis crosses the category axis.

Format
series axis

In a 3-D chart that contains the series axis as a third axis, you can change the number of series between the tick mark labels and the tick marks, and display the data series in reverse order.

To easily assign values to the axis, show the gridlines for major and minor tick marks by choosing *Chart/Chart Options*, and activating the *Gridlines* tab.

Formatting a Data Series

If you have included additional data series in a chart, or if you do not like the existing format any more, you can change the outward appearance of a data series.

All the elements in a data series contains the same values of the category they belong to, which means for example that all columns or bars or lines in a line chart are displayed in the same color.

In order to modify a data series, you first have to select it. Select the chart for editing, and click on any point on the data series.

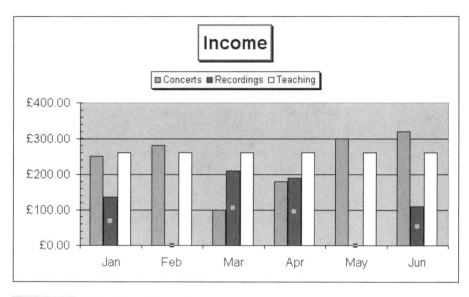

Selecting a data series

Then choose *Format/Data Series*. Instead of using the command from the *Format* menu you can also double-click the data series or right-click and choose the *Format Data Series* command from the shortcut menu.

Data Label

In the dialog box, you can determine the color and pattern for the selected data series and, if the chart is a two-dimensional one which contains axes, you can also decide upon the assignment to a primary or an additional secondary axis.

A secondary axis may be used for those data series whose values differ extremely from those of other series. You can determine whether you want to give a label to the data series by choosing the corresponding option on the *Data Labels* tab page. After setting the desired formatting close the dialog box by clicking *OK*.

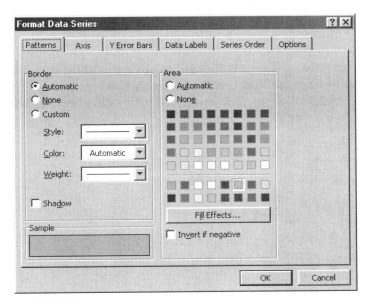

Formatting the selected data series

Formatting Data Points

A chart always contains at least one, and in most cases several data series. A data series is made up of several data points. You can format each data series of a chart, but also every single data point within the series. In a column chart, each data point forms a column. If the chart contains only one data series, you may, for example, choose a different color or a different pattern for each data point. You can change the following settings for a selected data point:

- pattern
- border
- color
- label

In order to format a data point, you must select it. First select the embedded chart. Then click the data series to which the data point belongs. Finally click again, this time on the data point.

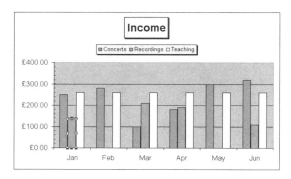

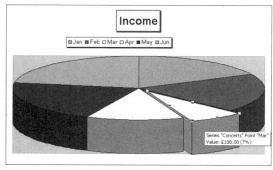

Fig. 8.27:   Selected data points

Double-click the selected data point or choose *Format/Data Point*. In the dialog box you can now change the setting of the various elements of the data point.

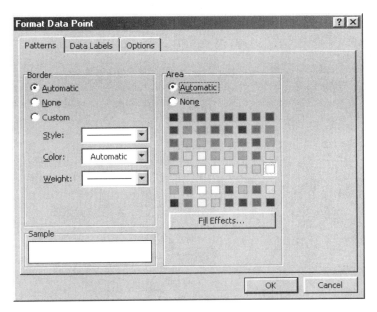

Fig. 8.28: Formatting a data point

Formatting Gridlines

In order to format the inserted major or minor gridlines, either double-click on one of these lines, or click the right mouse button and choose *Format Gridlines*.

The *Scale* tab affords you the option of scaling the axis to which the selected gridlines belong. The options you can choose from have already been introduced in the section on formatting axes.

Custom

On the *Patterns* tab, change from *Automatic* to *Custom* in the *Line* option group box. Then, from the drop-down list boxes, choose the *Style*, *Color* and *Weight* in which you want to display the selected gridlines.

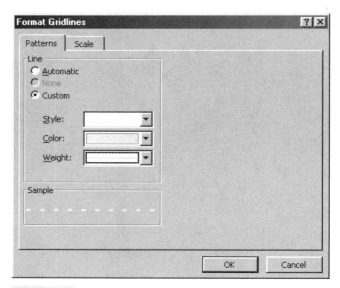

Fig. 8.29:   Formatting gridlines

In the *Sample* box, you can view the changes you made. If the results displayed there correspond to your idea of what you want the chart to look like, then close the dialog box by clicking *OK*.

Formatting a Data Table

Just like all the other elements of a chart, you can also display the data table in various ways. If you want to format the data table differently from the standard options, click on the data table or, in the *Chart* toolbar, choose the *Data Table* item in the *Chart Objects* drop-down list box.

Fig. 8.30: The selected data table

Font tab

Then choose *Format/Selected Data Table* or click the *Format Data Table* button. The *Format Data Table* dialog box contains two tabs. On the *Font* tab you will find the usual options for setting the fonts, style, size, color, etc. of the data table.

Formatting a Chart or a Chart Element with Fill Effects

You can insert a picture or a pattern as a background for a chart, a chart area, or into two- or three-dimensional chart objects. To do this, select the chart area or the appropriate chart element, such as:

- a data series

- a data point

- walls or floor of a 3-D-chart

- plot area of a surface chart

- background of a legend

In order to insert a picture as a background into a chart or a chart element, choose *Format/Selected Chart Area* or the command for the selected chart element. The *Format* dialog box will be opened, and the *Patterns* tab page will be active. Click the *Fill Effects* button in the *Area* group box to call up the *Fill Effects* dialog box.

The Gradient tab   The *Colors* option group box on the *Gradient* tab enables you to give *One color* or *Two colors* to the background of the selected element. In the *Shading Styles* option group box you can select the gradient fill style for the selected colors.

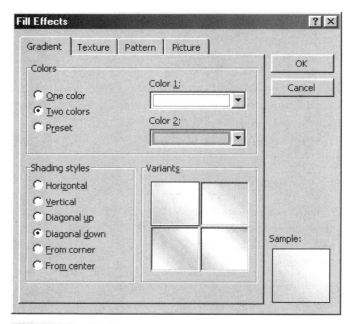

Fig. 8.31:   Fill effects

Preset colors   If you decide upon *Preset* in the *Colors* option group box, a list of predefined color sets will be displayed in the *Preset colors* drop-down list.

The Pattern tab   In order to fill the selected element with a pattern, select the *Pattern* tab. There you will find a multitude of buttons representing different patterns, as well as two boxes for determining the foreground and background colors for the selected pattern.

In order to insert a picture, select the *Picture* tab and click the *Select Picture* button. Select the type of picture files to display, then select the name of the picture file, and click *OK*.

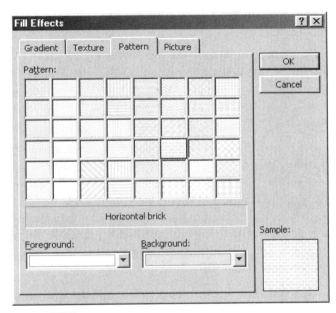

Fig. 8.32: Inserting a pattern

The Texture tab

On the *Texture* tab, you find various buttons with the help of which you can choose from a variety of predefined textures. Alternatively you can click the *Other Textures* button and make your choice from graphic files in which you have saved additional textures.

Delete fill effects

If you want to, you can later on clear the selected fill effects. Select the chart or the chart element, choose the *Format/Selected Chart Area* command, and in the *Pattern* tab select the *None* radio button in the option group box.

Deleting Formatting from a Chart

In *Excel 97*, there is an easy way to remove all the formatting you added to a chart or chart element. In order to delete the formatting which you added to the complete chart and to return to its original default settings, select the chart.

Undo Format

If you want to remove only the formatting which you have given to a certain chart element, select this element. Then choose *Edit/Undo Format*. All customized formatting is removed, and the selected element is displayed once again in its automatic format.

Chart Types

In *Excel*, there is a host of predefined choices for giving a shape to both tables and charts, which you can then further modify according to your requirements. In *Excel 97* these settings are not called *AutoFormat* anymore, but instead they are now termed *Chart Types*.

Customized
chart types

Excel distinguishes between the standard and the additional customized chart types which you can create yourself. If you have made a chart and adapted it to your particular ideas and needs, you can save its formatting in a customized chart type so that for other charts you might want to make in future you do not have to repeat the entire procedure again.

Standard Chart Types

In order to display or to use the standard chart types, choose *Chart/Chart Types* and activate the *Standard Types* tab. Select then the desired type from the *Chart Types* list and choose the corresponding chart sub-type which is shown on the right by clicking on it.

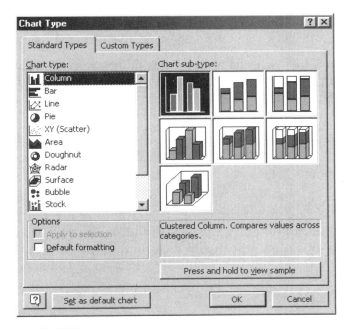

In *Excel 97*, in the list of the standard chart types as well on the *Custom Types* tab, you will find a broad range of new chart types, like for example:

- Bubble Chart
- Stock Chart
- Cylinder Chart
- Cone Chart
- Pyramid Chart

Description

In the *Chart Type* dialog box underneath the buttons for the sub-types, you will find a box in which the description of the select chart type is given.

419

Change
standard type

If you select a chart and then open the *Chart Type* dialog box, you can assign a different standard type to the chart.

Apply to selection

If you have selected a data series in an already created chart, you may choose a different type for this data series. In this case, check the *Apply to selection* check box in the *Options* group.

Default Formatting

In order to re-establish the standard format of a chart type or of a selected chart element, click the *Default formatting* check box in the same option group.

Customized Chart Types

In order to save the formatting of a chart as a new chart type, first create a chart which contains the exact formatting you are likely to want to use more often in the future.

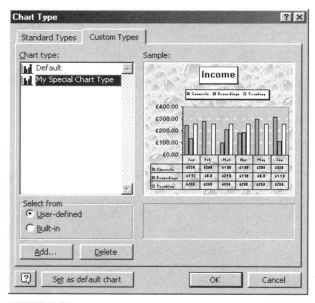

Fig. 8.34:   Creating a new chart type

Select from

Choose *Chart/Chart Type* and open the *Custom Types* tab. In the *Select from* option box click the *User-defined* radio button.

Add

Then click the *Add* button. A dialog box appears. Type the name you want to give to the new custom chart type in the *Name* box. In the box underneath that, enter its description.

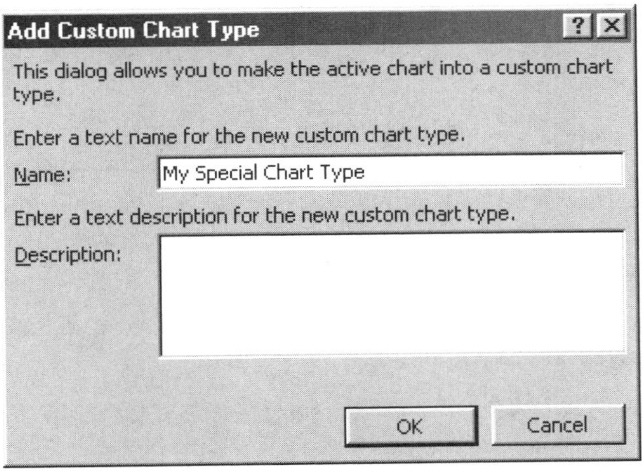

Add Custom Chart Type

This dialog allows you to make the active chart into a custom chart type.

Enter a text name for the new custom chart type.

Name: `My Special Chart Type`

Enter a text description for the new custom chart type.

Description:

OK   Cancel

Fig. 8.35:   Creating an Chart Type in *Excel 97*

Name and description

The name can contain up to 31 characters, while the description can contain up to 250 characters. Confirm the name for the new custom chart type by clicking *OK*, and close the *Chart type* dialog box by clicking *OK* as well.

Transferring AutoFormat

In *Excel 97*, in order to apply a saved chart type to a chart, choose *Chart/Chart Type*, select the *Custom Types* tab and then select the *User-defined* option button. Select the desired format in the *Chart type* list box, and click *OK*.

Default Chart Type

With the installation of *Excel 97*, you automatically have a default chart type. This default type will be assigned to a chart if you do not select any specific chart type but switch off the *Chart Wizard* beforehand.

**Built-in
default type**

The original default chart type consists of a two-dimensional column chart. You can choose any other chart type for your personal default type and later go back to the built-in default type.

Setting a New Standard Chart Type

In order to set a new default type, create a chart with the formatting elements which you want the default chart type to display in future.

In *Excel 97*, you can carry out the changes to a default chart type directly in the *Chart Type* dialog box.

User-defined

Choose *Chart/Chart type* and activate the *Custom Types* tab. Select the desired chart type from the list, or select the *User-defined* option button. In this case the selected chart will be displayed in the sample box.

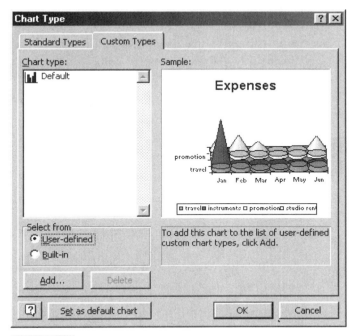

Setting a user-defined default chart

Set as default

chart

Click the *Set as default chart* button. You will be asked to confirm that you really want to replace the default chart type by a user-defined chart type.

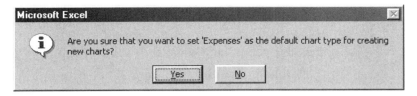

Fig. 8.37: Confirming the new chart type

In the dialog box, click on *Yes*, in order to change the default type. Close the *Chart Type* dialog box by clicking *OK*.

Resetting the Built-in Default Chart Type

If later on you want to reactivate the built-in chart type, choose *Chart/Chart Type* and select the *Custom Types* tab. Click the *User-defined* option button and then select the name you gave to the chart type in the *Chart Type* list. Click the *Delete* button.

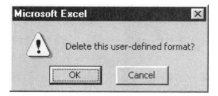

Fig. 8.38:   Resetting the built-in default type

Again, you will have to confirm the procedure by clicking on the *OK* button.

Using the Chart Toolbar

An embedded chart is displayed within the table worksheet. In order to edit such a chart, first point to the sheet tab that it is found on and then click.

In *Excel 97*, if you want to select an embedded chart in order to work on it, you simply have to click on it. A thin border appears around the chart with resize handles.

When you select an embedded chart for editing, the *Chart* toolbar shows buttons for the *Chart*.

Use these buttons on the toolbar in order to show or hide elements of the chart.

Use the toolbar buttons in order to quickly change the chart type or show or hide gridlines and the legend.

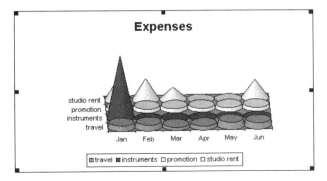

Fig. 8.39: The selected chart

In *Excel 97,* some buttons have disappeared from the *Chart* toolbar and others have been inserted. The button for the *Chart Wizard* can now be found on the *Standard* toolbar.

Fig. 8.40: The Chart toolbar

You can use the *Chart Objects* drop-down list box at the beginning of the toolbar to select the respective chart elements. If you choose one of the elements, *Excel* selects this element in the chart.

■ *Format Object*
The button is labelled with the name of the corresponding chart element which you selected. Click on this button in order to open the *Format Object* dialog box with the options for the formatting of the selected chart element.

■ *Data Table*
With this button you show or hide the data table displayed under the chart.

425

■ 🔲🔲 *By Row or by Column*
Click this button in order to change the sort of reference to the data series. Depending on which button you click, the data series are taken either from the rows or from the columns of the data table.

■ 🖉🖉 *Angle Text Downward, Angle Text Upward*
With these two buttons you can angle selected text of the chart in the indicated direction.

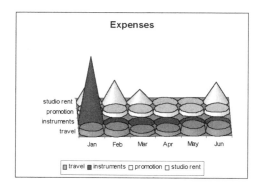

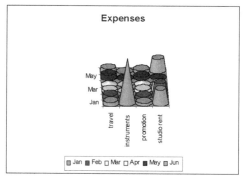

Fig. 8.41: The chart by rows and by columns

Two- and Three-dimensional Charts

Turning a 2-D Chart into a 3-D Chart

In *Excel*, you can create many types of charts, such as circular charts, bar charts, line or area charts, in either two or three dimensions. Even after the completion of a chart, you can turn a two-dimensional chart into a three-dimensional one whenever you want to.

Changing
dimensions

In some cases, for example before inserting an overlapping item, you should change the dimension of a chart, because certain commands, like inserting a secondary axis, cannot be applied to a three-dimensional chart.

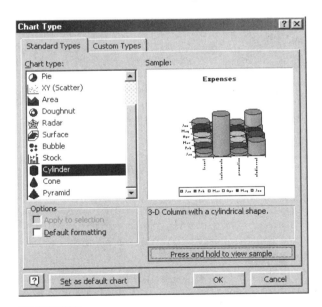

Fig. 8.42: Changing the dimensions

In order to change a two-dimensional into a three-dimen-sional chart or vice versa, select an embedded chart for editing with a single click. A separate chart sheet can be selected by clicking on the sheet tab.

Go to *Chart/Chart Type*, and select the chart type with the new dimensions on the *Standard Types* tab. In the *Chart Sub-type* box to the right you will see both the two- as well as the three-dimensional charts.

Chart Type

Instead of using this method you can also choose *Chart Type* in the *Chart* toolbar and open the *Chart Type* drop-down palette. Here you then click on the button repre-senting the chart type in the desired dimensions.

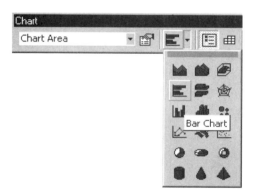

Fig. 8.43:   The Chart Type drop-down palette

Changing the View of a 3-D-Chart

The view of a 3-D chart is determined by the height of the view and by the angle of the chart elements. The height of the view determines the height of the observer's viewpoint in relation to the chart. The chart can be shown either as if the viewer were looking up at it from below, or looking down on it from some point above it.

Rotation

The rotation decides, for example in a column chart, whether the columns will be seen from the front, from the side or from behind. You can change the view of a 3-D chart in one of two different ways:

- By dragging one of the corners with the mouse.

- By changing the values for the elevation and rotation in the *Chart/3-D-View* dialog box.

Perspective

In order to change the perspective of a 3-D chart in one way or another, select the appropriate chart. An embedded chart can be selected by clicking on it, while a chart on a separate chart sheet can be selected by a click on its sheet tab.

In order to change the perspective of the chart using the mouse, hold the mouse button down on one of the corners, i.e., at the intersection of two axes, either at the starting point and the end point of an axis, and drag it in the direction in which you want to change the perspective.

In order to change the elevation, drag one of the corners upward or downward. In order to change the rotation, drag one of the corners to the right or to the left.

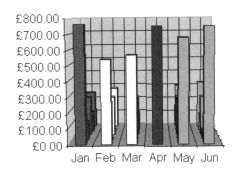 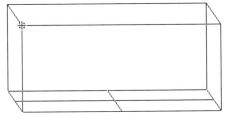

Fig. 8.44:   Rotating a 3-D-chart

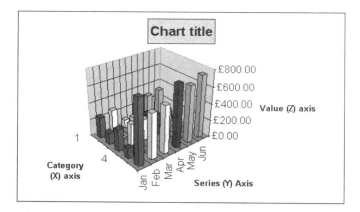

Fig. 8.45: The chart after rotation to the right

If you want to reset the change of perspective, or if you prefer to change it by setting the values in a dialog box, choose *Chart/3-D View*. Now you can either enter a value into the *Elevation* and *Rotation* text boxes, or change the values by clicking one of the corresponding arrow buttons. You can immediately see the effects of the change in the preview area of the dialog box.

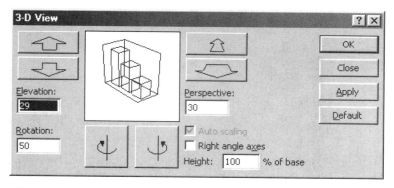

Fig. 8.46: Changing the perspective in the dialog box

Apply

If you are satisfied with the result displayed in the pre-view, click *OK* in order to transfer the changes made in the dialog box to the chart. You can also click on the *Apply* button, if you want to transfer the changes you have made so far to the chart before making any further modifications in the dialog box.

Standard

If you have opened the dialog box in order to reset the changes you made by dragging with the mouse, click the *Default* button. Afterwards, you can start all over again or carry on with the default settings.

Close

By clicking the *Close* button you can close the dialog box without applying any of the modifications you have made. The chart will then keep the perspective as it was set before you opened the dialog box.

Formatting the Floor of a 3-D Chart

In a 3-D chart, you can also format the floor. Select this chart element by clicking on the floor area among the data series, or, choose *Floor* from the *Chart Objects* drop-down list in the *Chart* toolbar.

Fig. 8.47:   The entry in the *Chart Objects* list

Then choose *Format/Selected Floor* or click on the *Format Floor* button ⊞. You can apply the following format options to a selected floor:

▪ Border

▪ Color

▪ Fill Effects

431

As soon as you click the *Fill Effects* button, the *Fill Effects* dialog box is opened. From the tab pages choose a pattern, a texture or a picture with which to fill the floor area. In the lower right-hand corner the *Sample* field gives you a preview of the selected effect.

Formating Walls

In the same manner, you can also format the walls of a 3-D chart. Activate these chart elements by clicking on one of the walls, or by choosing *Walls* from the *Chart Objects* drop-down list box in the *Chart* toolbar.

Fig. 8.48:   Formatting the walls of a 3-D-chart

Then choose *Format/Selected Walls* or click the *Format Walls* button. The options for formatting are identical to those for the floor of a 3-D chart given above.

Deleting Charts

If you want to use the space which is occupied by an embedded chart in a different way, you can remove the chart from the worksheet.

Chart sheet

You can also delete a chart sheet which you no longer need in order to increase the memory capacity of your workbook.

Embedded chart

Click onto an embedded chart in order to select it. Then press the Del key or choose *Edit/Clear/All*.

Delete sheet

In order to remove a chart sheet from the workbook, click on its sheet tab and choose *Edit/Delete Sheet*. You will be asked to confirm whether you really want to delete the chart sheet. If you do, click the *OK* button.

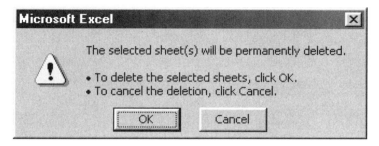

Fig. 8.49: Deleting a chart sheet

If you have deleted an embedded chart by mistake, you can retrieve the chart immediately after the *Edit/Clear/All* command by using the *Edit/Undo: Clear* command.

In *Excel 97*, deleting an embedded chart belongs to one of those commands which you can reset even after 16 actions by using the *Undo* command. Deleting a chart sheet, however, cannot be undone.

9. Data Exchange

The communication among the individual Windows applications has, since *Windows 95*, become even simpler than it used to be. Particularly the components of the *Office Suite* of which *Excel* is a part possess special functions to exchange information between individual modules.

You can always use the Windows clipboard to exchange data to and from *Excel*. In addition, *Excel* is capable of saving tables in various other formats.

Likewise, it can import formats from other table calculation programs, database files and files of various other programs.

If you use *Excel* as part of the *Office Suite*, then with the help of the data exchange you can do things like:

- Calculate a *Word* table in *Excel*

- Format an *Excel* table in *Word*

- Insert an *Excel* chart into a *Word* document

- Use an *Excel* database as a *Word* mail merge data source

- Import data from an *Access* database into an *Excel* table

- Create a query in order to integrate parts of an *Access* database in *Excel*

- Export data from an *Excel* database into an *Access* database

The easiest way to exchange data is by using the Windows clipboard. The Windows clipboard is a special reserved place in the memory that is always able to store an object which can then be pasted once, or even several times,

- into a different position in the same file;

- into another file of the same application;

- into a document of another application.

You can use the clipboard in different ways. You can copy data with the help of the clipboard, you can move data, and you can also link a destination and a source document.

Copying, Embedding, and Linking

With the clipboard, Windows provides an excellent instrument for exchanging data with other *Office* applications. You can either embed data or link it, whichever you prefer.

Embedding

Embedding an object into a document means that it is inserted and saved in the destination document. It loses its link with the source data, but is, however, inserted with an indication of the source application used to create it, so that later on you can edit or format it by double-clicking on the object.

Linking

A linked object continues to be saved in the original source file. In the destination document, there is only an indication of where this source data is located. This method of linking objects offers the following advantages:

- It takes little space in the destination document

- Changes are updated automatically

- Data is saved in only one file instead of many files.

The disadvantage of this method is that you always need to copy the source document together with the target document in order for the data to be displayed in the target document.

- *Copy*
  Copying an object means that a duplicate of the selected object is put in the clipboard. From there, it can subsequently be pasted at another position in the same or in a different document. The original object remains in its original location.

- *Cut*
  Cutting an object means that you remove a selected object from its original place and move it to another position by pasting it.

- *Paste*
  Pasting means inserting data into a document which you have previously put into the clipboard using the *Copy* or *Cut* commands. You can repeat this procedure as often as you like.

Exchanging Data Between Excel and Word

Since *Word* and *Excel* are both parts of the *Office Suite*, a data exchange between the two applications is rather simple. To exchange data, you can use either drag-and-drop or the Windows clipboard.

Link

Using the clipboard, you can insert tables or parts of tables, embedded charts or chart sheets into a *Word* document. When doing so, you can establish a link between the *Excel* workbook and the *Word* document so that changes which you make in the *Excel* workbook are, automatically, transferred to the *Word* document as well.

437

Copying an Excel-Table into a Word Document

In order to copy a table from *Excel* to *Word*, both *Word* and *Excel* should be running. Start them both through the *Start* button.

In *Excel*, open the source file, which is the workbook containing the table which you want to copy. In *Word*, open or create the target document, which is the file into which you want to copy the table.

Arrange windows By clicking the right mouse button on the taskbar and then selecting the appropriate windows arrangement command, you can arrange the windows in such a way that you can advantageously see both windows at the same time. Then select the appropriate cells in the *Excel* table.

Data Exchange by Drag-and-Drop

In order to copy the data from *Excel* to *Word* using drag-and-drop, drag the selected table range from *Excel* into the *Word* document while holding down the Ctrl key.

When you have arrived at the desired position, release the mouse button. The data is then embedded into the *Word* document. This means that it is saved in the *Word* document without any link to the *Excel* table.

Data Exchange via the Clipboard

If you use the clipboard to copy the data, you can choose whether you want to embed or to link the table.

In order to insert the selected table via the clipboard into the *Word* document, first select the desired cell range and choose *Edit/Copy*, or click the *Copy* button on the toolbar.

Paste special

Now activate the *Word* application window, and in the target document, click at the point where you want to insert the contents. Then choose *Edit/Paste Special*.

Paste link

If you want to insert the contents of the clipboard as a link, in the *Paste Special* dialog box, select the *Paste link* radio button.

If a link is established, the table remains saved in the *Excel* workbook.

Paste

If you want to insert the table as an embedded object so that it is saved directly in the *Word* document, select the *Paste* radio button.

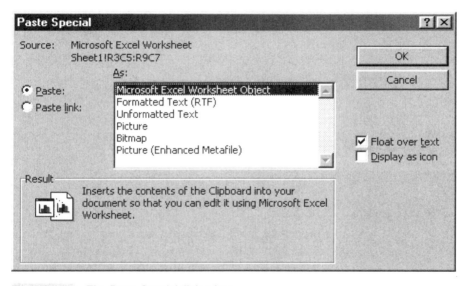

Fig. 9.1:   The *Paste Special* dialog box

In the *As* list box, select the *Microsoft Excel Worksheet Object*, and click *OK*.

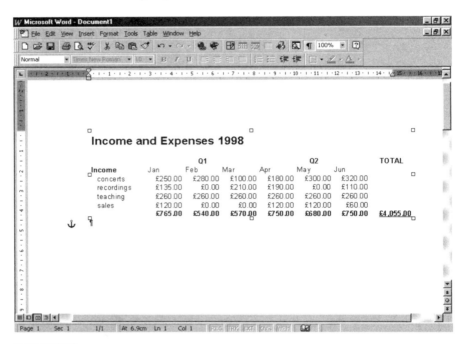

Fig. 9.2: A selected Excel table object in a Word document

Copying a Chart into a Word Document

The procedure is similar if you want to copy an embedded chart or a chart sheet into a *Word* document. Select the embedded chart by clicking on it, or by clicking on the sheet tab of the chart sheet in order to display it. Then choose *Edit/Copy*, and switch to the *Word* document. There, click at the desired insertion point and select the *Edit/Paste Special* command.

Paste or
Paste link

In order to save the chart as an embedded object in the *Word* document, choose the *Paste* radio button. In order to continue saving it in the *Excel* workbook and to only link it with the *Word* document, click the *Paste link* radio button.

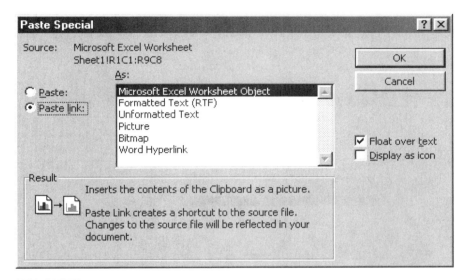

Fig. 9.3:   Pasting a chart as a link

Edit embedded
Excel objects

In the *As* list box, select the *Microsoft Excel Chart Object* entry. Then click the *OK* button. You can activate an embedded table object or embedded chart object by double-clicking it. In the *Word* application window, the *Excel* commands for the formatting and editing of tables or charts are then displayed.

Inserting a Word-Table into an Excel-Worksheet

Exchanging data between *Word* and *Excel* is just as easy as the other way round. You can copy a *Word* table via the clipboard into an *Excel* worksheet in order to calculate it there with commands that are more convenient. To do this, select the respective table in the *Word* document and choose the *Edit/Copy* command or click the *Copy* button on the toolbar.

Then switch to the *Excel* worksheet. There, click on the cell of the left upper corner where the table should be inserted, and select *Edit/Paste Special*. If you want to go on working with the table in *Excel*, in the *As* list box, select the *Text* or *Unicode Text* item.

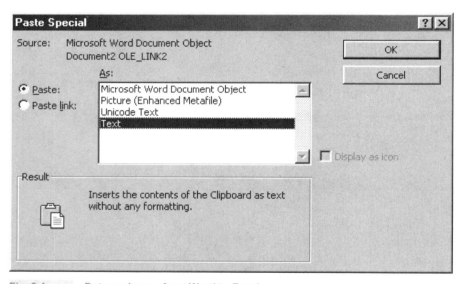

Fig. 9.4:   Data exchange from Word to Excel

Paste/

Paste link

Select the *Paste* option button in order to insert the table, or *Paste link* if you want to link the data with the original *Word* table. Finish the process by clicking *OK*.

Inserting Word Text Objects into an Excel Worksheet

Word text which you do not want to edit but only display in *Excel*, can be inserted as a picture or a *Word* document object in order to leave the formatting unchanged.

To do this, select the respective text sections in the *Word* document, and copy them into the Windows clipboard by using the *Edit/Copy* command, or by clicking the *Copy* button on the toolbar.

Select the desired insertion point in the *Excel* worksheet. Then choose the *Edit/Paste Special* command. In the *As* list box, select the *Microsoft Word Document Object* or *Picture (Enhanced Metafile)* command, depending on whether you want to insert the contents of the clipboard as a *Word* object or as a picture.

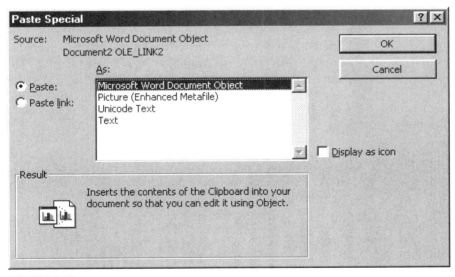

Fig. 9.5:   Inserting a Word object

Select the *Paste* radio button in order to create an embedded object. Select the *Paste link* radio button if you want to establish a link with the *Word* source document. Confirm the action with *OK*.

Exporting Data to Access

The tables in which databases store their records are very similar to the table structure of an *Excel* table. For this reason, you can without any difficulty prepare an *Excel* table so that it can be imported into a database.

Since *Excel* is sold together with *Access* in the *Office Suite*, the data exchange between these two programs is particularly easy. In spite of all the compatibility, however, *Excel* stores its data differently than *Access* does. Therefore, the data needs to be converted into an *Access* format before it can be loaded there.

Add-Ins

There is a wizard to guide you through the data conversion, however, so you should not have any difficulty at all. The data conversion wizard is an *Excel Add-In*. Check whether the *Add-In* is available for you. To do this, choose *Tools/Add-Ins* and see whether the following check box has a check mark:

```
Microsoft AccessLinks Add-In
```

If the check box is not marked, click in it. Should the item be missing altogether, click the *Browse* button and open the following folder:

```
Program\Microsoft Office\Office\Library
```

Select the *ACCLINK* or *ACCLINK.XLA* file and click the *Open* button. Then close the *Add-Ins* dialog box with *OK*. If you did not install the *Add-In* during the setup, or if you later deleted it, use the Setup program to install the file now.

Converting an Excel-Table into an Access-Table

New database

After loading the *Add-In*, choose *Data/Convert to MS Access*. In the *Convert to Microsoft Access* dialog box, select the *New database* radio button in order to convert the *Excel* table to a new database file.

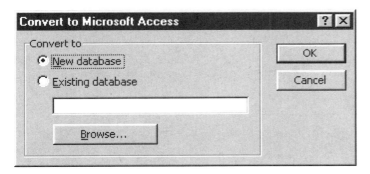

Fig. 9.6:   The first step to convert an Excel table to MS Access

Existing database

If you want to insert the table into an already existing database, select the *Existing database* radio button and enter the name of the *Access* target database or use the *Browse* button to select it.

Finally click the *OK* button. *Access* will then be started and a new database created or the existing one opened, depending on what you have chosen.

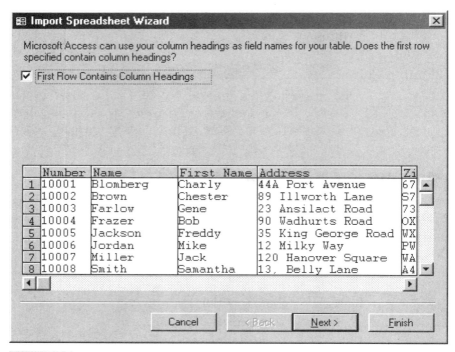

Fig. 9.7:   The first step of the *Import Spreadsheet Wizard*

First row contains
column headings
The *Import Spreadsheet Wizard* dialog box will be dis-played. Select the *First Row Contains Column Headings* check box if the *Excel* table contains column headings in the first row.

Then click the *Next* button to move to the second step of the *Import Spreadsheet Wizard*. Here you define whether the *Excel* data is to be inserted into a new or into an existing *Access* table. To insert the data into an existing table, select its name from the list.

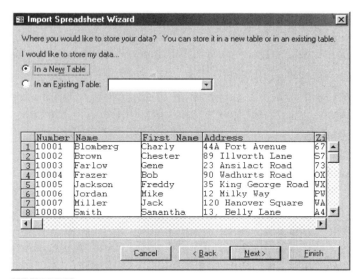

Fig. 9.8:   The second step

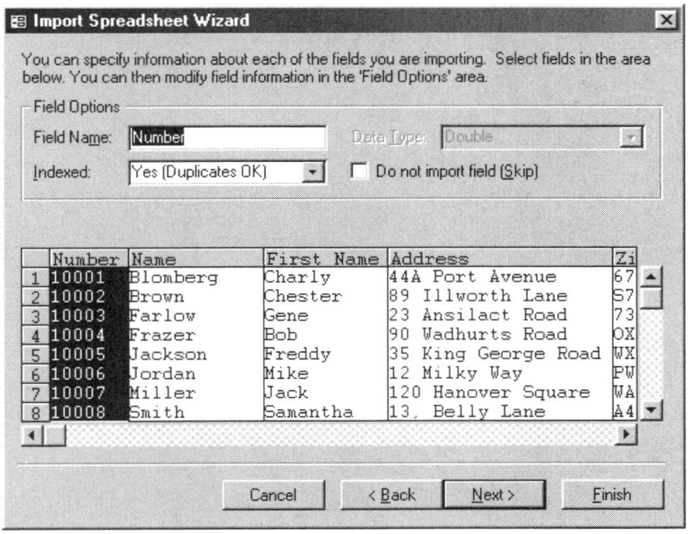

Fig. 9.9:   Setting the field options

In the next step of the Wizard, you can determine the data type that *Access* should use for each column separately, and whether the data is to be indexed according to the column for faster search results.

Click the *Do not import field* check box for all columns which you do not want to transfer to the *Access* database.

Primary key

After you have clicked the *Next* button once more, you have to decide whether you want *Access* to insert the primary key automatically, or whether you want to choose a primary key of your own, or even whether you do not want to define any primary key at all for the moment.

The primary key in an *Access* table is the data field which is used to uniquely identify a record. In such a column, each value must appear only once.

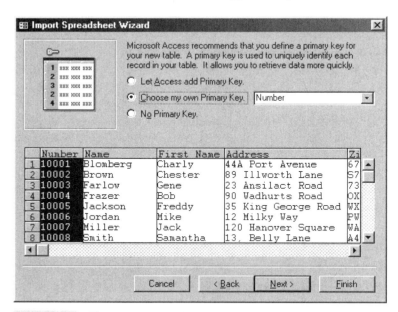

Fig. 9.10:   The customer number as primary key

Choose your own
primary key

If you want to create the field of the primary key from one of the *Excel* fields, select the *Choose my own primary key* radio button, and from the drop-down list select the desired name of the column. When you have determined the primary key, click once more on the *Next* button.

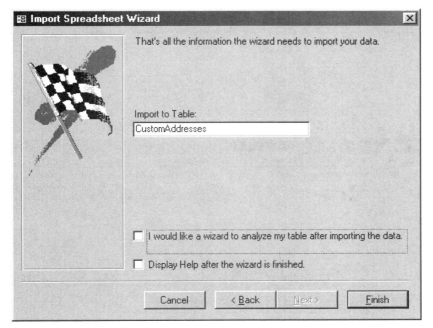

Fig. 9.11:   Selecting the target table

An *Access* database consists, just like an *Excel* workbook, of several tables. Therefore, you can now give a name to the target table in which the data of the *Excel* table is to appear.

Agree to the suggested table name or overwrite it with one of your own. Then click the *Finish* button.

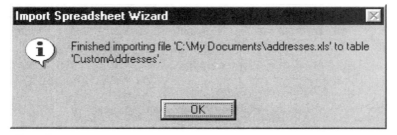

Import Spreadsheet Wizard

(i) Finished importing file 'C:\My Documents\addresses.xls' to table 'CustomAddresses'.

OK

Fig. 9.12: Message after importing

After the conversion has been completed successfully, *Access* displays a message to this effect. Confirm this message by clicking *OK*.

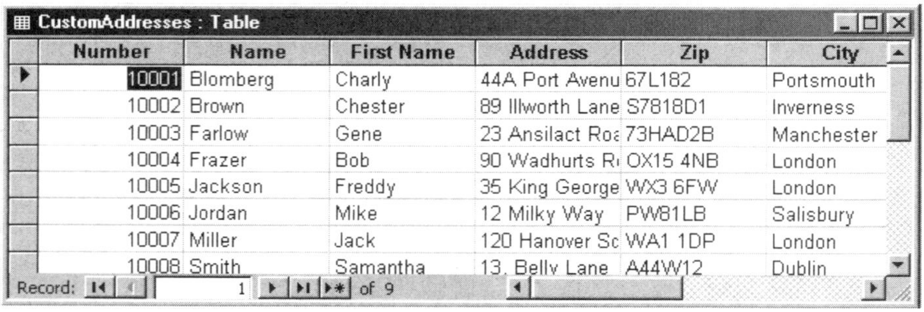

	Number	Name	First Name	Address	Zip	City
▶	10001	Blomberg	Charly	44A Port Avenu	67L182	Portsmouth
	10002	Brown	Chester	89 Illworth Lane	S7818D1	Inverness
	10003	Farlow	Gene	23 Ansilact Roa	73HAD2B	Manchester
	10004	Frazer	Bob	90 Wadhurts R	OX15 4NB	London
	10005	Jackson	Freddy	35 King George	WX3 6FW	London
	10006	Jordan	Mike	12 Milky Way	PW81LB	Salisbury
	10007	Miller	Jack	120 Hanover Sc	WA1 1DP	London
	10008	Smith	Samantha	13, Belly Lane	A44W12	Dublin

CustomAddresses : Table

Record: 1 of 9

Fig. 9.13: The converted records in the Access table

Now you can work on the *Excel* data in the *Access* database. In the original *Excel* table, a corresponding message is inserted.

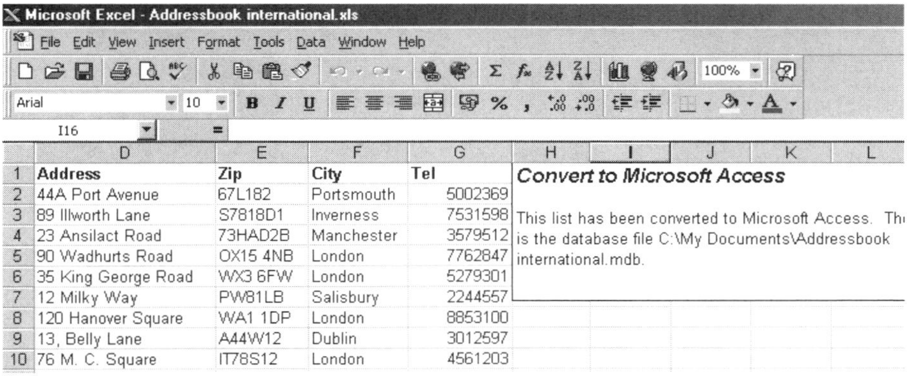

	D	E	F	G
1	Address	Zip	City	Tel
2	44A Port Avenue	67L182	Portsmouth	5002369
3	89 Illworth Lane	S7818D1	Inverness	7531598
4	23 Ansilact Road	73HAD2B	Manchester	3579512
5	90 Wadhurts Road	OX15 4NB	London	7762847
6	35 King George Road	WX3 6FW	London	5279301
7	12 Milky Way	PW81LB	Salisbury	2244557
8	120 Hanover Square	WA1 1DP	London	8853100
9	13, Belly Lane	A44W12	Dublin	3012597
10	76 M. C. Square	IT78S12	London	4561203

Fig. 9.14: The original Excel table

The indication is inserted as a text box and contains the path of the *Access* database into which the records have been exported.

Exchange of Data from Access to Excel

You can also additionally work on *Access* tables in *Excel*. *Access* has a special command to convert a table into a format which can be read in *Excel*.

Open the database and in the database window select the table which you want to use in *Excel*. In *Access*, select the *Tools/Office Links/Analyze it with MS Excel* command.

Another method of converting *Access* tables into a file which *Excel* can work on, is by saving the data in the *Excel* file format. To do this, choose the *File/Save As/ Export* command in *Access*.

Select the *To an External File or Database* radio button, and confirm by clicking *OK*. In the *Save as type* drop-down list box, select the *Microsoft Excel 97* item, and click the *Export* button.

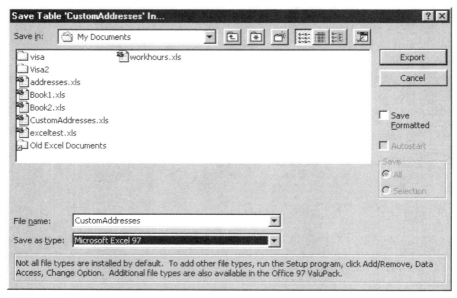

Exporting Data by Saving it in Another Format

Exporting data means saving a file in a different format which another application can read and edit. You can, for example, save an *Excel* table in such a way that it can afterwards be opened as a *Word* document, or in a database program.

Other formats

How you export data from *Excel* into an *Access* database has already been explained in the previous section on 'Exporting Data to *Access*'.

Excel can save files in many different application formats, such as file formats which can be opened by *dBase, Lotus 1-2-3, Quattro Pro*, or by earlier *Excel* versions.

Before you save a workbook in a different format, you should first save the changes in the *Excel* default format. Then, in the open workbook, choose the *File/Save As* command.

The *Save As* dialog box opens. The file formats you can use are determined in the *Save as type* drop-down list box. If you do not find the format of the target application, use one of the formats which is specifically designed for the exchange of data:

- *Formatted Text (Space delimited)*
  Saves text and values. Columns are separated by spaces, rows are saved as text lines; graphics, for-mattings, drawing objects, etc. are not saved at all

- *Text (Tab delimited)*
  Select the appropriate file type for Macintosh, OS2 or MS-DOS. This is like the *Formatted Text* option, except that columns are separated by tabs

- *CSV (Comma delimited)*
  Select the appropriate file type for Macintosh, OS2, or MS-DOS. Saves only text and values; rows are converted into text lines, columns are separated by commas

- *DIF (Data Interchange-Format)*
  Saves text and values, column width and some number formats

- *SYLK (Symbolic Link)*
  Saves text and values as well as most of the text formats and cell comments

When saving in a different format, keep in mind that most formats save only the current worksheet and not the whole workbook. This means that you may have to repeat the saving process in the case of several worksheets.

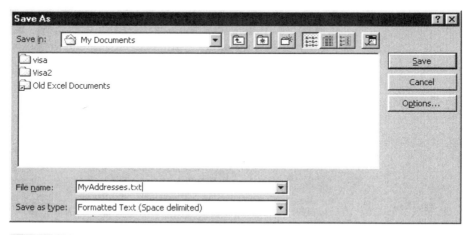

Saving in a different format

In the *Save as type* drop-down list, select a file type, and enter a new name for the file in the different format if necessary. If you want to save a worksheet so that it can be used as a Web page, choose the *Save as HTML* item from the *File* menu instead.

Copy is created

Excel does not save the original file, but creates a copy having the same name as the original which it then provides with a different extension. Select the folder for the converted file and click the *Save* button. *Excel* may point out to you that only the current worksheet, not the whole workbook, can be saved in the selected format. Confirm this with *OK*.

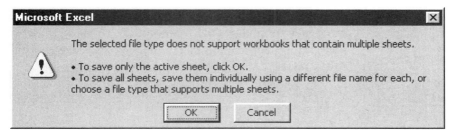

Microsoft Excel ✕

⚠ The selected file type does not support workbooks that contain multiple sheets.

• To save only the active sheet, click OK.
• To save all sheets, save them individually using a different file name for each, or choose a file type that supports multiple sheets.

[OK]   [Cancel]

Fig. 9.17:   A warning

When you close the workbook, you are asked whether you want to save it in the *Excel* format. Click the *Yes* button only if you want to replace the original *Excel* workbook by the data in the converted file.

Importing Data from Other Programs

Excel is capable of opening files which were created in a different application. You can see the file formats which you can import into *Excel* in the *Files of type* list box in the *Open* dialog box.

Source
applications

In this drop-down list, the names of the source applications of different files and certain formats are displayed. For more details on the various formats, read the previous section on 'Exporting Data'.

In order to be able to continue working on a file saved in a different format, the files of the different programs need to be converted to the *Excel* format.

While doing this work, you will be guided by a wizard which is automatically started.

Open

In order to open a file from another application, choose *File/Open* or click on the *Open* button. Open the *Files of type* drop-down list and select the file type in which the file is saved.

If you do not know in which format the file is saved, choose the *All Files* entry.

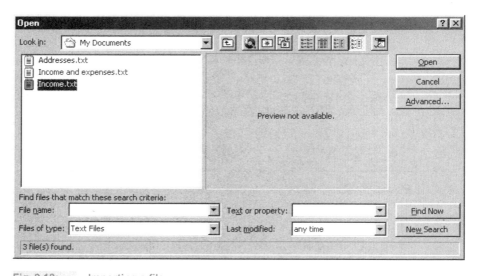

Fig. 9.18:   Importing a file

Then select the name of the file and click the *Open* button. If the file is saved in a text format, the first step of the *Text Import Wizard* is automatically displayed.

Delimited or
fixed width

In general, *Excel* recognizes the original data type automatically. Only if the correct source is not displayed should you choose another list entry. In the *Text Import Wizard* dialog box, define whether the records are separated by tabs or commas, or whether they are saved with a fixed column width. Also determine from which row onwards the data is to be imported. After the selection, activate the *Next* button.

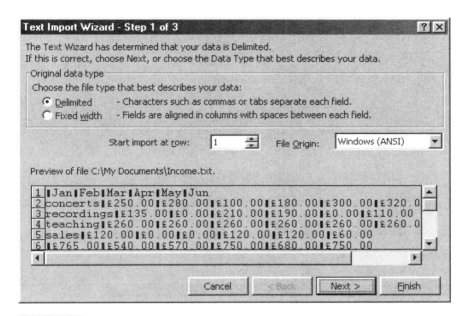

Fig. 9.19: The first step

Choose delimiter
or fixed column
width

If you import data which is separated by delimiters, you now need to define the type of delimiter to be used, such as a tab or a comma, by clicking the corresponding check box.

In a file which is saved with fixed column width, in the next step you will get an opportunity to adjust the column width. In both cases, afterwards click on the *Next* button.

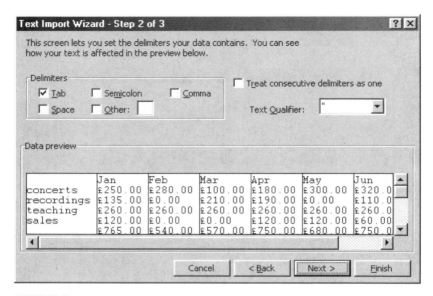

Fig. 9.20:   The second step

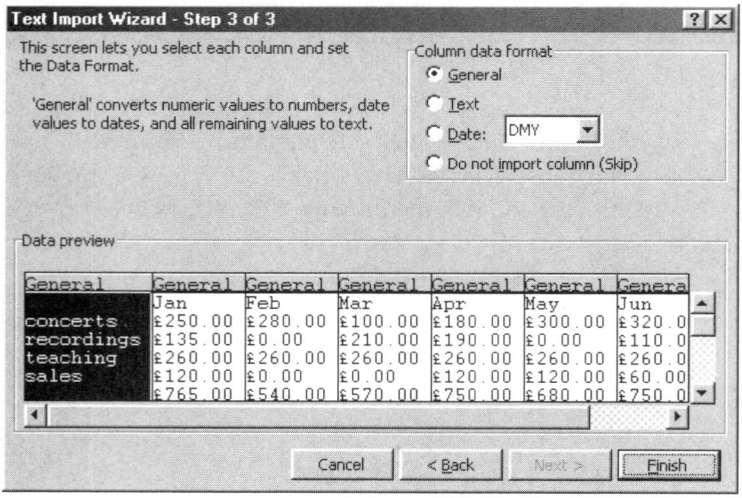

Fig. 9.21:   The third step

Check data type

In the third and last step of the *Text Import Wizard*, you can check each column to see whether *Excel* has recognized the correct data type.

The *General* default, imports values and date values into the corresponding *Excel* values, and imports all other data types as text.

If necessary, select a different radio button, for example, if you want to read some data recognized as a value as text.

Type of file workbook

Click on the *Finish* button. The process of converting is then completed. *Excel* displays the data in a workbook as a worksheet.

In order to save the data in the *Excel* format, choose *File/Save As*, and in the *Save as type* drop-down list box select *Microsoft Excel Workbook*.

After you have clicked the *Save* button, *Excel* saves the converted file as a normal workbook.

Creating a Query for an Access Database

In *Excel*, you can create a query in order to insert data from an *Access* database into an *Excel* worksheet. With the help of a query, you can filter, sort and link the records of an *Access* table.

Get External Data

In order to create a query, in the *Excel* target worksheet choose *Data/Get External Data/Create New Query*. In the *Choose Data Source* dialog box, choose the *MS Access 97 Database (not sharable)* entry. Confirm with *OK*.

By clicking in the *Use the Query Wizard to create/edit queries* check box, you activate a wizard to help you with the creation of a query.

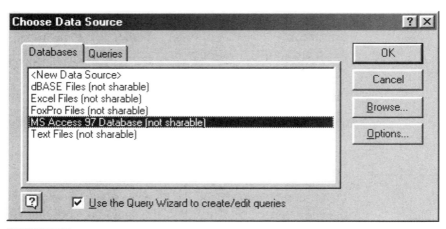

Query-wizard

Clear this check box in order to use *Microsoft Query* for the creation of the query. Close the dialog box by clicking on *OK*. In the *Select Database* dialog box, select the name of the *Access* database that contains the records you want to import into an *Excel* worksheet.

Select tables and columns

If you use the *Query Wizard*, in the next dialog box you can select the tables and columns to be included in the query.

In the *Choose Columns* dialog box, select the name of the *Access* table from which you want to import the records, and click on the ⟩ button in order to transfer all fields. You can click on the plus sign in front of the table name to display the available fields and transfer them one by one with the ⟩ button.

If you want to get information on the data contained in the fields before finally deciding on what to import, select the field name in the *Available tables and columns* list and click the *Preview Now* button.

In the *Preview of data in the selected column* list box, you then can view the individual list items by means of the scroll bar buttons. After you have chosen the fields you want to import, click the *Next* button.

If you want to use the *Query Wizard* in order to filter the records, then in the next step select the name of the field in the *Column to filter* list box according to which the data is to be filtered.

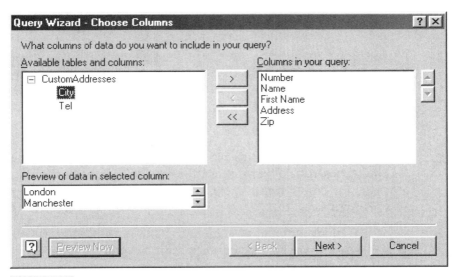

Fig. 9.23:   The preview of an imported column

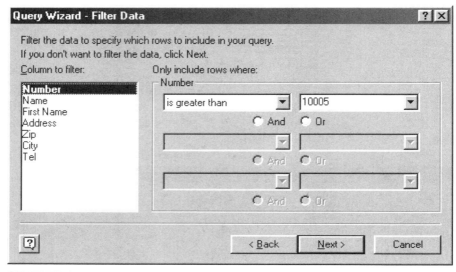

Fig. 9.24:   Filtering the records

In the drop-down list, under the group box with the chosen field name, select the comparison operator and in the drop-down list next to it, select the entry for the filter criterion.

Up to three
filter criteria

You can link up to three filter criteria with AND or OR. After you have determined the filter criteria, click again on *Next*, and in the *Sort by* drop-down list box select the name of the field by which the records are to be sorted.

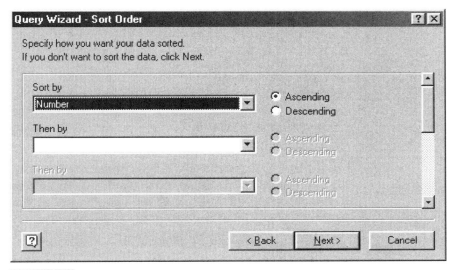

Fig. 9.25:   Sorting the records

Up to three
sort keys

In the sort order, you also have the possibility to fix three criteria, if more than one column entry needs to be sorted. After choosing the sort keys, click *Next* once more.

In the last step of the *Query Wizard*, you can decide whether you want to immediately return the data to *Excel*, or whether you want to first look at it and maybe edit it in *Microsoft Query*.

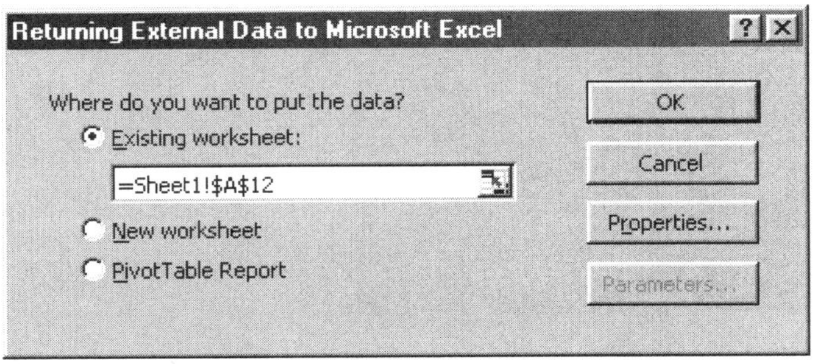

Fig. 9.26:   Setting the insertion point

Click the *Save Query* button in order to save the query you created in a file so that you can later use it again. Then click *Next* in order to display the last dialog box.

Existing worksheet

Here you determine where to insert the query result. *Excel* suggests the existing worksheet and in the entry box shows the active cell as the insertion point. Next to the *Existing worksheet* text box, you find the 🔳 button to reduce the dialog box in order to select a new insertion point.

New worksheet

If you do not want to insert the record into the current worksheet, select the *New worksheet* radio button. If you want to create a Pivot table from the query, click on the *PivotTable Report* radio button.

With the help of the *Properties* button, you can determine options for saving the query definition, for refreshing it in the future, and for the insertion of the records.

You can close the creation of the query by clicking *OK* and insert the external data in your worksheet.

By using the *Data/Refresh Data* command, you can update the inserted data, and by using the *Data/Get External Data/Edit Query* command you can change the query you created.

Using the help of *Data/Get External Data/Data Range Properties*, you can influence the refreshing of the data. Moreover, *Excel* offers you a new toolbar to edit your query.

Fig. 9.27: The *External Data* toolbar

Use this toolbar in order to refresh the data, edit the query, or to define the properties in the *External Data Range Properties* dialog box.

Inserting Hyperlinks

Excel 97 can now be represented on the Internet. This means that you can create and save *Excel* worksheets and charts in such a way that they can be published on the Web. The specific feature of documents on the Web, besides their multimedia composition, are the Hyperlinks, sometimes simply referred to as links.

What are
hyperlinks?

Hyperlinks are emphasized text passages, graphics, or other objects which contain links to other documents. A click on such a hyperlink jumps you to the linked file which may be on a totally different computer somewhere on the other side of the globe.

Why hyperlinks?

With the help of hyperlinks, you have the possibility to get background information on the ranges of a document which are of particular interest to you. In the background documents, you then find further hyperlinks with the help of which you can jump to other linked documents containing further information.

How to create
hyperlinks?

Even if you do not have access to the Internet, and even if you are not connected to a company's Intranet network, hyperlinks are still interesting for you.

With this sort of link, you can also link workbooks to one another, or create hyperlinks with files of other applications, such as background information which is saved in a *Word* document, or a hyperlink to graphics or other objects which are saved in a database outside the *Excel* workbook.

You can insert hyperlinks:

- from the clipboard by using the *Edit/Paste as Hyperlink* command

- by using the *Insert/Hyperlink* command

- by clicking the *Insert Hyperlink* button.

Insert hyperlink

Before inserting a hyperlink, you need to save a document. In order to create a hyperlink to another file in an *Excel* worksheet, choose *Insert/Hyperlink*, or click the *Insert Hyperlink* button.

Link to file or URL

In the *Link to file or URL* text box, enter the path to the file to which you want to link. Or click the *Browse* button, open the folder and select the file name.

Named location in file (optional)

With the help of the *Named location in file (optional)* text box, you can, in addition, define a certain area of the target file as the destination for the link.

If you want, for example, to create a link to a certain area in a *Word* document which is indicated with a bookmark, enter the name of the bookmark into this text box. This entry is optional.

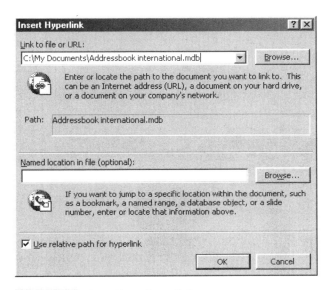

Inserting a hyperlink

ScreenTip

with path

After you have closed the dialog box by clicking *OK*, the hyperlink is inserted. If you move the mouse pointer over the hyperlink, it turns into a hand, and the path to the linked file is displayed as a *ScreenTip*.

E	F	G	H
Zip	**City**	**Tel**	
67L182	Portsmouth	5002369	
S7818D1	Inverne C:\My Documents\Portsmouth.doc		
73HAD2B	Manchester	3579512	
OX15 4NB	London	7762847	

Fig. 9.29: The mouse on a hyperlink

Web toolbar

When you click on the hyperlink, the linked file is opened and displayed. In addition, *Excel* automatically opens the Web toolbar so that you can return to the starting point of the hyperlink by clicking the *Back* button ⇐.

467

Fig. 9.30:   The Word document linked by hyperlink

Back ⇐

Click the *Back* button ⇐ in order to jump back to the *Excel* workbook. By clicking the right mouse button you can open the shortcut menu for a hyperlink in order to edit it.

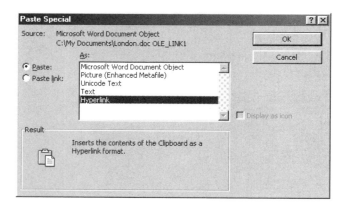

Fig. 9.31:   Creating a hyperlink via the clipboard

Hyperlinks via
the clipboard

In order to insert a hyperlink using the clipboard, select and copy the data in the data source file. In the *Excel* worksheet, select *Edit/Paste Special*. In the *As* list box, select the *Hyperlink* entry, and click *OK*.

10. Insert Objects

In order to make your *Excel* worksheets or charts look more attractive, you can insert various objects, some of which you can create with the help of the additional *Office* components. You can, for instance:

- Insert a picture into a worksheet or a chart sheet as a background

- Insert a map in order to show certain data in a geographical context

- Insert a *WordArt* object in order to create specific text effects

- Insert drawing elements and *AutoShapes* in order to illustrate your tables or charts with graphic symbols

- Insert an organization chart in order to illustrate hierarchical structures.

Insert Picture

Your *Excel* work- or chart sheets will look much more interesting if you insert additional objects such as pictures or drawing elements and symbols.

A chart would look quite unique if you inserted your own graphic symbols instead of using the default columns or bars to represent the data series.

There are various ways of inserting graphic elements into your worksheet or chart sheet:

- By means of the clipboard, if you have edited the image in another program or want to insert only a section of the picture from a graphic file;

■ By using the *Insert/Object* command which enables you to insert an existing graphic file as well as to create new graphics. The objects can be embedded or, if they constitute a file in themselves, they can be linked;

■ By using the *Insert/Picture* command which enables you to insert a picture file.

In *Excel 97*, the *Insert/Picture* command opens up an overlapping menu for the selection of pictures, symbols and other similar objects, such as *WordArt* objects, *AutoShapes* or organizational charts.

Fig. 10.1: Inserting a picture in *Excel 97*

To insert a picture file, from the overlapping menu choose the *From File* command. You will find picture files of the *Office Suite* in the following folder:

```
C.\Program Files\Microsoft Office\Clipart
```

Preview

In the *Insert Picture* dialog box, click on the *Preview* button so that the selected picture file will be displayed at the right of the list box.

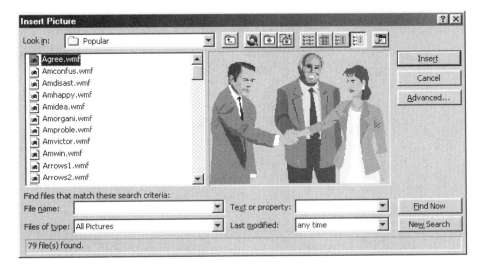

Fig. 10.2:   Inserting a picture

Select the name of the picture file you want to insert and click on the *Insert* button.

Editing the Picture

After you have inserted a picture file, *Excel 97* automatically displays the *Picture* toolbar with various buttons. You use these buttons to edit the selected picture.

The toolbar appears every time you select a picture, and disappears if you click into the worksheet outside the picture.

Formatting a Picture Using the Toolbar

Excel displays the *Picture* toolbar as soon as a picture is selected. Should the *Picture* toolbar not appear automatically, you can display it by using the *View/Toolbars* command, and then clicking onto the *Picture* item. You can use the buttons of the *Picture* toolbar in order to regulate the image control, the brightness, the contrast, to insert further pictures, and to open the *Format Picture* dialog box.

- *Insert Picture From File*
  Click this button in order to open the *Insert Picture* dialog box to insert another picture

- *Image Control*
  This button opens up a list from where you can choose how the picture is to be displayed. You can present the picture as a watermark, in grey scales or black and white

- *More Contrast*
  Click on this button in order to gradually increase the color contrast

- *Less Contrast*
  Click on this button in order to gradually reduce the color contrast

- *More Brightness*
  Click this button in order to gradually increase the brightness

- *Less Brightness*
  Click this button in order to gradually decrease the brightness

- *Crop*
  After clicking this button you can, by dragging the selection handles with the mouse, cut out a section of the picture

■ ☰ *Line Style*
A click on this button opens up a drop-list with a
palette of lines which you can use to shape the borders
of the picture

■ 🖼 *Format Picture*
This button opens the *Format Picture* dialog box. Here
you find various tab pages for the further formatting
of the picture

■ 🖼 *Reset Picture*
If you have changed the picture but do not like the
effects, click this button in order to reset it to its
former appearance

Formatting the Picture Using the Dialog Box

Instead of the buttons, you can also use commands to
format a picture. Besides, the dialog box offers additional
options which you cannot select by using the buttons.

After you have selected the picture, you can open the
dialog box in different ways.

■ By using the *Format/Picture* command

■ By using the *Format Picture* command in the shortcut
menu

■ By clicking the *Format Picture* button 🖼 on the
Picture toolbar

In the dialog box, you will find several tab pages in which
you can determine the color, the size and position as well
as the image control of the picture. On another tab page
you can lock the picture against further modifications.

The *Colors and Lines* Tab Page

On the *Colors and Lines* tab page, in the *Fill* option group, you can fill the picture with a color or with fill effects. As soon as you have selected a color, the *Semi-transparent* check box becomes active. If you select this check box, an opaque color becomes semitransparent.

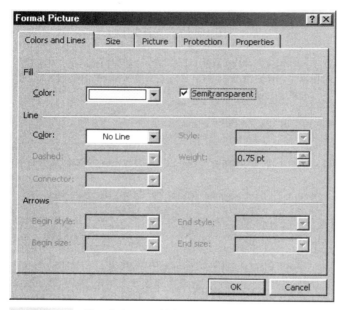

Fig. 10.3:   The *Colors and Lines* tab page

Lines

In the *Line* option group, you can choose a *Color* for the borders in order to frame the picture.

As soon as you have selected a color, the *Style, Dashed* and *Weight* drop-down list boxes become active and you can further define the type of line.

The *Size* Tab Page

On the *Size* tab page, you can determine the exact values for the size of a picture. Here you can work with either absolute values or with values relative to the original picture size. The values of the original size are displayed at the lower part of the dialog box.

The *Picture* Tab Page

On this tab page, you can cut out a section of the picture by entering the appropriate values for the trimming into the boxes in the *Crop from* option group.

The values which you set in the *Left*, *Right*, *Top*, and *Bottom* boxes determine how many centimetres are cut off from the respective border.

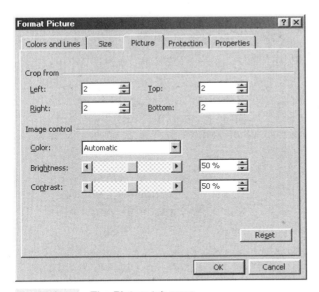

Fig. 10.4:   The *Picture* tab page

Image Control

In the *Image Control* option group, you can specify whether you want to present the picture in a *Grayscale*, in *Black & White*, or as a *Watermark*.

Brightness and Contrast

By means of the *Brightness* and *Contrast* scroll bars, or by changing the corresponding values in the boxes to the right, you can influence the presentation of the picture as an alternative to using the buttons on the *Picture* toolbar.

The *Protection* Tab Page

This tab page contains options to lock or unlock the selected picture against further changes. After locking, choose *Tools/Protection/Protect Sheet* in order to activate the protection.

The *Properties* Tab Page

On the *Properties* tab page you can determine whether the size and position of the selected picture is to be changed in relation to or independent from the cell.

- Select *Move and size with cells* if you want to change the size of the picture together with the height of the row and the width of a column of the underlying cells, and to automatically move the picture along with these cells.

- Select *Move but don't size with cells*, if you want to change the size of the picture independently from the height of the row and the width of the column, yet move the picture together with the cells.

- Select *Don't move or size with cells* if you want to maintain the size of the picture independently from the height of the row and the width of the column, and to keep the position of the picture even when moving the underlying cells.

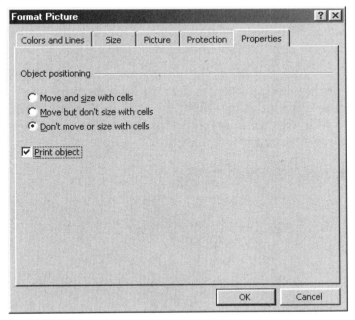

Positioning a picture dependently or independently of the cells

Print object

Clear the *Print object* check box if you want to suppress the picture in the printout.

Changing the Size of a Picture

After inserting a picture, it is displayed with a border and with sizing handles on the sides and at the corners. With these sizing handles, you can drag the picture to a new size.

Drag with the
mouse

Drag the sizing handles on one of the edges in order to change the height or the width of the picture. Drag the sizing handles in one of the corners in order to change the height and the width while maintaining the same proportions.

Format picture

With the *Format Picture* dialog box you have another way to change the picture dimensions. Click on the picture with the right mouse button, and choose *Format Picture*, or click the *Format Picture* button 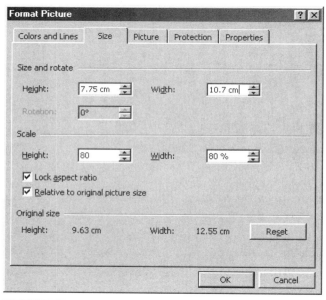.

Scale

Into the corresponding boxes of the *Size and rotate* option group, enter the *Height* and *Width* either as absolute values, or scale the size in proportion to the original size in the boxes of the same name under the *Scale* option group.

Fig. 10.6: Setting the size in the dialog box

By means of the *Relative to original picture size* check box, you can decide whether the scale of the size refers to the original size of the picture or to its current size.

Lock aspect ratio

Check the *Lock aspect ratio* checkbox so that a change of the height automatically implies a change of the width, thus maintaining the proportions.

Reset

If you have made changes and find they do not improve the presentation of the picture, you can return to the original picture size by clicking on the *Reset* button.

Changing the Position of a Picture

If you want to move the picture, point into it. At the tip of the mouse pointer a four-headed arrow will appear. Click and hold down the left mouse button, and drag the picture to any position in the worksheet.

Forming Data Series from a Picture

In order to shape the columns or bars of a chart with the assistance of inserted graphic objects, click onto the data series concerned in the chart. Choose *Format/Selected Data Series* and on the *Patterns* tab page click the *Fill Effects* button.

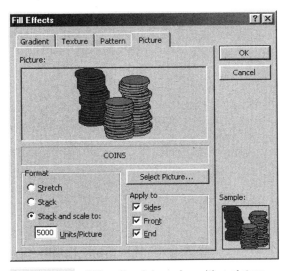

Fig. 10.7:   Filling the data series with a picture

On the *Picture* tab page, click the *Select Picture* button. Then in the *Select Picture* dialog box, select the desired picture and click on the *OK* button. In the *Fill Effects* dialog box you can now decide how the respective data points are to be filled with the picture.

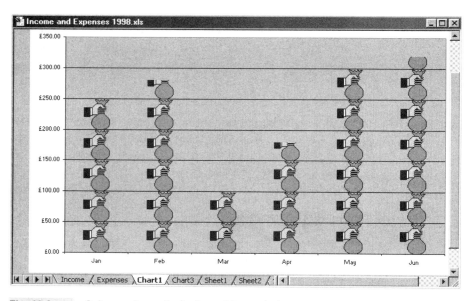

Fig. 10.8: Columns from stacked graphic symbols

▩ *Stretch*
Select this radio button in order to change the size of the picture so that one picture fills each data point entirely.

▩ *Stack*
Select this radio button in order to insert a varying number of copies of the picture to fill the data points, according to the values of the data point.

■ *Stack and scale to*
With this radio button you can determine how many value units you want per picture. Type the corresponding amount into the *Units/Picture* text box.

Apply to

The *Apply to* option group is only available for 3-D data series. Here you determine on which sides the inserted graphic objects are to be displayed.

Displaying Data in a Map

In order to insert a map, the data in the underlying table should contain at least one column made up from values and one column made up from geographical data.

Insert/Map

In the table, select the cell range you want to display in a map, and choose *Insert/Map*, or click the *Map* button.

In the worksheet, draw up a frame of a temporary size for the map. If *Excel* cannot automatically recognize the map selection, choose the desired map from the dialog box and click *OK*.

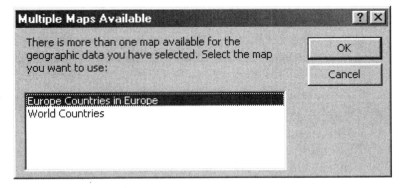

Fig. 10.9:   Selection of the map

481

The map is displayed, and a new *Map* toolbar appears with the following buttons:

- The *Select Objects* selects legends, titles, labels, or text for moving, sizing or deleting.

- The *Grabber* changes the position of the map within its borders.

- The *Center Map* specifies the center of the map.

- Click *Map Labels* in order to add labels to the map.

- Click the *Add Text* button if you want to enter text into the map.

- The *Custom Pin Map* button adds custom labels to the map.

- The *Display Entire* button centers the map and zooms so that all features are visible.

- With the *Redraw Map* button, you can redraw the map. Every flat map shows a stretched view of the earth. If you used the *Grabber* to move the map, you can click this button in order to reduce the stretching.

- *Map Refresh* updates your map after you change the data.

- *Show/Hide Microsoft Map Control* shows or hides the map control dialog box. This button is only available if you connected data to the map.

Together with the map and your inserted data the *Micro-soft Map Control* dialog box appears. Should the latter not open, choose *Insert/Data*, specify the cell range once more, and click *OK*. The data is then inserted. Now, in the *Microsoft Map Control* dialog box, drag the format button and the column buttons into the box in order to format the columns.

Drag the buttons for data which you do not want to show in the map out of the box.

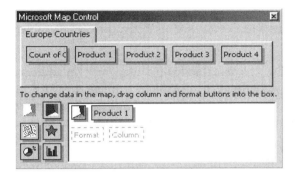

Fig. 10.11: The Microsoft map control

After you have finished compiling and displaying your data in the map, click outside the *Microsoft Map Control* into the worksheet.

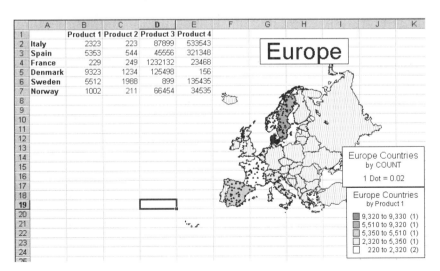

Fig. 10.12: An embedded map in a worksheet

Inserting AutoShapes

Already in *Excel 95*, it was possible to insert drawing and text objects such as circles, arrows or text boxes into tables and charts.

Excel 97 offers you an extended toolbar which, in addition to the normal buttons, makes the so-called *AutoShapes* available for simple graphic shapes. *AutoShapes* are preset shapes assembled in various categories that can be chosen from the palettes.

AutoShapes include lines, one- and two-dimensional (block) arrows, flowchart symbols, stars, banners, and callouts. After inserting them, the shapes can be formatted, moved around and adjusted in size. Two-dimensional *AutoShapes*, like for example block arrows, can also hold text just like text boxes.

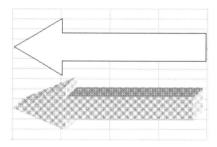

Fig. 10.13:   Block Arrows after inserting a 3-D effect and shadows

With the help of additional buttons, the *AutoShapes* can be displayed with shadows, either in two or three dimensions. By using a particular button, you can rotate an *AutoShape* in order to change its perspective.

Inserting Graphic Shapes

In order to insert a simple graphic shape like a rectangle or an oval into a worksheet or a chart, click on the button that displays the desired shape.

Then click into the worksheet and drag the mouse to create the shape. In order to create an even shape such as a square or a circle, hold down the ⇧ key while drawing.

AutoShape

In order to insert a readymade *AutoShape*, click the *AutoShapes* button and select the desired shape in the displayed palette.

Then click into the worksheet and drag the shape to the desired size.

Formatting AutoShapes and Drawing Elements with the Toolbar

Drawing toolbar

The method of inserting drawing elements and *AutoShapes* is very similar. First click on the *Drawing* button on the *Standard* toolbar.

Fig. 10.14: The *Drawing* toolbar

The *Drawing* toolbar in *Excel 97* contains buttons that already existed in earlier versions, for inserting and formatting drawing objects as well as buttons for the positioning of drawing objects, for adding shadows, and for the selection of dimensions.

- Draw *Draw*
  Click on this button to open a menu with commands for the grouping, as well as the order and the alignment of *AutoShapes* and other drawing elements.

■ ▢ *Select Objects*

Click on this button in order to activate the selection mode. You can then simply click on a particular object to select it or drag a selection rectangular around several objects to select them all.

■ ◔ *Free Rotate*

Click on an object and then click on this button in order to rotate it. After you have clicked this button, round handles appear in the corners of the object, enabling you to rotate the object.

■ AutoShapes ▾ *AutoShapes*

A click on this button opens a menu with the different *AutoShapes* categories. When you select one of these categories, a palette of the *AutoShapes* in that category is displayed.

■ ◳ *Line*

After clicking this button, you can draw a line by clicking on the point where the line is to begin, and dragging the mouse to the point where it is to end.

■ ◥ *Arrow*

Click this button and draw a line with an arrowhead at one end.

■ ▭ *Rectangle*

Click this button in order to draw a rectangle or, with the ⟨◇⟩ key held down, a square.

■ ◯ *Oval*

Click this button in order to draw an oval or, with the ⟨◇⟩ key held down, a circle.

■ ▤ *Text Box*

Click this button in order to draw a frame for a text box. After you release the mouse button, you can start entering the text.

■ ▲ *Insert WordArt*
This button opens the *WordArt* gallery from which
you can choose specially shaped text objects to insert
in your worksheet.

■ 🎨▾ *Fill Color*
Click on this button to fill a selected object with the
fill color displayed on the button, or click onto the
drop-down button and select another fill color or fill
effect from the palette.

■ 🖊▾ *Line Color*
Click on this button to display the border of a selected
object in the color given on the button, or click onto
the drop-down button and decide upon a different line
color from the palette.

■ ▲▾ *Font Color*
Use this button to format the selected object's labels
in the font color displayed on the button, or click on
the drop-down button and choose a different color for
the font.

■ ≡ *Line Style*
A click on this button opens a shortcut menu with
various line weights.

■ ▦ *Dash Style*
A click on this button opens a shortcut menu with a
variety of different styles such as dotted or dashed
lines.

■ ⇄ *Arrow Style*
A click on this button opens up a choice of arrow styles
which you can use to format a selected arrow object.

■ ◼ *Shadow*
This button opens a palette with possible shadow styles.

■ ◼ *3-D*

Clicking on this button opens a palette of possible 3-D representations.

Changing the Size of AutoShapes or Drawing Objects

You can select an *AutoShape* or a drawing object by clicking on it. It will then be surrounded by sizing handles. Drag these sizing handles in order to change the size of the object.

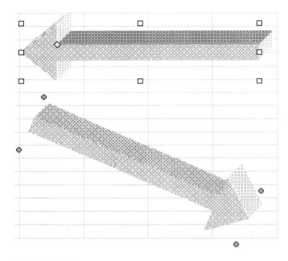

Fig. 10.15: The arrow from Figure 10.13 after rotation

An *AutoShape* which you can change retrospectively, displays a yellow handle in addition to the white ones. Drag this point in order to change the shape of the *Auto-Shape*.

AutoShape

default

You can reset an *AutoShape* you changed to its default shape by double-clicking on the yellow handle.

Free rotate

In order to freely rotate an object, first click the *Free Rotate* button ⟳. Then the object will be surrounded by round handles. As soon as you point to these handles with the mouse, the mouse pointer turns into a rounded arrow. If you now drag the handle with the mouse, the object will be rotated.

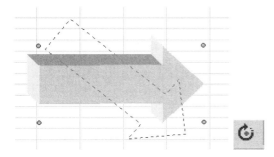

Fig. 10.16: Free rotate

Changing the Position of AutoShapes and Drawing Objects

To move an *AutoShape* or a drawing object, point to the object and then drag it to its new position with the mouse button held down.

Shadow Effects

In order to provide an object with a shadow effect, select it, then click on the *Shadow* button ▣. From the drop-down palette choose the style of shadow you want.

3-D Effects

If you want to represent a two-dimensional *AutoShape* or a two-dimensional drawing object in three dimensions, click the *3-D* button ▣. Choose one of the *3-D* effects shown in the palette, or click *No 3-D* if you want to display a three-dimensional object in only two dimensions.

Inserting Text into AutoShapes

If text is to be added to an *AutoShape*, click on the *Auto-Shape* with the right mouse button and choose *Add Text* from the shortcut menu. You can then enter the text which is to be displayed in the *AutoShape*.

Fig. 10.17:   Text in an AutoShape

When you have finished typing the text click outside the *AutoShape* into the worksheet.

Inserting a Graphic Object as a Background

Excel offers you the possibility to display a graphic object as a background in a worksheet. Since this background cannot be printed, this formatting is mainly interesting for Online documents, that is, for tables which are drafted for on-screen display and not for printing.

For a background picture, you can use any graphic or picture file in any of the usual graphic formats such as *WMF*, *EMF*, *JPG* or *BMP*. Likewise, you can display your logo or a picture you have made yourself, in the *Paint* Windows drawing program for example, as the background of an *Excel* table worksheet.

In order to insert a background graphic, select the work-sheet in which you want to display the background, and then choose *Format/Sheet/Background*.

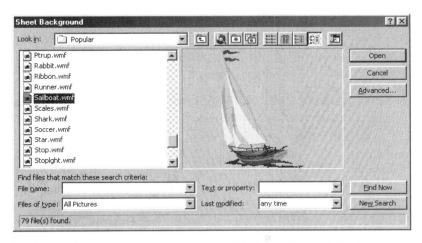

Fig. 10.18:   Choosing a background graphic for a table worksheet

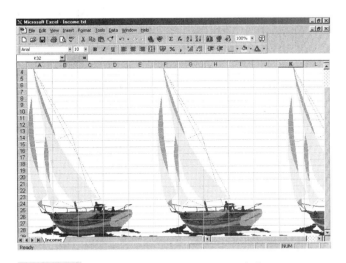

Fig. 10.19:   A background picture in a worksheet

In order to view the list of the background files you can import into *Excel*, in the dialog box open the *Files of type* drop-down list.

Open the folder which contains the graphic file, and select the the file you want to show as a background.

Preview

By clicking the *Preview* button 🔳 in the toolbar of the dialog box you can display the contents of the selected file.

Click the *Open* button in order to insert the file. In order to later on reset the inserted background, choose *Format/ Sheet/Delete Background*.

Inserting and Formatting WordArt Objects

The *WordArt* module is an integral part of the *Office Suite* and enables you to create text objects of extravagant or highly unusual effects, like, for example, arranging the fonts in waves or circles.

Inserting WordArt Objects

You can insert a new *WordArt* object either by using the *Insert/Picture/WordArt* command or by clicking the *Insert WordArt* button 🄌 on the *Drawing* toolbar.

WordArt-Gallery

The *WordArt Gallery* dialog box will be displayed. Click the box containing the desired *WordArt* style, and then click *OK*.

In the next step, you are asked to enter the text which you want to display in the *WordArt* object.

Overwrite the displayed text, and choose a font, font style and size using the buttons and the drop-down lists. Then close the *Edit WordArt Text* dialog box by clicking *OK*.

Formatting WordArt Objects with the Toolbar

Immediately after inserting, and every time you select a *WordArt* object, *Excel* automatically displays the *WordArt* toolbar.

Should this toolbar be missing, choose *View/Toolbars* and click on *WordArt* in the overlapping menu.

Insert WordArt

Click on this button in order to insert a new *WordArt* object.

Edit Text

Click this button in order to edit the text of a *WordArt* object you already inserted.

▪ 🔲 *WordArt-Gallery*
A click on this button opens the *WordArt Gallery*.

▪ 🔳 *Format WordArt*
This button opens the *Format WordArt* dialog box.

▪ 🔳 *WordArt Shape*
Select this button in order to display a variety of possible text arrangements.

▪ 🔳 *Free Rotate*
With this button you can rotate a selected *WordArt* object.

▪ 🔳 *WordArt Same Letter Heights*
This button displays upper and lower case letters at the same height.

▪ 🔳 *WordArt Vertical Text*
Displays your text vertical.

▪ 🔳 *WordArt Alignment*
Opens a shortcut menu with commands to arrange the *WordArt* text.

▪ 🔳 *WordArt Character Spacing*
Click on this button in order to change the spacing between the characters of the *WordArt* text.

Formatting WordArt Using the Dialog Box

As soon as you select a *WordArt* object and select the *Format/WordArt* command or click the *Format WordArt* button 🔳, the dialog box of the same name is opened.

There you will find the same tab pages already introduced in the *Format Picture* section. Note that the *Size* tab page allows you to rotate the object.

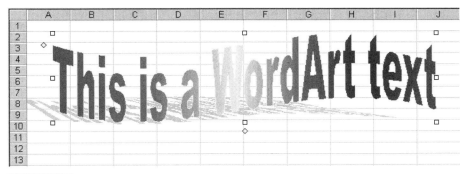

Fig. 10.21:   A WordArt object in the worksheet

You can also make use of the buttons on the *Drawing* toolbar in order to add and shape shadows or 3-D effects.

Inserting an Organization Chart

Organizational charts display hierarchical structures, such as the decision-making process in an enterprise, using a graphic illustration.

An organizational chart is created by the *Microsoft Organization Chart* Office component and can be inserted into an *Excel* worksheet as an embedded object.

Creating an
organization
chart

In order to create an organizational chart, choose *Insert/ Picture/Organization Chart*.

The *Microsoft Organisation Chart* program is started and displayed in a separate window, containing the standard chart with placeholders.

495

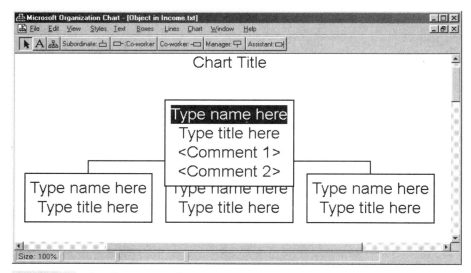

Select the placeholder and enter a chart title as well as the data for the name, the title, and the comments in the respective boxes.

With the help of the buttons on the toolbar or the function keys, you can insert additional boxes of the same order, subordinate order, or higher order.

Subordinates

Co-workers

Manager

Assistants

You can end the editing of a box by clicking the [Esc] key and then select the next box for editing.

In order to format a box or its contents, or in order to draw connectors among the boxes, use the following commands from the menu:

▥ *Styles*
In order to open a palette for grouping the boxes. Here you determine the kind of arrangement you want for the boxes of a group, of the assistant and/ or the co-managers

▥ *Text*
In order to open a menu with commands for the selection of fonts, color and alignment

▥ *Box*
In order to determine the box color, the border line, its color and line weight, and to add a shadow

▥ *Line*
In order to format the weight, style and color of the connecting lines

▥ *Chart*
In order to select a background color for the chart

After you have inserted and formatted all the information, select the *File/Close and Return to Workbook XY* command. Confirm the updating by clicking *Yes*.

If you want to change the embedded organizational chart later on, double-click on it.

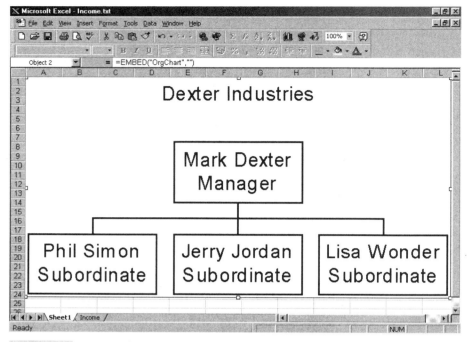

11. Automatic Functions

Now that you have grown accustomed to the basic functions of *Excel*, you will want to find ways to accelerate and simplify your entries and formatting, or to adjust certain *Excel* formats to your specific needs.

There are various automatic facilities to make your work more efficient and simple, such as *AutoFill*, *AutoFormat*, and *AutoCorrect*.

The recording of macros, the installation and use of *Add-Ins* as well as the customizing and extension of the toolbars offer additional facilities to expand the range of *Excel*'s utilities.

An Overview of Automatic Functions

Every *Office* application has certain automatic functions. These functions accelerate entering and formatting data, or automatically saving it. Some functions, like the spelling checker or *AutoCorrect*, work for many programs, while others, like *AutoFill* or *AutoComplete*, are typical *Excel* functions. Here is an overview of the most important *Excel* functions which perform certain tasks automatically:

■ *AutoComplete*
This function automatically completes an entry to a certain character chain already existing in the column.

■ *AutoCalculate*
This function displays a statistical evaluation of a selected cell range on the status bar.

■ *AutoFormat*
Use *AutoFormat* in order to automatically format tables and emphasize labels and totals.

▓ *AutoCorrect*
This function automatically corrects typing errors or replaces an entry.

▓ *AutoSave*
This function automatically saves your workbooks at intervals determined by you.

▓ *Spelling Checker*
The spelling checker searches the contents of a worksheet for typing errors and automatically suggests corrections.

▓ *Add-Ins*
This includes any additional program functions that are installed.

▓ *Macros*
Records in a macro a series of commands which you frequently use while performing specific tasks.

AutoComplete

Excel is equipped with a function which helps you while you are entering new data and which continuously checks whether a particular entry has already been made in a different cell or column.

Excel compares the text character by character with the one you enter into a specific cell. As soon as it finds a match with an entry made earlier in the same column, *Excel* suggests the remainder of the text which already exists as a possible completion.

Pick from list

Then all you need to do is confirm the completion by pressing the enter ↵ key, thus sparing yourself from having to repeat the entry. In addition, by clicking the right mouse button the function offers you a list of all the items already entered in the column.

The function completes only text, not numeric values. It is particularly useful for lists and database-like tables in which certain entries, like the type of address, is often repeated.

	A	B	C	D	
1	Address	City	Postal Code	Country	Phone
2	Walserweg 21	Aachen	52066	Germany	0241-I
3	2817 Milton Dr.	Albuquerque	87110	USA	(505)
4	2743 Bering St.	Anchorage	99508	USA	(907)
5	Smagsløget 45	Århus	8200	Denmark	86 21
6	Rambla de Cataluña, 23	Barcelona	8022	Spain	(93) 2
7	Carrera 52 con Ave. Bolívar #65-98 Llano Largo	Barquisimeto	3508	Venezuela	(9) 33
8	Via Ludovico il Moro 22	Bergamo	24100	Italy	035-6
9	Obere Str. 57	Berlin	12209	Germany	030-0I
10	Hauptstr. 29	Bern	3012	Switzerland	0452-I
11	Monumentenstr. 18	Berlin			
		Albuquerque			
		Anchorage			
		Barcelona			
		Barquisimeto			
		Bergamo			
		Berlin			
		Bern			
		Århus			

Fig. 11.1:   AutoComplete in the *City* column

In other cases, the automatic completion can be more of a hindrance than a help. All you have to do to cancel the automatic completion is just to go on typing. You can also press the backspace key ⌫ in order to delete the automatically entered characters.

Enable AutoComplete for cell values

If this automatic suggestion irritates you, for example because you have to enter many similar, yet different names of items into a list, you can turn off *AutoComplete* for the length of this task and reactivate it later on.

Options

To do so, select *Tools/Options* and activate the *Edit* tab page. Clear the *Enable AutoComplete for cell values* check box and close the the dialog box by clicking *OK*.

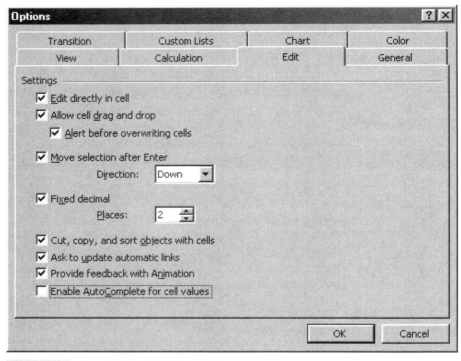

Fig. 11.2: Deactivating AutoComplete

In order to later reactivate *AutoComplete*, open the dialog box again, select the check box, and then click *OK*.

AutoCalculate

If you select any range in a worksheet, you can, without even giving a command, obtain information on the total, the average value or the maximum value of this range.

It is the *AutoCalculate* function which supplies you with this information.

Using AutoCalculate

Surely you will have noticed the *SUM=X* displayed in the status bar. This display is supplied by a function called *AutoCalculate*. Besides showing totals, it can give you further statistical results.

Sum=297735

Fig. 11.3: Display of the *AutoCalculate* function

The display of the sum is set as the default. You can, however, display instead another function which you need more frequently. The *AutoCalculate* function can alternatively calculate and display one of the following functions:

- *Average*
- *Count*
- *Count Nums*
- *Max*
- *Min*
- *Sum*

Changing AutoCalculate

In order to select the *AutoCalculate* function, click onto the stats bar with the right mouse button and choose the desired function from the shortcut menu. The COUNT NUMS function provides the values contained in a selected range. The COUNT function is the only one that can be used for the interpretation of text and it provides the number of cells in the list that contain text.

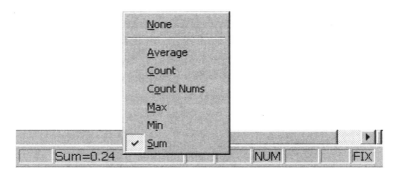

Shortcut menu for AutoCalculate

You can, for example, use the function to get quick information on the number of entries in a long list. Unlike *Excel 95*, in the *Excel 97* version the result of the *Auto-Calculate* function is only displayed when a cell range is selected.

AutoFormat

Tables are often arranged in a similar way. They contain labels of the rows in the first column and titles of the columns in the first row. The last rows and columns frequently contain the summaries, for example the column and row totals.

Since tables are often arranged in a similar way, they are also frequently formatted in a similar way. In most cases, the column and row titles, as well as the summaries in the last row/column, are emphasized.

What are
AutoFormats?

In order to be able to format such tables more quickly, *Excel* offers you a choice of preset formats via a function called *AutoFormat*. Not only can you transfer these ready-made styles to your whole table, but in addition you can exactly determine which format styles you want to take

from *AutoFormat* while maintaining others which you
have already set yourself.

Applying AutoFormat

In order to apply an *AutoFormat* to a table, select the
table and choose *Format/AutoFormat*.

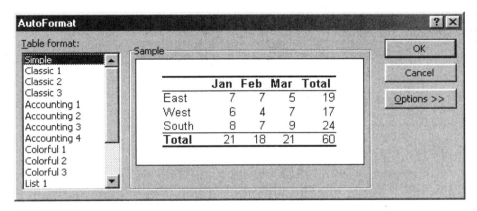

Fig. 11.5:   The *AutoFormat* dialog box*t*

In the *Table format* list you find all the *AutoFormats*
available. When you select one of these formats, an
example is displayed in the *Sample* box to the right, containing all the corresponding formattings.

Options

With the *Options* button you can enlarge the dialog box.
At the bottom, check boxes will appear. Clear the check
boxes next to the formats which you do not want to
transfer to your table. If, for example, you have already
perfectly adjusted the width of the columns to the cell
contents, clear the *Width/Height* check box so that this
format is not changed by *AutoFormat*.

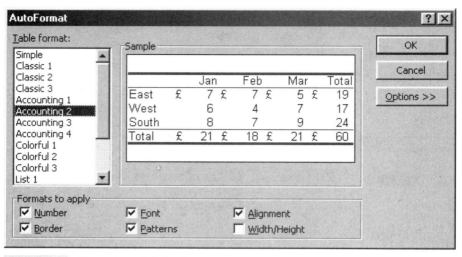

Fig. 11.6:   The enlarged dialog box

After you have thus selected the desired format and adjusted the *AutoFormat* to your specific needs by checking or clearing the check boxes, close the dialog box by clicking *OK*.

	A	B	C	D	E	F	G	H	I
4	**Income**	Jan	Feb	Mar	Apr	May	Jun	Jul	Aug
5	concerts	£250.00	£280.00	£100.00	£180.00	£300.00	£320.00	£0.00	£180.0
6	recordings	£135.00	£0.00	£210.00	£190.00	£0.00	£110.00	£0.00	£0.0
7	teaching	£260.00	£260.00	£260.00	£260.00	£260.00	£260.00	£0.00	£260.0
8	sales	£120.00	£0.00	£0.00	£120.00	£120.00	£60.00	£0.00	£0.0
9		**£765.00**	**£540.00**	**£570.00**	**£750.00**	**£680.00**	**£750.00**	**£0.00**	**£440.0**

	A	B	C	D	E	F	G	H	I	J
4	***Income***	*Jan*	*Feb*	*Mar*	*Apr*	*May*	*Jun*	*Jul*	*Aug*	*Sep*
5	*concerts*	£250.00	£280.00	£100.00	£180.00	£300.00	£320.00	£0.00	£180.00	£180.00 £
6	*recordings*	£135.00	£0.00	£210.00	£190.00	£0.00	£110.00	£0.00	£0.00	£190.00 £
7	*teaching*	£260.00	£260.00	£260.00	£260.00	£260.00	£260.00	£0.00	£260.00	£260.00 £
8	*sales*	£120.00	£0.00	£0.00	£120.00	£120.00	£60.00	£0.00	£0.00	£60.00 £
9		£765.00	£540.00	£570.00	£750.00	£680.00	£750.00	£0.00	£440.00	£690.00 £

Fig. 11.7:   A table before and after applying an AutoFormat

Removing AutoFormat

You can later remove an *AutoFormat* from your table. To do this, open the *AutoFormat* dialog box and from the *Table format* list select *None*, and click *OK*.

AutoCorrect

The *AutoCorrect* function primarily takes care of correcting typing errors. This is done on the basis of a list in which both the erroneous as well as the correct spellings of certain words are saved.

Replacement list

When *AutoCorrect* recognizes an entry contained in this list, it automatically replaces the entry by the correctly spelled word. You can open and add words to this replacement list by choosing *Tools/AutoCorrect*. If necessary, you can also delete words from the list so that they are not replaced automatically anymore.

The Features of AutoCorrect

All *Office* applications are equipped with a function which automatically corrects typing errors and other similar mistakes. This function is called *AutoCorrect* and it works throughout the different programs.

Two initial capitals

This function makes sure, for example, that if a word begins with two capital letters because you held down the *Shift* key ⬆ for too long, this oversight will be corrected automatically.

Likewise many typing errors are corrected automatically, mainly those which have occurred because two or more characters were transposed within a word by mistake.

Special keys

Besides corrections, the function also inserts special characters which cannot be entered with the normal keyboard keys. The following automatic replacements can be done by *AutoCorrect*:

▦ Correcting two initial capitals at the beginning of a word.

    `HOuse` → `House`

▦ The first letter of the weekdays is always capitalized.

    `wednesday` → `Wednesday`

▦ When you type (c), it will be automatically turned into the character for 'Copyright'.

    `(c)` → ©

▦ If you type (r), it will be automatically changed into the special character for 'registered trademark'.

    `(r)` → ®

▦ If you type (tm), this will be automatically changed into the special character for 'trademark'.

    `(tm)` → ™

In *Excel 97*, the function has been expanded. Now the first letter of a sentence is automatically capitalized too. And mistakes which occur because of accidentally pressing the *CAPS LOCK* key are automatically corrected.

Adding to the *AutoCorrect* List

In order to extend the *AutoCorrect* list and enter your own corrections, choose *Tools/AutoCorrect* and type the misspelled word into the *Replace* text box. Next click into the *With* box or jump there by pressing the *Tab* key ⇥ .

Add

Type the word once more, this time, though, with the correct spelling. Then click the *Add* button. In this way you can customize the list and automatically correct typing errors that you make now and then. The dialog box will remain open until you close it by clicking *OK*.

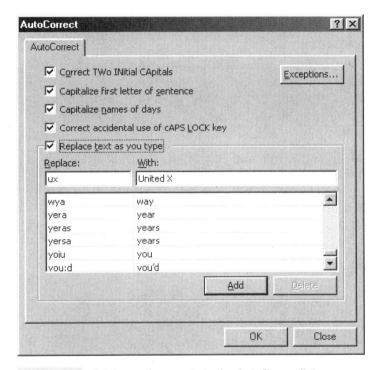

Replace text
as you type

The *Replace text as you type* check box in the *Auto-Correct* dialog box must be selected if *AutoCorrect* is to correct your typing errors immediately. Once it is checked, you need not bother anymore about recurring typing errors which you have added to the list. As soon as you have mistyped the word and then press the spacebar, type a punctuation mark or press the *Enter* key ⏎, *Auto-Correct* will replace the misspelled word.

Strictly speaking, *AutoCorrect* is an automatic replace-ment function. Therefore you can also use *AutoCorrect* to enter an abbreviation into the *Replace* box and write out the full text in the *With* box.

Deactivate AutoCorrect

In some cases, you will not want the automatic replace-ment. You then can deactivate *AutoCorrect*, either for specific terms or altogether. In order to partially or com-pletely prevent automatic replacements, choose *Tools/ AutoCorrect*.

In order to suppress the replacements indicated by the check boxes, clear the corresponding check box.

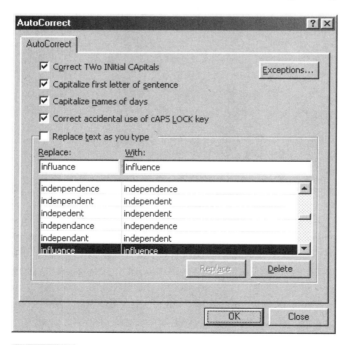

Fig. 11.9:   Deactivating the replacement function

If there is an entry in the list which you not longer want to be replaced, you can delete it. Select the entry in the list by clicking on it, then click the *Delete* button. Close the dialog box by clicking *OK*.

Replace text
as you type

If you want to deactivate the replacements of the *Auto-Correct* function altogether, clear the *Replace text as you type* check box and close the dialog box by clicking *OK*.

Deciding on Exceptions

In *Excel 97*, you have the opportunity to define exceptions in order to specify in which cases the first letter after a punctuation mark should not be capitalized. Use this function in order to be able to go on with your sentence after using, for example, an abbreviation like approx. or esp.

In order to define an exception, choose *Tools/Auto-Correct* and in the *AutoCorrect* dialog box, click the *Exceptions* button.

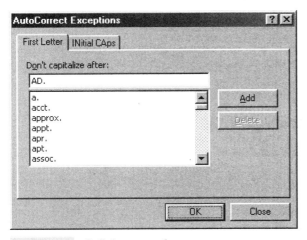

Fig. 11.10:   Defining exceptions

Add

Type the exception you want into the text box and click *Add*. Later you can remove the exception from the list again by clicking the *Delete* button.

AutoSave

One of the reasons why some people still prefer a calculator and paper spreadsheets to the calculation programs of a computer is because they are afraid of an unexpected program crash, its accidental wrong handling and any probable loss of data due to that.

Very often *Excel* is used to work on important data, such as a company's accounts, a cashbook of a society or association or charity, as well as private accounts. A loss of data could in fact have disastrous effects.

Therefore, you should always protect yourself against any possible loss of data by regularly saving your entries, and by creating additional copies which you keep in other folders.

Nevertheless, there is no reason why you should do without the many advantages which a spreadsheet calculation program, unlike any traditional calculator, has to offer you.

In order to be protected against the accidental deletion of workbooks, you can create backup copies.

Automatic saving function

With an automatic saving function, *Excel* makes sure that you are also protected against the loss of any data in the event of a program failure.

Excel provides this protection by saving either only the active or all open workbooks at certain time intervals. This time interval can be determined by you. In addition, you can specify that you want to be asked each time before the saving occurs.

Installing

The automatic saving function is an *Add-In*, that is, an additional program function which is activated or deactivated in the *Add-In* dialog box . In order to enable the saving function, choose *Tools/Add-Ins*, and select the *AutoSave* check box

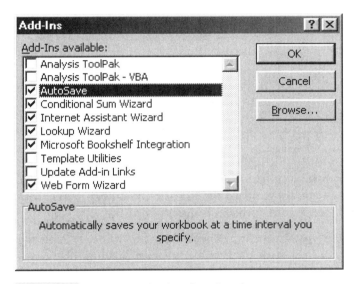

Should the entry in the *Add-Ins available* list be missing, click on the *Browse* button. During the *Office* setup the *AUTOSAVE.XLA* Add-In is by default saved in the folder *...PROGRAM FILES\MICROSOFT OFFICE\OFFICE\LIBRARY*.

The *AutoSave* Add-In is part of the default setup. When it is installed, it is saved in the above mentioned folder. If the Add-In has not yet been installed, open this folder, select the name of the *AutoSave* Add-In, and click *OK*.

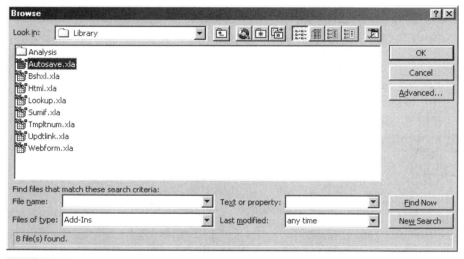

Installing the *AutoSave* function

After the installation, the Add-In is automatically loaded. Once you have closed the *Add-Ins* dialog box by clicking *OK*, the loading process is displayed in the status bar.

Activating
AutoSave

If the *AutoSave* item is displayed in the *Add-Ins* dialog box but not selected, click onto the corresponding check box and then click *OK*. Now you can call up the function via the *Tools* menu.

If *AutoSave* is activated, you will find a check mark in front of its name on the *Tools* menu. Immediately after loading it, this function is automatically activated. In order to specify the time interval, you open the *Tools/ AutoSave* dialog box.

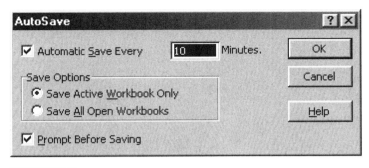

Configuring the *AutoSave* function

By selecting or clearing the *Automatic Save Every X Minutes* check box you can activate or deactivate *Auto-Save*. Into the text box in front of *Minutes*, enter the interval you want to set for the automatic saving. You can choose any time between 1 and 120 minutes. Ten (10) minutes is the default value.

Setting the interval

Which interval you choose depends on the speed with which you work, and on the amount of changes you make. If you are not sure how often the function should save your work for you, do not change the default setting. After a certain working period you can then decide whether automatic saving every 10 minutes is enough or whether you should change the interval.

Prompt before saving

Check the *Prompt Before Saving* check box if you want *Excel* to wait for your confirmation before saving. If the confirmation function is activated, a dialog box is displayed after the specified save interval and you can either click *Save*, or cancel the save by clicking *Skip*. The confirmation appears for every single workbook.

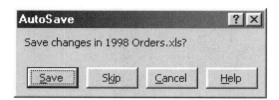

Fig. 11.14:   Save confirmation

In the *Save Options* option group you decide whether only the active workbook or all workbooks are to be automatically saved at the given time interval. After you have specified the saving functions according to your needs, close the dialog box by clicking *OK*.

If the *Prompt Before Saving* option is activated, *Excel* will ask you to confirm when the save interval has lapsed. If you have cleared the *Prompt Before Saving* check box, the status bar will indicate when the function is saving.

Add-Ins

Add-Ins are additional program functions extending the range of *Excel* functions. They can be installed or un-installed individually.

Installing

As with the earlier versions of *Excel*, in *Excel 97*, you can extend the normal range of commands by using *Add-Ins*. Among others, the following commands will then be available to you:

- *AutoSave*

- Simplified data exchange with *Access* (*AccessLinks*)

- Analysis functions (*Analysis ToolPak*)

- *Solver*

- *Report Manager*

- *Template Utilities*

Tip!

If you have Internet access, the *Internet Assistant Wizard* and the *Web Form Wizard* Add-Ins of *Excel 97* will be of special interest to you.

Not all of the *Add-Ins* are installed in the default setup. If you have set up a customized installation, or if some *Add-Ins* are missing, you can use the Setup program of *Office* or *Excel* respectively in order to install the *Add-Ins* later on. Insert the CD or the floppy disk, choose *Start/Run* and enter the letter of the drive, followed by the *Setup* command. If you used an installation from the CD drive, it would look like this if your CD was on drive D:

`D:\SETUP`

Add

In the setup program, click the *Add/Remove* button. Select the *Add-Ins* or *Microsoft Excel* in the *Office Suite* respectively. Click the *Change Option* button, and in the *Office* setup select the *Add-Ins*. Click the *Change Option* button.

Check boxes

Now either select all the check boxes one by one, or click the *Select All* button. Click *OK* two times, then *Continue* in order to finish the installation. You will get the message that the installation has been successfully completed. Click *OK*.

Making Add-Ins Available

Should the *Add-Ins* be installed but not be available in the menus, choose *Tools/Add-Ins* and click the check boxes

517

for the *Add-Ins* you want to use. *Add-Ins* with selected check boxes are loaded automatically when *Excel* is started. With the *Browse* button you can look for *Add-Ins* which are not displayed in the *Add-Ins* dialog box.

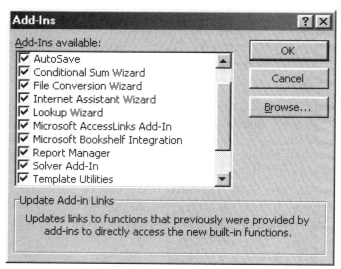

Fig. 11.15:   The *Add-Ins* dialog box*r*

After you have installed all the *Add-Ins* you want, close the dialog box by clicking *OK*. You can then call up the *Add-Ins* from the menus.

Spelling Checker

It is true that although *Excel* is primarily a spreadsheet calculation program, it also contains an integrated spell checker in order to correct typing errors.

In the *Office Suite*, the spelling checker is set up to work throughout the various programs. This means that words which you add to the dictionary while working in *Excel* will later on also be available in other applications such as *Word*, and vice versa.

How does the spelling checker work?

The spelling checker compares the text in your table with the entries in the built-in dictionary. Each word not contained in this dictionary is highlighted for examination, and you can decide whether it needs to be corrected or, if it is correct and moreover it is a word you frequently use, then you should add it to the dictionary.

AutoCorrect

A particularly convenient point here is the fact that you can transfer a correction directly from the spell checker into the *AutoCorrect* function so that in the future the corresponding word is immediately corrected as you type it.

Starting the Spelling Checker

To activate the spell checker, use one of the following procedures:

- Choose the *Tools/Spelling* command.

- Click on the *Spelling* button .

- Press the F7 key.

If the spelling checker does not find any typing errors or unknown words in the table, a message to this effect is displayed on the screen.

However, if it finds a word it does not know and which is not contained in the dictionary in the way you spelled it, the *Spelling* dialog box is opened and the word is displayed.

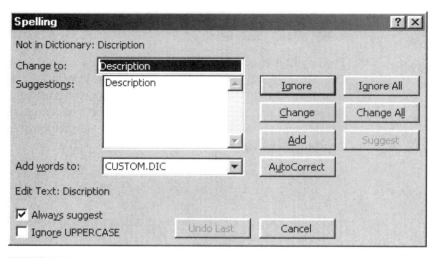

Suggestions

The unknown word is displayed next to the *Not in Dictionary* label. If the spelling checker has suggestions, these will be displayed in the *Suggestions* list box. You can either double-click on the correct suggestion or select it and click the *Change* button in order to replace the wrong word.

Change and
change all

If the spelling checker cannot suggest a correction, click into the *Change to* text box and correct the word manually. By clicking the *Change* button, you transfer the correction into the current cell in the table. Clicking the *Change All* button will correct the word in every cell of the table in which it appears.

Add to
AutoCorrect

When the spelling checker displays a typing error which occurs repeatedly, you can include the correction made by hand or made by selecting the highlighted suggestion, in the *AutoCorrect* function by clicking the corresponding button. In future, this word will be automatically corrected as soon as you have typed it.

Ignore

It often occurs that the spell checker displays words which are typed correctly but which are not contained in the dictionary. In this case, click the *Ignore* button if the word appears only in the current cell, or click *Ignore All* if the word recurs in other cells as well.

Add

If the spell checker displays a word which is correctly typed and which you use frequently, such as your company's name or parts of your address, you can add this word to the dictionary so that in the future the spell checker will not display it anymore. To do this, click the *Add* button.

Always suggest
corrections

In order to accelerate the spell checker, clear the *Always suggest* check box. The suggestions will then be displayed only after clicking the *Suggest* button.

Using Macros

If there is a certain command, a certain function or a certain series of commands which you use over and over again in the same order, you can make your work easier by creating a *Macro* which saves you having to repeat these working steps and executes them automatically after you press a key or click a button.

How a macro is created and how it functions can best be understood by an example. In order to insert a sample macro which can later be activated by a click and inserts the current date into the active cell, choose *Tools/Macro/Record New Macro*.

Enter a name for the new macro and click *OK*.

521

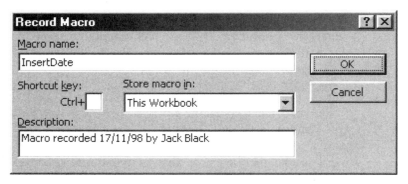

Fig. 11.17: Fig. 11.17:   Naming the macro

Click the *Relative Reference* button in the *Stop Recording* toolbar so that later the date is inserted in each selected cell. Next choose *Insert/Function*, and in the *Function category* list box select *Date & Time*. Then in the *Function name* box select *TODAY*. Now close the dialog box by clicking *OK*. Close the *Formula Palette* by clicking *OK* as well.

Macro recording   Finish the macro recording by clicking the *Stop Recording* button in the toolbar which is automatically displayed during the recording.

Fig. 11.18:   The *Stop Recording* toolbar in Excel 97

In order to assign a button to the macro, choose *View/ Toolbars/Customize*. In the *Customize* dialog box, switch to the *Commands* tab page and select the *Macros* item in the *Categories* list box.

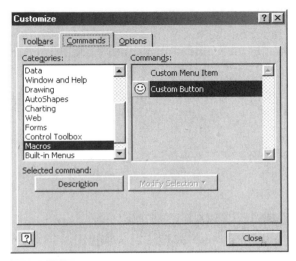

Fig. 11.19: The *Customize* dialog box

From the *Commands* list box, drag the *Custom Button* onto a toolbar, and click on it with the right mouse button.
From the shortcut menu, select *Assign Macro*.

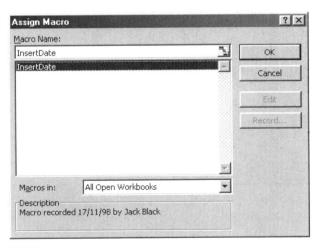

Fig. 11.20: Assigning a macro

Select the name of the macro and click *OK*. Now right-click once more on the button, open the *Change Button Image* palette on the shortcut menu and select a different image.

With the *Edit Button Image* command on the shortcut menu, you can design your own image in the *Button Editor*.

After completing your changes close the *Button Editor* by clicking *OK*. Close the *Customize* dialog box by clicking *Close*.

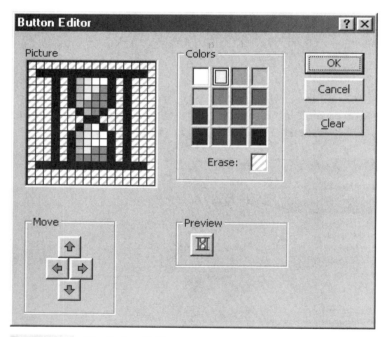

Fig. 11.21:   The Button Editor

Using a Macro

You can start a recorded macro in three different ways. If you want to activate the macro using a shortcut key, then before recording it, you should give it a shortcut key together with a name.

The usual way of running a macro to which you have assigned neither a button nor a shortcut key, is by selecting *Tools/Macro/Macros*. In the *Macro* dialog box, select the name of the macro you want to run, and click the *Run* button.

You can, however, at a later time assign a button and/or a key combination to a macro to access it more easily.

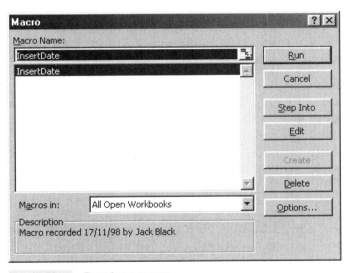

Fig. 11.22:   Running a macro

In order to assign a shortcut key to an already recorded macro, choose *Tools/Macro/Macros*. Select the name of the corresponding macro and click the *Options* button.

Assigning a shortcut key to a macro

In the *Shortcut key: Ctrl+* text box, press the key which should be used in conjunction with the `Ctrl` key in order to run the macro. Close the dialog box by clicking *OK*.

In order to include a macro into a menu, choose *View/ Toolbars/Customize*. On the *Commands* tab page, select *Macros* from the *Categories* list box.

Custom menu item

Then from the *Commands* list box, drag the *Custom Menu Item* entry onto the menu where you want to insert the macro. The menu will be automatically opened. Drag the item to the desired position in the menu, and release the mouse button. Then right-click on the new item and choose *Assign Macro*.

Name

In the *Assign Macro* dialog box, double-click on the name of the macro in the list. Right-click again on the item, and in the *Name* box overwrite the entry with the command which should display and activate the macro in the menu. Press the *Enter* key `↵` to confirm the entry and then close the *Customize* dialog box by clicking *Close*.

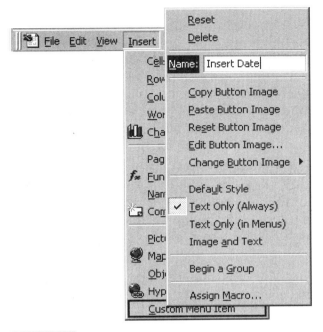

Fig. 11.24: Assigning a menu command for a macro

You can then choose the macro from the menu just like any other built-in *Excel* command.

If you later want to remove a macro button or a macro command from the menu, again choose *View/Toolbars/Customize*. Drag the macro button out of the toolbar or the command out of the opened menu. After you have changed your menu or toolbar entries close the *Customize* dialog box by clicking *Close*.

If you only want to remove a button from a toolbar, it is not necessary to open the *Customize* dialog box. While pressing down the ⟨Alt⟩ key you can simply drag the button out of the toolbar.

Opening a Workbook Automatically After Starting

Normally, you open a workbook by using the *File/Open* command or by clicking the *Open* button. You then have to open the folder in which the workbook is saved, and choose the name of the workbook, then finally complete the action either by double-clicking the selected name, or by selecting the file and clicking *Open.*

It goes without saying that this procedure of opening workbooks which you use regularly over a long period of time is rather cumbersome. Therefore there are faster ways to automatically open a workbook or several workbooks respectively, as soon as *Excel* starts.

Document menu

A quick way to start *Excel* along with one of the workbooks you are currently using, is by selecting the name of the workbook from the *Documents* menu in the *Start* menu. To do so, click on the *Start* button, and select *Documents*, followed by the name of the workbook.

XLSTART

You can open a workbook even more quickly by putting it in the *XLSTART* folder. All the workbooks contained in this folder are automatically loaded when *Excel* starts.

In order to establish a link between the workbook in the current folder and the *XLSTART* folder, you can use the *Open* or *Save As* dialog box of *Excel*, if the workbook which you want to open automatically in future is closed.

Create Shortcut

Choose *File/Save As* and open the folder in which the workbook is currently saved. With the right mouse button click on the name of the workbook, and select the *Create Shortcut* item from the shortcut menu. *Excel* will insert a new file with the following name:

```
Shortcut to [Workbook Name]
```

Right-click onto the shortcut and select *Cut*. Now open the *XLSTART* folder. After the *Office* installation, it is automatically located in the following path:

```
C:\Program\Microsoft Office\Office\XLSTART
```

Up one level

Click the *Up One Level* button until the icon for the hard disk is displayed in the *Look in/Save in* drop-down list. Then you can one by one open the corresponding folders. Right-click in the open *XLSTART* folder and from the shortcut menu, choose *Paste*. Then close the *Save As* dialog box by clicking *Cancel*. The workbook will now be automatically opened every time you start *Excel*.

Changing Basic Excel Settings

Excel is not a rigid program made up of fixed settings but is very flexible. You can always customize it to suit your needs. Thus you can, for example, change the view or certain calculation or formatting settings.

Customize

The settings which you can change are, for the most part, contained in the *Options* dialog box. Additional options are also accessible in the *Customize* dialog box.

Individual screen elements can be changed using the *View* menu. Click *View* and then on the item you want to display in addition to the others on the screen. With the help of this menu you can show or hide the *Standard* and *Formula* toolbars. The settings will only be valid for the current workbook. You can, however, also change these elements in the *Options* dialog box.

Options

In order to open the *Options* dialog box, choose *Tools/ Options*. Select the tab page containing the items you want to change.

Select the desired radio button or click the corresponding check box. In the following list, some important settings are shown:

- On the *View* tab page you find window options to show or hide screen elements, such as *Page breaks*.

- On the *Calculation* tab page you can set the way calculations and iterations are done and how link values are saved.

- On the *Customs Lists* tab page you can create a series of items which you can then transfer into your worksheet using the fill handle.

- On the *Chart* tab page you can determine the chart type and set a new default chart.

- On the *Edit* tab page you can determine how inserted values are to be treated, whether you can edit directly in the cell, and whether drag-and-drop moving and copying cells with the mouse is possible.

- On the *Color* tab page, you can select default colors, e.g., for charts, and create your own custom colors.

- On the *General* tab page, you can change the default file location and set the default number of worksheets in a workbook. Here you can also change the default font.

- The *Transition* tab page offers options for those who are switching to *Excel* from other programs.

Customizing Toolbars

The most important basic commands can be quickly activated using the buttons on the *Standard* toolbar. For formatting, you find corresponding buttons on the *Formatting* toolbar.

For further specific tasks, such as the creation of drawing objects or the formatting of charts, there are additional toolbars which are displayed either automatically while such a task is being performed, or which can be shown using the shortcut menu of the toolbars or with the *View/ Toolbars* command.

Apart from the buttons displayed by default on the toolbars, *Excel* has additional buttons that can be used.

Since every user uses *Excel* in a different way, so each of the commands will be used more or less frequently. In order to accommodate these differences, the toolbars can be extended and changed to suit the needs of individual users.

- You can add buttons for commands which you use frequently.

- Buttons which you do not need at all can be removed in order to make space for other buttons.

- You can move buttons to other locations in the toolbars.

- You can create your own toolbars.

Extend toolbar

In order to change toolbars, choose *Tools/Customize* and activate the *Commands* tab. From here you can drag buttons out from the displayed toolbars in order to remove them or to move them to another position on the toolbar.

In the *Customize* dialog box, select a category and drag a button from the *Commands* list box onto a toolbar in order to make the corresponding command available there.

After you have completed your changes, close the dialog box by clicking the *Close* button. You can reset a toolbar to its default settings by clicking the *Reset* button in the *Customize* dialog box (*Tools/Customize*) on the *Toolbars* tab page. You have to confirm the resetting so that you do not accidentally remove buttons you still want to use.

Icon Size, Animation and ScreenTips

On the *Options* tab page of the *Customize* dialog box, you find two check boxes for displaying *Large icons* and for showing or hiding the *ScreenTips* on the toolbars.

In the *Menu-Animation* drop-down list, you can choose among various animations which can be used to open a menu.

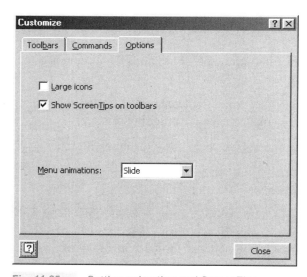

Fig. 11.25:   Setting animation and ScreenTips

12. Protection Features

Modern computer systems need to offer comfortable and convenient commands for the processing of electronic data, as well a wide range of formatting options for the visual appearance.

Another important component an application should offer is the protection of data. A good calculation program is obliged to include a protection against unauthorized access as well as a protection against the loss of data.

Excel can offer you both, and in various ways. By creating passwords, you can prevent other users from deactivating a protection which you have established for your data.

In order to guarantee an extensive protection, you can additionally use passwords already in Windows which are associated, for example, with a screen saver, and which prevent general access to your personal computer.

Protection of Data

If you use *Excel* in your office for working on delicate data, such as personal data concerning the wage slips, if for no other reason than to protect the data, you should see that no unauthorized person can read the data.

Protection against access

In order to guarantee this, you can provide your workbook with password protection which will open the workbook only if the correct password has been entered.

This sort of protection is called a *Password to open* protection, because without the password it is not possible to either view or change the file.

Another function serves to protect you from the loss of data. This is called write protection. In this area, *Excel* offers you different options, starting with the simple *Read-only recommended* option to the *Password to modify* write protection.

Additional methods of preventing loss of data include creating backup copies, which *Excel* can make automatically for every workbook. Also, the automatic saving at regular intervals determined by you can help to prevent data loss.

In order to protect individual cells or cell ranges from any changes, you can lock them. You can protect the spreadsheet or the workbook against any changes by entering a password.

If you work in a team, you can protect a distributed workbook in such a way that all changes made are recorded in detail. The various protections options are shown below:

- *Read-only recommended*
  This is the weakest protection you can use to protect a workbook from accidental change. Since it is merely a recommendation, it can just as well be refused when opening the file.

- *Password to modify*
  A *Read-only* protection can be defined for the duration of a session. It is automatically deactivated when the workbook is opened the next time. The *Read-only* write protection can be connected to a *Password to modify*. Then it is established for good and makes it impossible to save the file under the original name if the workbook was not opened using the password.

- *Password to open*
  This type of protection is principally connected with a password and prevents the opening of files by persons who do not know the password.

- *Protect Sheet*
  The sheet protection works to the effect that locked cells and certain other objects cannot be changed anymore. This protection can be set up with or without a password.

- *Protect Workbook*
  A workbook protection protects the composition and the arrangement of the windows. It can be established with or without a password.

Passwords

If you want your protection to be efficient, you should use a password so that the protection can only be cancelled by persons who are in possession of the password.

Entering a password in *Excel* is principally connected to a saving process. To enter a valid password, keep the following rules in mind:

- The password can have up to 15 characters.

- The case has to exactly match.

- It can be a combination of letters, numbers and symbols.

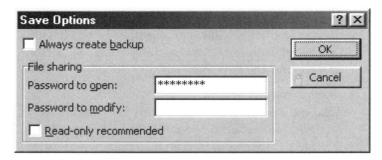

Fig. 12.1:   Entering a password to open for file sharing

The entry appears as asterisks '*'. The password must be entered a second time in order to prevent typing errors, and finally confirmed by clicking *OK*.

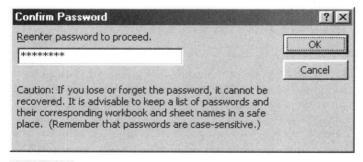

Fig 12.2:   Confirming the password

Afterwards, activate the saving process of the workbook in the *Save As* dialog box by clicking the *Save* button.

Activating Read-only Recommended

You can define a differentiated protection for your *Excel* workbooks. You can, for example, protect the workbooks in such a way that they can be opened only after entering a password.

You can also protect workbooks to the extent that they cannot be saved under the original name if they have not been opened using a password.

You should mainly work with these two protection features if you work with a personal computer to which other people also have access.

If you want to provide your workbooks with a read-only protection in order to merely prevent your saving any accidental changes, you can, instead of entering a password, activate the read-only recommendation.

As the name already suggests, a read-only recommendation is merely a recommendation which is displayed during the opening of a file, but which can be refused. It is not connected to a password.

In order to set up a read-only recommendation for the current workbook, choose *File/Save As*, and click the *Options* button. Check the *Read-only recommended* check box, and close the dialog box by clicking *OK*.

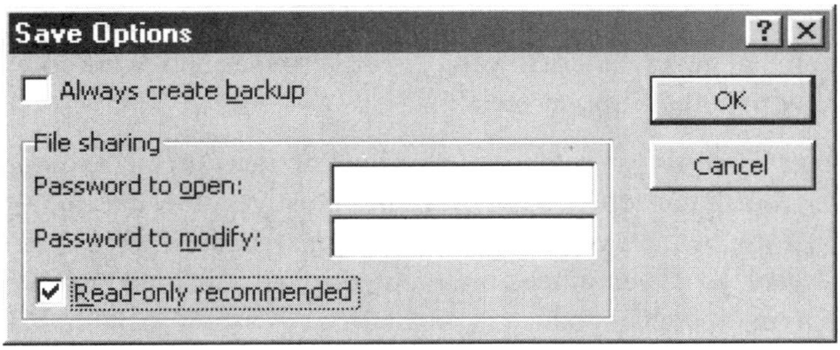

Fig. 12.3: Activating the *Read-only* recommendation

Now save the file by clicking the *Save* button. Before the workbook is opened the next time, a message will be displayed which brings the read-only recommendation to your attention.

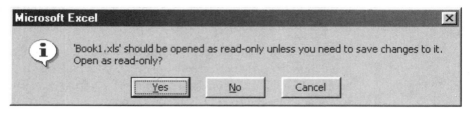

Fig. 12.4:   Read-only protection is activated

Click the *Yes* button in order to open the workbook in *Read-only* mode. Click the *No* button if you want to be able to make changes and want to save them in the workbook.

Providing *Read-only* Protection

If a workbook contains tables with important data which must never be lost, you should provide the workbook with a *Read-only* protection.

A *Read-only* protection does not prevent the workbook from being opened. It prevents, however, the workbook from being saved under the original name again. This way it is guaranteed that the original file will always remain unchanged.

Open a File with a *Read-only* Protection

There are several ways of opening a workbook with a *Read-only* protection. You can either activate the *Read-only* protection just for the length of the current session, or you can set it up permanently. If you activate it permanently, you can connect it with a password so that the *Read-only* protection can be removed only by you and by those persons to whom you have given the password.

Read-only for the current session

In order to open a workbook in such a way that you want the *Read-only* protection to be valid only for the current session, choose *File/Open* or click the *Open* button 🗁 on the toolbar.

Open the folder containing the workbook and select the corresponding file name.

Commands and settings

Click the *Commands and Settings* button 🔡 in the dialog box toolbar, and select the *Open Read-Only* command.

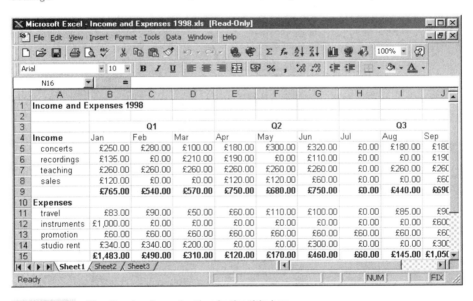

Fig. 12.5: The Read-only protection in the title bar

539

The status of a *Read-only* workbook is displayed in the title bar of the document window. If the document window is maximized, the protection is displayed in title bar of the application. You can still make changes to the *Read-only* workbook, by when you try to save the changes, *Excel* will display an error message.

Permanent *Read-only* Protection with Password

In order to provide a permanent *Read-only* protection, first open the workbook which you want to protect. Then choose *File/Save As*, and click the *Options* button.

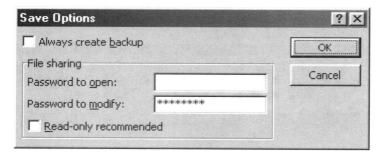

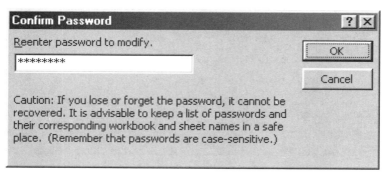

Fig. 12.6:   A password to modify and the confirmation

Into the *Password to modify* text box, enter a password according to the following rules:

- A maximum length of 255 characters.
- Use exact case.
- Can be composed of letters, numbers and symbols.

After entering the password and clicking *OK*, you have to re-enter the password again using the same spelling. Since the password you entered is displayed by asterisks, this procedure is used to make sure that no error occurred during the first entry.

Click the *OK* button again, and then save the workbook by clicking the *Save* button. You need to confirm the replacement of the original file with the changed file by clicking *Yes*. In order to activate the protection, the workbook must first be closed and then reopened.

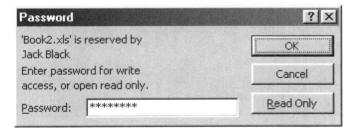

Fig. 12.7:   Opening of a workbook protected with a password to modify

In the dialog box, you can choose whether you want to open the workbook with or without *Read-only* protection. In order to open the file without *Read-only* protection, you have to enter the password and then click *OK*.

Fig. 12.8: A wrong password

Read-only

If you enter the wrong password, *Excel* refuses to open the workbook without *Read-only* protection. If you open the file with the *Read-only* protection, or if you want to open a workbook whose password you do not know, click the *Read Only* button.

As soon as you then try to save the workbook without any change of name or folder, a message appears which reminds you of the *Read-only* protection. *Excel* then opens the *Save As* dialog box so that you can enter a new name for the modified file.

Fig. 12.9: The workbook is read-only.

In order to cancel the *Password* protection of a workbook, open it without *Read-only* protection. To do this, you must, of course, know the password. Then choose *File/Save As* and click the *Options* button. Delete the displayed password, and then save the workbook.

Activate the Access Control

The access control prevents the opening of a workbook by users who are not in the possession of the valid password. An access control is also called *Read/Write* protection and always goes along with a password.

In order to activate an access control, select the *File/Save As* command, and then click the *Options* button.

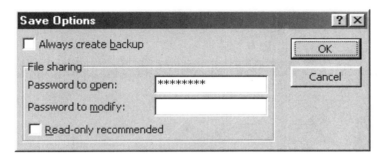

Fig. 12.10:   Enter a password to open

Into the *Password to open* text box, enter a password which adheres to the following rules:

- A length up to 255 characters

- Upper and lower case must match

- Composed of letters, numbers, and symbols

After you have completed the entry and clicked *OK*, you are asked to repeat the password a second time. The repeated entry serves to exclude any mistakes or errors.

Type the password again in exactly the same spelling and case as you did the first time. Then click the *OK* button once more. Now save the workbook by clicking the *Save* button, and confirm the replacement of the original work-book with the changed file by clicking the *Yes* button. In order to activate the access control, you need to first close and then reopen the workbook.

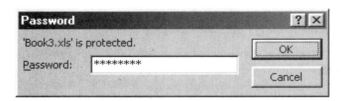

Fig. 12.13:   Opening a workbook with access control

Fig. 12.14:   A wrong password

After choosing the *Open* command, a dialog box is displayed, into which you must enter the password. Then click the *OK* button, and if the password is incorrect, *Excel* will refuse to open the file.

Protect Sheet

Creating and formatting a table with all its formulas and charts can take a lot of time and involvement. If you have completed the worksheet, and if a modification of the formulas is no longer necessary, except perhaps in rare cases, you should protect your worksheet from being changed.

This does not mean, however, that you cannot enter any further data in the future. You have the option to define in detail which cells can still be changed, and which cannot.

If you always enter data into a table at the same time as other people, it is advisable to protect at least the existing formulas. Even if you are the only one working on the table, you should consider whether or not a sheet protection is practical. With this sheet protection you can prevent the deletion of an extensive formula which took you a long time to create – should you accidentally click on the wrong cell, for instance.

Conditions

Excel can protect a worksheet against entries and changes. In order for the sheet protection to work, two conditions need to be fulfilled:

- The cells which you want to protect must be locked.

- The sheet protection must be active.

Only if you activate the sheet protection does the locking of the cells becomes effective. In *Excel* all cells are locked by default. You probably did not realize this fact because you have not activated the sheet protection before. If you activate the sheet protection without any further preparation, no cell can be selected any longer. If this corresponds to your wishes, you can activate the sheet protection without any further preliminaries.

As a rule, however, some cells should be locked and others should be open to continue working with them. Therefore, first unlock those cells which still need to be worked upon after the sheet protection has been activated. To do so, select the cells which will need to be changed in the future. You can select non-adjacent cells by clicking and dragging the mouse across the cell ranges with the Ctrl key held down.

Choose *Format/Cells*, and activate the *Protection* tab page. Then clear the *Locked* check box.

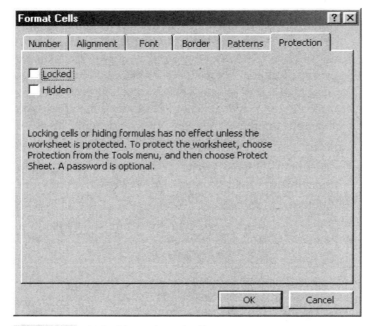

Fig. 12.15:   Unlocking selected cells

Close the *Format Cells* dialog box by clicking *OK*, and choose *Tools/Protection/Protect Sheet*.

In the *Protect Sheet* dialog box, you can, by clicking or clearing the corresponding check boxes, specify that only certain contents of the worksheet should or should not be protected respectively.

If you do not want any other user to simply change your protection settings, you should add a password.

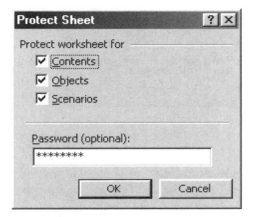

Activating a password for the sheet protection

Enter a password according to the following rules:

- A maximum length of 255 characters
- Case should match
- Composed of letters, numbers, and symbols

Instead of displaying the password you enter, the asterisks will be shown on the screen. In order to make sure that no typing error has occurred as well as see that you remember the password, you will need to retype the password a second time before confirming the entry by clicking *OK*.

Now the sheet will be protected. If you try to change a locked cell, a dialog box opens with the message that any modification is refused.

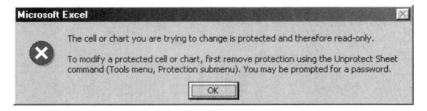

Microsoft Excel

The cell or chart you are trying to change is protected and therefore read-only.

To modify a protected cell or chart, first remove protection using the Unprotect Sheet command (Tools menu, Protection submenu). You may be prompted for a password.

OK

Fig. 12.17: Protected cells cannot be modified

In addition, in many menus all commands leading to a change are displayed in light grey to show that they are deactivated. You can cancel the sheet protection by using the *Tools/Protection/Unprotect Sheet* command.

Protecting a Workbook

Like all the other elements, you can also protect the arrangement of the windows and the structure of a workbook itself. With this protection, the following actions in worksheets are prevented:

▨ Deletion

▨ Moving

▨ Hiding

▨ Showing

▨ Renaming

▨ Insertion

For windows, the following commands are prevented:

▨ Move

▨ Maximize and minimize

▨ Hide or show

▨ Close

The protection of a workbook can be linked with a password, too.

Structure

In order to protect a workbook, choose *Tools/Protection/ Protect Workbook*. Check the *Structure* check box in order to protect the structure of the sheets in the workbook against any changes.

Windows

Select the *Windows* check box in order to prevent any changes to the arrangement of the windows.

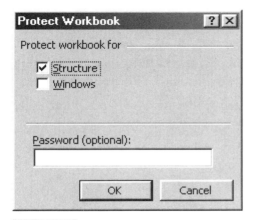

Fig. 12.18: Protecting a workbook

Password

If you want to connect the protection of the workbook with a password, enter it into the *Password* text box and then click *OK*. You need to repeat the entry of the password in order to exclude any potential typing errors.

In order to later deactivate the protection of the workbook, choose *Tools/Protection/Unprotect Workbook*. If you had connected the protection of the workbook with a password, you will need to enter it.

Changing or Deleting Passwords

You can provide *Excel* workbooks or worksheets with passwords. You can choose among a *Read-only* protection, an access control, or a sheet protection.

All of these protection options can be connected to a password. If you want to change or delete the assigned password, you need to know the original password, and the file needs to be opened without *Read-only* protection.

Open workbook without *Read-only*

In order to delete a previous password, open the file by selecting the *File/Open* command. If the workbook is protected with a password, you need to enter it before opening the workbook. Then click *OK*.

If the file is protected with a *Read-only* password, enter the password in order to open the file without *Read-only*.

In order to change or delete a *Read-only* or an access control password, choose *File/Save As* and click the *Options* button.

Delete password

Delete the password in the *Password to modify* or *Password to open* text box, depending on what area the password is valid for. If you want to change the password, overwrite it with a new password. You will then be asked to repeat this new entry once more. Do so, and click *OK*.

Click the *OK* button in order to close the *Save Options* dialog box, and click the *Save* button to save the file. A message appears: *The file [file name] already exists. Do you want to replace the existing file?*

Confirm the question by clicking *Yes*.

In order to delete or change the protection of a worksheet, open the file and choose *Tools/Protection/Unprotect Sheet*. Then enter the password so that it is deleted. You can then enter a new password.

Share Workbook

If you work with directly connected personal computers or in a network, you can make *Excel* workbooks available to other users too. The making available of workbooks is called *Sharing*.

If several persons are working on a workbook at the same time and each one is modifying it, *Excel* takes care of organizing which change is transferred to the workbook and when. Conflicts may arise, particularly if two users are trying to work on the same cell.

For this reason, you can define a log for the shared workbook in which such conflicts are recorded. In order to share a workbook with other users, open it and choose *Tools/Share Workbook*.

Select the *Allow changes by more than one user at the same time* check box.

On the *Advanced* tab page of the *Share Workbook* dialog box, you can determine in detail how conflicts are to be recorded and treated.

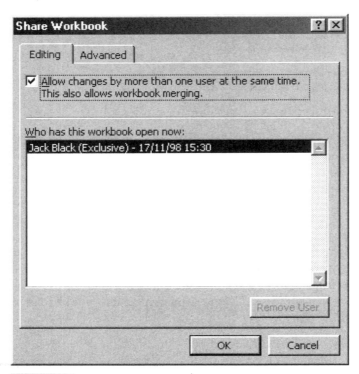

Fig. 12.20   Sharing a workbook

Tracking Changes in a Shared Workbook

In *Excel*, you can, in a workbook that you have allowed other network users to use as well, track all changes, for example, so that later on you can decide which changes to finally put in the workbook.

The history of changes keeps track of:

- the sort of changes,

- the time of the change,

- who made the changes,

- in which cells they were carried out,

- the value before and after the change.

Keep change history

In *Excel 97*, you can activate a history of changes for shared workbooks by using the *Tools/Share Workbook* command. To do so, on the *Advanced* tab page click the *Keep change history for x days* radio button. By means of the *Tools/Track Changes/Highlight Changes* you can then determine which information should be recorded in the change history.

List changes on a new sheet

In order to create a change history on a separate sheet, select the *List changes on a new sheet* check box.

The changes can be also highlighted directly in the table. In order to do this, in the *Highlight Changes* dialog box, select the *Highlight changes on screen* check box.

Fig. 12.21: Keeping a change history

You can then display information on all selected changes by using the *ScreenTips*. With the *Tools/Track Changes/ Accept or Reject Changes* command, the changes can be examined and accepted or rejected respectively.

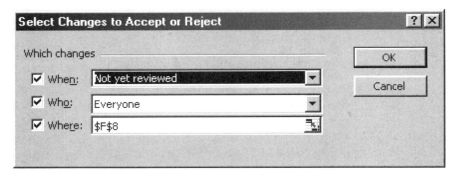

Fig. 12.22:   Reviewing changes

Comments

If you should discover, while creating a table, that you want to get more information on certain topics, or if you are working on the workbook together with other users, it is helpful to insert a note in the respective cell to say which data should be displayed in it, for example, or in which way a formula works. If you or one of the other users later selects the cell, the note will be displayed.

Inserting a Comment

The *Notes* of the earlier *Excel* versions have become *Comments* in *Excel 97*. In order to insert a comment into a workbook, choose *Insert/Comment*, and enter the text of the comment into the text box. After you have finished your entry, click outside the text box.

Cells containing a comment are indicated with a red mark. When you move the mouse pointer over such a cell, the note is displayed as a *ScreenTip*.

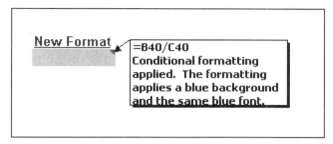

New Format

=B40/C40
Conditional formatting
applied. The formatting
applies a blue background
and the same blue font.

Fig. 12.23:   A comment

Show or Hide Comments

You can show or hide the comments and the red marks by selecting *View/Comments* or the *Tools/Options/View* command. If you select the *View/Comments* command, the *Reviewing* toolbar is automatically displayed.

On the *View* tab page in the *Options* dialog box, select one of the following radio buttons in the *Comments* option group:

■ *None*
In order to hide the comments as well as the red indicators.

■ *Comment indicator only*
In order to display only the red indicator.
The comment will be displayed as a *ScreenTip* as soon as the mouse pointer is moved over the cell.

■ *Comment & indicator*
The indicators as well as the comments are displayed.

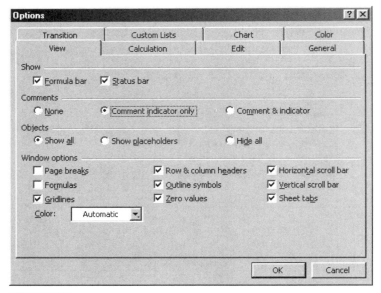

Fig. 12.24: Show and hide comments

Printing a Comment

Before you start printing a worksheet containing comments, you can decide whether or not these comments are to be printed.

In order to do this, activate the worksheet you want to print, and select *File/Page Setup*. Activate the *Sheet* tab page, and in the *Print* option group open the *Comments* drop-down box. Select one of the following items:

- *None*
  In order to supress all comments and comment indicators. This is the default setting.

- *At end of sheet*
  In order to print all comments not at their actual position, but underneath the last cell of the table.

■ *As displayed on sheet*
In order to print all comments at the positions where they actually occur.

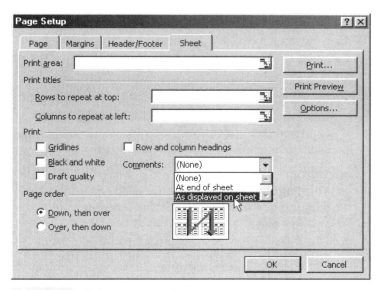

Remove Comments

You can remove a comment by right-clicking onto the cell containing the comment. From the shortcut menu that appears, select the *Delete Comment* command.

Edit a Comment Using the Toolbar

Excel 97 offers you a special toolbar to insert and edit comments. You can display this toolbar by using the *View/Toolbars/Reviewing* command or via the *Comments* item on the *View* menu.

The *Reviewing* toolbar

Use the buttons of the toolbars in order to create new comments, and to show or hide, edit or delete existing comments.

■   🗂 *Edit Comment*
This button is displayed as soon as you highlight a comment that is already inserted. Click the button in order to activate the comment text box for editing.

■   🗂 *New Comment*
This button is displayed instead of the *Edit Comment* button if you select a cell without a comment in order to insert one.

■   🗂 *Previous Comment*
Click on this button to display the previous comment.

■   🗂 *Next Comment*
A click on this button displays the next comment.

■   🗂 *Show/Hide Comment*
With this button you show and hide the comment of the active cell.

■   🗂 *Show/Hide All Comments*
With a click on this button you show or hide all comments.

■   🗂 *Delete Comment*
Click on this button in order to delete the selected comment. The comment is deleted immediately without further confirmation requested.

Sending Workbooks

If you use *Excel* in a team and you are connected to a network, you can use *Excel* together with *Exchange* or *Outlook* in order to send workbooks to other network users.

In order to do so, you have the choice of whether to send the workbook to a single user, or to insert it as an attached file and send copies to many recipients at once.

Sending Files to E-mail Recipients

In order to send a workbook by E-mail, open the workbook and choose *File/Send To/Mail Recipient*. Choose a profile or confirm the existing one by clicking *OK*.

Select the E-mail recipient, overwrite if necessary the subject of the text, and add an accompanying text for the workbook.

You can use the *Format* and *Spelling* commands in order to edit the message and check it for typing errors.

When you have completed the E-mail, click the *Send* button.

After the workbook and message has been sent, you will automatically be returned to your *Excel* workbook.

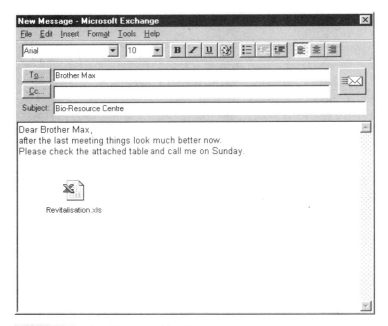

Fig. 12.27: Sending a workbook

Sending a File to Routing Recipients

To send a document as a *Routing Slip*, open the document and choose *File/Send To/Routing Recipient*. Choose a *Profile* or confirm the *Profile* offered with *OK*.

Click the *Address* button and select in the *Show Names from the* drop-down list box, the address book from which you want to take the addresses. After that select one by one all the desired names of the recipients from the list box on the left side of the dialog box and click on the *To* button.

The selected names will be displayed in the right list of the dialog box. After you have summarized the names, activate the *OK* button.

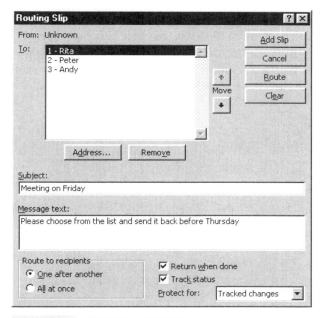

Routing Slip

From: Unknown

To:
1 - Rita
2 - Peter
3 - Andy

Move

Add Slip
Cancel
Route
Clear

Address... | Remove

Subject:
Meeting on Friday

Message text:
Please choose from the list and send it back before Thursday

Route to recipients
- One after another
- All at once

☑ Return when done
☑ Track status
Protect for: Tracked changes

Fig. 6.19: Selected recipients

Order

You can change the order of the recipients in the *To* list box with the help of the *Move* arrow buttons. Move the selected recipient up or down the routing list. If you click the *One after another* radio button, the document goes to recipients in the order they appear in the *To* list.

Message text

If necessary overwrite the *Subject* and type the text of your mail into the *Message text* box.

In the *Route to recipients* options group, you can choose whether you want to send the documents to *All at once* or *One after another*.

Route

To add the routing slip to the document and send it according to the currently selected options, click the *Route* button. This button is unavailable if the *To* list is empty.

To send the routing slip later on, click the *Add Slip* button instead. The routing slip will be added to the document and the *Rountig Slip* dialog box will be closed without sending the document. In the *File* menu the submenu of the *Send To* command offers the *Other Routing Recipient* option to add new recipients and send the routing slip later on.

13. Help and Troubleshooting

We all make mistakes in the course of our daily life, even while we are creating tables and diagrams in a spreadsheet program. Among some of the most common errors are:

- Entry errors

- Syntax errors in formulas

- Logic errors

- Handling errors

- Formatting errors

To work as effectively as possible you should try to avoid mistakes right from the start. To help you out here, *Excel 97* offers a new feature that limits the range in which data can be entered.

If mistakes have already occurred, you should be informed about the meaning of the various error messages and about how to correct these errors.

Typing errors

Some of the mistakes which occur most frequently during the creation and editing of worksheets are simple typing mistakes and errors when creating cell references.

Excel provides you with excellent methods for finding mistakes and correcting them. To eliminate typing mistakes, run the spelling checker with *Tools/Spelling*. You will get suggestions for alternative spellings, and the opportunity to correct the mistakes yourself.

AutoCorrect

With *Tools/AutoCorrect*, you can prevent your 'favorite' typing mistakes with an automatic correction. Enter any of the mistakes which you frequently make into the *Replace* text box and the correction into the *With* box, then click the *Add* button.

Avoiding Wrong Entries as a Matter of Principle

If you want to create a worksheet that will be used by others or if you rarely enter new data into your worksheet, mistakes can happen particularly easily. This can mean:

- Text might be entered into a cell that is used as an argument for a function, and the function expects a numeric value.

This will result in an error message. Well, at least you get a message.

- Data is entered into entirely wrong cells and the cell references are incorrect.

This mistake does not produce an error message if you have configured the worksheet in such a way that error messages do not appear when there is no data entered.

- The values are not in the valid range; say, somebody enters 80% for VAT. This would still be an error.

These errors would not be displayed because the data would conform to the *Excel* rules, meaning that there are no logic or syntax mistakes.

Here is a list of things you (or another user) can do to avoid having to 'manually' search for the cause of every single mistake.

- Limit the entry to particular types of data or to a value range.

■ Let *Excel* display a help message indicating the valid data range.

■ Let *Excel* display the appropriate error message.

All three features can be used separately or combined. To activate one or more of these features, select the cell or cell area that you want to validate and choose *Data/ Validation.*

Settings tab   On the *Settings* tab page, choose from the *Allow* drop-down list the data type that should be allowed in the selected area. Choose for example *Whole number* to suppress the entry of decimal numbers or *Text length* to allow only character sequences. Depending on your choice of data type and operator, the additional content of this dialog box changes.

To allow only a particular range of values, choose for example *Whole number* or *Decimal* and select in the *Data* drop-down list the *between* operator.

Enter one or more values to limit the range of validity. To set a value range, enter the lower limit into the *Minimum* text box and the upper limit into the *Maximum* text box. Instead of entering constant values you can also enter cell references.

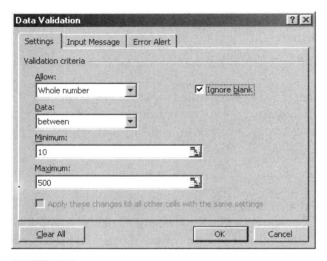

Fig. 13.1:   Determining the validation range

Input Message   On the *Input Message* tab page, you can create a supporting message which will be displayed as a *ScreenTip* when the mouse moves over cells with validation rules.

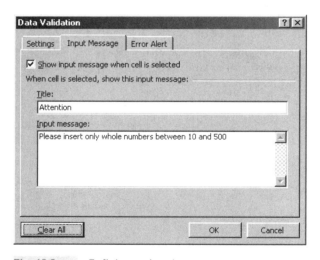

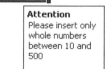

Fig. 13.2:   Defining an input message

In addition to, or instead of, the input message you can set an error message on the *Error Alert* tab page that draws the user's attention to the wrong entry.

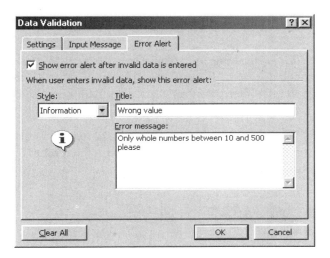

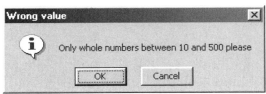

Fig. 13.3: The definition on the left hand, the result on the right

In the *Style* drop-down list, you can choose from among three icons for the warning. Close the dialog box by clicking the *OK* button.

If a worksheet already contains data that do not conform to a rule, you can highlight these cells with *Edit/Go To/ Special* or with the *Circle Invalid Data* button on the *Auditing* toolbar.

Finding Mistakes with Auditing

You can also use the *Auditing* feature to trace the cause of error messages that appear in a cell instead of a proper result.

Auditing menu command

Choose *Tools/Auditing* and from the overlapping menu the commands *Trace Precedents* and *Trace Dependents* in order to trace faulty cell references back to their origin and to view the disastrous results in the dependent cells.

Auditing toolbar

Choose *Tools/Auditing/Show Auditing Toolbar*, to trace the mistakes with the help of the buttons on the toolbar.

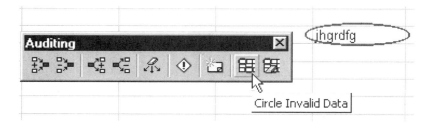

Fig. 13.4:   The Auditing toolbar

The *Auditing* toolbar contains buttons to mark cells that contain references or that refer to references. It also contains a button to mark cells that create errors.

- *Trace Precedents*
  Click this button to trace cells to which the currently selected cell refers.

- *Remove Precedent Arrows*
  Use this button to remove the traces created with the above button.

■ ⁺⁼ *Trace Dependents*
Click this button to trace cells that depend on the currently selected cell.

■ ⁺⁼ *Remove Dependent Arrows*
Use this button to remove the traces created with the *Trace Dependents* button.

■ ⁺⁼ *Remove All Arrows*
Click this button to remove all arrows in the worksheet in one go.

■ ◈ *Trace Error*
Select a cell that displays an error message and click the *Trace Error* button. Each time you click, you can trace the error back one more step.

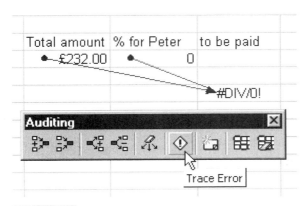

Fig. 13.5:   A traced error

Displaying and Checking Formulas

In order to display all formulas and any errors they might contain, either press the Ctrl+` key combination or choose *Tools/Options* and select the *Formulas* check box on the *View* tab page. After confirming with the *OK* button, the formulas will be displayed.

AutoFit Selection

Since formulas usually require more space than their results, the column width is increased automatically. To check as many formulas as possible select the whole worksheet with the *Select All* button above the row headings and choose *Format/Column/AutoFit Selection*.

Remove All

Arrows

Now, with the help of *Auditing*, you are able to trace any errors and correct them. After the search and correction has been done, you can remove all traces from your worksheet with a click on the *Remove All Arrows* button 🔏. Using the ⌗Ctrl⌗+⌗`⌗ key combination will revert the display to the formula results.

Suppressing and Correcting Error Values

If you create a worksheet that has to serve as a template, most of the time the actual data will only be entered later. Only constant text and formulas make up the basic structure of the worksheet and have to be saved with the template worksheet. The still unentered data, however, can produce error messages in the formulas. The cells will display #N/A like in Figure 13.6.

Information

functions

In such a case, *Excel* provides a number of functions to suppress the error messages that are created by missing data. These functions can be found in the *Information* function category. Before using such a function, determine what type of information has to be entered into the cell that produces the error message.

In this example, the error message #N/A is displayed in C5 because the data for column C are taken automatically by *Excel* from a separate item list. But to do that *Excel* first needs the item number, which is still missing in A5. The moment the item number is entered, the error message will disappear and the formulas will be executed.

	A	B	C	D	E	F	G	H
1	**Item**	**Qty**	**Unit Rate**	**Total**				
2	A110	3	£3.00	£9.00				
3	A198	6	£0.23	£1.38				
4	A123	6	£1.56	£9.36				
5			#N/A	#N/A				
6				#N/A				
7								

Fig. 13.6:   An error message

But to suppress the unnecessary error message even be-fore the data entry, you need the ISTEXT() function. This function is inserted together with a condition, and checks whether data is already entered into the cell. Only if such is the case is the calculation executed; otherwise the execution is cancelled.

To supplement the formula in our example, so that the error messages are suppressed, insert a condition and the ISTEXT() function. To do that, click in the formula be-hind the equal sign and insert an IF() function that con-tains as arguments:

- for the *Logical test*, the information function;

- for the *Value_if_true*, the calculation formula; and

- as instruction for the *Value_if_false*, two empty quotation marks to suppress the error message.

In the example, the following formula is used in C5:

```
=VLOOKUP(A5,Sheet3!$A$2:$B$5,2)
```

The error is created by the reference to A5 as long as there is no data entered. The formula is completed as follows:

```
=IF(ISTEXT(A5),VLOOKUP(A5,Sheet3!$A$2:$B$5,2),"")
```

571

You can insert the functions with the *Paste Function* dialog box and the *Formula Palette* or type it directly into the *Formula* bar.

Further functions and their application are listed in the following overview. Here *Error causing cell* means always the cell that produces the error due to missing data. The *Calculation formula* is always the cell that displays the error message until data is entered into the *Error causing cell*.

- ISBLANK()
  This function tests whether a cell already contains data. The type of data, be it text or numerical, is ignored. The function returns the TRUE value if the cell is empty and the FALSE value if there is any content in the cell.

```
=IF(ISBLANK(Error causing cell),Calculation
formula,"")
```

- ISTEXT()
  Use this function to check whether text has been entered into a cell. The function returns the TRUE value if the cell contains text and the FALSE value if the cell is empty or contains anything other than text, such as values, formulas or error messages.

```
=IF(ISTEXT(Error causing cell),Calculation formula,"")
```

- ISNONTEXT()
  This function is sort of the opposite of the previous one. It checks whether there is no text in a cell. It returns the TRUE value if the cell contains anything other than text and the FALSE value if the cell contains text.

```
=IF(ISNONTEXT(Error causing cell),Calculation
formula,"")
```

- ISNA()
  This function tests whether a cell contains the error
  message #N/A and returns TRUE if the cell contains it
  and FALSE if the cell contains anything else.

```
=IF(ISNA(Error causing cell),Calculation formula,"")
```

To get the complete list of all *Information* functions,
choose *Insert/Function* or click the *Paste Function* button
fx to display the *Paste Function* dialog box. Select
Information in the *Function category* list.

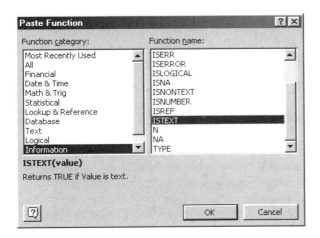

Fig. 13.7:   The information category

In the *Function name* list, you can find all functions that
you can use to check within a formula, whether data and
if so which data is contained in a cell. Depending on the
result of this check, calculations can be executed or not.

Recognizing and Treating Errors

When a formula cannot be calculated because it contains an error, or because it refers to a cell that creates the error, *Excel* will display an error message instead of the proper result. An error can be recognized by the preceding '#' sign.

Instead of a Cell Content

This error message is displayed if the current column width is not sufficient to display the complete cell contents. This can happen after entering a formula, after assigning a number format or after changing the font size.

You have to change the column width to make the error message disappear and to display the correct result. To do so, you can use one of these procedures:

- Drag the right boundary of the column heading of the column which contains the error-causing cell. Move it to the right until the error message disappears and the cell content is displayed.

- Double-click the right boundary of the column heading to *AutoFit* the column width.

- Highlight the column by clicking on the column heading and choose *Format/Column/AutoFit Selection*.

- After selecting the column you can also set the column width manually by choosing *Format/Column/ Width*. Increase the value and close the dialog box by clicking the *OK* button.

Date and time values

The error message #### will also be displayed when calculating with time values that lead to a negative result.

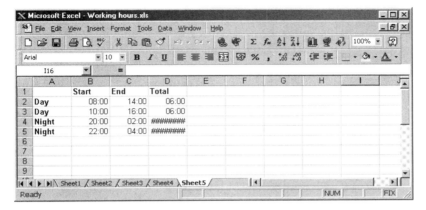

Excel then fills the whole cell independent of its width with the error sign '#'.

To correct this error, choose *Format/Cells* and assign a different format from another category to the cell, for example *General*. After confirming with *OK* the error message will disappear and the formula result will be displayed.

Correcting #N/A Errors

If a cell displays the #N/A error value instead of the expected result, a formula is referring to a non-existent value so that the value is not available to the function or the formula.

This error appears in the following functions:

- MATCH
- LOOKUP
- HLOOKUP
- VLOOKUP

Possible cause

In any of these functions, the cause of the error can be that you are using a wrong type of lookup value or that you are searching an unsorted table. If you are developing a formula for a template, use the ISBLANK() function or ISNUMBER(), for example, to suppress the error message until the data is entered into the cell in question.

Correction

If the error message resulted from a different reason, try using the following steps to correct the error:

- Test whether the cell with the lookup value contains data of the correct type, if the search column contains values at all.

- Test whether the reference for the lookup value has been made to a cell area instead of a single cell.

- When using the VLOOKUP and HLOOKUP functions, add the FALSE value as the last (optional) argument if you are searching in an unsorted list.

- Sort the list that has to be searched in ascending order.

- If you use the LOOKUP functions with an array formula, check to see whether the arguments use the same number of rows and columns as the range in which the array formula is contained.

If you use macros or user-defined functions, the cause of an error can also be a missing argument in a user-defined function. It can also be returned by a macro. In this case make sure that:

- the workbook that contains the worksheet is opened;

- the user-defined function works correctly;

- no argument is missing;

- all arguments for the user-defined function have been entered in the proper order.

Lookup Wizard

In *Excel 97*, you can call up the *Lookup Wizard* to help you to write a formula that finds a value in a list. This function is an *Add-In* and has to be activated via *Tools/ Add-Ins* before you can use it.

If you want more exact information on the #N/A error message or other error messages, open the *Help* menu and click *Contents and Index*. On the *Index* tab page choose the first entry *#####error* from the list box and click the *Display* button.

Correcting #REF! Errors

The #REF! error value appears instead of a result if the formula contains invalid references. This happens when you add or delete cells to which the formula refers.

It also happens when the formula refers to a worksheet or workbook that has been deleted or moved to a different location.

Undo

If you realize your mistake immediately after pasting or deleting a cell, use the *Undo* button ◙▾, or choose *Edit/Undo*.

If you realize the error too late, so that *Undo* is not available anymore, use the ⌨Ctrl+⌨ key combination to display the formulas with the references and check the references with the help of the auditing feature. Choose *Tools/Auditing/Trace Precedents* to check which references still exist and which references are missing and are therefore causing the error. Clean up after you finish by removing the traces with *Tools/Auditing/Remove All Arrrows*.

If the cause of the error is a missing worksheet, you have no choice but to recreate this sheet and assemble the required values there.

If the cause of the error value is a reference to a workbook whose location has been changed, you are more fortunate. Just choose *Edit/Links* and click the *Change Source* button.

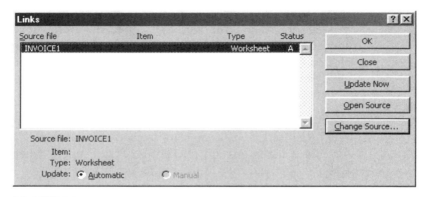

Fig. 13.9:   Editing links

Open the folder that now contains the workbook your formula refers to and select the name of the workbook. Close the dialog box by clicking the *OK* button.

If the whole workbook has not been moved, but has disappeared, recreate it and link it as described above.

Correcting #Div/0! Errors

If you get the #DIV/0 error value instead of a valid result, the formula in the cell executes a division by zero or a division by a cell that returns a zero. Division by zero is mathematically impossible, therefore the formula cannot return a proper result.

Zero

If this error value appears, you should first check whether the formula contains a zero as a constant operand. Maybe you just mistyped the entry, it happens. If so, double-click the cell that contains the error value, click into the point where the zero is displayed and delete it. Then type in the correct value.

Display zero values

You can display zeros by choosing *Tool/Options,* and on the *View* tab page selecting the *Zero Values* check box in the *Window options* group box.

Tracing the error

If the zero is not a constant value in the formula but is derived from a reference, select the cell with the error value and choose *Tools/Auditing/Trace Error.*

If you do not spot the trouble-maker immediately, double-click the trace itself to select the cell that caused the error.

If you find that the error value is caused by a reference to the wrong cell, replace the wrong reference by the correct one. Double-click the cell in order to edit it.

Colored cell reference

Double-clicking on the error cell will display the referenced cells in different colors so as to distinguish them easily.

Correcting the cell reference

In order to replace a wrong reference with a correct one, select the cell reference that is causing the error by clicking at the point where it begins and dragging the mouse over it while holding down the left mouse button. Then, in the worksheet, select the correct cell and confirm by pressing the *Enter* key ⏎.

If the error is caused by an empty cell in a template-like worksheet that is supposed to be filled in later, suppress the display of the error value with a suitable function until the data has been entered.

IF() Function

Use an IF() function so that division with the error causing cell is only executed once the cell contains data.

The following formula causes the error message #DIV/0, as long as cell B4 is empty:

```
=34/B4
```

ISNUMBER()

Adding a condition and the ISNUMBER() function will suppress the resulting message:

```
=IF(ISNUMBER(B4),34/B4,"")
```

The IF() function tests whether a number has already been entered into cell B4. Only if this is the case will the division be executed. The empty quotation marks suppress the error message until data is entered into cell B4.

By complementing the formula with the following expression, even entering a zero into B4 will not cause an error message:

```
=IF(B4<>0,34/B4,"")
```

With this condition the division is only executed if the cell contains a number which is not equal to '0'.

Correcting #NAME? Errors

One of the most frequent errors that occurs during the entry of data and the creation of formulas is the #NAME? error. This error value always appears, when you use a character sequence in a formula that cannot be recognized as a formula or cell name. This error may be due to the following reasons:

- You are using a text argument without quotation marks.

- You have mistyped a function name.

- You are using a cell name that you have deleted.

- You have misspelled the cell name you are using.

- You forgot to put a colon in a reference to a cell area.

Source of error

Character sequences in formulas are automatically interpreted as function names. If there is no function with that name, the character sequence is interpreted as a cell range name.

In *Excel*, you can name cells and cell areas in order to use these names as cell addresses in formulas. If the character sequence in the formula does not correspond to either a formula name or to one of these user-defined names, the error message will be returned.

If you want to find out which names are already defined in your table, click the drop-down button of the *Name* box at the left end of the *Formula* bar.

The drop-down list contains all names used in the worksheet. You can use the *Insert/Name/Paste* command to paste names in the correct spelling into a formula and thus avoid mistakes.

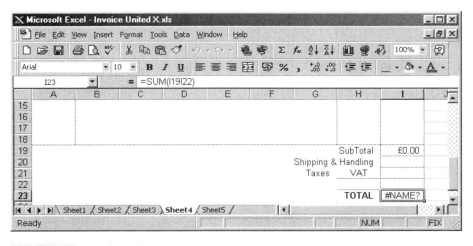

Fig. 13.10:   The #NAME? error value

Fig. 13.11:   The *Paste Name* dialog box

To avoid typing errors with function names, always click at the point in the formula where you need to insert the function, then click the *Paste Function* button 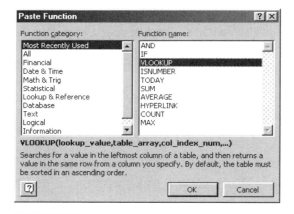.

Fig. 13.12:   Use the *Paste Function* dialog box to avoid typing errors

Select the category to which the required function belongs and double-click the function name in the list. Then enter the function arguments if necessary.

Further functions   Besides the described procedure, you can also open the *Function* drop-down list in the *Formula Palette* to select a function from there. From the drop-down list choosing *More Functions* you can and call up the *Paste Function* dialog box.

Missing quotation marks

Missing quotation marks or a missing colon in a reference can be corrected manually. Double-click the cell with the error value, place the insertion point where the mistake is and insert the correction.

With the command *Insert/Names/Define*, you can recreate a deleted name. Read more about the creation of names in Chapter 2.

Correcting #NULL! Errors

If a formula returns the '#NULL!' error value instead of the expected results, the formula refers to an empty intersection. This error value occurs when you specify an intersection of two areas that do not intersect.

Empty intersection

The source of the error is the use of a wrong reference operator or a missing reference operator or a wrong cell reference:

- Use a single space as an intersection operator between two references whose intersection is the reference area.

- Use a comma as a union operator to refer to two areas that do not intersect.

Correcting the error

To correct the error, first check the formula. You might have just mistyped something and entered a space instead of a comma. In that case replace the space by a comma and press enter ⏎.

To correct an erroneous reference to an empty intersection, you can mark the error-causing cells with *Tools/ Auditing/Trace Error*. Subsequently correct the cell reference to create an intersection and press *Enter* ⏎.

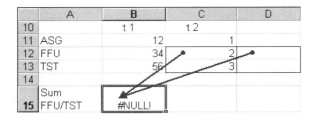

	A	B	C	D
10		t 1	t 2	
11	ASG	12	1	
12	FFU	34	2	
13	TST	56	3	
14				
15	Sum FFU/TST	#NULL!		

Fig. 13.13:   Error value and Trace Error

In *Excel 97*, a double click on the cell displaying an error is enough to highlight the cells to which the formula refers. This way you can see immediately whether or not there is an intersection.

In Figure 13.14, the #NULL! error value is displayed in the cell B15. It is caused by a reference to an empty intersection. In the next figure below it, after double-clicking on the cell, the empty intersection is immediately visible.

	A	B	C
10		t 1	t 2
11	ASG	12	1
12	FFU	34	2
13	TST	56	3
14			
15	Sum FFU/TST	#NULL!	

	A	B	C	D
10		t 1	t 2	
11	ASG	12	1	
12	FFU	34	2	
13	TST	56	3	
14				
15	Sum FFU/TST	=SUMME(D12:D13 C12:C13)		

Fig. 13.14:   #NULL! error value due to a missing comma

Correcting #VALUE! Errors

The #VALUE! error value is displayed instead of the proper result when the type of data in an argument is incorrect, when an array formula has been entered as a normal formula, or when a cell reference has been entered as an argument for an array constant.

Trace error

You can use the *Auditing* feature to check the cell references of the formula. Choose *Tools/Auditing/Trace Error*. In *Excel 97*, you can also see the cell references when you double-click on a cell.

Subsequently, examine the formula and its references for the following error sources:

- A calculation with the operators + - / * that refers to a cell that contains text. Replace an addition by the SUM() function; for example,

```
=A3+A4:A10
```

can be replaced by

```
=SUM(A3,A4:A10)
```

- You have entered text or referred to a cell containing text for a function argument that has to be a value (or a logical value).

ISTEXT()

Correct the cell references so that no cell that contains text is addressed. If the error is caused in a template, where text has to be replaced later on by respective values, suppress the error message with the ISTEXT() function. Use the following syntax:

```
=IF(ISTEXT(Cell Reference),"",Calculation Formula)
```

For example, an error message in the formula '=C5*12%' could be caused by a text in the cell C5 which says, 'Please insert value here'. In such a case, extend the formula to include the following expression:

```
=IF(ISTEXT(C5),"",C5*12%)
```

- A formula that was intended as an array formula has been entered as a normal formula.

Array: {}

This mistake is easily recognizable because the formula is not enclosed between braces. You probably ended the entry of the formula by pressing the ⏎ key and not the Ctrl+⇧+⏎ key combination required for array formulas. Double-click the cell that displays the error value and press the Ctrl+⇧+⏎ key combination. Now the formula is displayed in braces and the error value is removed.

- In an array, you used a formula for a constant, or a reference to a single cell and not, as required here, a cell area.

Error in an array formula

This error can be traced with the arrows produced by the *Auditing* feature.

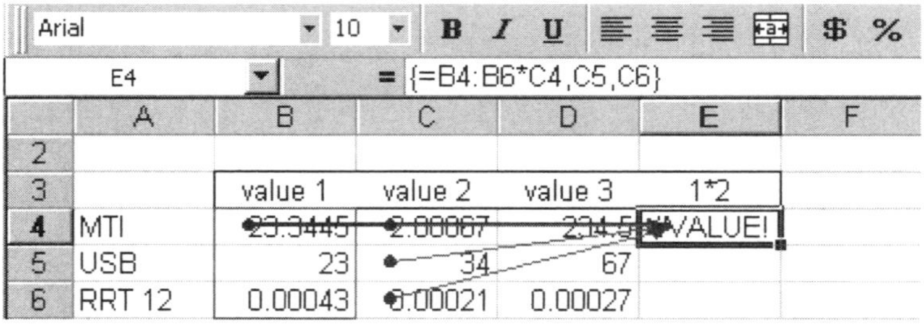

Arial		▼ 10 ▼	**B** *I* U	≡ ≡ ≡ ⊞	$ %	
E4	▼	= {=B4:B6*C4,C5,C6}				
	A	B	C	D	E	F
2						
3		value 1	value 2	value 3	1*2	
4	MTI	23.3445	2.00007	234.5	#VALUE!	
5	USB	23	34	67		
6	RRT 12	0.00043	0.00021	0.00027		

Fig. 13.15:   A wrong array formula

Double-click the cell with the error value and select the wrong reference. Then select the range or cells from which the array formula has to get the constants. Finish the creation of the formula with Ctrl+⇧+⏎.

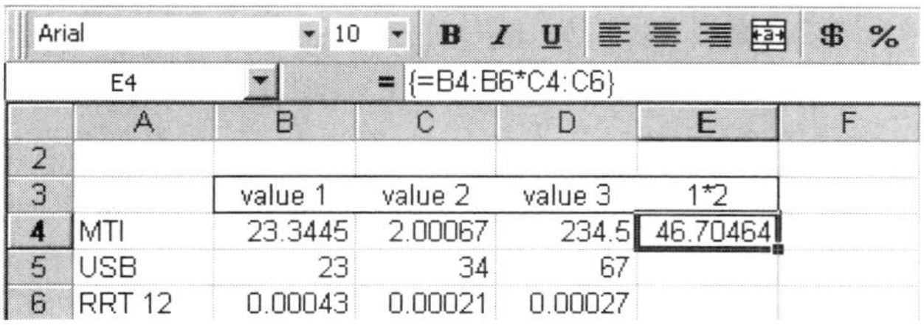

Fig. 13.16:   The corrected reference

In Figure 13.15, the reference to single cells is the source of the error. In Figure 13.16, the reference has been extended or reformulated to the respective cell area. If this was not the source of the error message, you can check whether all cell references refer to the correct cells and cell areas or whether a mistake has occurred while selecting and copying the formula. Check to see whether a relative reference, after copying, now refers to a cell containing text. If this is the case, replace the relative reference by an absolute reference.

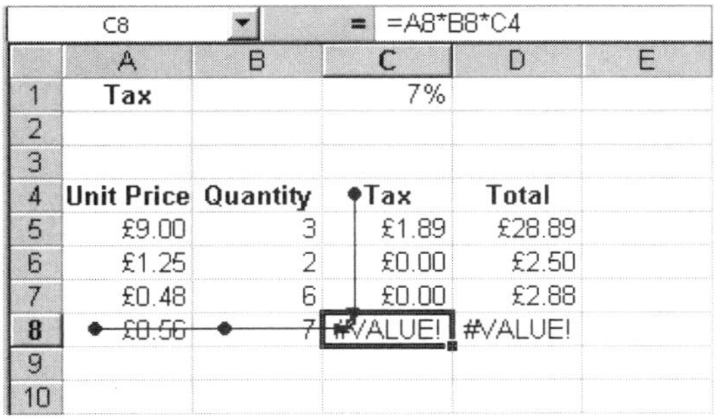

Fig. 13.17:   The #VALUE! error

In Figure 13.17, the cell C8 displays the #VALUE! error because by copying the formula from C5 to C6:C8 the references do not refer anymore to the *Tax* in C1, but to the cell C4, which contains text.

Double-click the cell with the original formula and select the reference which causes the error when copied.

Next press the [F4] function key to convert the relative reference to an absolute reference. Finish the editing with *Enter* [↵] and copy the formula again.

C8	▼	=	=A8*B8*$C$1	
	A	B	C	D	E
1	Tax		7%		
2					
3					
4	Unit Price	Quantity	Tax	Total	
5	£9.00	3	£1.89	£28.89	
6	£1.25	2	£0.18	£2.68	
7	£0.48	6	£0.20	£3.08	
8	£0.56	7	£0.27	£4.19	
9					
10					

Fig. 13.18: The relative cell reference has been replaced by an absolute reference

Correcting #NUM! Errors

The #NUM! error value means that the result of the formula is too big or too small to be properly displayed by *Excel*.

Unacceptable argument

An unacceptable argument in a function that requires a numeric argument can also be the source of the error.

Another source of error can be that you used a function such as RATE(), which executes an iteration but cannot return a result. In *Excel* the successive results of RATE() have to converge to within 0.0000001 after 20 iterations, otherwise RATE returns the #NUM! error value.

Incorrect data type

If an argument does not contain the correct type of data you will have to rectify that. Check all arguments to determine whether:

- the right order of the arguments is respected;

- no argument is missing;

- no number constants have been entered without the currency symbol;

- references have been entered correctly and the proper cell is addressed.

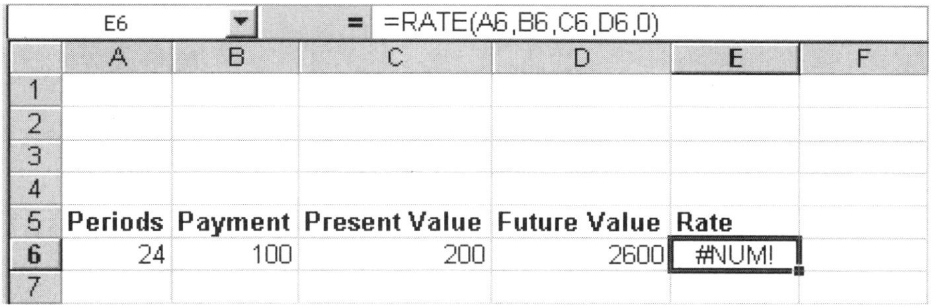

	E6	▼	=	=RATE(A6,B6,C6,D6,0)		
	A	B	C	D	E	F
1						
2						
3						
4						
5	Periods	Payment	Present Value	Future Value	Rate	
6	24	100	200	2600	#NUM!	
7						

Fig. 13.19: The #NUM! error value

If an iteration does not return a result, because the number produced by the formula is too large or too small, use a different starting value for the worksheet function.

Circular References

A common source of error is the creation of a circular reference. A circular reference is a reference that refers to itself. That means that you incorporate the cell in which the formula is located into the formula.

Excel 97 reacts to the creation of a circular reference with a dialog box and the display of the respective Help window when you close the dialog box with *OK*.

The *Circular Reference* toolbar also appears after closing the Help window.

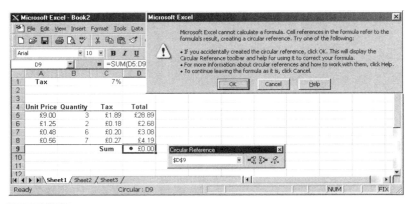

Fig. 13.20: A cell with a circular reference

The toolbar contains a drop-down list which allows you to jump to any cell of the circular reference. Additionally, there are button sto show the traces to the *Precedents* and to the *Dependents* to help you to make out the reference that causes the error.

Excel Help Options

If you want to manage a new task in *Excel*, or to apply a feature for the first time, or if an error message appears on your screen and you do not know what to do, there are various Help options which come to your assistance:

- The *Office Assistant*
  This Help bubble appears automatically after installation and provides information about all new functions. In addition, the *Office Assistant* will display tips to help you work more efficiently. This Help feature is available in all *Office* applications.

- The context-sensitive Help
This Help feature enables you to display a short piece
of information about a selected screen element. In
dialog boxes this feature shows information about a
particular option without your having to open a Help
window.

- Help for specific topics
This is a hierarchical Help feature that branches out
into subtopics from a main topic.

- Help using keywords
An alphabetical index in which you can find specific
words you are looking for.

- Help keyword database
A database in which you can find words you are
searching for.

- Help from the Web
A new Help feature that offers access to Help pages
for *Microsoft Excel* and other *Office* applications on
the *World Wide Web*.

The Office Assistant

The *Office Assistant* appeared in the *Welcome* window
immediately after you started *Excel* for the first time. The
Office Assistant shows up in a little window and assists
you with your daily work in *Excel*.

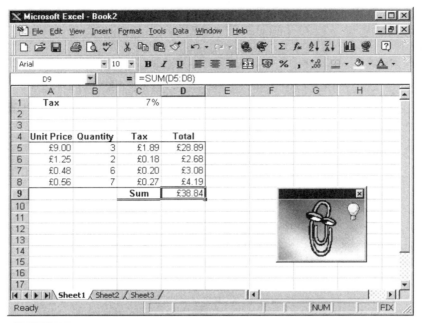

Fig. 13.21: The Office Assistant

This Help feature provides information about the new functions that you are using for the first time, but it also displays tips to help you work more efficiently and gives you step-by-step explanations.

With this feature, you can also receive answers to your questions.

Click the button 🔲 if you want to call up the *Office Assistant*.

In dialog boxes in which the 🔲 button is displayed, you can also access the *Office Assistant* directly if it is not visible.

To hide the *Office Assistant*, click the *Close* button on the title bar of the *Assistant* window.

Finding a Help Topic

You can ask the *Office Assistant* questions about a specific topic. To do this, click the *Assistant* window and insert the question or topic that you are looking for in the *What would you like to do?* text box.

Fig. 13.22: Searching for a topic

Next, click the *Search* button. The Assistant searches through the Help file and displays the related Help topics. If the Assistant does not find anything relevant to your query, then a message to this effect will appear, in which case you should reformulate your question.

Click the relevant Help topic and read the Help text.

Searching for Tips

The *Office Assistant* permanently surveys everything you do and checks whether you are carrying out your tasks efficiently or in a rather roundabout way. If the Assistant is able to propose an easier or faster method for executing a certain operation, a yellow light bulb will appear in the *Assistant* window.

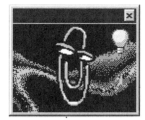

Fig. 13.24: The Assistant has a tip

If this happens, click on the Assistant to display the tip.

To be able to view a list of already displayed tips at a later stage, right-click the window of the *Office Assistant*. Select *See Tips* from the shortcut menu, or click the Assistant and then on the *Tips* button in the bubble that appears.

Shortcut: As a shortcut, you can use the Trace Precedents button on the Auditing toolbar.

Click here to try it.

Back   Next   Close

Fig. 13.25: Example of a tip

Next or back   After you have read the first tip, you can scroll forwards or backwards through the tip list by clicking the *Next* or *Back* buttons.

Test a tip   Some tips can be tried out immediately and this will be indicated. If you want to try it, click on the button displayed.

Hide the tip list   To hide the tip list, click on the *Close* button.

Selecting a Different Office Assistant

The default Assistant called *Clippit* appears immediately after starting *Excel*. You can use a different Assistant if you want a change.

To select a different Assistant, right-click the Assistant and select *Choose Assistant* from the shortcut menu to bring up the *Office Assistant* dialog box.

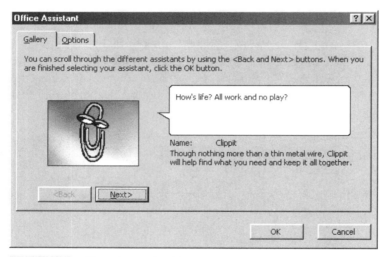

Fig. 13.26: Choosing an Assistant

Click the *Next* button to display a different Assistant. The relevant animation automatically appears.

If you want to go back to a previous Assistant, click *Back* again.

Once you have selected an Assistant, click the *OK* button to display the Assistant and close the dialog box.

Fig. 13.27:   The new Assistant

Not all Assistants are installed in the default installation. If, after selecting another Assistant, a message appears that the chosen Assistant could not be found, then run the setup program so that the Assistant can be automatically installed.

Assistant-Options

You can influence the way the *Office Assistant* is displayed on the *Options* tab page. To do so, right-click the Assistant and select the *Options* command.

Assistant
capabilities

In the *Assistant capabilities* option group, you can, using the check boxes, determine how the *Office Assistant* operates. Check the *Respond to F1 key* check box, if you want to activate the Assistant by pressing F1, but be sure to disable this if you want to use that key to call up the *Excel* Help.

Display tips

In the *Show tips about* and the *Other tip options* option groups, you can set which type of tips the Assistant should display and in which way. You can, for example, display only the tips for using the mouse or the keyboard.

Click the *Reset my tips* button to restore the tips that have already been displayed, if you want to view them again.

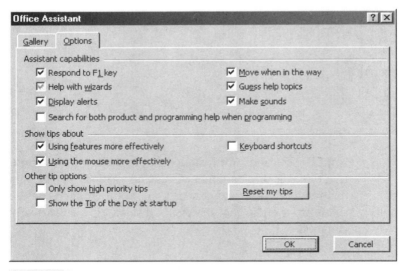

Fig. 13.28:   The *Options* tab page

Context-Sensitive Help

If you want to quickly get some information about an unknown button on a toolbar, a menu command or any other screen element, use the context-sensitive Help. It gives a brief explanation of the screen element you selected, and you do not have to bring up the Help window in order to do this.

To activate the context-sensitive Help, open the *Help* menu and select *What's This?* or press the ⬧+F1 key combination. A question mark appears next to the mouse pointer.

With this Help cursor, you can click the screen element or the command for which you want information. With another click, you can hide the context-sensitive Help again.

Worksheet area

The entire worksheet and all its elements, including cells, gridlines, row and column headings, scroll bars, and sheet tabs.

Ffg. 13.29: Mouse pointer and context-sensitive Help

Help in Dialog Boxes

Every now and again, you will come across an option in a dialog box that you have never used before and for which you may require some information.

In this case, you can also take advantage of the context-sensitive Help. You will find the *Help* button **?** in every dialog box.

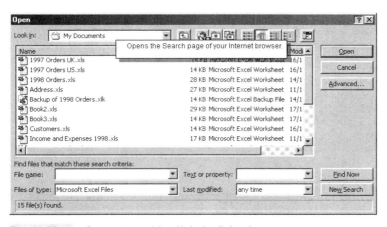

Fig. 13.30: Context-sensitive Help in dialog boxes

Instead of clicking **?**, you can also right-click an element in a dialog box and select *What's This?*.

If the dialog box displays the button ⊡, click it to display the Help of the *Office Assistant* or to ask the Assistant a question.

The *Contents* Tab Page

You can access a comprehensive Help that appears in its own window by clicking the *Help* item on the menu bar and selecting *Contents and Index*.

Fig. 13.31:   The *Contents* tab page

Double-click a Help topic on the *Contents* tab page to open the book icon ❧. This will display a subtopic. If a book does not contain the topic you are looking for, you can close it again by double-clicking on it. Repeat these steps until you have found the topic you are looking for.

Help topic [?]

Then double-click the page icon [?] to display the relevant Help topic. After reading it, click the *Close* button.

In some cases, an overview of the Help topic is displayed. Click on the text or the button next to it to display the actual topic.

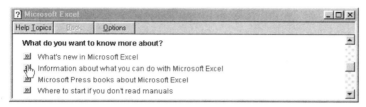

Fig. 13.32:   The mouse pointer in Help

Some Help topics highlight specific terms in green. If you point the mouse to such a word, the mouse pointer changes into a hand, too. With this hand, click on the highlighted word to display its definition.

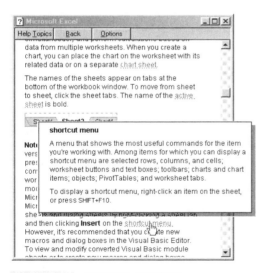

Fig. 13.33:   Display a definition

After reading a definition, you can hide it again by clicking on the Help window.

Tool bar

The Help window displays a bar with three buttons. You can always return to the main Help list by clicking the *Help Topics* button. You can move through the Help topics that you have previously accessed one by one, by clicking on the *Back* button. The *Options* button opens a menu which offers you various options, for example, to insert bookmarks and annotations or print the Help.

The *Index* Tab Page

The *Index* tab page offers you a different method of finding Help topics. This tab page displays a list of topics in alphabetical order. Type the first letter of the topic that you are looking for.

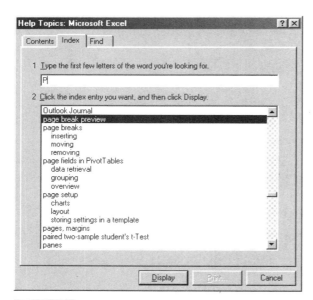

Fig. 13.34: The *Index* tab page

The list will then display the items that are available for this letter. Double-click on an item to view the relevant Help topic. You can also type the complete keyword you are looking for to accelerate the search.

The *Find* Tab Page

The *Find* tab page offers access to the Help word list. When you display the *Find* tab page for the first time *Excel* has first to create a word list. Afterwards insert one or several search words into the text box, and make sure you insert spaces between each word.

The first list that appears displays words that correspond to the words searched for. Click on an item in this list to display the topics associated with this word in the bottom list.

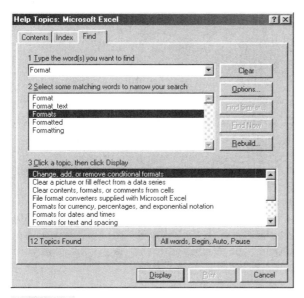

Fig.13.35:   The *Find* tab page

To display the selected Help topic, double-click the item in the bottom list or select it and click on the *Display* button. Choose the *Options* button to define different ways in which *Excel* can execute the search.

Printing a Help Topic

Just viewing the Help on the screen is not always sufficient. In some cases it is advantageous to print out the displayed Help topic, for example, in order to obtain an overview in black and white of the new functions or the shortcut keys for specific jobs.

Select a Help topic to print and click the *Options* button. Choose *Print Topic* and confirm the *Print* dialog box by clicking the *OK* button.

Displaying Help Simultaneously with Your Work

If you are working on a specific task for the first time and have to apply new functions you do not know, you can display the *Help* window simultaneously with the *Excel* application window. This will enable you to carry out your work steps according to the Help information displayed.

Go to the Help topic that you found and click the *Options* button. Select the *Keep Help on Top* command and in the overlapping menu click the *On Top* item.

You can resize the *Help* window and the *Excel* application window accordingly by using the resizing cursor on a window edge. With the help of the window title bar you can relocate the *Help* window to a position of your choice on the Desktop.

Help on the Web

You will find the *Microsoft on the Web* item on the *Help* menu, accessible by selecting the *Help* command on the menu bar. An overlapping menu appears if you select this item.

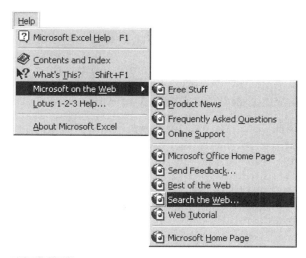

Fig. 13.36:   Help options on the Web

If you have access to the *Microsoft Network* or the Internet, you should take advantage of these options to access help and support directly from the Web.

You are given the following options:

- Obtain Online support.

- Start a tutorial.

- Visit the *Microsoft Home Page* or the *Microsoft Office Home Page*.

- Download *Office* accessories from the Web to your computer free of charge.

Selecting a command on the overlapping menu starts *Internet Explorer* and opens the dialog box requesting a connection to your service provider.

You can only take advantage of these online facilities if you have a Modem or an ISDN adapter and an online service installed in the Windows *Control Panel.*

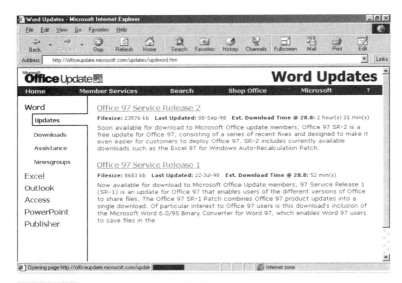

Fig. 13.37:   Assistance on the Web

With the help of hyperlinks that are available on each page, you can link to more pages. You can also move between the already displayed Web pages with the help of the buttons of *Internet Explorer* or the *Web* toolbar.

Glossary

#

In *Excel*, this symbol indicates an error value. An error value consisting of only this symbol indicates a too narrow column width. If the column width is increased, the error value disappears, and the cell contents are displayed again.

#DIV/0!

This error value points to the fact that a formula carries out a division by zero – which is mathematically impossible.

#N/A

This error value is displayed if a value to which the formula refers is not available, for example, because a lookup value in a list was not found.

#NAME?

Instead of the result of a formula, *Excel* displays this error value if text that cannot be identified was entered into a formula. In most cases, this is caused by missing quotation marks or typing errors in a function name.

#NUM

This error value appears if a number within a formula or a function prevents a calculation, because it is either too large or too small to be displayed by *Excel*.

#REF

This error value is displayed when an invalid reference has been entered into a cell, for example, if cells to which a formula refers were deleted.

#VALUE!

This error value is displayed instead of the formula result, if a wrong type of data was used as an argument or operator, for example if text was entered where a numeric value was expected.

*

The arithmetic operator for multiplication.

,

The comma is used as a reference operator to combine as a union operator multiple references into one reference.

/

The arithmetic operator for division.

:

The colon is used as a reference operator to produce as a range operator one reference to all the cells between two references, including the two references.

^

The '^' (caret) symbol is used as an operator for exponentiations. It connects the basic number and the exponent.

3-D Reference

A three-dimensional reference refers to a cell or a cell range in more than one worksheet. It can be used in formulas with certain functions, like SUM().

3-D View

A dialog box which you use to change the perspective of a 3-D chart. It can be opened with the *Chart/3-D View* command.

Absolute Reference

An absolute cell reference consists of a dollar sign, the column letter, a second dollar sign and the row number. An absolute reference, unlike a relative reference, does not change when it is copied.

Access Protection

An *Access* protection password prevents the opening of a file by an unauthorized person. It is requested each time before the opening of a workbook, or before displaying the preview in the *Open* dialog box. You can define an *Access* protection password by using the *Save As* dialog box and clicking the *Options* button.

Add-In

Program that adds optional commands and features to *Excel*, extending the performance and enabling, for example, the data exchange, or the *AutoSave* function. Before you can use an add-in, you must install it on your computer and then load it in *Excel*.

Add-Ins

A dialog box to install, make available or remove *Add-Ins* from the memory. *Add-Ins* which have been removed from this dialog box are still available on the hard disk.

Advanced Filter

A filter for databases and lists that works with a search criteria range. You can work with extended filter conditions, for example by using several filters for a column or using more than two filter criteria. In addition, you can copy the filtered records to a new location.

Alignment

The horizontal alignment determines the arrangement of the cell contents between the left and the right column edge. The vertical alignment determines the arrangement of the cell contents between the upper and the lower cell edges. *Excel* automatically aligns text to the left and values to the right.

AND

A logical operator that links conditions in such a way that all arguments must return the TRUE value in order for the total result to evaluate to TRUE .

AND()   AND(TRUE1,...TRUEt30)

Excel offers an AND() function which can carry out up to 30 TRUE calculations. The function returns the TRUE value only if all arguments evaluate to TRUE .

Arithmetic Operators

A calculation symbol that a formula uses. In *Excel*, the following arithmetic operators are used:

+	and -	Addition and subtraction
*	and /	Multiplication and division
%		Percent
^		Exponentiation

Arrange Windows

If more than one window is open, you can choose the *Window/ Arrange* command in order to place all open windows next to each other, underneath each other or overlapping each other.

Array Formula

A formula which returns more than one result. It is confirmed by [Ctrl]+[⇧]+[↵] and put in curly brackets.

Auditing

Commands of the *Tools/Auditing* menu or the buttons of the *Auditing* toolbar to display references and error values in the form of tracer arrows.

Auto Outline

A function that automatically groups and summarizes table contents into individual hierarchical levels. In doing so, the function is oriented towards the summarizing formulas contained in the cells, and it assigns the respective next higher level to those cells and columns containing these summarizing formulas.

AutoCalculate

A function that displays a statistic evaluation of the selected cell range in the status bar. This summary function can calculate, for example, the grand totals as well as the minimum, maximum, or average values.

AutoComplete

The *AutoComplete* function automatically completes cell entries. It recognizes the entered text automatically. If the first few characters you type in a cell match an existing entry in that column, *AutoComplete* fills in the remaining characters for you in the current cell.

AutoFill

A function that recognizes linear and growth series and date values as soon as two values have been entered and then fills in the rest of the cells automatically. *AutoFill* can be activated by dragging the fill handle of the selected cell.

AutoFilter

A function that is activated from the *Data* menu and inserts a drop-down list box into each column. These drop-down lists contain all column entries as well as some default entries and can be used as a filter criterion.

AutoFit

You can adjust the row height and the column width to the longest or widest entry. To make the row height or column width fit the entry, double-click the boundary below the row heading or the right boundary of the column heading.

AutoFormat

A combination of formatting that can be applied to tables by selecting *Format/AutoFormat*, choosing an item in the *Table format* list box and confirming with *OK*.

AutoSave

An *Add-In* that automatically saves the workbook at regular intervals which you define yourself.

AutoShapes

A new drawing feature in *Excel 97* with preset shapes that can be changed after being inserted. There are *AutoShapes*, for example, for hearts, arrows, legends, rectangles and ovals, etc. *AutoShapes* are inserted by using a button on the *Drawing* toolbar.

AutoSum

The fastest way to get sums is by clicking the *AutoSum* button on the *Standard* toolbar. After double-clicking this button, the cell range to the left of the current cell is added, up to the next blank cell.

AVERAGE() AVERAGE(Num1,...Num30)

The AVERAGE() function returns the average of all values entered as number arguments. You can give up to 30 values to this function.

Backup Copies

Excel can be set in such a way that the last version of a workbook is always kept as a backup, so that you always have the current and the previous version of the workbook. You create backup copies by using the *Save As/Options* command. In addition to the name of your saved workbook, you then get a *Backup of* file.

Cell Address

The address of a cell describes its position in the worksheet . It consists of the row number and the column letter. B3, for example, is the address of the cell in the third row of the second column.

Center

The cell contents can be centered horizontally as well as vertically. You find the corresponding options on the *Alignment* tab page via *Format/Cells*. For titles, use the *Merge and Center* button on the toolbar.

Chart Sheet

A chart which is displayed on a separate sheet, unlike an embedded chart which is displayed within the current worksheet containing the data table.

Chart Wizard

A button that activates an integrated wizard for the creation of a chart. All the necessary information is asked for in various dialog boxes, step by step. You will find the button for this on the *Standard* toolbar.

Clipboard

A protected area of the memory that temporarily saves copied or cut data so that it can be inserted at another position in the same or another document.

Column Heading

The grey button on top of a column labelled with a letter. A click on the column heading selects an entire column. Dragging the right boundary of a column heading changes the column width.

Columns to Repeat at Left

The columns that you want to be printed at the left border of each page. You find the command on the *Sheet* tab page in the *Page Setup* dialog box.

Comment

Remarks that can be added to a cell. Comment indicators are displayed in the upper-right corners of the cells with comments to show that a cell contains a comment. When you rest the pointer over the cells that contain remarks, the comments will be displayed in a *ScreenTip*.

Comparison Operators

Comparison operators carry out a comparison between the value on the right and the value on the left side of the operator. They are used in conditional operations, to filter and to search for records. *Excel* supports the following comparison operators:

=	Equal to
>	Greater than
<	Less than
>=	Greater than or equal to
<=	Less than or equal to
<>	Not equal to

Condition

A condition is formulated, for example, by the IF() function and carries out a conditional test that returns either a TRUE or a FALSE evaluation. For each of the two cases, different instructions can be entered.

Conditional Formatting

An option that exists only in *Excel 97*. It assigns a particular format, for example a specific font color, pattern or border, to cells but only when a certain condition is met.

Consolidation

The summarizing calculation of data which links and calculates data from several worksheets with the selected function. You can establish a link to the source data. The command to consolidate data is activated from the *Data* menu.

Copy to location

A specified range of cells of an *Advanced Filter* into which the filtered records that meet your criteria are copied. Make sure that the range is spacious enough to accommodate all the records found.

Criteria

The data that is entered as a comparison value in a filter, a condition, a search, for a group, or for a sort order. It consists of values and comparison operators which define how the content has to behave in relation with the value in order to meet the criterion. The comparison '>1200', for example, defines that the cell contents must be greater than 1200 in order for the criterion to be fulfilled.

Criteria Range

The range of an *Advanced Filter* into which the search criteria are entered. It contains a row with the same column labels as the list, and at least one more row in which the filter criteria are entered.

Currency Style

The default currency style in *Excel* can be assigned by clicking the currency style button on the toolbar. It formats values with a thousand's separator, two decimal places and the currency symbol.

Custom Lists

A list of a user-defined series of entries which is created in the *Tools/Options* dialog box on the *Custom Lists* tab page. It can be used on the one hand for the creation of automatic series, and on the other hand for the customized sorting.

Data Form

A dialog box in which the records of a database or a list are displayed and can be edited individually. Thus they can be added to, changed, searched for or deleted.

Data Point

Any individual item in a line chart, any segment of a pie chart and any bar or column in a bar or column chart forms a data point. A data point contains one of the individual bits of information from which a data series is made up.

Data Series

The connected data in a chart which is represented in a line, a column or a bar, or by a pattern respectively. A pie chart can represent only one data series.

Database

A table which is built in such a way that the column labels are entered in the first row and the list entries are entered in the rows underneath, can be called a database. The *Excel* database functions can be applied to such a database.

Date and Time Values

Date values which are entered in the 01/12/97,01.12.97 or, 01-12-97 formats, or time values that are entered in the 12:01 format, are automatically recognized by *Excel*. Internally, *Excel* organizes date and time values as serial numbers. Therefore, you can use them to carry out calculations. You can select a number format for date and time values on the *Number* tab page in the *Format Cells* dialog box.

Decimal places

Excel supports fixed decimal places. By choosing *Tools/Options* you can, on the *Edit* tab page, set a fixed number of decimal places which *Excel* should use, in order to save yourself the hassle of entering the decimal separator every time.

Default Margins

The default margins in *Excel* are 2.5 cm from the top and the bottom of a page, and 1.9 cm from the left and the right edge of the page. The settings can be changed on the *Margins* tab page in the *Page Setup* dialog box.

Default Workbook

All workbooks created by clicking on the *New* button or by choosing the *File/New* command and then selecting the *Workbook* item, are default workbooks.

Desktop

A Windows object that forms the highest level in the Window hierarchy. At the bottom of the desktop, the taskbar appears with buttons for each running application. A click on a button changes to the corresponding program. The desktop also takes in scraps with the help of which you can drag data from one program into another using drag-and-drop.

Drag-and-Drop

With this function you can move or copy selected data with the help of the mouse. Drag-and-drop means drag and paste, because the selected data is dragged to the new position and pasted there. If you want to copy, press and hold down the Ctrl key at the same time.

Drawing Elements

On the *Drawing* toolbar, *Excel* has buttons to draw simple shapes like ovals, rectangles, lines, arrows and text boxes in a table or a chart.

Embedded Chart

An embedded chart is created and displayed within an *Excel* worksheet and not on a separate sheet. In *Excel 97*, it is activated by a simple click on its area. An embedded chart can later be transferred to a separate chart sheet, and vice versa.

Embedding

An object consisting of foreign data which is inserted into another file in such a way that it is saved within this destination file, but can be activated and edited with the commands of the source application by double-clicking it.

Export

The data exchange from one application to another is called data exchange. *Excel* can save tables in the file formats of other applications, or in specific data exchange formats. From the *Files of type* drop-down list in the *Save As* dialog box, you can see which formats are supported by *Excel*.

EXT

Excel displays this entry in the status bar if the selection extension was activated with [F8]. It can also be deactivated by pressing [F8] again.

External Data

Get External Data is a command on the *Data* menu. With it, you can create a query for databases in order to insert records into an *Excel* table. The command opens a menu in which the data can later be updated and the query refreshed. Moreover, *Excel* offers a toolbar with buttons for the editing of external data ranges.

Fill Effects

A formatting option for the table background and the filling of two- and three-dimensional objects in charts or worksheets. This formatting makes it possible to insert patterns, special hues, and background pictures.

Fill handle

The little rectangle in the bottom right corner of the selected cell. It can be dragged across cells in order to copy the contents of the selected cell, or to create a series.

Find

Excel supports several search functions. In the *Open* and the *Advanced Find* dialog boxes you can search for files. You can search for any cell contents using the *Edit/Find* command. Records can be searched for with the help of the *Data Form* after you turn it into a search criteria form. This is accessed by using the *Data/Form* command.

Footer

A line at the bottom of the print page in which *Excel* prints, for example, the page number of the current page or the name of the workbook or the sheet. You can set footers by choosing *File/ Page Setup/Header/Footer*, or by using the *View/Header and Footer* command.

Formula bar

The bar above your table in which the formula for the currently selected cell is displayed and can be worked on. It contains buttons to confirm or cancel entries.

Formula Palette

A new feature in *Excel 97*. It enables the calling up and structuring of formulas, the entry of function arguments, and the control and editing of existing formulas. It contains buttons to reduce or enlarge its size so that cell references can be selected. The *Formula Palette* provides a description of a chosen function and displays the current result when selecting the arguments.

Formulas

A formula always begins with an equal sign and is made up of constants, functions, names and references, operators and parentheses. Formulas perform operations such as addition, multiplication, and comparison on worksheet values A formula returns a result that is displayed in the cell containing the formula while the formula itself is displayed in the *Formula* bar.

Freeze Panes

In extensive tables, you can freeze row and column labels in such a way that they maintain their position while the rest of the table is scrolled. Activate this setting by choosing the *Window/Freeze Panes* command.

Function

A function is a predefined expression with the help of which a calculation (like SUM) or a comparison (like IF) can be carried out, or which checks cells (like IS). A function is always made up of the function name followed by the function arguments.

Function Arguments

The arguments of a function signify the values with which the function is to work. These are enclosed in parentheses and separated by commas. Certain functions work without arguments, or have required or optional arguments.

Grouped Sheets

Worksheets can be grouped if entries or commands are to involve more than one sheet. You group worksheets by clicking the relevant sheet tab while holding down the `Ctrl` key.

Header

Data which is printed at the top of each print page. You can create and edit headers on the *Header/Footer* tab page in the *Page Setup* dialog box.

Hide

Rows, columns, and worksheets can be shown or hidden via the *Format* menu, while whole workbooks can be shown or hidden using the *Window* menu.

Hyperlink

In *Excel 97*, you have the possibility to link files in the same way that Web documents are linked. The link is emphasized, usually by highlighting it in a different color. A click on this link activates the linked document and thus enables you to read the linked information.

IF()   **IF(logical_test, value_if_true, value_if_false)**

A function to carry out a logical test. If the test turns out positive, the function returns the TRUE value. If the test turns out negative, the function returns the FALSE value. For both cases, you can determine the proper action to be taken.

Import

The data exchange from a different application into *Excel* is called data import. *Excel* can import the formats of several applications and special exchange formats. Which formats you can import into *Excel* can be seen from the *Files of type* drop-down list box in the *File/Open* dialog box.

Indents

In *Excel 97*, you can specify a left indent for cell contents. To do this, choose the *Format/Cells/Alignment* command. Each increment in the *Indent* box is equivalent to the width of one character.

Landscape

Excel supports printing in *Landscape* mode. To change from *Portrait* to *Landscape* mode, use the *File/Page Setup* command, switch to the *Page* page tab and click the corresponding button in the *Orientation* option group.

Line Break

You can insert a line break by using the ⌈Alt⌉+⌈↵⌋ shortcut keys. The cell contents is then displayed and arranged into several rows.

Link

If formulas of a table refer to data in another table of another worksheet in the same or a different workbook, this is called a link. Linking also refers to objects stored in an *Excel* workbook in such a way that they remain saved in the source file.

Lock

By default, all cells of a workbook are locked against any change. The lock, however, is only activated if the worksheet is protected. You can unlock cells by choosing *Format/Cells* and then activating the *Protection* tab page and clearing the *Locked* check box.

Macros

Macros save a series of commands of any length that are frequently used. You can then carry them out in the saved order by 'running' the macro. They can be linked to a button or a shortcut key in order to be run more quickly.

Map

An object that is created with *Microsoft Map* and can be embedded in a worksheet. It represents the data in a demographic arrangement on a map, for example, of the U.S.A., Europe, or on a world map.

MAX()   **MAX(Num1,...Num30)**

This function returns the greatest value of the values entered with the *Num* arguments. You can give up to 30 values to this function.

MIN()   **MIN(Num1,...Num30)**

The MIN() function calculates the smallest of all values entered as number arguments. You can assign up to 30 values to this function.

Mixed Reference

A reference which has both an absolute and a relative part. It consists either of an absolute column reference and a relative row reference, or vice versa. In a mixed reference only the relative part changes when you copy it.

Multiple selection

The selection of non-adjacent cells is called a multiple selection. In *Excel*, you can create a multiple selection by highlighting the cells while holding down the Ctrl key.

Names

Cells and cell ranges can be named so that a reference can be established by using their name. Names of cells can be up to 255 characters long, can begin with a letter or an underscored letter and can consist of letters, numbers, periods or underscored characters.

The name of a worksheet can be up to 31 characters long. It may contain letters, numbers, single spaces and symbols, but it cannot contain \ / ? *, nor can it be enclosed in brackets [ ]. In names, *Excel* does not distinguish between uppercase and lowercase characters.

Number Format

The formatting that defines how a value is displayed in a cell. You can decide how many decimal places will be displayed, whether a currency symbol will appear, whether the comma will be the thousands separator, and if percentage signs or a minus sign will be displayed.

Office Assistant

A new sort of Help feature which works in all of the *Office* components and which displays comments and tips in relation to the current work situation.

Operators

The signs or symbols that define how a calculation or comparison operation is to be carried out. *Excel* supports arithmetic, logical, comparison and reference operators.

Options

A dialog box you use to adjust the different *Excel* settings to your personal needs. View options, calculation and formatting options, the creation of customized series and sort orders, chart options, color palette and special settings for persons who previously used other calculation programs – all these belong to the settings you can adjust to your needs. You open the *Options* dialog box from the *Tools* menu.

OR

A logic operator linking conditions in such a way that only one of the conditions needs to return the TRUE value in order for the total result to evaluate to TRUE.

OR()   **OR(TRUE 1,...TRUE 30)**

With the OR() function, *Excel* offers a function that can carry out up to 30 TRUE calculations, returning the TRUE value as soon as it finds one argument that evaluates to TRUE.

Organization Chart

A command in the *Insert/Picture* menu to insert an organization chart into an *Excel* worksheet. The command starts an additional *Office* module that enables the presentation of hierarchical structures.

Outline

A function called up from the *Data* menu. It structures a table by rows and columns into different levels. By using the *Data/Group and Outline* command, you can summarize and evaluate selected rows or columns.

Page Break

A page break indicates the boundary between two print pages. In *Excel*, they are inserted automatically as soon as a table exceeds the height or width of a single page. You can, however, insert a page break manually at another location by using the *Insert/Page Break* command.

Page Break Preview

A special view in *Excel 97* which reduces the table and displays it with marks indicating the page break. The page breaks can be moved by dragging the boundaries with the mouse.

Page Layout

The page layout defines what a print page will look like in terms of the paper size, the print orientation, the margins and the orientation of the table.

Page Numbers

Page numbers are added to the header or footer of a page. In *Excel 97*, the page numbers are inserted in the footer by default. You can add or remove page numbers and the total amount of pages by choosing the *Page Setup* command and then activating the *Header/Footer* tab page.

Page Order

The page order defines whether in an extensive table that is broader and longer than one print page, you first want to print the sheets underneath each other or the sheets next to each other. Choose the page order on the *Sheet* tab page in the *Page Setup* dialog box.

Passwords

Passwords are entered for *Read-only* protection, *Access* protection and for *Worksheet* protection. Passwords can be up to 15 characters long and consist of letters, numbers and symbols. Passwords are case-sensitive.

Paste Special

A command you use to insert objects from the clipboard and embed or link them. If there is a selected cell contents in the clipboard, this command opens a dialog box in which you can choose which parts of the cell contents you want to insert. The command can replace a formula with its result if you choose *Values*.

Pick from List

A list you can open via the *Pick from List* item in a cell's shortcut menu. This list displays all text entries already in the column, and which you can repeat again for other entries.

Print area

A selected range in the worksheet that is prepared for printing by using the *File/Print Area/Set Print Area* command. The command inserts page breaks above, below, to the right and to the left of the highlighted cell range so that only the selected area is printed.

Print Preview

A view used to display and give a final once-over to the entire page before printing. The *Print Preview* shows the table or the chart in the way the installed printer will print it. In the *Print Preview*, you can change the margins as well as the headers and footers of the page.

Print Titles

Row and column headings which are printed on each page are called print titles in *Excel*. They can be determined on the *Sheet* tab page of the *File/Page Setup* dialog box.

Properties of Workbooks

File properties help you find workbooks. Some properties are defined by Windows automatically, like for example the date of creation, while others you can determine yourself. To do so, choose *File/Properties*.

Read-Only (Password to modify)

A *Read-only* protected workbook cannot be saved under the same name unless the password is entered. *Excel* supports the *Read-only* protection in connection with a password. You can activate the corresponding command by choosing *File/Save As* and then clicking the *Options* button.

Read-Only Recommended

The *Read-only* recommendation displays a message that suggests opening the workbook in *Read-only* mode. The recommendation can be refused, however. You can activate the *Read-only* recommendation by choosing *File/Save As*, clicking the *Options* button and selecting the corresponding check box.

Reference Operators

Reference operators link cells which are given to a formula or a function.

: The colon creates one reference to all the cells located in between the two cells connected by the colon, including the two references.

, The comma separates individual references and unites them into a single reference.

Single space: A single space is used as an intersection operator. The intersection is formed by the references to the right and to the left of the single space.

Relative Reference

A reference to a cell or cell range which consists of the column letter and the row number, and is adjusted to the new location in the worksheet when copied. The relative reference is, unlike the absolute reference, always defined in relation to the current location of the cell. A10+A11, for example, is a relative reference. When it is copied into one column further to the right, this reference becomes B10+B11.

Row Heading

The grey button to the left of each row. A click on the row heading highlights an entire row. Dragging the lower boundary of the row heading extends the size of the row height.

Rows to Repeat at Top

The rows that you want to be printed as a print title at the top of each page.You find the command on the *Sheet* tab page in the *Page Setup* dialog box.

Scrap

A scrap is a selected part of the table containing data that you dragged with drag-and-drop from a workbook or another file onto the desktop. The data is represented by an icon on the desktop and can later be pasted into another workbook or into another application.

ScreenTip

A short information which is displayed in a little box to explain buttons on the toolbar, the scroll bar, the taskbar, and, in *Excel*, also additional table elements such as comments.

Select All

The grey unlabelled button on top of the first row heading and to the left of the first column heading. A click on this button highlights the whole worksheet.

Series

Each list of values with a regular distance between its members is called a series. In an linear series, the next increment is made by addition or subtraction, while in a growth series it is made by multiplication or division. *Excel* supports the forming of series by automatic functions which can complete a series automatically already after one or two members have been entered.

Sheet Tabs

The sheet tabs at the bottom of the worksheet window show how many sheets are contained in the workbook and which sheet is currently active. You use the sheet tabs to activate, move, copy and group the individual worksheets.

Shortcut Menu

The shortcut menu is opened with a click on the right mouse button. It contains commands connected to the respective object or the specific working step. For example all toolbar names appear in the toolbar shortcut menu.

Split

You can divide a window into several panes so that it is possible to look at different ranges of the table at the same time. To do so, either use the *Window/Split* command, or use the split boxes which are located on top of the vertical scroll bar and to the right of the horizontal scroll bar.

Standard Column Width

The standard column width is 8.43 characters and can be changed by using the *Format/Column/Standard Width* command.

Standard Font

The standard font in a workbook is defined by the font of the *Normal* style. The standard font for all workbooks can be changed on the *General* tab page in the *Tools/Options* dialog box.

StartUp

A Windows folder that is located in the *Windows/Start Menu/ Programs* folder. All programs with shortcuts in this folder are automatically started when Windows starts.

Styles

Styles save formatting such as fonts, number formats, alignment, borders, protection, etc., under a name selected by the user. If the user later selects the name, the current cell is formatted with the saved formattings.

Subscript

Excel supports subscript characters. You find the corresponding check box on the *Font* tab page in the *Format Cells* dialog box.

Subtotals

An *Excel* function for the evaluation of sorted lists. Identical list entries are summarized in groups and evaluated with a function such as SUM() or COUNT(). At the end a grand total of all groups is returned.

Summary

A tab page in the *File/Properties* dialog box which saves the title, author, company, keywords, and other information. These entries can later be used when organizing your files.

Superscript

Excel supports superscript signs, for example within a scientific formula. You find the corresponding check box on the *Font* tab page in the *Format Cells* dialog box.

Template

A sample workbook that is created as a template for new workbooks and saved in a template folder as a *Template* file of type. When choosing the *File/New* command, a copy of the selected template will be created.

Text Operator

The '&' symbol is used as a text operator to connect several text values to one single piece of text.

TODAY()

The TODAY() function provides the current date. It is entered into a formula as: =TODAY() and inserts the date into a cell in such a way that it is updated every day.

Top 10

A feature of the *AutoFilter* function used to evaluate the highest or lowest values of a table. The function can be chosen from the filter drop-down list of the *AutoFilter* function.

Traces

Traces are markings in the form of arrows which are inserted to trace references or indicate the source of errors.

Validation

A new command in *Excel 97* which enables the checking of entries. You can set rules for the validation to determine which entries are allowed in a cell. In addition, you can define an input message and an error alert if invalid data is entered.

View

A view saves the current screen settings and restores them when calling up the view. You can save and activate a view by using the *View/Custom Views* command.

What's This?

Activate this Help feature by choosing *Help* on the menu bar and then selecting *What's This?*. Next to the mouse pointer a question mark will appear. If you click on a screen element with this *Help* cursor, a *ScreenTip* will be displayed with the corresponding information.

Wildcards

Wildcards can be used for searching in tables, or, for searching for workbooks in the *Open* dialog box. Use '?' as a wildcard for a single character and '*' for any sequence of characters.

Wizard

Integrated Help functions that lead you step by step through certain operations, such as the *Lookup Wizard* and the *Chart Wizard*. The *Chart Wizard* can be started by clicking the corresponding button on the *Standard* toolbar.

WordArt

An additional *Office* module used to insert special font effects into an *Excel* table. You activate this module via the *Insert/Picture/WordArt* command or by clicking the *Insert WordArt* button on the *Drawing* toolbar.

Workbook

An *Excel* file is referred to as a workbook. In *Excel 97*, it contains three worksheets by default. A workbook can contain up to 255 worksheets.

Worksheet

A single spreadsheet in an *Excel* workbook, made up of gridlines of rows and columns that form cells, thus creating a table. A table also refers to a connected data range within a worksheet.

Worksheet Protection

The worksheet protection prevents the accidental overwriting of locked cells. It should only be activated after unlocking those cells which are to be worked on further. Activate it by choosing *Format/Cells* and clearing the *Locked* check box on the *Protection* tab page. The worksheet protection is activated via *Tools/Protection/Protect Sheet* and can be used with a password.

Workspace

A workspace is saved in a particular file and contains the names, positions, arrangements and print areas of all open workbooks of a project. You can create a workspace by using the *File/Save Workspace* command.

XLSTART

Files that are saved in this folder are automatically opened when you start *Excel*. A workbook template of the name *WORKBOOK. XLT* saved in this folder will be used as the default template.

Zoom

Changing the size of the display is called *Zooming*. In *Excel* you can choose zoom values between 10% and 400%. You can do this via a drop-down list on the *Standard* toolbar or by choosing the *View/Zoom* command.